Building Skills for the New TOEIC® Test

SECOND EDITION

Lin Lougheed

Building Skills for the New TOEIC® Test, Second Edition

Pearson Education, 10 Bank Street, White Plains, NY 10606

Staff credits: The people who made up the ***Building Skills for the New TOEIC® Test, Second Edition*** team, representing editorial, production, design, and manufacturing, are Pietro Alongi, Angela Castro, Dave Dickey, Nancy Flaggman, Ann France, Lise Minovitz, and Michael Mone.

Cover and Text Design: Ann France
Text Composition: S4/Carlisle
Text font: 11/14 Plantin Light

Photo Credits: Cover: Robert Churchill/iStockphoto.com (background) Shutterstock.com; page 3 Shutterstock; page 7 ICI; pages 10, 12 John Davis; page 15 (above and below) Sally and Richard Greenhill, page 16 (above) The Wellcome Foundation Ltd., (below) McDonald's Restaurants Ltd.; page 17 (above) The Wellcome Foundation Ltd., (below) Sally and Richard Greenhill; pages 123, 130, 131, 132, 133, 143, 146, 149, 156 Shutterstock; page 165 iStockphoto; page 166 (above) Shutterstock, (below) iStockphoto; page 167 (above and below) Shutterstock; page 185 (above) Japan Information and Cultural Centre, (below) Louise Elkins; page 186 (above and below) Japan Information and Cultural Centre; page 187 (above) British Petroleum, (below) Press Division of the Taipei Representative Office in the UK; page 188 (above) Japan Information and Cultural Centre, (below) British Petroleum; page 189 (above) Nissan Motor (GB) Ltd., (below) Louise Elkins; page 225 (above) Japan Information and Cultural Centre, (below) Hyatt International Hotels; page 226 (above) American Airlines, (below) Nissan Motor (GB) Ltd.; page 227 (above) Hyatt International Hotels, (below) Japan Information and Cultural Centre; page 228 (above) Glaxo Holdings p.l.c., (below) Shutterstock; page 229 (above and below) Hyatt International Hotels; pages 265, 270, 275, 280, 283, 284 Shutterstock; page 285 (above) Dreamstime, (below) Shutterstock; pages 291, 292, 293 Shutterstock.

Library of Congress Cataloging-in-Publication Data

Lougheed, Lin, 1946–
Building skills for the new TOEIC test/Lin Lougheed.—2nd ed.
p. cm.
Rev. ed. of: Building skills for the TOEIC test/Gina Richardson.
Harlow, England: Longman, 1995.
ISBN-13: 978-0-13-813625-3 (paper back)
ISBN-10: 0-13-813625-4 (paper back)
1. English language—Textbooks for foreign speakers. 2. Test of English for International Communication—Study guides. 3. English language—Examinations—Study guides. I. Richardson, Gina. Building skills for the TOEIC test. II. Title.
PE1128.L64364 2008
428.0076—dc22 2008038700

Printed in the United States of America
3 4 5 6 7 8 9 10–V012–12 11

Contents

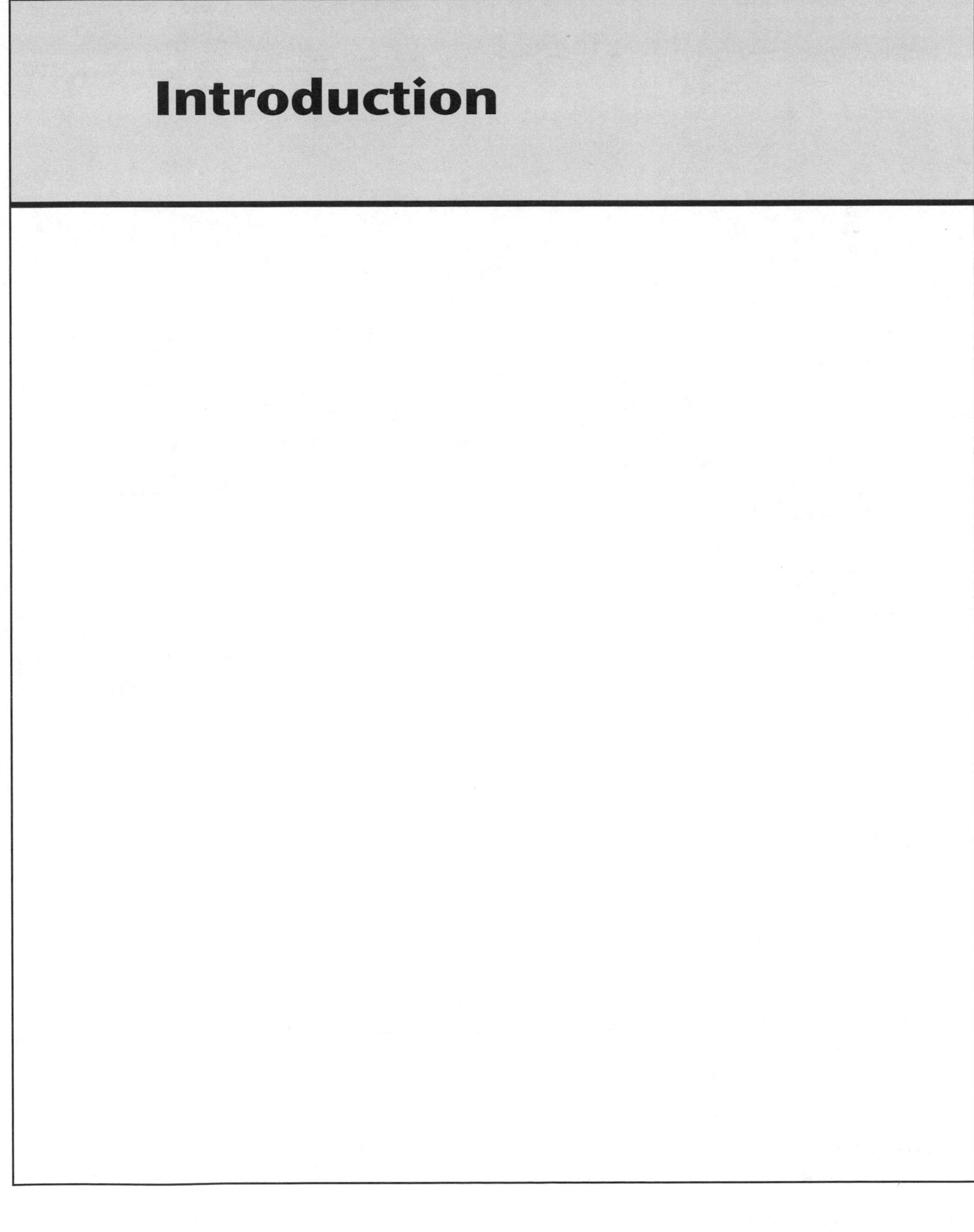
Introduction

About the New TOEIC® Tests

The Test of English for International Communication, or TOEIC® test, assesses English language skills for business. It covers the vocabulary and situations business people encounter when using English all over the world.

Listening and Reading

Like the old TOEIC test, the new TOEIC test is a paper-and-pencil, multiple-choice assessment. It has two sections: Listening Comprehension and Reading. However, there have been some changes to each section.

Listening section changes include:

- fewer photograph questions in Part 1
- both recorded and written questions in Part 3 and Part 4
- sets of questions in Part 3
- American, Canadian, British, and Australian accents in the audio material

Reading section changes include:

- deletion of error recognition questions in Part 6
- addition of text completion questions in Part 6
- addition of "double-passage" questions in Part 7

The following chart shows the parts of the new TOEIC test, the number of questions, and the total time to work on each part.

Section	Questions	Time
Listening Comprehension		45 minutes
Part 1: Photos	10	
Part 2: Question-Response	30	
Part 3: Conversations	30	
Part 4: Talks	30	
Reading		75 minutes
Part 5: Incomplete Sentences	40	
Part 6: Text Completion	12	
Part 7: Reading Comprehension • Single Passages • Double Passages	 28 20	
TOTAL	**200**	**120 minutes**

TOEIC scores range from 10 to 990. The score you receive for the Listening Comprehension section is added to the score you receive from the Reading section. Only your correct responses are counted toward the final score.

Section	Score
Listening Comprehension	5 to 495
Reading	5 to 495
TOTAL	**10 to 990**

Speaking and Writing

The new TOEIC Speaking and Writing tests are delivered through the Internet. They measure the ability to communicate clearly in spoken and written English. The Speaking Test consists of 11 questions which involve speaking tasks such as reading aloud, answering questions, and expressing original ideas. The Writing Test consists of 8 questions which involve writing tasks such as sentence writing, responding to requests, and expressing original ideas.

TOEIC tests are administered by regional representatives of the TOEIC offices of the Educational Testing Service (ETS®) in Princeton, New Jersey. To take a TOEIC test, go to the website (www.ets.org) or write to ETS at the address below:

TOEIC Service International
Educational Testing Service
Princeton, New Jersey 08541
USA

To the Teacher: Using the Book in Class

Building Skills for the New TOEIC® Test, Second Edition provides students with a clear, systematic approach to help you prepare them for the TOEIC test step by step.

- Students will build skills for taking the new TOEIC test and the new TOEIC Speaking and Writing tests.
- Students will learn and practice the business vocabulary used on the new TOEIC test.
- Students will learn Test Tips—ways to choose the correct answer and avoid traps that can cause problems for test takers.
- Students will learn how to manage their time while taking the TOEIC tests.
- Students will take Practice TOEIC Tests, Practice TOEIC Speaking Tests and Practice TOEIC Writing Tests.
- Students will improve their overall knowledge of English.

Organization of Book

This book is very easy to use. Sections I through IV are the skill-building sections of the text. Sections I and II cover the listening and reading sections of the new TOEIC test. Section III covers the new TOEIC Speaking Test, and Section IV covers the new TOEIC Writing Test. There are two practice tests for each test, and there are complete audioscripts and answer keys for each.

Section I Listening Comprehension

This section builds skills for the listening portion of the new TOEIC test. It is divided into four parts; each part represents a part of the new TOEIC test. Each part consists of a sample TOEIC test item, focused skill development, exercises, and comprehensive practice to help students develop strategies to improve their scores. Each sample TOEIC test item answer is thoroughly explained in the text. Every practice item is explained in depth in the answer key at the end of the book.

Section II Reading

This section builds skills for the reading portion of the new TOEIC test. It is divided into three parts; each part represents a part of the new TOEIC test. Each part consists of a sample TOEIC test item, focused skill development, exercises, and comprehensive practice to help students develop strategies to improve their scores. Each sample TOEIC test item answer is thoroughly described in the text. Every practice item is explained in depth in the answer key at the end of the book.

Section III Speaking

This section builds skills for the new TOEIC Speaking Test. Each part of Section III consists of sample TOEIC test items, focused skill development, exercises, and comprehensive practice to help students develop strategies to improve their scores. Sample answers for the exercises and practice items are found in the answer key at the end of the book.

Section IV Writing

This section builds skills for the new TOEIC Writing Test. Each part of Section IV consists of sample TOEIC test items, focused skill development, exercises, and comprehensive practice to help students develop strategies to improve their scores. Sample answers for the exercises and practice items are found in the answer key at the end of the book.

Practice Tests

There are two Practice TOEIC Tests, two Practice TOEIC Speaking Tests, and two Practice TOEIC Writing Tests. The format of each of the tests is similar to the actual TOEIC tests. For the Listening Comprehension sections of the Practice TOEIC Tests and the Practice TOEIC Speaking Tests, use the audio CDs (in the back of the book).

Appendix

The Appendix includes the audioscripts for the Listening Comprehension skills section as well as the Listening Comprehension portion of the two Practice TOEIC Tests. Audioscripts are also included for all exercises, practice, and test items for Questions 7–10 in Speaking. The Appendix also includes the answer keys for the skills and the practice tests. Answer sheets for the two Practice TOEIC Tests and the Audio CD Tracking List are found at the end of the Appendix.

Sample Syllabus

The following chart presents a possible syllabus for this course. Of course, the precise amount of time you will want to devote to each skill depends on the skill level of your students, whether the material is to be covered entirely in class or in class and at home, and, of course, the amount of time available to you per course and class session.

Skill 1, Developing Business Vocabulary, can be covered in two hours in class, or you can cover it in one hour by assigning the exercises as homework or by beginning in class and having the students complete them at home. Most of the other skills can be covered in a one-hour class period. Practice and the practice tests can be assigned for homework or done in class.

Listening Comprehension		
Introduction		1 hour
Part 1	Skill 1	2 hours
	Skill 2	1 hour
	Skill 3	1 hour
	Skill 4	1 hour
	Practice	1 hour
Part 2	Skill 1	2 hours
	Skill 2	1 hour
	Skill 3	1 hour
	Skill 4	1 hour
	Practice	1 hour
Part 3	Skill 1	2 hours
	Skill 2	1 hour
	Skill 3	1 hour
	Skill 4	1 hour
	Practice	1 hour
Part 4	Skill 1	2 hours
	Skill 2	1 hour
	Skill 3	1 hour
	Skill 4	1 hour
	Practice	1 hour

Reading		
Introduction		1 hour
Part 5	Skill 1	2 hours
	Skill 2	1 hour
	Skill 3	1 hour
	Skill 4	1 hour
	Skill 5	1 hour
	Skill 6	1 hour
	Skill 7	1 hour
	Practice	1 hour

Part 6	Skill 1	2 hours
	Skill 2	1 hour
	Skill 3	1 hour
	Skill 4	1 hour
	Skill 5	1 hour
	Skill 6	1 hour
	Practice	1 hour
Part 7	Skill 1	2 hours
	Skill 2	1 hour
	Skill 3	1 hour
	Skill 4	1 hour
	Skill 5	1 hour
	Practice	1 hour
Speaking		
Introduction		1 hour
	Skill 1	2 hours
	Skill 2	1 hour
	Skill 3	1 hour
	Skill 4	1 hour
	Skill 5	1 hour
	Skill 6	1 hour
	Skill 7	1 hour
	Practice	1 hour
Writing		
Introduction		1 hour
	Skill 1	2 hours
	Skill 2	1 hour
	Skill 3	1 hour
	Skill 4	1 hour
	Skill 5	1 hour
	Practice	1 hour
Practice TOEIC Test 1		2 hours
Practice TOEIC Test 2		2 hours
Practice TOEIC Speaking Test 1		2 hours
Practice TOEIC Speaking Test 2		2 hours
Practice TOEIC Writing Test 1		2 hours
Practice TOEIC Writing Test 2		2 hours
		80 hours

To the Student: Using the Book for Self-Study

There are many ways to use this book, depending on how much time you have and your level of English proficiency. Here are two methods you might try.

Method A

- Study the skills sections carefully. Learn to focus on each part.
- Take a practice test.
- Note those parts where you made the most errors.
- Review those parts in the book.
- Take another practice test.

Method B

- Take a practice test.
- Note those parts where you made the most errors.
- Study those parts in the book.
- Take another practice test.

Please note that this book focuses on specific areas of the new TOEIC test; it is not a complete textbook of English. When you read the explanatory answers for a practice test, write down the particular item you missed. If you consistently make mistakes in a particular area, such as use of conjunctions, you should review that area in a standard English textbook.

A Final Word on Improving Your Score

After you have studied this book carefully, continue using English as much as you can. Go to movies in English, watch television in English, read newspapers and magazines in English, correspond by e-mail with English speakers around the globe. The more you use English, the better your score on the TOEIC test will be.

I Listening Comprehension

The Listening Comprehension section of the new TOEIC® test is a paper-and-pencil, multiple-choice assessment. There are four different listening sections that give you the chance to show how well you understand spoken English. You will have approximately 45 minutes to answer 100 questions. The four parts to this section are:

- Part 1: Photos 10 questions
- Part 2: Question-Response 30 questions
- Part 3: Conversations 30 questions
- Part 4: Talks 30 questions

For all four parts, you will listen to audio. You will choose the correct answer from four written answers: (A), (B), (C), or (D) in Parts 1, 3, and 4; and from three written answers in Part 2.

Part 1: Photos

OBJECTIVES

You can improve your score in Part 1 by:

- developing business vocabulary
- analyzing the photo
- distinguishing similar sounds
- making inferences

In Part 1 of the new TOEIC® test, you will see a photo in your test book. You will hear four short statements, but you will not see these four statements in your test book. You will hear the statements just once. Listen carefully to understand what the speaker says.

When you are listening to the four statements, look at the photo in your test book. Choose the statement that best describes the photo. Then, on your answer sheet, find the number of the question and mark your answer. You will have five seconds to answer each question.

Sample TOEIC Test Question

You will hear: (A) *They're working on computers.*
(B) *They're having a meeting.*
(C) *They're eating in a restaurant.*
(D) *They're moving the furniture.*

Answer

Choice (B), *They're having a meeting*, best describes what you see in the photo. Choice (A) is incorrect because they are working, but there are no computers. Choice (C) is incorrect because although they are at a table, they are not eating, and the setting is a conference room, not a restaurant. Choice (D) is incorrect because they are not moving furniture.

Types of Statements

The statements in Part 1 may have any of these five characteristics:

Characteristics	Examples
The statements are often in the present continuous tense.	The man *is signing* his name. The people *are watching* a presentation.
The statements often use pronouns instead of names.	*She's* watching television. *They're* eating at a café.
The statements are brief; they rarely use more than five or six words.	They're at the bank. She's on a bus.
Contractions are often used.	*It's* going to rain. *He's* talking on the phone.
The definite article *the* is often used.	*The* cars are being towed. *The* train is crowded.

Skill 1: Developing Business Vocabulary

Exercise 1

Write the letter of the correct definition next to each word. Then complete the passage with the correct words.

Group A

_d_	1. board	a. late
____	2. change	b. money in the form of coins
____	3. delayed	c. a place where a train arrives
____	4. discussion	d. get on a train or plane
____	5. station	e. a conversation about a topic

A man and a woman are standing in the (6)__station__. The train is (7)____________, and they have been waiting for it for a long time. They bought their tickets from a machine. They used bills and (8)____________ to pay for the tickets because the machine doesn't take credit cards. They are having an interesting (9)____________ about business. They often talk about their business as they ride the train to work. As soon as the train arrives, they will (10)____________ it and look for a seat in the dining car.

Group B

____	1. attendant	a. clothing style
____	2. check in	b. a situation where things can't move
____	3. fashion	c. a person who provides personal service
____	4. hairdresser	d. register at a hotel
____	5. jam	e. a person who cuts, washes, and arranges hair

A woman has just arrived at the hotel and wants to (6)____________. She hopes they will give her a room on the first floor. She has arrived later than she expected because there was a big traffic (7)____________, and she had to drive very slowly. The (8)____________ takes her credit card number and gives her a room key. The woman asks if there is a (9)____________ in the hotel. She has to go to a party soon, and she wants to look nice. She is a famous (10)____________ designer. The clothes she designs are popular all around the world. The party is for other designers like her.

Group C

____ 1. address a. the window in the front of a car

____ 2. elevator b. speak to

____ 3. experiment c. scientific test

____ 4. puddles d. water on the ground

____ 5. windshield e. a machine that carries people up and down in buildings

A man is driving in the rain. There are (6)____________ everywhere, and the man's shoes got very wet when he walked to his car. He is driving slowly because it is raining very hard and he can't see clearly through the (7)____________. He is on his way to a conference. He is going to (8)____________ a group of scientists. He is going to talk about the (9)____________ he has been working on. He is late. When he gets to the conference, he won't take the time to wait for the (10)____________. It is faster to run up the stairs.

Exercise 2

Complete the sentences with the correct word form.

attendant (*noun*) **attendance** (*noun*) **attend** (*verb*)

1. About 500 people will ___attend___ the conference.
2. We will need a large room because we expect the ___attendance___ to be high.
3. The ___attendant___ at the desk will help you.

discussion (*noun*) **discussant** (*noun*) **discuss** (*verb*)

4. Each ___discussant___ at the conference had a different point of view.
5. It was such a boring ___discussion___ that I almost fell asleep.
6. They usually like to ___discuss___ politics together.

experiment (*noun*) **experiment** (*verb*) **experimental** (*adjective*)

7. Several scientists worked on the ___experiment___ together.
8. They decided to ___experiment (verb)___ with using a different type of material.
9. It was an ___experimental___ project; no one had ever tried anything like it before.

Skill 2: Analyzing the Photo

Some TOEIC test questions ask for information about the photo. You will need to analyze the photo and practice describing what is happening in the photo.

Sample TOEIC Test Question

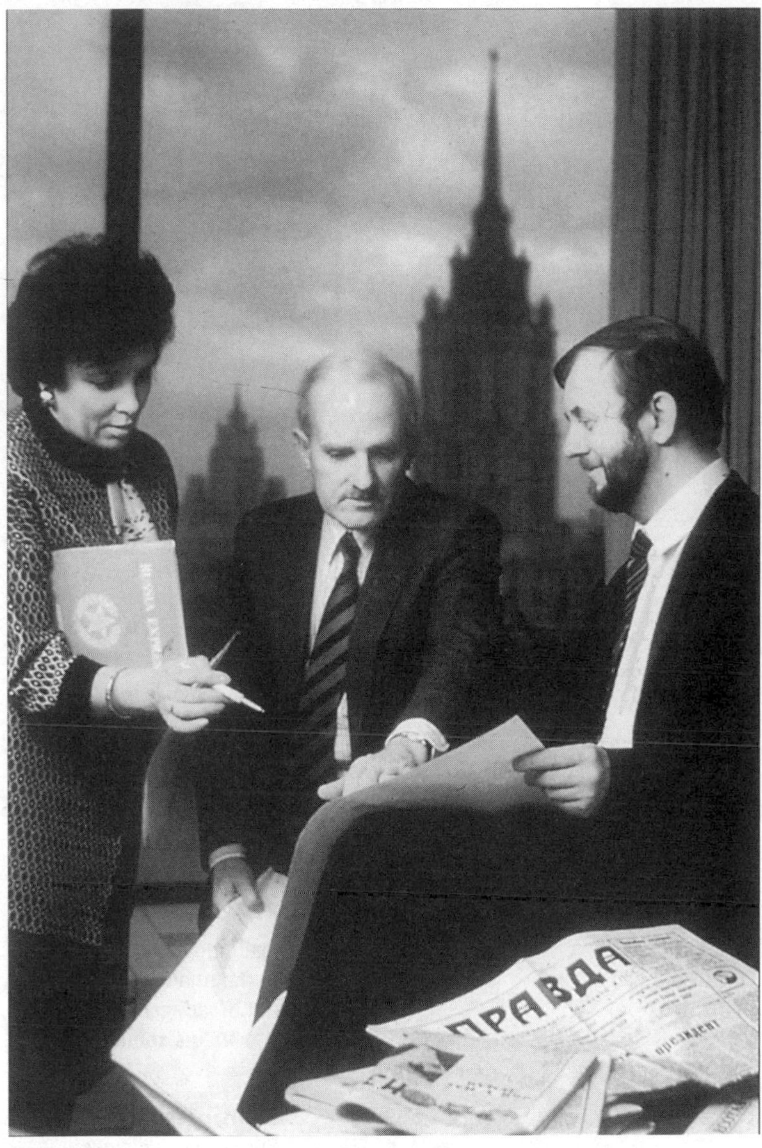

<u>You will hear</u>: (A) *They're looking at some papers.*
(B) *They're standing outside.*
(C) *They're looking out the window.*
(D) *They're delivering newspapers.*

Answer

Choice (A), *They're looking at some papers,* best describes what you see in the photo. Choice (B) is incorrect because they are standing inside, not outside. Choice (C) is incorrect because they are talking, not looking out the window. Choice (D) is incorrect because one man is holding papers, but he is not delivering newspapers.

Skill Focus

When you analyze the photo, look for the overall focus. This is the main idea. Look at what seems to be happening and what people are doing. Describe the scene to yourself, but try to differentiate between key ideas and details. You may want to use *there is/there are* or the present continuous in your descriptions.

Here are some examples of main idea statements that fit the photo on page 7.

- Three people are looking at some papers.
- They are having a business meeting.
- A woman and two men are talking.
- They are discussing a document.

Now read the following detail statements. Compare them to the main idea statements.

- The woman is holding a pen.
- There are newspapers on the table.
- The men are wearing ties.
- There is a large window.

Both the main idea statements and the detail statements are true and fit the photo, but the main idea statements tell us important information about the photo.

For practice, look at other photos in the book and describe each scene to yourself. Concentrate on the main ideas.

Skill 2: Exercise

Circle the main idea in the following choices. Be prepared to explain your choices.

1. (A) They're having a discussion.
   (B) There are cups on the table.
   (C) Their suits are very nice.
   (D) They're wearing glasses.

2. (A) A calendar is on the wall.
   (B) It's a sunny day outside.
   (C) A woman is on the phone.
   (D) She has pens on her desk.

3. (A) The plane is ready to leave.
   (B) Pilots wear uniforms.
   (C) It's ten o'clock in the morning.
   (D) Flying is expensive.

TEST TIP

Main ideas are specific to the photo. They are not broad, general statements about a topic.

Examples:
Businesspeople make presentations. (broad, general statement)

The businessman is making a presentation. (main idea about a photo)

4. (A) The woman is drinking coffee.
   (B) The woman's hair is long and dark.
   (C) The man is applying for a job.
   (D) The man is wearing a white shirt.

5. (A) The speaker is tall and thin.
   (B) Some speakers are interesting.
   (C) Three people have coats on.
   (D) People are listening to a speaker.

6. (A) The man is looking at some plans.
   (B) The man is short.
   (C) It is a sunny day.
   (D) The man is outside.

7. (A) A man is wearing a hat.
   (B) They're waiting for a train.
   (C) A woman is holding an umbrella.
   (D) There are two children.

8. (A) Bus drivers should be courteous.
   (B) One man has a leather briefcase.
   (C) Buses are not very comfortable.
   (D) Passengers are getting off a bus.

TEST TIP

It is often possible to choose the main idea without looking at a photo. Carefully read each of the four choices. Cross out any statements that are simply details. Then decide which of the remaining choices is probably the main idea.

Skill 3: Distinguishing Similar Sounds

In the new TOEIC test, you may have to choose among statements that contain similar-sounding words. Some English words have similar pronunciations. To distinguish similar-sounding words, listen carefully for the differences in sounds. Then think about what will make sense in the sentence.

Sample TOEIC Test Question

You will hear: (A) *The station is crowded.*
(B) *They're planning a vacation.*
(C) *They'll take a plane.*
(D) *They're waiting for the train.*

Answer

Choice (D), *They're waiting for the train,* best describes what you see in the photo. You see people standing on the platform at a train station. Choice (A) talks about a station, but it is incorrect because there aren't a lot of people at the station in the photo. Choice (B) is incorrect because it confuses *vacation* with *station.* Also, you cannot tell by the photo if the people are planning anything. Choice (C) is incorrect because it confuses the similar-sounding *plane* and *train.*

Skill Focus

To learn how to distinguish similar sounds, you should hear the words pronounced in pairs. The pairs of words that follow all have similar sounds. Read these pairs of words aloud or listen as a friend reads them. Pay attention to the different sounds.

Words that sound similar at the beginning

personal	personnel
magnetic	magnitude
respectively	respectfully
than	then
devise	device

Words that sound similar at the end

hand	brand
cab	tab
large	charge
pay	say
place	pace
grain	drain
date	rate
then	yen
dine	fine
rest	guest

Words that sound similar when combined with other words

(he is)	he's	his
(he will)	he'll	hill
(we will)	we'll	well

Skill 3: Exercise

Circle the word in each row that doesn't have a similar sound.

1. zip	tip	ship	pipe
2. night	write	high	flight
3. how	show	now	plow
4. box	socks	locks	smokes
5. trunk	brunch	hunch	lunch
6. five	strive	glib	drive
7. coast	most	cost	post
8. chose	choose	close	those
9. bin	dime	rhyme	time
10. ram	jam	lame	lamb

TEST TIP

Reading aloud and listening to poetry that rhymes are good ways to practice listening for different sounds.

Skill 4: Making Inferences

In the new TOEIC test, you may be asked to make inferences about the photos. When you make an inference, you think ahead or predict what might happen next. You may not SEE the action, but you can make a guess about the action. Determine the facts presented in the photo and make inferences accordingly.

Sample TOEIC Test Question

You will hear: (A) *The waiter is changing his clothes.*
(B) *He's about to give them change.*
(C) *They're parking their car on the sidewalk.*
(D) *Coffee beans are sold.*

Answer

Choice (B), *He's about to give them change*, best describes what you see in the photo. The waiter has served them and could be looking for change. Therefore, the waiter is probably about to give the customers their change. Choice (A) is incorrect because it confuses *change* (money) with *changing his clothes*. Choice (C) is incorrect because you may see a car and a sidewalk, but the sentence doesn't make sense for the photo. Choice (D) is incorrect because it confuses the similar-sounding *coffee* with *café*.

Skill Focus

To make an inference about the future, listen for the future tense of the verb. This will tell you which action we can infer will happen in the future. Study these structures that show future time in English.

Structures for Future Tense	Examples
will + base form of verb	He *will go.* They *will pay.* She *will shake* hands.
(*to be*) + *going to* + base form of verb	She*'s going to ask* a question. They*'re going to discuss* the experiment.
(*to be*) *about to* + base form of verb	He *is about to speak.* They *are about to land.*
(*to be*) + infinitive	He *is to leave* at four o'clock. They *are to plan* the meeting.

Look at other photos in this book. Make inferences about what might happen next.

Skill 4: Exercise

Choose the best inference based on each photo description.

____ 1. a cloudy sky

(A) The sun will shine for the picnic.

(B) It's going to rain.

(C) The stars will come out.

(D) There isn't a cloud in the sky.

____ 2. cars in a traffic jam

(A) The cars will move quickly.

(B) The drivers will wait patiently.

(C) Someone will be late.

(D) No one is driving slowly.

____ 3. people in line at an airport gate

(A) They're going to board a plane.

(B) Their flight is delayed.

(C) They're about to go home.

(D) They're traveling on business.

TEST TIP

An inference should be something that is likely to happen. It should not be something that is possible but not probable or not related closely to the topic.

____ **4.** a housekeeper entering a messy hotel room

(A) She will check into the hotel.

(B) She's about to leave a tip.

(C) She's going to clean the room.

(D) She's going to go to bed.

____ **5.** a courier with a package going down a hall

(A) He will open the package.

(B) He's about to deliver the package.

(C) He's going to drop the package.

(D) He's going to keep the package.

____ **6.** a woman running after a bus

(A) She missed the bus.

(B) She likes to chase buses.

(C) She wants some exercise.

(D) She is going to the movies.

____ **7.** a man carrying a shopping bag

(A) He stole the bag.

(B) He is going to play tennis.

(C) He is an accountant.

(D) He bought a new shirt.

____ **8.** a man wearing a heavy coat

(A) He's going swimming.

(B) It's cold outside.

(C) It's summer time.

(D) His car broke down.

Part 1 Practice

You will hear four statements about each photo. Choose the statement that best describes what you see in the photo.

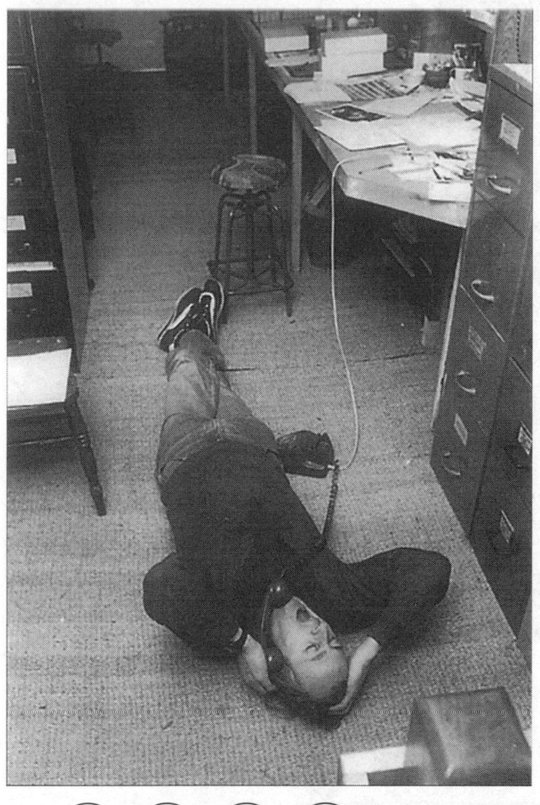

TEST TIP

The correct answer is one of four choices: (A), (B), (C), or (D). You have a 25 percent chance of guessing correctly. Eliminate one choice, and you have a 33⅓ percent chance. Eliminate another choice and you have a 50 percent chance.

1. (A) (B) (C) (D)

2. (A) (B) (C) (D)

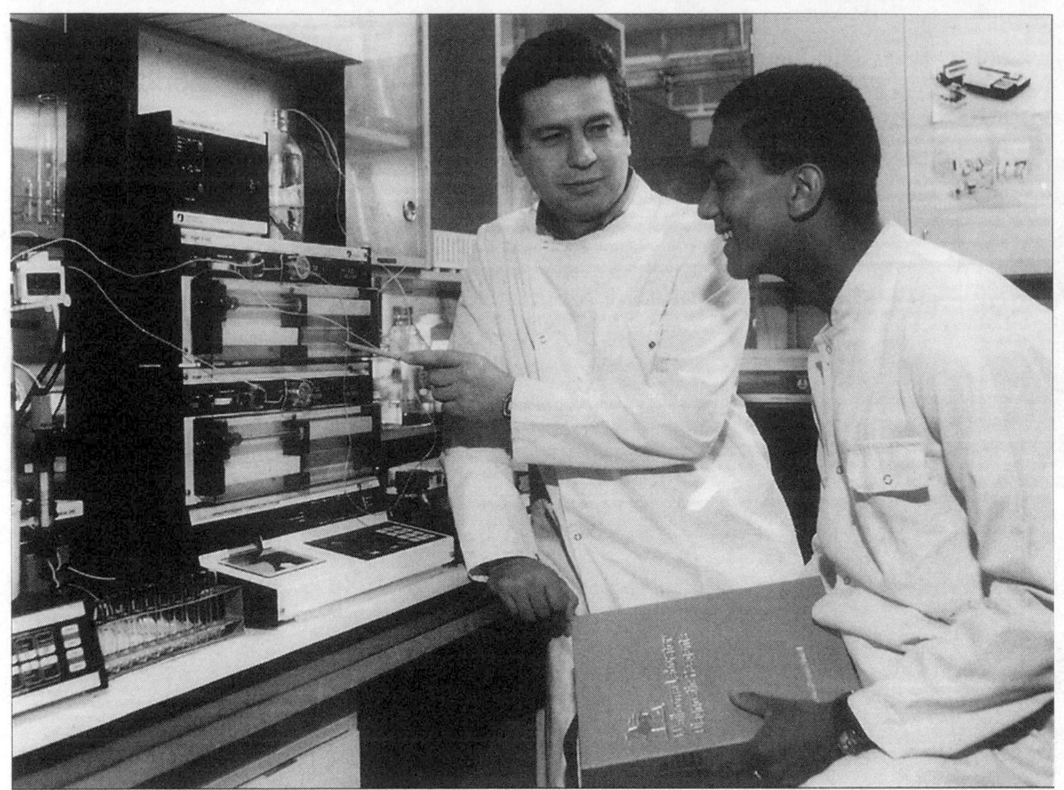

3. Ⓐ Ⓑ Ⓒ Ⓓ

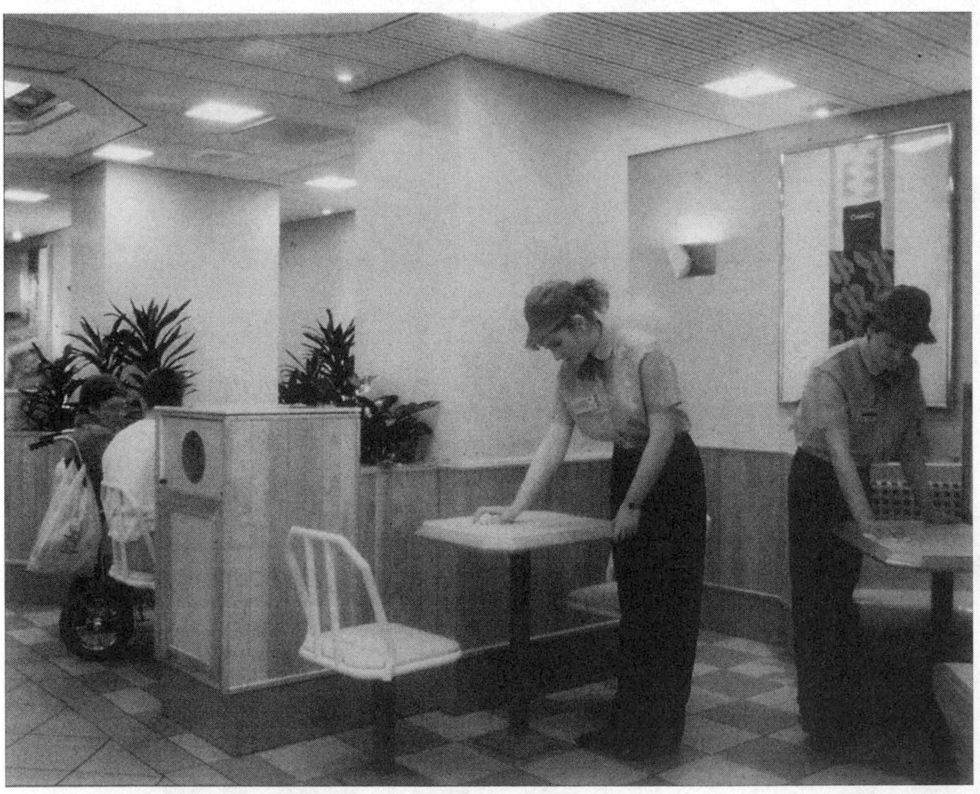

4. Ⓐ Ⓑ Ⓒ Ⓓ

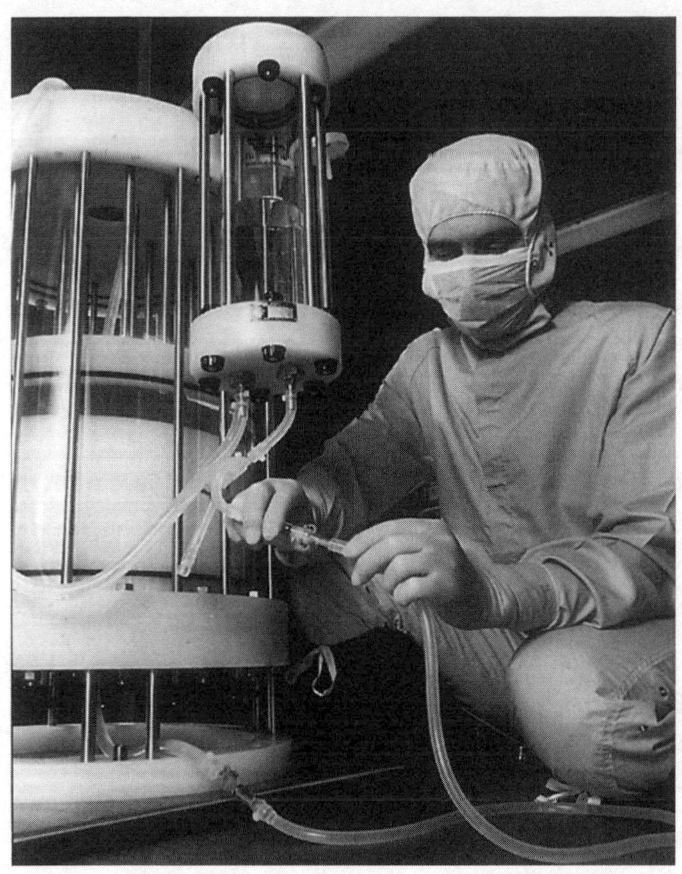

5. Ⓐ Ⓑ Ⓒ Ⓓ

6. Ⓐ Ⓑ Ⓒ Ⓓ

Part 2: Question-Response

OBJECTIVES

You can improve your score in Part 2 by:

- developing business vocabulary
- distinguishing *Wh-* and Yes/No questions
- identifying homophones
- recognizing negative meaning

In Part 2 of the new TOEIC® test, you will hear a question and three responses. You will hear the question and the responses one time only. You will not be able to read them, so listen carefully and choose the best response to each question. You will have five seconds to answer each question.

Sample TOEIC Test Question

You will hear: *How can I get to the airport from here?*
You will also hear: (A) *Take a taxi. It's just a short ride.*
(B) *No, I don't.*
(C) *You can get on easily.*

Answer

Choice (A), *Take a taxi. It's just a short ride,* is the best response to this *Wh-* question. Choice (A) directly answers the *Wh-* question *How.* Choice (B) is incorrect because this is a response to a Yes/No question. Choice (C) is incorrect because it confuses the similar-sounding *get on* with *get to.*

Types of Questions

There are two types of questions in Part 2: *Wh-* questions and Yes/No questions.

_Wh-_ Questions

Wh- questions ask for information. These questions begin with *Wh-* words.
Who . . . ? *What . . . ?* *Where . . . ?* *When . . . ?* *How long . . . ?*

Yes/No Questions

These questions expect a *Yes* or *No* response. Yes/No questions begin with auxiliary verbs.
Does he . . . ? *Can you . . . ?* *Will she . . . ?* *Have we . . . ?* *Are they . . . ?*

Skill 1: Developing Business Vocabulary

Exercise 1

Write the letter of the correct definition next to each word. Then complete the passage with the correct words.

Group A

____ 1. invoice a. a bill asking for payment
____ 2. loyal b. take away a number
____ 3. revenue c. faithful
____ 4. shipment d. things that are sent
____ 5. subtract e. money earned in a business

Customers expect to receive their orders in a timely manner, and a good business always sends out each (6)________ on time. It is important to include the (7)________ with each order sent. This encourages timely payment. When customers don't pay their bills on time, the company's (8)________ goes down. Some companies (9)________ a small percentage from the money owed when bills are paid on time. This discount encourages timely payment. Sending orders on time and giving discounts keeps customers happy. Every company wants (10)________ customers who will continue to bring their business to it.

Group B

____ 1. agency a. the space between rows
____ 2. aisle b. a business that provides a particular service
____ 3. calculate c. an arrangement made ahead of time
____ 4. raze d. tear down a building
____ 5. reservation e. find the answer to a math problem

Easy Going Tours is the top tourist (6)________ in the area. Join us for a day-long bus tour of the major points of interest in our city. We will begin in the historic district. Don't miss this opportunity to see some interesting old buildings. The city plans to (7)________ several of these soon to make way for modern offices. We will then visit several museums, government buildings, and City Park. This is a popular tour, so make your (8)________ early to make sure that you get a place on the date of your choice. Please let us know if you prefer a seat by a window or on the (9)________. When you (10)________ the cost of your tickets, remember that there is a 15 percent discount for groups of four or more.

Group C

____	1. contact	**a.**	identify; know who someone is
____	2. functioning	**b.**	forget; leave out
____	3. microphone	**c.**	talk to or write to someone
____	4. omit	**d.**	performing; in working order
____	5. recognize	**e.**	a machine that makes sounds louder

When you prepare for a conference, you will want to make sure that all equipment is (6)________. You should (7)________ a repairperson to fix any broken equipment well ahead of time so that everything will be ready on the day of the conference. If you expect a large audience, you will need a (8)________ so that everyone will be able to hear the speakers. Don't (9)________ video and computer equipment since your speakers will probably want to use these, too. It's a good idea to prepare some background information about your speakers. Even if they are famous, not everyone in the audience will (10)________ them.

Exercise 2

Complete the sentences with the correct word form.

calculation (*noun*) **calculator** (*noun*) **calculate** (*verb*)

1. I don't need to know how to do arithmetic because I always use a ________.
2. Some math problems are very difficult to ________.
3. The numbers don't match because this ________ is incorrect.

recognition (*noun*) **recognize** (*verb*) **recognizable** (*adjective*)

4. His voice wasn't ________ over the telephone.
5. It isn't always easy to ________ people you haven't seen for years.
6. He looked at her but showed no ________.

shipment (*noun*) **ship** (*verb*) **shippable** (*adjective*)

7. This order will be ________ as soon as the customer pays.
8. We sent out a large ________ yesterday.
9. They will ________ the order as soon as possible.

Skill 2: Distinguishing *Wh-* and Yes/No Questions

In the new TOEIC test, you may have to determine the type of the question asked in order to choose the correct response. The wording of an answer has to be appropriate for the type of question asked. Make sure you can distinguish *Wh-* questions from Yes/No questions.

Sample TOEIC Test Question

You will hear: *When will the package arrive?*
You will also hear: (A) *Any minute.*
(B) *No, not yet.*
(C) *I'll pack it now.*

Answer

Choice (A), *Any minute,* is the correct answer because it has the correct form and answers the *Wh-* question *When.* Choice (B) is incorrect because its form is appropriate for answering Yes/No questions. It could be the correct answer if the question were *Has the package arrived?* Choice (C) is incorrect because it confuses the similar sounds of *pack it* and *package.*

Skill Focus

The first words of a question are very important. They let you know immediately whether the question is *Wh-* or Yes/No. When you know what kind of question you have, you can predict the structure of your answer and the kind of information it should have.

***Wh-* Questions**	**Possible Responses**
Who . . . ?	The sales director.
What . . . ?	A meeting.
Where . . . ?	On the second floor.
When . . . ?	At 10:00.
Why . . . ?	Because I was late.
How long . . . ?	For one hour.

Yes/No Questions	**Possible Responses**
Does he . . . ?	Yes, he does.
Can you . . . ?	No, I can't.
Will she . . . ?	Yes, she will.
Have we . . . ?	No, we haven't.
Should they . . . ?	Yes, they should.

Skill 2: Exercise

Read each question. Then circle the correct question type.

1. Who is talking?

   (A) *Wh-*
   (B) Yes/No

2. Are they prepared?

   (A) *Wh-*
   (B) Yes/No

3. Where are they?

   (A) *Wh-*
   (B) Yes/No

4. Have you ever been abroad?

   (A) *Wh-*
   (B) Yes/No

5. What will the tour be like?

   (A) *Wh-*
   (B) Yes/No

6. Would you like some coffee?

   (A) *Wh-*
   (B) Yes/No

7. Will he call when he is ready?

   (A) *Wh-*
   (B) Yes/No

8. Why were you late for work?

   (A) *Wh-*
   (B) Yes/No

9. How often do you come here?

   (A) *Wh-*
   (B) Yes/No

10. Isn't that her boss?

    (A) *Wh-*
    (B) Yes/No

TEST TIP

The answers to Yes/No questions begin with *yes* or *no*. Sometimes, the *yes* or *no* is understood but not spoken.

Example:
Should we arrive early?

(Yes,) you should definitely come early.

Skill 3: Identifying Homophones

In the new TOEIC test, you may have to recognize the different meanings of homophones. Homophones are words that sound alike but have different meanings and spellings. You cannot distinguish homophones by their pronunciation. You must distinguish them by the meaning of the sentence.

Sample TOEIC Test Question

You will hear: *What will the weather be like tomorrow?*

You will also hear: (A) *He'll be here at seven.*
(B) *I think it's going to rain.*
(C) *She doesn't know whether she'll go.*

Answer

Choice (B), *I think it's going to rain*, is the best response to the question. The *Wh-* question is asking for a weather forecast. Choice (A) is incorrect because it confuses the similar-sounding *will the weather be* with *He'll be*. Choice (C) is incorrect because it confuses the homophones *whether* and *weather*.

Skill Focus

Homophones can always be distinguished by their meanings, even when you do not see them written down. Because each homophone in a pair has a different meaning, the words around a homophone in a sentence will indicate which homophone is being used. If the homophones are different parts of speech (and many of them are), the position of the word in the sentence will also help. You will see why this is true when you read the following example questions and responses.

Homophones (meaning)	Examples
ad (advertisement) *add* (addition)	Did you see this *ad* in the paper? Did you *add* and subtract the numbers correctly?
allowed (permitted) *aloud* (audible)	No one is *allowed* in the building after dark. No one was willing to read *aloud* to the group.
band (orchestra) *banned* (prohibited)	The *band* gave a concert in the park. Dogs without leashes are *banned* from the park.
board (leaders of a firm) *bored* (uninterested)	The *board* is meeting in the conference room. Everyone got *bored* at the meeting.
cents (money) *sense* (intelligence)	It costs 50 *cents* to ride the bus. It makes *sense* to ride the bus.
sight (ability to see) *site* (location)	People's *sight* tends to change as they age. That *site* had three houses on it over the years.
fair (just, honest) *fare* (cost)	The decision should be *fair* for everyone. The *fare* has increased for everyone.
find (discover) *fined* (given a penalty)	People sometimes *find* lost items when they are not looking for them. People can be *fined* for crossing the street without a signal.

(Continued on next page)

Homophones (meaning)	Examples
guessed (supposed) *guest* (visitor)	Mr. Ho *guessed* that Mr. Yoder was visiting. Mr. Ho knew that Mr. Yoder was our *guest*.
higher (above, greater) *hire* (employ)	The revenue from sales of the product is *higher* this year. We must *hire* more employees.
knew (past tense of *know*) *new* (opposite of *old*)	He *knew* where to buy a computer. He just bought a *new* computer.
mail (send by post) *male* (opposite of *female*)	The *mail* was delivered at 11:00. The person who delivered the package was *male*.
meat (food) *meet* (to get acquainted with or spend time with someone)	I don't eat much *meat* at lunch. I *meet* her every day for lunch.
overseas (abroad) *oversees* (supervises)	Ms. Dechaine is working on a project *overseas*. Ms. Dechaine *oversees* a new project at work.
pear (fruit) *pair* (two)	I need to buy a *pear* and some apples at the market. I need to buy a new *pair* of shoes.
road (street) *rode* (past tense of *ride*)	The country *road* needed to be repaired. He *rode* into the country to look at the scenery.
sale (low prices) *sail* (travel by boat)	Mr. Sulka bought his boat on *sale*. Mr. Sulka likes to *sail* his boat on weekends.
some (part) *sum* (total of addition)	You should get *some* help calculating those invoice totals. Your *sum* does not match the total on the invoice.
suite (group of rooms or offices) *sweet* (taste of sugar)	Please make a reservation for the Presidential *Suite*. Please bring me something *sweet*.
wear (dress in) *where* (tells place)	What should I *wear* to the party? *Where* is the party taking place?
weigh (number of pounds) *way* (direction)	I don't want to tell the doctor what I *weigh*. I don't know the *way* to the doctor's office.
weak (lack of strength) *week* (seven days)	She has been *weak* since her illness. She has been ill for a *week*.

Skill 3: Exercise

Circle the correct response to each question. Then underline the homophones.

1. You will hear: *Do you know where we are to meet?*
   (A) In the conference center.
   (B) Wear a suit.
   (C) I don't want meat.

2. You will hear: *Where can I hire a guide?*
   (A) I can make it lower.
   (B) Go to the tourist agency across the street.
   (C) It won't go higher.

3. You will hear: *What's the total sum?*
   (A) It's over a thousand.
   (B) We can't omit any of it.
   (C) Some of us are loyal.

4. You will hear: *Did they raise the fare?*
   (A) Yes. It costs 50 cents more.
   (B) It's not fair to anyone.
   (C) They razed the building.

5. You will hear: *Do you prefer an aisle seat or a window seat for your guest?*
   (A) He guessed correctly.
   (B) I'll see where he is.
   (C) It doesn't matter.

6. You will hear: *Did he have a long wait?*
   (A) At the airport.
   (B) No, he lost weight.
   (C) About three hours.

TEST TIP

Sometimes homophones are stated directly in incorrect choices. Other times, homophones are stated indirectly, or implied.

Examples:
The boat was at full *sail*.

I paid full price for the shipment. (Implied: I didn't get it on *sale*.)

Skill 4: Recognizing Negative Meaning

In the new TOEIC test, you must determine whether statements you hear have positive or negative meanings. To do this, you will need to learn to recognize negative expressions and understand how they change meaning.

Sample TOEIC Test Question

You will hear: *Why didn't the presentation start on time?*
You will also hear: (A) *That clock is never wrong.*
(B) *Nobody was late for the presentation.*
(C) *The microphone was not functioning.*

Answer

Choice (C), *The microphone was not functioning*, is the best explanation for the presentation not starting on time. Choice (A) is incorrect because *is never wrong* means *is always correct*. This does not explain why the presentation did not start on time. Choice (B) is incorrect because *Nobody was late* means *everyone was on time*. This does not explain why the presentation did not start on time.

Skill Focus

Usually, English sentences have only one negative word. Verbs are negative when they are used with the negative word *not* (such as *do not*). Other words indicate other negative ideas (for example, *nobody* means *no people*). Study the following negative expressions. Remember that these expressions make the meaning of a sentence negative.

Negative Expressions

not	not all
no	not at all
no one	none
never	nor
not ever	neither
nobody	

Choose some positive statements from this book. Rewrite them so their meanings are negative, for example:

That clock is always right. = That clock is never wrong.

Skill 4: Exercise

Read each sentence. Then circle the letter of the sentence that means the same thing.

1. There's no one in the office.
   (A) Only one person is there.
   (B) Nobody is there.

2. Neither Yoshi nor I know.
   (A) We don't know.
   (B) I know.

3. He's not at all happy.
   (A) He's unhappy.
   (B) He's not unhappy.

4. She didn't recognize anybody.
   (A) She didn't recognize all the people.
   (B) She recognized no one at all.

5. Not all members participated.
   (A) Some members participated.
   (B) No one participated.

6. No one was in the room.
   (A) The room had no people.
   (B) There were some people in the room.

7. They are never on time.
   (A) They aren't ever late.
   (B) They are always tardy.

8. I wasn't at all uncomfortable.
   (A) I was comfortable.
   (B) I was uncomfortable.

TEST TIP

Prefixes can also be negative. The most common negative prefix is *un-*, as in *unfriendly*. Be careful about negative verbs in sentences with words that have negative prefixes as they actually express a positive meaning in English.

Example:
She's not unfriendly. = She's friendly.

Part 2 Practice

You will hear a question, followed by three responses. Choose the best response to each question.

1. Ⓐ ● Ⓒ
2. Ⓐ Ⓑ ●
3. Ⓐ ● Ⓒ
4. ● Ⓑ Ⓒ
5. Ⓐ Ⓑ ●
6. Ⓐ ● Ⓒ
7. ● Ⓑ Ⓒ
8. ● Ⓑ Ⓒ
9. ● Ⓑ Ⓒ
10. Ⓐ ● Ⓒ

Part 3: Conversations

OBJECTIVES

You can improve your score in Part 3 by:

- developing business vocabulary
- listening for the main idea
- understanding *Wh-* questions
- understanding modal verbs

In Part 3 of the new TOEIC test, you will hear ten conversations. The conversations are between two people. Listen to the conversations carefully. You will hear each conversation only once.

Then, in your test book, you will read three questions about each conversation. You will also read four answer choices. Choose the best answer for each question. You will have eight seconds to answer each question.

Sample TOEIC Test Questions

You will hear:

WOMAN: *When are you leaving on your trip?*

MAN: *Tomorrow evening on the five o'clock train. I'll be gone for 12 days.*

WOMAN: *Wow. That's close to two weeks. It must be exciting to travel to faraway places.*

MAN: *To tell you the truth, I'm not happy about this trip. At this point in my career, long trips like this just aren't interesting anymore.*

You will read:

1. How long will the man's trip last?
   (A) Four days.
   (B) Five days.
   (C) Almost two weeks.
   (D) Exactly two weeks.

2. How will he travel?
   (A) By car.
   (B) By bus.
   (C) By plane.
   (D) By train.

3. How does he feel about his trip?
   (A) Bored.
   (B) Happy.
   (C) Excited.
   (D) Interested.

Answers

1. Choice (C) is the correct answer. The man will be gone for 12 days, which is almost two weeks. Choice (A) confuses *four* with *for*. Choice (B) is confused with the time the man will leave, *five* o'clock. Choice (D) repeats the phrase *two weeks*.

2. Choice (D) is the correct answer. The man says he will leave *on the five o'clock train*. Choice (A) confuses *car* with *far*. Choice (B) is not mentioned. Choice (C) sounds similar to the correct answer.

3. Choice (A) is the correct answer. The man says that he is *not happy* about the trip and that he thinks trips *like this just aren't interesting*. Choices (B) and (D) are how the man says he doesn't feel. Choice (C) is how the woman thinks he must feel.

Types of Questions

In Part 3, the questions ask either about the general idea of the conversation or for specific information from the conversation. These questions have three common characteristics.

Characteristics	Examples
The questions are often very short.	Who is talking? Where are they? What day is it?
The questions often ask for information. (The first word may be a *Wh-* word.)	When is the man's vacation? What does the client want? Where is the meeting?
The questions are often in the simple present or the present continuous tense.	Where does the woman work? Why is she changing her job? When is he leaving?

Knowing these characteristics will help you to predict the types of questions you might see. This will help you find the answer more quickly.

Skill 1: Developing Business Vocabulary

Exercise 1

Write the letter of the correct definition next to each word. Then complete the passage with the correct words.

Group A

____	1. appetizers	a. small servings of food served before the main meal
____	2. check	b. look at
____	3. illustrated	c. many
____	4. numerous	d. suggest
____	5. recommend	e. used pictures for

Rosie's Restaurant has been voted the most popular restaurant in the city! Start your meal with some of our famous (6)____________. Don't forget to (7)____________ our daily specials board to see what special dishes we are serving, or choose your meal from the menu. Don't know what to order? Your waiter will be happy to (8)____________ a dish that you will surely enjoy. We have (9)____________ the menu with photographs so you can know exactly what your meal will look like. Do you like sweet things? Then choose one of the (10)____________ desserts on the menu to end your meal. With so many dessert choices, you just might have to order two!

Group B

____	1. graphics	a. studied
____	2. presentation	b. suggested plan
____	3. proposal	c. pictures, charts, etc.
____	4. researched	d. hand in; give
____	5. submit	e. speech

Anyone interested in giving a (6)____________ at the next Business Owners' Conference should contact the conference organizers soon. Send us a (7)____________ to let us know what you want to talk about, and include the exact topic and length of time you will need. You will have to show that you have (8)____________ your topic well, and you should plan to use (9)____________ to make your information clearer. Please (10)____________ your ideas to the Conference Committee before the end of this month.

Group C

____ 1. contract a. a move to a higher job

____ 2. employee b. ask

____ 3. inquire c. a document showing a formal agreement

____ 4. postpone d. a person who works for a company

____ 5. promotion e. put off to a later date

It's exciting to be hired for a new job, but don't let your excitement lead you to mistakes. As a new (6)____________ you probably are not familiar with many things about the company. First, it is important to read your (7)____________ carefully before you sign it. Make sure you understand everything in the agreement, and (8)____________ about any areas that are not clear to you. Don't (9)____________ this until later. It is important to understand everything before you sign. Make sure you know what salary you will be paid and how the company decides on making an employee's (10)____________. You need to know what you will have to do to move up in the company.

Exercise 2

Complete the sentences with the correct word form.

employee (*noun*) **employer** (*noun*) **employ** (*verb*)

1. It is up to the ____________ to decide a worker's salary.
2. A new ____________ needs some time to learn the new job.
3. International companies ____________ people who speak several languages.

illustration (*noun*) **illustrator** (*noun*) **illustrate** (*verb*)

4. They chose a famous artist to ____________ the book.
5. We need a large ____________ to make this information clearer.
6. The ____________ drew some beautiful pictures.

presentation (*noun*) **presenter** (*noun*) **present** (*verb*)

7. The ____________ will speak about world politics.
8. He will ____________ information that will shock you.
9. The ____________ is scheduled to last for almost an hour.

Skill 2: Listening for the Main Idea

In Part 3, you may be asked questions about the main idea of the conversation. To answer these questions, focus on the whole conversation, not just part of it.

Sample TOEIC Test Question

You will hear:

MAN: *My car won't start. And look at the time. I'll be really late for work.*

WOMAN: *There's a garage around the corner that has a very good mechanic.*

MAN: *I guess I'll have to have the car towed there. But then I'll still have to find a way to get to work.*

WOMAN: *The subway station isn't far from here. That should get you anywhere you want to go fairly quickly.*

You will read:

1. What is the problem?
   (A) He is lost.
   (B) He needs a job.
   (C) The car needs repair.
   (D) The garage is closed.

Answer

Choice (C) is the correct answer. *My car won't start* means something is wrong with the car and it needs to be repaired. Choice (A) incorrectly infers that the man is lost from the fact that the woman gives him directions to a garage. Choice (B) confuses the idea of needing a job with the mention of going to work. Choice (D) is probably incorrect. Since the woman suggests the garage as a solution, she expects it to be open and helping motorists.

Skill Focus

It is very helpful to distinguish questions that ask for main ideas from other types of questions. If you know you have to answer a main idea question, you will know what kind of information to listen for. Study these common main idea questions.

- What are the speakers planning to do?
- Where are the speakers?
- Where does this conversation take place?
- What are the speakers talking about?

Skill 2: Exercise

Read the conversations. Then read questions (A) and (B). Circle the question that asks about the main idea. Finally, think about possible answers to the question.

1. MAN: *I'll be back in a few minutes. I have to stop by the Service Department to check an order.*
   WOMAN: *What's the trouble?*
   MAN: *The order was delivered two weeks late. I need to find out what's going on there. It was a simple order to fulfill.*
   WOMAN: *All right. I'll wait for you here.*

   Which question asks the main idea?
   (A) How late was the order?
   (B) What is the man going to do?

> **TEST TIP**
>
> Practice summarizing in one sentence what you hear (or read) in a conversation. Then turn your summary sentence into a main idea question. This will help you anticipate questions on the new TOEIC test.
>
> **Example:**
> The man is going to the Service Department to check on an order.
>
> What is the man going to do?

2. WOMAN: *You won't forget to stress the importance of design, of course.*
   MAN: *Of course not. It's an important part of my presentation.*
   WOMAN: *And remember to illustrate your speech with good graphics. That really helps the audience follow what you're talking about.*
   MAN: *I know, I know. Don't worry, I was up all night preparing everything. It'll be fine.*

   Which question asks the main idea?
   (A) What are the speakers talking about?
   (B) Why should the man use graphics?

3. MAN: *She has ten years of experience, and she works well with people.*
   WOMAN: *And you can tell she's good with numbers, too.*
   MAN: *I think she's got everything we've been looking for. Let's recommend her for the job.*
   WOMAN: *Yes, let's. We need her skills immediately. She's definitely the best candidate.*

   Which question asks the main idea?
   (A) What are the speakers planning to do?
   (B) How much experience does the woman have?

4. WOMAN: *Do you think we'll get what we want on this contract?*
   MAN: *I'm not sure. We disagree on some key points. It may be tricky.*
   WOMAN: *Well, we'll have to do the best we can to at least get something satisfactory.*
   MAN: *We'll work something out. Bill has a lot of experience with contracts.*

   Which question asks the main idea?
   (A) What do the speakers disagree on?
   (B) What are the speakers discussing?

5. WOMAN: *Do you have exercise facilities at this hotel?*
   MAN: *No, but we offer guests a courtesy pass for the gym next door.*
   WOMAN: *Great. I'd like one for tonight, please. I really need a good workout after that long plane ride.*
   MAN: *I'm sorry, the gym isn't open this late, but it does open fairly early in the morning, at 5:30, I think. You can use it then.*

   Which question asks the main idea?
   (A) What is the woman inquiring about?
   (B) How many passes does the woman request?

Skill 3: Understanding *Wh-* Questions

In Part 3, you may be asked information questions. Information questions start with *Wh-* words. To answer information questions, focus on the meaning of the *Wh-* words *(what, why, who, where, when, how much,* and *how long)*. These types of questions ask for either the main idea of the conversation or specific information from the conversation.

Study these example *Wh-* questions.

- What is Mr. Rozicer angry about?
- What are the women discussing?
- Who are the speakers talking about?
- Why is the man going by train?

Sample TOEIC Test Question

You will hear:

WOMAN: *I have tickets for the one o'clock flight. Can you tell me which gate it's leaving from?*

MAN: *I'm sorry. That flight has been delayed for two hours. We won't announce the gate until about 30 minutes before departure.*

WOMAN: *Oh, no. That means I'll have a long wait.*

MAN: *There are several nice restaurants right here where you can relax during your wait.*

You will read:

1. How long has the flight been delayed?

(A) Until one o'clock.
(B) Until two o'clock.
(C) For two hours.
(D) For three hours.

Answer

Choice (C) is the correct answer. The man says the flight has been delayed for two hours. Choice (A) gives the time that the flight was scheduled to leave. Choice (B) confuses *two o'clock* with *for two hours*. Choice (D) confuses the time the flight will leave, *three o'clock*, with *three hours*. The plane was to leave at one o'clock, but there is a two-hour delay. Now it will depart at three o'clock.

Skill Focus

Wh- words refer to specific information. Knowing how information is expressed by *Wh-* words helps you understand the meaning of *Wh-* questions. Notice how the statements in the following chart are changed into *Wh-* questions.

Statements	*Wh-* Questions
Ms. Gulbrandsen left a message.	*Who* left a message?
We should discuss *the latest marketing report.*	*What* should we discuss?
The project is due *by 12 noon on the eighteenth.*	*When* is the project due?
The office supply store is *on State Street.*	*Where* is the office supply store?
The picnic is postponed *because it is raining.*	*Why* is the picnic postponed?
You turn the machine on *by pressing this button.*	*How* do you turn this machine on?
I stayed at the party *for three hours.*	*How long* did you stay at the party?
My son is *almost as tall as I am.*	*How tall* is your son?

Skill 3: Exercise

Circle the correct *Wh-* word for each question.

1. ____________ will he look into the problem?
(A) What
(B) When

2. ____________ are they discussing?
(A) What
(B) Where

3. ____________ wasn't the shipment sent?
(A) Why
(B) Which

4. ____________ is the man talking to?
(A) Where
(B) Who

5. ____________ do I get to the art museum?
(A) Where
(B) How

TEST TIP

Reread conversations such as the one on page 35. Write as many *Wh-* questions as you can think of for the conversation. Then practice answering the questions. This will help you prepare for *Wh-* questions on the new TOEIC test.

Skill 4: Understanding Modal Verbs

In Part 3, there are questions that use the modal verbs *should, can, could, will, would, may, might,* and *must.* To answer these questions, focus on the meaning of the modals. A modal can express necessity, ability, possibility, permission, probability, obligation, willingness, or intention. Knowing the meaning of the modal can help you understand the purpose of the conversation.

Sample TOEIC Test Question

You will hear:

WOMAN: *I have to catch a plane at six o'clock. Can't you drive any faster?*

MAN: *I don't think so. Just look at this traffic jam we're stuck in. We can't make it to the airport on time with the roads like this.*

WOMAN: *Oh dear. I guess I'll have to take a later flight.*

MAN: *Yes, it looks like you'll have to do that. I'm sorry.*

You will read:

1. What must the woman do?
   (A) Catch a six o'clock flight.
   (B) Get out of the traffic jam.
   (C) Find a taxi.
   (D) Take a later flight.

Answer

Choice (D), *Take a later flight,* is the correct answer. The modal verb *must* indicates necessity. It is necessary for the woman to take a later flight because she will miss the six o'clock flight. Choice (A) is incorrect because the woman cannot get to the airport in time for her six o'clock flight. Choice (B) is incorrect because it is usually not possible to get out of traffic jams once you are in them. Choice (C) is incorrect because the woman probably would not be able to find a taxi in a traffic jam, and she already has transportation. A taxi probably would not be any faster. Notice that these explanations use modals such as *cannot* and *would not.*

Skill Focus

Modal verbs convey ideas about obligation and possibility. Because modal verbs are auxiliary verbs, they are used with main verbs. Sometimes the main verb can be deleted but only if it is clearly understood (as in answer to Yes/No questions). Study the following chart.

Modal Verbs	Meanings	Examples
can, could	ability, permission, willingness, or possibility	*Can* we meet in the small conference room? I *can* call her for you. This loose screw *could* have been the problem.
will, would	intention or probability	*Will* you type this letter for me? On the train, we *would* see more scenery.
should	obligation, intention, or probability	We *should* mail this letter before the post office closes. The package *should* arrive tomorrow. Maybe we *should*.
must	obligation, necessity, or probability	I *must* give Mr. Platig this urgent message. It *must* be noon by now.
may, might	possibility or permission	You *may* leave early today. Our company *might* bid on the contract.

Skill 4: Exercise

Read each conversation. Then circle the best response.

1. WOMAN: *There are numerous new projects starting this spring, more than we've ever had before.*
   MAN: *Our staff is already working very hard. I don't see how we'll be able to manage all the new work.*
   WOMAN: *Let's think about hiring more staff then.*
   MAN: *Yes, we'll have to do that. It's the only way we can do all this work.*

   What should the speakers do?
   (A) Start new projects.
   (B) Plan more projects.
   → (C) Hire more staff.
   (D) Work harder.

2. Man: *The proposal has to be submitted by Monday. I'm going to need some help to get it ready by then.*

Woman: *I'll ask Mina to help with the research.*

Man: *Mina works in marketing. She can't just move over to research.*

Woman: *Well, what do you suggest then? Everyone else is busy on other projects.*

Why can't Mina help?

(A) She has to submit the proposal by Wednesday.
(B) She doesn't work in research.
(C) She doesn't know the facts.
(D) She hasn't been asked.

3. Woman: *Would you like to see the dessert list? Our pastry chef is very talented.*

Man: *It sounds tempting, but no thank you. After that appetizer and main course, I'm full. A cup of coffee would be good, though.*

Woman: *All right. There's a fresh pot in the kitchen. Cream and sugar?*

Man: *No, thank you. I take it black.*

What will the man do?

(A) Look at the dessert list.
(B) Speak with the chef.
(C) Have a cup of coffee.
(D) Visit the kitchen.

4. Man: *I met with the employees yesterday. It didn't go well at all.*

Woman: *What happened? Are they unhappy with the terms of the contract?*

Man: *They certainly are. I'm afraid this means that they may walk off the job.*

Woman: *That would not be good at all, especially now when we're right in the middle of our busy season.*

What might happen?

(A) The employees might be unhappy.
(B) The woman might meet with the employees.
(C) The employees might go for a walk.
(D) There might be a strike.

5. Woman: *We have to track last week's shipment. It was lost in transit.*

Man: *You're kidding! Did you check the paperwork?*

Woman: *Yes, I did, and everything's in order. I just don't understand how something like this could happen.*

Man: *The next step is to look at the computer tracking system. That should give us some clues.*

What must the speakers do?

(A) Find the shipment.
(B) Check the paperwork.
(C) Lose the transfer.
(D) Place an order.

Part 3 Practice

You will hear conversations between two people and read three questions about each conversation. Choose the best answer to each question.

1. What are the speakers discussing?
   (A) A future meeting.
   (B) A lunch date.
   (C) A conference.
   (D) A new employee.

2. What does the man want to show the woman?
   (A) Pictures from overseas.
   (B) His apartment.
   (C) The project plans.
   (D) A new work schedule.

3. What time will they meet?
   (A) 9:00.
   (B) 9:15.
   (C) 11:00.
   (D) 11:30.

---

4. Where does this conversation take place?
   (A) In an elevator.
   (B) At the receptionist's desk.
   (C) On the telephone.
   (D) In a parking lot.

5. What does the man give the woman?
   (A) A sign.
   (B) A book.
   (C) A pass.
   (D) An appointment.

6. Where is Ms. Salam's office?
   (A) On the right.
   (B) On the left.
   (C) Downstairs.
   (D) Next door.

---

7. What are the speakers discussing?
   (A) A pool.
   (B) A school.
   (C) A present.
   (D) A presentation.

8. How many questions were there?
   (A) Two.
   (B) Four.
   (C) Almost ten.
   (D) Over twelve.

9. How does the man feel now?
   (A) Happy.
   (B) Worried.
   (C) Mad.
   (D) Nervous.

---

10. What did Mr. Ling do this morning?
    (A) He paid a tax.
    (B) He sent a fax.
    (C) He took a taxi.
    (D) He bought new shoes.

11. How does Mr. Ling feel about the deal?
    (A) Unhappy.
    (B) Uncertain.
    (C) Confident.
    (D) Mistaken.

12. How many years has Mr. Ling worked for this company?
    (A) Four.
    (B) Nine.
    (C) Fifteen.
    (D) Sixteen.

Part 4: Talks

> **OBJECTIVES**
>
> You can improve your score in Part 4 by:
>
> - developing business vocabulary
> - listening for answers to *Wh-* questions
> - following the questions chronologically
> - making inferences

In Part 4 of the new TOEIC test, you will listen to talks. These are not conversations. They are talks on the weather, advertisements, recorded announcements, and so on. There is only one speaker. Each talk will be spoken only once. Listen carefully because the talk is not written out.

In your test book, you will find three questions about the talk. You will also read four answer choices. Choose the best answer to the question. There are 30 questions in Part 4. You will have eight seconds to answer each question.

Sample TOEIC Test Questions

You will hear:

Attention, shoppers. We have a special sale today on women's coats. Please visit the Women's Department on the second floor, where you will find all women's winter coats are 25 percent off. This special deal is for today only. Don't forget to visit our newly opened café on the fourth floor. Enjoy hot coffee, tasty baked goods, sandwiches, and other delicious treats while you take a rest from shopping. Remember, our customers are not charged for parking in the mall garage, but you must have your ticket validated by a cashier. Enjoy your shopping!

You will read:

1. How long is the sale?
(A) One day.
(B) Two days.
(C) Three days.
(D) Four days.

2. What is on the fourth floor?
(A) A bakery.
(B) The restroom.
(C) A small restaurant.
(D) The Women's Department.

3. What is free for store customers?
(A) Coffee and sandwiches.
(B) Parking.
(C) A coat.
(D) Movie tickets.

Answers

1. Choice (A) is the correct answer. The sale is for today only. Choice (B) confuses *two days* with the similar sound of *today*. Choice (C) is not mentioned. Choice (D) confuses *four* with *for*.

2. Choice (C) is the correct answer. The speaker mentions a café on the fourth floor. Choice (A) associates *bakery* with *baked goods*. Choice (B) confuses *restroom* with *take a rest*. Choice (D) is on the second floor.

3. Choice (B) is the correct answer. The speaker tells us that *customers are not charged for parking*. Choice (A) is what is served in the café, but there is no mention that it is served for free. Choice (C) is on sale for a discount. Choice (D) repeats the word *ticket*, but it is parking tickets the speaker refers to, not movie tickets.

Types of Questions

In Part 4, you may be asked questions about facts. Examples of factual questions are:

- What is going on sale?
- Who is attending the meeting?
- When does the increase go into effect?
- Where are the people going?
- How long will she be gone?

Factual questions have the following three characteristics.

Characteristics	Examples
The questions often begin with a *Wh-* word.	*Who* got a promotion? Ms. Mills.
The questions are often in the present continuous tense.	*What* are the people doing? They're paying their bill.
The answer choices are usually short (two to five words).	*When* is the ferry leaving? At noon.

Skill 1: Developing Business Vocabulary

Exercise 1

Write the letter of the correct definition next to each word. Then complete the passage with the correct words.

Group A

____	1. commuters	a. place
____	2. construction	b. the act of building
____	3. increase	c. price
____	4. location	d. people who travel from home to work
____	5. rate	e. grow; get larger

The City Transportation Office announced that the cost of parking at the train station will (6)____________ next month. The new parking (7)____________ will be 15 percent higher than it is now. This will have a big effect on (8)____________ who take the train to work every day. City officials say that they raised the parking fees in order to pay for the (9)____________ of the new parking garage. The new parking garage has more parking spaces than the old one, but it is not in a good (10)____________. It is one block away from the train station. City officials say this was done because there was not enough room for a large parking garage right next to the station.

Group B

____	1. approximately	a. one hundred years
____	2. century	b. the state of being
____	3. demonstrates	c. an act that hurts or harms
____	4. existence	d. about; more or less
____	5. injury	e. shows

Wilson Family Enterprises is one of the oldest businesses in our town. It was started more than a (6)____________ ago by brothers Tom and John Wilson. The company's original factory building is still in (7)____________, but it is now used as a museum. The factory has grown and now takes up space in two large buildings downtown. It has (8)____________ 300 employees. The Wilson family is proud to say that no employee has ever suffered any serious (9)____________ on the job, even though the work is sometimes dangerous. This (10)____________ the truth of the company motto: "We always put safety first."

Group C

____	1. advisors	a.	more than half; most
____	2. investments	b.	people who work at a company
____	3. majority	c.	money used to make a profit
____	4. personnel	d.	workshop; special class
____	5. seminar	e.	people who give advice or suggestions

It isn't always easy to know where to put your money. If you would like help with your (6)____________, we have the answer for you. In our financial (7)____________, you will learn everything you need to know to make your money grow. This special class is taught by some of the country's top financial (8)____________. They can answer all your questions and make suggestions for each person's specific financial situation. This is a very popular class. The (9)____________ of people who have attended it in the past have returned to us for more financial advice. There is a special offer for everyone who works at this company. All (10)____________ who sign up this week will receive a 10 percent discount on the fee.

Exercise 2

Complete the sentences with the correct word form.

investment (*noun*) **investor** (*noun*) **invest** (*verb*)

1. It is not a good idea to ____________ all your money in one place.
2. A smart ____________ puts money into several different things.
3. It's a good idea to do some research before you make a big ____________.

advisor (*noun*) **advice** (*noun*) **advise** (*verb*) **advisable** (*adjective*)

4. An ____________ can help you make a decision about your career.
5. It is not ____________ to change jobs at a time like this.
6. She usually gives very good ____________.
7. I ____________ you not to take that job because it doesn't pay well.

injury (*noun*) **injure** (*verb*) **injurious** (*adjective*)

8. Smoking is ____________ to your health.
9. She fell and hurt her leg, but it wasn't a serious ____________.
10. It is not unusual for people to ____________ themselves even in the safety of their own homes.

Skill 2: Listening for Answers to *Wh-* Questions

As you listen to the talks in Part 4, keep the *Wh-* words in mind. The answers to these questions are the specific facts found in the talks.

Sample TOEIC Test Question

You will hear:

May I have your attention, please? Because our flight today is fully booked, we must require that passengers limit their carry-on items to one per person. If you have more than one carry-on item, please report to the counter now so that attendants may check your extra bags.

You will read:

1. Who should report to the counter?
- (A) Passengers who want to read.
- (B) Passengers with two bags.
- (C) Parents traveling with children.
- (D) Attendants who are ready to leave.

Answer

Choice (B) is the correct answer. Passengers with more than one carry-on item should report to the counter. The announcement states that carry-on bags will be limited to one per person. Choice (A) incorrectly associates *fully booked* with *read*. Choice (C) is a group of passengers with special concerns, but they are not mentioned here. Choice (D) is incorrect because the attendants are checking bags, not leaving work.

Skill Focus

Wh- question words appear in Parts 2, 3, 4, and 7 of the new TOEIC test. They tell you not only that specific information is required, but what kind of information to look for. Knowing what kind of information will answer each *Wh-* question word will help you listen for the right information. Study the following *Wh-* words and possible answer types.

Wh- Words	Answer Types	Examples
Who	name, title, identification	Ms. Engle, the manager, the man in the gray cap
What	object, idea, event	the computer, the manufacturing process, the theory, the banquet
When	time, day, month, year	1:00 on Tuesday, in the afternoon, in April, on the fifteenth, in 2006
Where	place, location	in the park, on the table, in a meeting
Why	reason, explanation	because the copier is broken, so that he will know how to get here
How	method, means, way	pull this handle, follow these directions, do this first
How + adj.	length of object or time	11 inches, three hours
How + adv.	quantity or size	4 pints, enough, some for everybody

Skill 2: Exercise

Circle the best response to each question.

Questions 1–3 refer to the following introduction.

I'd like to present Bob Atwood, the general manager of Stansfield Company. We all know Stansfield Company as a compact disc manufacturing firm located outside of Sydney, Australia. Mr. Atwood has been on our board of directors for over ten years. We are honored to have Bob assigned here as consultant.

1. Who is being introduced?
(A) Mr. Atwood.
(B) Mr. Stansfield.
(C) Mr. Sydney.
(D) Mr. Fields.

2. How long has he been on the board of directors?
(A) Approximately two years.
(B) Exactly two years.
(C) Exactly ten years.
(D) More than ten years.

3. Why is he assigned here?
(A) He is the general manager.
(B) He is on the board of directors.
(C) He wanted a vacation.
(D) He is serving as a consultant.

TEST TIP

Write as many additional *Wh*-questions as you can think of for each conversation. Then practice answering the questions. This will help you prepare for *Wh*-questions on the new TOEIC test.

Questions 4–6 refer to the following advertisement.

How do you know which mutual fund to invest in this year? There are over 3,000 mutual funds to choose from. If you can't stand the confusion, come to the trained experts at Townsend Fund for investment advice. There are four convenient Townsend locations to meet your needs. For over 25 years, the people of Townsend Fund have been successful at making your money work for you.

4. What kind of advisors does Townsend Fund have?
(A) Trained.
(B) Confused.
(C) Busy.
(D) Rich.

5. How many locations does Townsend have?
(A) One.
(B) Three.
(C) Four.
(D) Five.

6. How long has Townsend Fund been in existence?
(A) A year.
(B) A decade.
(C) A quarter of a century.
(D) A century.

Skill 3: Following the Questions Chronologically

In Part 4, try to skim the questions quickly before the talk begins. The questions are in the same order as the information presented in the talk. When the talk begins, go back to the first question for the talk. You can follow the talk by following the questions.

Sample TOEIC Test Questions

Questions 1–3 refer to the following announcement.

You will hear:

> *Kakuyama Parking Company announces an increase in the charges for monthly parking spaces in its lot. The changes will not go into effect until the first day of July of this year. The new fee will reflect a 7 percent increase on your current parking rate.*

You will read:

1. What kind of company is making the announcement?
   (A) Gardening.
   (B) Parking.
   (C) Car sales.
   (D) Banking.

2. When will the new rate start?
   (A) Immediately.
   (B) Next month.
   (C) July 1.
   (D) Next year.

3. How much will the increase be?
   (A) One percent.
   (B) Seven percent.
   (C) Seventeen percent.
   (D) Seventy percent.

Answers

1. Choice (B) is the correct answer. Kakuyama is a *parking* company. Choice (A) is not related to this talk. Choice (C), *car sales,* is incorrectly associated with the words *car, park, lot, rates,* and *increase.* Choice (D), *banking,* is incorrectly associated with the words *fee, rate, increase,* and *7 percent.*

2. Choice (C) is the correct answer. The announcement says the increase will start on the first day of July of this year. Choices (A), (B), and (D) are all contradicted by *the first day of July of this year.* For Choice (B), we cannot assume that next month is July.

3. Choice (B) is the correct answer. The announcement says the increase reflects a *7 percent increase* on current rates. Choice (A) is not mentioned in any context. Choices (C) and (D) confuse *seven* with *seventeen* and *seventy* because of the similar sounds.

Skill Focus

Most of the talks will start out with general information and move on to specific information. Sometimes there may be a result or prediction at the end. The questions will follow this pattern, too. Knowing when to expect different kinds of questions can make it easier to follow the information in a talk. Study the common question patterns in the following chart.

Question Types	Questions	Listen for	Examples
General	Who is making this announcement?	the people	teachers speaking in classrooms, businesspeople speaking in meetings
	Where is this talk taking place?	the setting	a business meeting, an airport
	What is the discussion about?	a problem, an object, or an idea	a deadline, a menu, a marketing strategy
Specific	How much is the increase?	amounts	ten dollars
	When is it due?	time expressions	next Friday
Result or Prediction	What will happen next?	a logical or probable outcome	They will hire more personnel.
	How will they probably solve the problem?		They will have the fax machine repaired.

Skill 3: Exercise

Choose the best answer for each question.

Questions 1–3 refer to the following speech.

Welcome to our annual sales meeting, everyone. After lunch and a brief business meeting, a team from our Research and Development Department will join us and demonstrate our newest products. Each of you will have the chance to try samples from our new line and ask questions of the team. Now please help yourselves to the delicious buffet that has been set up in the adjoining dining room.

1. How often does the meeting take place?
   (A) Once a year.
   (B) Twice a year.
   (C) Three times a year.
   (D) Once every two years.

2. Who is attending the meeting?
   (A) Sales personnel.
   (B) Food service staff.
   (C) Bank executives.
   (D) Factory workers.

3. What will people do first?
   (A) Try out some new products.
   (B) Eat a meal.
   (C) Visit the Research Department.
   (D) Discuss salaries.

Questions 4–6 refer to the following recorded message.

Thank you for calling Buffington's, the dependable retail store. Our hours are Monday through Saturday, nine o'clock to six o'clock. On Sundays, our hours are one o'clock to six o'clock. If you know the extension of the person you want to talk to, press the three digits of the extension. If you want customer service, press 2 now. If you need an operator, stay on the line.

4. What is Buffington's?
   (A) A shopping mall.
   (B) A repair shop.
   (C) A store.
   (D) A bank.

5. When is Buffington's open?
   (A) Monday through Friday.
   (B) Monday through Saturday.
   (C) Saturday and Sunday only.
   (D) Every day.

6. What number do you press for customer service?
   (A) 1.
   (B) 2.
   (C) 6.
   (D) 9.

Skill 4: Making Inferences

In Part 4, you may be asked questions for which you must make inferences. These questions will not be about stated facts, but about conclusions or judgments you must make.

Sample TOEIC Test Question

You will hear:

If you are ambitious and want to move ahead in your career, or if you want to enter a new field of business, we guarantee that you will gain a competitive edge by attending our seminars on professional development. The seminars are offered at many locations in the metropolitan area, at convenient evening hours. Choose the entire program of seminars, or select only the areas that interest you.

You will read:

1. Who will be interested in this advertisement?
   (A) Teachers.
   (B) Farmers.
   (C) Athletes.
   (D) Businesspeople.

Answer

Choice (D) is the correct answer. The seminars are for those interested in new fields of business and in professional development. They would probably work in the city during the day. All these ideas are associated with business. Choice (A) makes an inference about who will be giving the seminars, not who will be taking them. Choice (B) incorrectly interprets *new field.* Choice (C) draws an incorrect inference from the phrase *competitive edge.*

Skill Focus

Questions about inferences make you think about what is probable, based on the information in the talk. Questions about inferences are often *Wh-* questions that ask about ideas or impressions conveyed in the passage. Study these common questions about inferences.

- What will happen next?
- Who is the intended audience?
- What happened before?
- What is the probable result?

Skill 4: Exercise

Choose the best answer for each question. You will need to make inferences.

Questions 1–3 refer to the following report.

Those of you who are driving into the city from the northeast, please take notice that, because of highway construction on Route 312, traffic will be closed in the southbound lane at 9:30 tomorrow morning. That's Route 312, tomorrow morning at 9:30. You may want to find another route into the city tomorrow morning.

1. Who is this report for?
   (A) Commuters driving into work.
   (B) Construction workers.
   (C) Subway riders.
   (D) Joggers.

2. What is the announcer trying to prevent?
   (A) Highway construction.
   (B) A traffic jam tomorrow.
   (C) Train delays.
   (D) Accidents.

3. What does the speaker think that listeners should do?
   (A) Enter the city from the northeast.
   (B) Visit the city tomorrow morning.
   (C) Tour the construction site.
   (D) Use a different road.

TEST TIP

Remember to choose the most likely inference. Try assigning probabilities if needed. Use relative percentages or a range from 1 to 5, for example, with 5 being most likely.

Questions 4–6 refer to the following talk.

We asked your customers about their favorite vacations. The majority said they preferred to travel in the months between June and September. Very few customers said they preferred to take vacations between the months of November and February. We think you could increase your business by offering more discounts during those low-activity months.

4. Who is the audience?
   (A) Travel agents.
   (B) Vacationers.
   (C) Students.
   (D) Pilots.

5. What is the speaker doing?
   (A) Giving advice.
   (B) Explaining a process.
   (C) Showing pictures.
   (D) Demonstrating a product.

6. What might happen next?
   (A) Vacations in November will increase.
   (B) The audience will ask questions.
   (C) Listeners will purchase tickets.
   (D) Customers will ask for discounts.

Part 4 Practice

You will hear talks given by one speaker and answer three questions about each talk. Choose the best answer to each question.

1. What kind of injury is mentioned?
   (A) Wrist injuries.
   (B) Injuries to the mouse.
   (C) Keyboard injuries.
   (D) Monitor problems.

2. What products are offered?
   (A) Computer operators.
   (B) Work habits.
   (C) Computer accessories.
   (D) Catalogs.

3. Who is the audience for this advertisement?
   (A) Computer operators.
   (B) Computer repairpersons.
   (C) Catalog salespersons.
   (D) Producers.

4. Where will the meeting take place?
   (A) Palm Springs.
   (B) Rio de Janeiro.
   (C) Hawaii.
   (D) Los Angeles.

5. How many timeshares were sold last year?
   (A) 50.
   (B) 90.
   (C) 500.
   (D) 10,000.

6. What can you get by calling the Timeshares International office?
   (A) Tickets to the event.
   (B) A fifty percent discount.
   (C) The names of the sponsors.
   (D) A list of timeshares for sale.

II Reading

The Reading section of the new TOEIC® test is a paper-and-pencil assessment. It consists of three parts. Part 5 is Incomplete Sentences, Part 6 is Text Completion, and Part 7 is Reading Comprehension.

Parts 5 and 6 test both knowledge of grammar and the ability to interpret meaning correctly. Part 5 consists of 40 sentences, each with a blank and four possible answer choices. Part 6 consists of four longer passages. Each passage has three blanks, and each blank has four possible answer choices. The total number of test items in Part 6 is 12.

Part 7 tests comprehension and understanding of function as they relate to a particular theme. This part consists of single and double reading passages followed by a series of questions. The passages are those commonly used in business: advertisements, schedules, agendas, and business correspondence such as letters, memos, and e-mails. The four single passages are followed by two to five questions each, for a total of 28 questions. The four pairs of double passages have five questions each, for a total of 20 questions. The total number of questions in Part 7 is 48.

Part 5: Incomplete Sentences

OBJECTIVES

You can improve your score in Part 5 by:

- developing business vocabulary
- understanding prefixes
- understanding suffixes
- recognizing time markers
- understanding the passive voice
- identifying the correct prepositions
- using relative pronouns

In Part 5 of the new TOEIC® test, your knowledge of both vocabulary and grammar will be tested. This part consists of 40 incomplete sentences. Under each sentence, you will see four words or phrases, marked (A), (B), (C), and (D). You should choose the best word or phrase to complete the sentence.

Try not to spend more than 30 seconds per question. You will have only 75 minutes for all of Parts 5, 6, and 7, so use your time wisely.

Sample TOEIC Test Question

1. Before he joined our firm, Mr. Guzman _______ Maltex Corporation.
   (A) belonging to
   (B) worked
   (C) served
   (D) was employed by

Answer

Choice (D) is the correct answer. The sentence should read, *Before he joined our firm, Mr. Guzman was employed by Maltex Corporation. Was employed by Maltex Corporation* is in the passive voice. It means the same thing as *Maltex Corporation employed Mr. Guzman.* Choice (A) is incorrect because the verb *belong* does not indicate employment. In addition, stative verbs like *belong* are rarely used in the continuous form. Choice (B) is incorrect because the verb *work* would be followed by a preposition such as *worked at* or *worked for.* Choice (C) is not correct because the verb *serve* may be used with job positions, such as *served as marketing director*, but not with company names.

Skill 1: Developing Business Vocabulary

Exercise 1

Write the letter of the correct definition next to each word. Then complete the passage with the correct words.

Group A

____	**1.** appreciate	**a.**	be thankful for
____	**2.** fill in	**b.**	robbery; stealing
____	**3.** handle	**c.**	take someone's place
____	**4.** invented	**d.**	made up something new
____	**5.** theft	**e.**	manage; carry out

To: Don Reynolds
From: Mary Sawyer
Subject: Next week

Hi Don,

Thank you for agreeing to run the store next week while I am on vacation. I **(6)**____________ your help. I don't think you will have any difficulties. Peter Jones has agreed to (7)____________ the website and all online orders, so you won't have to worry about that. He has also agreed to (8)____________ for you one day if you want to take a day off. Please don't forget to turn on the burglar alarm every night when you close the store. We have had problems with (9)____________. I am glad somebody **(10)**____________ burglar alarms. I would not feel safe without one. Thanks again for your help.

Mary

Group B

____ 1. applicant a. form an opinion; believe

____ 2. judge b. make sure something is true or correct

____ 3. previous c. a person who makes a formal request; one who applies

____ 4. supervisor d. earlier

____ 5. verify e. boss; person in charge

When you are looking for a new job, you want to present yourself as well as possible. You are not the only (6)_____________ for the job. The person who interviews you will likely be your (7)_____________ if you take the new job. This is the person who will (8)_____________ whether or not you are prepared for the job. He or she will look over your papers and (9)_____________ important information about your work history and education. This person will need to contact your (10)_____________ boss, for example, and will probably also call your university.

Group C

____ 1. eliminate a. something to help someone remember

____ 2. negotiations b. a suggestion for a plan

____ 3. proposal c. a person who changes words from one language to another

____ 4. reminder d. remove

____ 5. translator e. discussions to come to an agreement

To: Harry Billingsley
From: Myrna Michaels
Subject: Marketing Plan

Harry,

Please don't forget that there will be a meeting to discuss the new marketing plan on the 20th of next month. It's very important not to forget this, and I will send you another (6)_____________ a week before the meeting. I will need to see your ideas for the plan before the meeting, so please send me your (7)_____________ by the end of next week. Also, you will need to get a good (8)_____________ since the Tokyo office wants to see everything in Japanese as well as English. That will (9)_____________ any problems of misunderstanding because of language. As soon as we have completed the plan, we will begin (10)_____________ with the client. I expect they will agree with most of our ideas. Thanks for all your hard work.

Myrna

Exercise 2

Complete the sentences with the correct word form.

application (*noun*) **applicant** (*noun*) **apply** (*verb*)

1. We expect over 100 people to ____________ for the new position.
2. Please send in your ____________ before the end of the month.
3. This ____________ does not seem to be qualified for the job.

invention (*noun*) **inventor** (*noun*) **invent** (*verb*)

4. The computer was the most important ____________ of the twentieth century.
5. Nowadays, technology develops very quickly, and people ____________ new things all the time.
6. The company hired a well-known ____________ to come up with new products.

negotiations (*noun*) **negotiator** (*noun*) **negotiable** (*verb*)

7. He is a skilled ____________ and always gets what he wants.
8. Some items on the contract are not ____________; we will not agree to change them.
9. After several hours of ____________, they finally came to an agreement.

Skill 2: Understanding Prefixes

In Part 5 of the new TOEIC test, your knowledge of the meanings of prefixes will help you choose the word or phrase that matches the meaning of the sentence. A prefix is a word part that is added to the front of a word to change its meaning.

Sample TOEIC Test Question

1. We should have that document on file, but it seems to have been _______.
   (A) misplaced
   (B) displaced
   (C) replaced
   (D) placed

Answer

Choice (A) is the correct answer. The sentence should read, *We should have that document on file, but it seems to have been misplaced.* The coordinating conjunction *but* adds contrasting information to the first part of the sentence. You should understand that the document is not on file. The prefix *mis-* adds a negative meaning to *place.* The document was not placed in the proper place; consequently it is not on file. Choice (B) is incorrect. The prefix *dis-* also adds a negative meaning to *place,* but *displaced* usually refers to people. Choice (C) is incorrect because the prefix *re-* means *again.* Choice (D) is incorrect because *placed* should be followed by a location, as in *placed in the wrong file.*

Skill Focus

Prefixes increase vocabulary very efficiently because they are a combination of a word part and a word whose meanings are already known. You can use this information to understand words that you have not seen before. Study the prefixes and meanings in the following chart. Then look at the examples of words with the prefix. Think about what the words probably mean.

Prefix	Meaning	Examples
after-	after	afternoon, aftermath, afterward
ante-	before or in front of	antedate, antechamber, antecedent
anti-	against	antisocial, antibiotic, antidote
auto-	by itself or self	automobile, automatic, autobiography
bene-	good	benefit, beneficial, benefactor
bi-, bin-	two	bifocal, bicycle, binoculars
circu-	around	circulate, circular, circus
co-, col-	together	cooperate, coworker, collect
contra-	against	contradict, contrary, contrast
counter-	opposite	counteract, counterfeit, counterpart
dis-	opposite or negative	disagree, disgrace, dishonest

Prefix	Meaning	Examples
hyper-	excessive	hypercritical, hyperbole, hypersensitive
hypo-	too little or beneath	hypoactive, hypodermic, hypoglycemia
il-	not	illogical, illegal, illegible
in-	not	incorrect, inhumane, inability
inter-	among or between	international, interaction, interfere
ir-	not	irresponsible, irregular, irrelevant
mal-	bad or wrong	malfunction, malpractice, malnourished
mis-	bad or wrong	misfortune, mistake, misplace
multi-	many or much	multilingual, multiple, multinational
omni-	all	omniscient, omnivorous, omnipotent
over-	too much	overactive, overflow, overdraw
poly-	many	polyglot, polygon, polytechnic
post-	after	postpone, postpaid, postscript
pre-	before	prefix, prefer, prehistoric
pro-	before or in favor of	prologue, procedure, pronoun
re-	again	rewrite, repeat, replace

Skill 2: Exercise

Classify the prefixes from the chart by meaning.

1. Write eight prefixes that express a negative meaning.

   _______ _______ _______ _______

   _______ _______ _______ _______

2. Write two prefixes that express a positive meaning.

   _______ _______

3. Write two prefixes that express a quantity.

   _______ _______

4. Write four prefixes that express time.

   _______ _______

   _______ _______

TEST TIP

Be careful! Some prefixes look almost the same, but their meanings are different.

For example, the prefix *anti-* means "against," but the prefix *ante-* means "in front of."

Examples:
Anti-smoking laws ban smoking in public places. (*anti-smoking* = against smoking)

We waited in the anteroom. (*anteroom* = a small room in front of a larger room)

Skill 3: Understanding Suffixes

In Part 5, your knowledge of suffixes will help you choose the word or phrase that matches the meaning of the sentence. A suffix is a word part that is added to the end of a word. Many suffixes change the part of speech of the word. Suffixes can help you determine whether the word is a noun, adjective, verb, or adverb. Suffixes can sometimes add meaning, too.

Sample TOEIC Test Question

1. Office managers expect accuracy, efficiency, and _______ from those they supervise.
   (A) dedication
   (B) dedicated
   (C) dedicatedly
   (D) dedicate

Answer

Choice (A) is the correct answer. The sentence should read, *Office managers expect accuracy, efficiency, and dedication from those they supervise.* The first two words, *accuracy* and *efficiency*, are nouns. We need to choose the same part of speech, a noun form, to complete the list. The suffix *-ation* indicates a noun. Choice (A), *dedication*, is the noun form of the verb *dedicate*. Choice (B) is incorrect because the suffix *-ed* in this case indicates an adjective. Choice (C) is incorrect because the suffix *-ly* indicates an adverb. Choice (D) is incorrect because the word *dedicate* is a verb.

Skill Focus

Suffixes change a word's part of speech. This means that you can often turn the same idea into a noun, verb, adjective, or adverb. You can use this information to understand words that you have not seen before. Study the suffixes and meanings in the following chart. Then look at the examples of words with the suffix. Think about what the words probably mean.

Suffix	Meaning	Part of Speech	Examples
-al	relating to	adjective	influential, provincial, financial
-ance	state or quality of	noun	resistance, acceptance, extravagance
-ancy	state or quality of	noun	vacancy, pregnancy, redundancy
-ary	relating to, quality of	adjective or noun	primary, fiduciary, visionary
-ate	to make	verb	activate, reciprocate, elevate
-ation, -tion	state or quality of	noun	inspiration, separation, translation
-en	to make	verb	shorten, lengthen, fatten

Suffix	Meaning	Part of Speech	Examples
-ency	state or quality of	noun	expediency, leniency, latency
-hood	state or quality of	noun	childhood, adulthood, manhood
-ic	relating to	adjective	economic, scientific, scenic
-ify	to make	verb	beautify, clarify, specify
-ity	state or quality of	noun	authenticity, publicity, civility
-ize	to cause to become	verb	computerize, modernize, legalize
-ly	in the manner of, at intervals of, having the quality of	adjective or adverb	friendly, yearly, clearly, ordinarily
-ment	process or state of	noun	enjoyment, procurement, experiment
-ness	state or quality of	noun	kindness, darkness, likeness
-ous	full of	adjective	nervous, anxious, jealous
-ship	state or quality of	noun	friendship, relationship, kinship

Skill 3: Exercise

Classify the suffixes from the chart by parts of speech.

1. Write ten suffixes that indicate noun forms.

_______ _______ _______ _______ _______

_______ _______ _______ _______ _______

2. Write five suffixes that indicate adjective forms.

_______ _______ _______ _______ _______

3. Write one suffix that indicates an adverb form.

____

4. Write four suffixes that indicate verb forms.

_______ _______ _______ _______

TEST TIP

Some suffixes are spelled exactly the same, but they indicate different parts of speech.

When *-ly* is added to *week,* it becomes *weekly.* (adverb meaning "every week")

When *-ly* is added to *love,* it becomes *lovely.* (adjective meaning "having pleasing qualities")

Skill 4: Recognizing Time Markers

In Part 5, your understanding of time markers will help you choose the correct verb tense for the sentence. Time markers are words that reflect the time of the verb.

Sample TOEIC Test Question

1. We usually _______ that brand available.
   (A) has had
   (B) have been having
   (C) have
   (D) are having

Answer

Choice (C) is the correct answer. The sentence should read, *We usually have that brand available.* The word *usually* is a time marker. It is an adverb of frequency that suggests habit. The simple present tense suggests habitual action. Choice (A) is incorrect for two reasons: first, the present perfect tense does not carry the habitual idea of *usually*; and second, the subject *We* is a plural pronoun which does not agree in number with the singular verb *has had*. Choices (B) and (D) are incorrect because *have* is rarely used in the continuous form when it indicates possession.

Skill Focus

Time markers can indicate different kinds of time. Some indicate periods of time, others indicate points in time, and still others indicate recurring time—things that happen repeatedly. This means that different kinds of time markers answer different kinds of time questions. Study the time markers in the following chart. Notice which time questions they answer.

Time Questions	Time Markers
When . . . ?	ago, already, before, after, during, while, as soon as, next month, last week, yesterday, on Tuesday
How long . . . ?	for, since, until
How often . . . ?	always, usually, often, sometimes, never, generally, rarely, every day, weekly, once a day

Skill 4: Exercise

Circle the time marker that completes each sentence.

1. How long has Mr. Block been working on the report?
   Mr. Block has been working on the report ______.
   (A) three hours ago
   (B) for three hours

2. When did the housekeeper clean the room?
   ______ we left the room, she cleaned it.
   (A) After
   (B) Usually

3. How long will Ms. Colinas fill in?
   Ms. Colinas will fill in ______ Ms. Irzel is out of the hospital.
   (A) until
   (B) already

4. When does the secretary take notes?
   The secretary takes notes ______ the meeting.
   (A) often
   (B) during

5. How often does he travel on business?
   He ______ travels once a month.
   (A) generally
   (B) while

TEST TIP

Since is used as a preposition with the present perfect tense. It is also used as a subordinate conjunction to mean *because*.

Examples:
We have been here *since* 10 o'clock. (preposition)

They didn't want to come *since* they weren't invited. (subordinate conjunction)

Skill 5: Understanding the Passive Voice

In Part 5, your understanding of the passive voice will help you choose the verb form that fits the context of the sentence. The passive voice is often used in formal and business communication. It is used when you do not need (or want) to mention who does the action.

Sample TOEIC Test Question

1. Before the dam _______, the river overflowed its banks every spring.
   (A) was built
   (B) built
   (C) was building
   (D) builds

> **TEST TIP**
>
> The verb *be* is used both in the passive voice and in the continuous tense. Don't confuse them! Look at the whole sentence.
>
> **Examples:**
> The reservations *were confirmed*. (passive voice)
>
> They *were confirming* the reservations when the phone went dead. (past continuous tense)

Answer

Choice (A) is the correct answer. The sentence should read, *Before the dam was built, the river overflowed its banks every spring.* The verb *was built* is the past tense of the passive voice. The emphasis is on the dam. It's not important who built the dam. Choices (B), (C), and (D) are all incorrect because they are active voice. That is, they all mean that the dam built something (which is illogical). We know that someone built the dam, so the sentence requires the passive voice. Choice (D) is illogical for another reason also. The main verb, *overflowed*, is in the past tense, so we cannot use the present tense in the subordinate clause, which begins with *before*.

Skill Focus

It is important to know how to recognize the passive voice. Think of the grammatical structure of a sentence—subject, verb, and object. Also think of the role of these words in the meaning of the sentence. In an active sentence, the subject is the agent (the person or thing that does the action), the verb is the action, and the object is the receiver (the person or thing that the action affects). In a passive sentence, the agent and the receiver have changed positions. Study the following clues for recognizing a passive sentence.

Clues	Examples	Explanations
1. The subject of a passive sentence is NOT the agent (the person or thing that does the action).	*The letters* were typed by the secretary.	Who typed? Letters can't type, but a secretary can. The subject (*the letters*) is not the agent.
2. The object (agent) of a passive sentence follows the preposition *by*.	The announcement was made *by the director.*	*By the director* means that the director is the agent.

Clues	Examples	Explanations
3. The object (agent) of a passive sentence may be omitted from the sentence if it is understood, unknown, or unimportant. It may also be omitted if we do not want to name the agent.	The mail was delivered. The crime was committed at midnight. Mistakes were made.	We understand that the mail carrier delivered the mail. Therefore, the agent (*the mail carrier*) is not important. We don't know who committed the crime. Therefore, there is no agent. We don't want to say who made the mistakes.
4. The verb consists of a form of *be* and the past participle of the main verb.	Our company *has been mentioned* in that magazine.	The passive voice can be in any tense. *Has been* tells us that this is the present perfect form of the passive voice.

Skill 5: Exercise

Circle the correct active or passive voice verb.

1. The viewers _______ the opportunity to judge the performance.
   (A) were given
   (B) gave

2. The shipment must _______ carefully.
   (A) handle
   (B) be handled

3. The food manager _______ to eliminate theft.
   (A) was told
   (B) has told

4. The flight _______ on time.
   (A) was left
   (B) left

5. The proposal _______ now.
   (A) can be mailed
   (B) can mail

TEST TIP

The past participle (the verb form with *-ed*) is used in the passive voice, in the simple past tense, and as an adjective. Don't confuse them! Look at the whole sentence.

Examples:
The meal was *cooked* before we came. (passive voice in simple past tense)

They *cooked* the meal before we came. (active voice in simple past tense)

The *cooked* food was on the table when we came. (adjective)

Skill 6: Identifying the Correct Prepositions

In Part 5, your understanding of the context of the sentence will help you choose the correct preposition. Prepositions are words used to show the relationship between things in a sentence. They are commonly used in prepositional phrases to show relationships of time or location.

Sample TOEIC Test Question

1. We are so glad you could come. Welcome _______ Rome.
   (A) in
   (B) at
   (C) to
   (D) of

Answer

Choice (C) is the correct answer. The sentence should read, *Welcome to Rome.* The combination of *Welcome* and *Rome* indicates that Rome is a destination. Destinations use the preposition of place, *to*. Choice (A) is also a preposition of place, but it is not used with destinations. Use it after you get there: *I vacationed in Rome.* Choice (B) is a preposition of place (but not with cities) and time. Choice (D) is a preposition that shows possession.

Skill Focus

There are many prepositions in English. Pay attention to the prepositions that you hear and read every day; that is the best way to learn them. There are a few rules, however, about the use of prepositions. Study the prepositions in the following chart for common ways to express location and time. Notice the contrasts in the ways the prepositions are used.

Prepositional Phrase	Use	Examples
to Rome	destination	I went *to* Rome.
in Rome	within a location	While I was *in* Rome, I saw many Roman ruins.
from Rome	direction away	I went *from* Rome to Vienna.
from Rome	source	I brought you this souvenir *from* Rome.
to the meeting	destination	I went *to* the meeting.
in the meeting	within a location	I was *in* the meeting all morning.
from the meeting	direction away	I went *from* the meeting to my office.
at the meeting	during	Some people got bored *at* the meeting this morning.
at the airport	general location	I can catch a cab *at* the airport.

Prepositional Phrase	Use	Examples
at 9:00	specific point in time	*At* 9:00, I arrived at work.
at night	specific period of time (night, noon, dawn, sunrise, sunset)	It gets chilly *at* night.
from 9:00 *to* 12:00	boundaries of a time period	I attended a seminar *from* 9:00 *to* 12:00.
until Tuesday	end of a time period	I decided to stay *until* Tuesday.
for one hour	duration of time	I stopped *for* one hour to eat lunch.
since 10:00	time starting at a point in the past and continuing to the present	I have been working on this proposal *since* 10:00.
on February 6	with dates	I start my new job *on* February 6.
in one day	with a period of days	I wrote the memo *in* one day.
in two weeks	with a period of weeks	The package should arrive *in* two weeks.
in April	with a specific month, year, decade, or century	His birthday is *in* April.
in the morning	with a period of the day (morning, afternoon, evening)	I ride the train *in* the morning.

Skill 6: Exercise

Complete the sentences with the correct preposition from the chart.

1. Ms. Legesse is ____________ a meeting right now.
2. Class starts ____________ one month.
3. Meet me ____________ noon.
4. The meeting continued ____________ 5:30.
5. She's been the director ____________ Mr. Lee retired.
6. I'll meet you ____________ the train station.
7. She went ____________ the office to the party.
8. We have been waiting for him ____________ two hours.

TEST TIP

For and *since* are both prepositions of time. *For* shows a duration of time, and *since* shows an exact starting point in time. Don't confuse them. Look at the meaning of the verb and the length of time.

Examples:
We have been talking *for* an hour.

We have been talking *since* 11:00.

Skill 7: Using Relative Pronouns

In the new TOEIC test, you may need to determine which relative pronoun correctly completes a sentence. Relative pronouns are words used to introduce subordinate clauses. The relative pronouns are *that*, *which*, *who*, *whose*, and *whom*.

Sample TOEIC Test Question

1. Mr. Wang spoke with the man _______ called yesterday.
   (A) which
   (B) who
   (C) whose
   (D) why

Answer

Choice (B) is the correct answer. The sentence should read, *Mr. Wang spoke with the man who called yesterday.* The relative pronoun *who* replaces *the man* in the subordinate clause *the man called yesterday*. Choice (A) is incorrect because *which* is not used for people. Choice (C) is incorrect because you do not need to show possession. Choice (D) is incorrect because *why* is not a relative pronoun.

TEST TIP

Who can be used only for people, and *which* can be used only for things. However, *that* can be used for both people and things.

Skill Focus

Relative pronouns replace nouns. We can combine sentences with a relative pronoun to avoid repeating a noun. Study how the relative pronouns in the following sentences replace the repeated nouns.

1. Ms. Ling signed for <u>the package</u>. <u>The package</u> arrived this morning.

   Ms. Ling signed for the package *which* (*that*) arrived this morning.
2. This line is for <u>the passengers</u>. <u>The passengers</u> bought their tickets in advance.

   This line is for the passengers *who* (*that*) bought their tickets in advance.
3. Ms. Riad received <u>some letters</u>. <u>The letters</u> were mailed last week.

   Ms. Riad received the letters *that* (*which*) were mailed last week.
4. <u>The message</u> is on your desk. I took <u>the message</u> for you.

   The message *that* (*which*) I took for you is on your desk.
5. The director interviewed <u>an applicant</u>. <u>The applicant's</u> computer skills are strong.

   The director interviewed an applicant *whose* computer skills are strong.

Skill 7: Exercise

Choose the correct relative pronoun for each sentence.

1. Here is the report _______ you wanted to read.
   (A) that
   (B) it

2. Mr. Peri is the chef _______ created this dish.
   (A) which
   (B) who

3. The person _______ computer is still on must be working late.
   (A) whose
   (B) why

4. The plants, _______ are rare and exotic, require meticulous care.
   (A) they
   (B) which

5. The tables _______ are by the window are the most popular.
   (A) who
   (B) that

6. That is the woman _______ daughter won the competition.
   (A) who
   (B) whose

7. The conference call _______ was scheduled for today has been canceled.
   (A) that
   (B) whom

8. The new store, _______ is having a big sale, was opened last week.
   (A) which
   (B) that

9. My brother, _______ is named Joe, will be arriving next week.
   (A) which
   (B) who

10. The book _______ you want is on the table.
    (A) that
    (B) whose

TEST TIP

A nonrestrictive relative clause, which provides additional information about the subject, begins and ends with a comma. It can use *who*, *whose*, *whom*, and *which*, but it cannot use *that*.

Examples:
These chairs, *which* do not match the desks, must be replaced.

The speaker, *who* lives far away, arrived late.

Part 5 Practice

Choose the word or phrase that best completes each sentence.

1. The restaurant ______ has just opened has a famous chef.
   (A) whose
   (B) who
   (C) it
   (D) that

2. Negotiations will take place ______ London.
   (A) at
   (B) in
   (C) by
   (D) to

3. We were in ______ with our supplier.
   (A) agree
   (B) agreeing
   (C) agreement
   (D) agreed

4. Mrs. Dubois is a ______ supervisor.
   (A) confident
   (B) confidence
   (C) confidentially
   (D) confidently

5. Our store gets more business ______ our new location.
   (A) of
   (B) to
   (C) from
   (D) in

6. The proposals ______ by messenger.
   (A) delivered
   (B) have delivered
   (C) are delivered
   (D) are delivering

7. On what date did you ______ the shipment?
   (A) perceive
   (B) deceive
   (C) receive
   (D) recede

8. Two weeks ago, Mr. Uto ______ his reservations.
   (A) makes
   (B) was made
   (C) made
   (D) has made

9. All the members have arrived ______ Mr. Sampson.
   (A) accept
   (B) expect
   (C) not
   (D) except

10. She expressed her ______.
    (A) appreciate
    (B) appreciative
    (C) appreciation
    (D) appreciated

11. Eliza Donato ______ to vice president in January.
    (A) will promote
    (B) will be promoting
    (C) will be promoted
    (D) promotes

12. Mr. Yung sent a reminder to customers ______ didn't pay their bills.
    (A) what
    (B) whom
    (C) which
    (D) who

13. Mr. Weber hired a new ______.
    (A) assist
    (B) assistance
    (C) assisted
    (D) assistant

14. Send a fax to ______ the prices.
    (A) verily
    (B) verify
    (C) verifying
    (D) has verified

15. That product ______ until recently.
(A) wasn't invented
(B) invented
(C) didn't invent
(D) has invented

16. We're sending Mary Sula to participate ______ the seminar.
(A) at
(B) to
(C) from
(D) in

17. The employees ______ by the director to give suggestions.
(A) are asking
(B) asking
(C) are asked
(D) be asked

18. Mr. Caputo usually ______ with a translator.
(A) is traveled
(B) travel
(C) is traveling
(D) travels

19. Her ______ employer gave her a good recommendation.
(A) prevalent
(B) prevent
(C) preview
(D) previous

20. Flight 201 will be arriving at Gate 7B ______ time.
(A) by
(B) on
(C) at
(D) within

Part 6: Text Completion

OBJECTIVES

You can improve your score in Part 6 by:

- developing business vocabulary
- using the correct verb tense
- identifying pronouns
- identifying the appropriate meaning
- analyzing word families
- identifying coordinating conjunctions

Part 6 of the new TOEIC® test evaluates your knowledge of vocabulary and grammar. It is different from Part 5 in that it tests this knowledge in the context of paragraphs rather than individual sentences. You will need to understand the context of the passages in order to choose the correct answer. Part 6 consists of four passages with three incomplete sentences each. For each incomplete sentence, you will see four words or phrases marked (A), (B), (C), and (D). Choose the best word or phrase to complete each sentence.

Try not to spend more than 30 seconds per question. You will have only 75 minutes for all of Parts 5, 6, and 7, so use your time wisely.

Sample TOEIC Test Questions

Notice

For your shopping convenience, we at Reynolds Electronics are pleased to announce that free parking is now available in the mall parking garage for all of our ____________.

1. (A) customs
   (B) costumes
   (C) customers
   (D) cosmetics

Please remember that ____________ parking ticket must be stamped by the cashier at

2. (A) its
   (B) our
   (C) her
   (D) your

checkout time. Those without a stamped ticket will be charged the full parking rate. Free parking is ____________ only while shopping at Reynolds and only in those

3. (A) valid
   (B) validity
   (C) validate
   (D) valuable

spaces marked "Reynolds Electronics." Violation of this rule will result in your car being towed. Please address any questions about this policy to the manager. Thank you.

The Manager

Answers

1. Choice (C) is the correct answer. This notice is about parking for shoppers, or *customers*, at a store. The other choices look similar to the correct answer but have very different meanings. Choice (A) means *habits*. Choices (B) means *special clothing*. Choice (D) refers to *beauty products*.

2. Choice (D) is the correct answer. The parking ticket belongs to the person reading the notice, or *you*, so it is *your* ticket. Choice (A) refers to a thing. Choices (B) and (C) refer to the wrong person.

3. Choice (A) is the correct answer. This is an adjective modifying the phrase *free parking*. Choice (B) is a noun. Choice (C) is a verb. Choice (D) is from a different word family and does not make sense in this context.

Skill 1: Developing Business Vocabulary

Exercise 1

Write the letter of the correct definition next to each word. Then complete the passage with the correct words.

Group A

____ 1. bulk		a. show
____ 2. convenience		b. things for sale
____ 3. display		c. large size or quantity
____ 4. merchandise		d. remodeling of a building
____ 5. renovations		e. ease of use

Wetherell Design Build, Inc. did the recent (6)____________ for Gourmet Groceries. The store was expanded and repainted. New, larger windows were added to the front so that the store can more attractively (7)____________ its products to passersby. Several more aisles were added to the interior to enable the store to stock a greater selection of (8)____________ for its customers to buy. In the back of the store, special larger shelves were built to hold (9)____________ items. The entire store was reorganized for the (10)____________ of customers. "We designed a store where shopping would always be easy and comfortable," said Madeline Wetherell, president of the firm.

Group B

____ 1. desire		a. reasonable; allowed
____ 2. mood		b. feeling; state of mind
____ 3. properly		c. wish for something
____ 4. temporary		d. correctly
____ 5. valid		e. not permanent

Most people experience a depressed (6)____________ from time to time. This feeling of sadness is usually (7)____________, lasting only a day or two. We often try to hide our sad feelings, but it is important to understand that they are (8)____________; there is nothing wrong or unreasonable about them. Naturally, we all (9)____________ to feel happy, but it is also natural to feel sad from time to time. When our feelings are (10)____________ understood, they are easier to manage.

Group C

D	1. agenda	a.	diploma from a college or university
A	2. degree	b.	produced and distributed written work
E	3. extensive	c.	made final
C	4. finalized	d.	schedule for a meeting
B	5. published	e.	large; wide; far-reaching

Welcome. The first speaker on our (6) agenda today is Dr. Mi Ja Kim. Dr. Kim received her (7) degree in international economics from Wycliffe University. Her (8) extensive research on economics in East Asia has made her one of the world's foremost authorities in the field. She has (9) published two books and numerous journal articles on East Asian economics. She has recently (10) finalized plans to lead a group of international economists on a tour of East Asia next month. We are pleased that this long-awaited tour will take place soon. And now I give you Dr. Kim.

Exercise 2

Complete the sentences with the correct word form.

publisher (*noun*) **publication** (*noun*) **publish** (*verb*)

1. We are a small company and publish only five or six books a year.
2. The publisher has decided to increase the money paid to authors.
3. I read this publication every month.

extension (*noun*) **extend** (*verb*) **extensive** (*adjective*)

4. The entrance to the building is very small, so they decided to add an extension.
5. His knowledge of the subject is extensive; he is definitely an expert.
6. We will sell more if we extend the store hours.

propriety (*noun*) **proper** (*adjective*) **properly** (*adverb*)

7. They will not consider the application unless it is completed properly.
8. She won't get the job because she didn't give proper answers during the interview.
9. The propriety of their behavior was greatly appreciated.

Skill 2: Using the Correct Verb Tense

In Part 6 of the new TOEIC test, you may be asked to choose the correct verb tense. The context clues to help you choose the correct tense may be in another sentence in the passage.

Sample TOEIC Test Question

Mr. Marsden started working here six months ago. He ______________ in the mailroom from the beginning. We hope to give him a promotion soon.

1. (A) worked
   (B) will work
   (C) had worked
   (D) has worked

Answer

Choice (D) is the correct answer. The sentence should read, *He has worked in the mailroom from the beginning*. A present perfect verb indicates an action that started in the past and continues to the present. We know from the first sentence that the action started six months ago. We know from the last sentence that the action continues to the present, but it may change in the near future. Choices (A) and (C) indicate actions that were completed in the past. Choice (B) indicates an action that will occur in the future.

Skill Focus

There are four verb tense groups in English: simple, continuous, perfect, and perfect continuous. Each of these can be expressed in the past, present, or future. With the exception of the simple tenses, English verb tenses generally deal with relational time. That is, the tense of a verb is determined by its relationship to another action or point in time.

Simple tenses indicate an action without particular emphasis on duration or relationship to other actions.

Examples:
During the rainy season, it *rains* every day. (present)
I stayed home yesterday because it *rained* all day. (past)
According to the weather forecast, it *will rain* tomorrow afternoon. (future)

Continuous tenses emphasize that the action is happening or continuing.

Examples:
Look out the window. It*'s raining*. (present)
It *was raining* until midnight. (past)
Take an umbrella. It *will be raining* when you leave work. (future)

Perfect tenses emphasize that an action is completed before a reference point (another time or action).

Examples:
It *has rained* every day for almost a week now. (present)
When we left work, it *had stopped* raining. (past)
The rain won't stop until tomorrow. By then, it *will have rained* every day for a week. (future)

Perfect continuous tenses emphasize the happening or continuing of an action that occurs before a reference point (another time or action) in the same time frame.

Examples:
It *has been raining* for six hours. (present)
It *had been raining* for almost six hours when the sun came out. (past)
In two more days, it *will have been raining* long enough to set a world record. (future)

Skill 2: Exercise

Choose the correct verb to complete each sentence.

1. We got to the train station just one minute late, but our train ________. We had to wait two hours for the next train.
   (A) left
   (B) was leaving
   (C) had left
   (D) has left

2. Ms. Kovacs plans to leave this job to return to school. Friday will be her last day at work. By then she ________ here for six months.
   (A) works
   (B) has worked
   (C) will be working
   (D) will have worked

3. Mr. Lopez was the owner of a small publishing company. He ________ books about economics and politics. After he died, his family sold the company.
   (A) publishes
   (B) published
   (C) has published
   (D) is publishing

4. Linda has been studying at the university for several years now. If all goes well, she ________ her degree in June. Then she hopes to get a better job.
   (A) will get
   (B) gets
   (C) was getting
   (D) got

5. I arrived at the meeting late. The director ________ the agenda. I entered the room and sat down quietly.
   (A) explained
   (B) was explaining
   (C) explains
   (D) has explained

TEST TIP

Sometimes verbs in subordinate clauses are in the simple present tense, even though the sentence refers to the future.

Example:
The assistant *will tell* us when Mr. Lee *arrives*.

The main verb *will tell* is in the simple future tense. The verb in the subordinate clause, *arrives*, is in the simple present tense.

Skill 3: Identifying Pronouns

Knowing the different types of pronouns can help you understand how pronouns are used on the new TOEIC test. Pronouns take the place of nouns. Different types of pronouns indicate different functions in the sentences. A closely related group of words is the group of possessive adjectives. They replace the possessive form of nouns and therefore modify nouns. The noun to which the pronoun refers may be in another sentence in the paragraph.

Sample TOEIC Test Question

Mr. Madison works for a small company in New York. ____________ job is challenging but interesting.

1. (A) His
   (B) Her
   (C) Its
   (D) My

Answer

Choice (A) is the correct answer. We know from the first sentences that the job belongs to Mr. Madison, so it is *his job*. This third person possessive adjective, *his*, refers to a man. Choice (B) refers to a woman. Choice (C) refers to a thing. Choice (D) is first person.

Skill Focus

Pronouns must be the same person and number as the nouns they replace. A pronoun must be singular or plural and first, second, or third person, according to the noun. This is also true for possessive adjectives. Study the following chart. Notice that some pronouns have different singular and plural or subject and object forms.

	Subject Pronouns		Object Pronouns		Possessive Adjectives	
	Singular	Plural	Singular	Plural	Singular	Plural
First person	I	we	me	us	my	our
Second person	you	you	you	you	your	your
Third person	he she it	they	him her it	them	his her its	their

Skill 3: Exercise

Complete the sentences with the correct pronoun.

1. Complete the form carefully. When you have finished, turn _______ in to the receptionist. She can also answer any questions you may have.
   (A) her
   (B) it
   (C) them
   (D) you

2. All these items are on sale. _______ cannot be returned to the store.
   (A) It
   (B) We
   (C) They
   (D) Their

3. Mr. Kim will be giving a lecture tonight. I have heard that _______ lectures are very interesting.
   (A) my
   (B) its
   (C) his
   (D) her

TEST TIP

In imperative sentences, the subject is not mentioned but is understood to be *you*. Therefore, any pronoun or possessive adjective referring to the subject of an imperative sentence must be in the second person.

Example:
(*You*) Please stay on the line. *Your* call will be taken in turn.

4. All new merchandise is displayed on the shelves by the entrance for our customers' convenience. In that place, _______ can be easily seen.
   (A) it
   (B) them
   (C) they
   (D) he

5. Ms. Lewiston has worked for this company for five years. We are sorry to see _______ leave.
   (A) us
   (B) it
   (C) him
   (D) her

Skill 4: Identifying the Appropriate Meaning

In Part 6, you may be asked to choose from a list of words that look similar but are actually very different in meaning. You will have to choose the word with the meaning that is appropriate for the context.

Sample TOEIC Test Question

Here at Professional Career Services we offer expert ____________ to help you move ahead in your career.

1. (A) advance
   (B) advertise
   (C) advice
   (D) advent

We can help you write a résumé, prepare for job interviews, and focus your job search.

Answer

Choice (C) is the correct answer. Professional Career Services gives help, or *advice*, to help its clients find jobs. Choice (A) means *progress*. Choice (B) means *announce*. Choice (D) means *beginning*.

Skill Focus

The context of a sentence will help you understand new vocabulary. When you read, you can understand the meaning of a sentence or paragraph even if you don't understand every word. When you understand the context, often you can guess the meaning of an unknown word.

Read the following groups of sentences. Try to understand the meaning and guess what words might complete the sentences.

1. Winter is often uncomfortable, but the ____________ is very pleasant in the autumn. You usually don't need to wear a jacket.
2. This job is just ____________. It will be finished in six months.
3. She has an even ____________. She rarely gets upset about anything.
4. He knew he couldn't afford the car, but the ____________ was too strong. He had to have it. He borrowed a lot of money so he could buy it.
5. He danced too slowly for the music. He couldn't keep up with the ____________.

We understand the general meaning of the sentences even without reading every word.

Example 1 is about comfort in different seasons.
Example 2 is about something that is not permanent.
Example 3 is about someone's personality.
Example 4 is about a strong desire.
Example 5 is about musical beat.

Skill 4: Exercise

Choose the correct word to complete each sentence.

temperament   temperature   tempo   temporary   temptation

1. Winter is often uncomfortable, but the ____________ is very pleasant in the autumn. You usually don't need to wear a jacket.
2. This job is just ____________. It will be finished in six months.
3. She has an even ____________. She rarely gets upset about anything.
4. He knew he couldn't afford the car, but the ____________ was too strong. He had to have it. He borrowed a lot of money so he could buy it.
5. He danced too slowly for the music. He couldn't keep up with the ____________.

TEST TIP

If the context still isn't clear, think about the part of speech that is needed for the blank. A noun will be a person, place, or thing. A verb will be an action. An adjective will describe, and an adverb will tell how. Thinking about the part of speech will help you approximate meaning.

Skill 5: Analyzing Word Families

In Part 6, you may need to complete a sentence with the correct word from a word family. You will have to identify the part of speech of each word.

Sample TOEIC Test Question

All of us at the Play Day Corporation ___________ everything you have done for our company.

1. (A) appreciate
   (B) appreciation
   (C) appreciative
   (D) appreciatively

Answer

Choice (A) is the correct answer. It is the main verb of the sentence, following the subject *All of us at the Play Day Corporation.* Choice (B) is a noun. Choice (C) is an adjective. Choice (D) is an adverb.

Skill Focus

The suffix often tells you a word's part of speech. A suffix can change a word into a noun, a verb, an adjective, or an adverb. Study the following chart, which includes some of the common suffixes in English.

Noun	Verb	Adjective	Adverb
-ance	*-ate*	*-able*	*-ly*
-ence	*-en*	*-al*	
-ity	*-ify*	*-ent*	
-ment	*-ize*	*-ful*	
-ness		*-ive*	
-sion		*-less*	
-tion		*-ly*	
		-ous	

Skill 5: Exercise

Complete the chart. Write the words from each word family in the correct column.

Noun	Verb	Adjective	Adverb
1. *enjoyment*	*enjoy*	*enjoyable*	*enjoyably*
2.			
3.			
4.			
5.			
6.			
7.			
8.			
9.			
10.			

1. enjoy, enjoyable, enjoyment, enjoyably
2. national, nation, nationally, nationalize
3. bright, brightly, brightness, brighten
4. simplify, simply, simple, simplicity
5. politicize, political, politics, politically
6. active, activate, actively, activation
7. confide, confident, confidently, confidence
8. pure, purity, purify, purely
9. conclusively, conclude, conclusion, conclusive
10. theory, theoretical, theorize, theoretically

TEST TIP

Be careful! Some word families have two or more words that are the same part of speech.

Examples:
Careful (adjective) means "full of care."
Careless (adjective) means "not careful."

Validity and *validation* are both nouns.
Other words have the same spelling for different parts of speech.

Example:
Moderate (verb) sounds like *ate* on the last syllable; *moderate* (noun-adjective) sounds like *it* on the last syllable.

Skill 6: Identifying Coordinating Conjunctions

In the new TOEIC test, you may be asked to choose the correct coordinating conjunction to complete a sentence. You will have to identify which conjunction gives the correct meaning to the sentence. The context clues that will help you choose the correct conjunction may be in another sentence in the paragraph.

Sample TOEIC Test Question

Mr. Rogers worked hard to make a delicious meal, ____________ Mrs. Rogers thought it was too spicy. She asked him to use fewer spices next time.

1. (A) or
(B) but
(C) and
(D) so

Answer

Choice (B) is the correct answer. The conjunction *but* connects two opposing ideas. We expect that after working hard, Mr. Rogers would create a delicious meal. From the second clause, we understand that Mrs. Rogers did not like the spiciness of the food, so the result was the opposite of what we might expect. Choice (A) connects two choices. Choice (C) connects two similar ideas. Choice (D) connects a cause with a result.

Skill Focus

Coordinating conjunctions are used to connect two parts of a sentence that are grammatically similar. For example, they may connect two clauses, two similar parts of speech, or two phrases.

Examples:

He worked hard all day, *so* he is very tired now. (two clauses)
The day was cold *but* beautiful. (two similar parts of speech)
We can meet in the boardroom *or* in my office. (two phrases)

Different conjunctions are used in different ways. Study the following chart.

Conjunction	Use	Example
and	connects two similar ideas	There were books on every shelf *and* in every cupboard.
but	connects two opposing ideas	I take the bus to work, *but* I usually walk home.
or	connects two choices	We can eat now *or* later.
so	connects a cause with a result	It was raining hard, *so* my shoes got wet.

Skill 6: Exercise

Complete the sentences with the correct coordinating conjunction.

1. You can order soup _______ salad. On a hot day like today, you might be in the mood for salad.
   (A) and
   (B) but
   (C) or
   (D) so

2. It's a nice building, _______ the neighborhood is too quiet. We need to locate our business in a busier part of town.
   (A) and
   (B) but
   (C) or
   (D) so

3. I didn't read the report, _______ I can't answer your questions.
   (A) for
   (B) but
   (C) or
   (D) so

4. The presenter spoke very quickly _______ softly. Nobody could understand her.
   (A) and
   (B) but
   (C) or
   (D) so

5. We can buy a new photocopier, _______ we can order more computers. Which do you think is the best way to spend our budget?
   (A) and
   (B) but
   (C) or
   (D) so

Part 6 Practice

Choose the one word or phrase that best completes each sentence.

Questions 1–3 refer to the following article.

A contract _____________ with the Quechee Development Corporation to renovate

1. (A) signed
   (B) has signed
   (C) will sign
   (D) has been signed

several downtown buildings, city officials announced last night. The city library will be torn _____________ and rebuilt, and extensive renovation work will be

2. (A) down
   (B) up
   (C) off
   (D) in

done to City Hall and the train station. "We are pleased to have finally reached an agreement about this work," said Mayor Clark at a City Council meeting last night. "Our city's downtown _____________ greatly improved as a result."

3. (A) is
   (B) will be
   (C) was
   (D) has been

There has been a great deal of controversy surrounding this project. Historic preservationists have protested the razing of the library, and city council members could not agree on the size of the budget. "After months of negotiation, I think we now have a valid plan that everyone will be happy with," said the mayor.

Questions 4–6 refer to the following letter.

Dear Potential Homeowner,

Why pay rent when you can own your own home? For thirty years we at Ridgefield Realtors have been in the business of ____________ homes in

4. (A) sell
   (B) to sell
   (C) selling
   (D) have sold

this city. Our agents are ready to help you find the perfect home for you and your family. ____________ you are looking for a condo,

5. (A) Whether
   (B) Although
   (C) Until
   (D) Unless

townhouse, or single-family home, we can find the right home in the right ____________ for you. Call us today at 800-555-7321 to make an

6. (A) neighbor
   (B) neighborly
   (C) neighboring
   (D) neighborhood

appointment with an experienced realtor. Or visit us online to start looking at listings immediately. Before you know it, you will be living in the home of your dreams.

Sincerely,

Roger Milton

Roger Milton
President

Questions 7–9 refer to the following e-mail.

To: Sam Jones
From: Cynthia Wilsen
Subject: Trip Plans

Hi Sam,

I just wanted to let you know that I have finalized my travel plans for next week. I will be arriving at the airport Monday afternoon at 3:05. You don't need to send anyone to meet me ____________ I plan to rent a car. I'll be staying at the

7. (A) since
   (B) when
   (C) despite
   (D) so

Spring House Hotel. There's a great restaurant there. Why don't we meet there for dinner at 6:30? I'll have a copy of the project plan with me, and we can go over it then. That way, we will be completely ____________ for the next day's

8. (A) prepare
   (B) prepared
   (C) preparation
   (D) preparer

meeting. I am really looking forward to this meeting. I know we have a great project to present. I know it will be well ____________ by the board members.

9. (A) deceived
   (B) believed
   (C) received
   (D) conceived

Cynthia

Questions 10–12 refer to the following notice.

To all Palm Acres residents:

It is time once again for the annual spring ____________ trash pickup, which

10. (A) weekly
    (B) bulk
    (C) dirty
    (D) paper

will take place during the week of April 23. Please place all large items intended for trash pickup on the curb in front of ____________ house before 6:00 on the

11. (A) his
    (B) its
    (C) our
    (D) your

morning of April 23. Please make sure that the items do not obstruct the sidewalk or the road. All items that are ____________ placed on the curb will be picked

12. (A) proper
    (B) property
    (C) properly
    (D) properness

up by 5 P.M. Friday, April 27. Items left on the curb before April 23 or after April 27 will be subject to fine. Please address any questions or problems to the maintenance office. Thank you.

The Management

Part 7: Reading Comprehension

OBJECTIVES

You can improve your score in Part 7 by:

- developing business vocabulary
- recognizing the main idea
- understanding the facts
- making inferences
- understanding the purpose

Part 7 of the new TOEIC® test contains different types of reading materials. These readings are the kind you would find during the course of a normal day in an English-speaking environment. These readings might include:

advertisements	announcements
calendars	charts
faxes	forms
graphs	brochures
letters	memos
articles	e-mails

Part 7 contains two types of reading passages—single passages and double passages. Each single passage is followed by two to five questions, for a total of 28 questions. The single passages are followed by a series of four double passages. Each pair of double passages is followed by five questions, for a total of 20 questions.

The questions for both kinds of passages are similar. When you answer questions about double passages, you have to understand the relationship between the two passages in order to answer the questions correctly.

Try not to spend more than 30 seconds per question. You will have only 75 minutes for all of Parts 5, 6, and 7, so use your time wisely.

Sample TOEIC Test Questions

Questions 1–4 refer to the following passage.

The White House, the official home of the president of the United States, was designed by the architect James Hoban, who is said to have been influenced by the design of a palace in Ireland. The building was begun in 1792 and was first occupied by the second president of the United States, John Adams, in November 1800. The house received its present name when it was painted white after being damaged by fire in 1814.

1. What is the main idea of the reading passage?
   (A) The White House has an interesting history.
   (B) President Adams was the first occupant of the White House.
   (C) The architect of the White House was from Ireland.
   (D) The White House was damaged by fire.

2. When was the White House first occupied?
   (A) 1776
   (B) 1792
   (C) 1800
   (D) 1814

3. Which of the following statements is probably true?
   (A) Palaces in Ireland are painted white.
   (B) All American presidents have lived in the White House.
   (C) John Adams was not president in 1800.
   (D) The White House was not white prior to 1814.

4. What is the author's purpose?
   (A) To inform
   (B) To persuade
   (C) To criticize
   (D) To praise

Answers

1. Choice (A) is the correct answer. This is a main idea question. To find the main idea, you must look at the complete reading passage, not just one part or one sentence. The reading passage states many facts. Choice (A) contains the most general, and true information. Choices (B), (C), and (D) are true, but each contains only part of the information of the passage.

2. Choice (C) is the correct answer. This is a factual question. To find this specific fact, scan the passage for the specific date. The reading passage states: *The building . . . was first occupied . . . in November 1800.* Choices (A), (B), and (D) are incorrect because the dates do not match the question.

3. Choice (D) is the correct answer. This is an inference question. You must infer the answer because the answer is not directly stated. The last sentence of the reading passage says that the White House . . . *was painted white . . . in 1814.* This implies that the official house of the president had been another color, but this information is not stated. Choice (A) is incorrect because the design, not the color, of the White House was influenced by a palace (one palace, not several). Choice (B) is incorrect because the first president did not live in the White House. Choice (C) is incorrect because Adams was president when he moved into the White House in 1800.

4. Choice (A) is the correct answer. This question asks for the author's purpose in writing the passage. The purpose is not stated directly, so you must infer the answer. The information in the reading passage is general: what the White House is, who the architect was, what the design influences were, when it was begun, who the first occupants were, and how it received its name. Choice (B) is incorrect because the author does not try to persuade us to believe or do something. Choices (C) and (D) are incorrect because there is no criticism or praise. There are simply facts in the passage.

Types of Questions

There are basically two types of questions in Part 7 of the Reading section of the new TOEIC test. The questions in Part 7 are based on what is *stated* (main idea and factual questions) and what is *implied* (inference and purpose questions). Study the examples in the chart below.

Question Types	Examples
Stated Main Idea Questions	The main idea of this article is . . . . The main topic of this article is . . . . The author believes . . . .
Stated Fact Questions	What happened . . . ? Who did what? How much . . . ? How many . . . ? How short . . . ? Which of the following is NOT mentioned? According to the article, what . . . ?
Implied Inference Questions	What does the author imply? What do you think . . . ? It can be inferred from the article that . . . . What can we infer from this passage?
Implied Purpose Questions	Why was this article written? What is the purpose of this article? Why did the author write this memo?

Skill 1: Developing Business Vocabulary

Exercise 1

Write the letter of the correct definition next to each word. Then complete the passage with the correct words.

Group A

____	1. accommodations	a. choices
____	2. consumers	b. a study of people's opinions or preferences
____	3. investigate	c. hotel rooms
____	4. options	d. buyers
____	5. survey	e. study; research

The Hotel Owners Association did a recent (6)__________ of hotel guests. The group wanted to find out what kinds of services and (7)__________ hotel guests generally prefer. One interesting result was that guests are willing to pay extra for more comfortable beds. They also prefer hotels that give them (8)__________. For example, many respondents said that they like to be able to choose between a plan that includes meals and one that doesn't. For its next study, the association plans to (9)__________ the effect of pricing on hotel choice. Do hotel guests act the same as (10)__________ of other products and services when it comes to the effect of price?

Group B

____	1. access	a. opinion that others have of you
____	2. discourage	b. provide
____	3. equip	c. proper; right for a situation
____	4. suitable	d. right to use; entry
____	5. reputation	e. try to stop

To: All personnel
From: B. Jones, Director
Re: New office policies

First, starting next month, we will have Casual Friday weekly, meaning you can dress less formally for work on Fridays. However, this is still an office and you should always wear (6)__________ clothes. We (7)__________ you from wearing sandals and T-shirts, especially when you meet with a client. We want to maintain our company's good (8)__________ and not lead people to think this is a playground.

Second, (9)__________ to the supply closet has been limited. The only person allowed to enter it regularly will be the office manager. If you need special supplies for a meeting or workshop, the manager will (10)__________ you with the necessary items.

Group C

_c_ 1. apologize a. help; doing what is asked
_e_ 2. budget b. origin; where something comes from
_A_ 3. cooperation c. say you are sorry
_D_ 4. entitle d. give the right to something
_b_ 5. source e. plan for spending money

To: Department personnel
From: Sue Buzzi, Department Manager
Re: Finances

We have just completed the company's financial planning for the year and have made several money-saving changes. There will be less money in each department's (6)_budget_ for extras such as office parties. In the future, we will have to plan our celebrations more economically. We will need everyone's (7)_cooperation_ for this. I thank you in advance for your help and (8)_apologize_ for any difficulties this may cause. We are also looking for another (9)_source_ for office supplies as the place we order from now charges higher prices than other stores. On a better note, we have made an agreement with the local health club. Your employee card will (10)_entitle_ you to a 20 percent discount on your health club membership.

Exercise 2

Complete the sentences with the correct word form.

apology (*noun*) **apologize** (*verb*) **apologetic** (*adjective*)

1. She accepted his _apology_, and they shook hands.
2. I want to _apologize_ for my late arrival.
3. He gave her an _apologetic_ look and said he was sorry.

cooperation (*noun*) **cooperate** (*verb*) **cooperative** (*adjective*)

4. The receptionist was very _cooperative_ and answered all our questions.
5. We will need everyone's _cooperation_ to finish the project on time.
6. Your boss will ask you to _cooperate_ on many projects.

option (*noun*) **opt** (*verb*) **optional** (*adjective*)

7. Many people _opt_ for higher-priced but more comfortable accommodations.
8. The car comes with heating, but air-conditioning is _optional_.
9. Skipping the meeting is not an _option_; everyone must attend.

Skill 2: Recognizing the Main Idea

In Part 7 of the new TOEIC test, you may be asked to determine the main idea of a reading passage. To answer factual questions, focus on the main idea, or what the passage is about. The main idea usually appears in the first paragraph.

Sample TOEIC Test Question

This question refers to the following announcement.

> The Marmax Group is a private family-held company that sells versions of the world's most treasured and expensive ladies' and men's colognes at a fraction of the original prices. Since our family started the business in 1993, we have been marketing our interpretations of famous perfumes under the brand name of "Aromas."

1. What is the main idea of the passage?
   (A) The Marmax Group sells scents.
   (B) Colognes are a fraction of Marmax's business.
   (C) The company started in the 1990s.
   (D) The company has its own brand name.

Answer

Choice (A) is the correct answer. The company sells ladies' and men's colognes. The generic term for colognes and perfumes is *scents*. This is the main idea of the passage. Choice (B) is incorrect because it is a detail. It is also incorrect because the company sells colognes at a discount that is a fraction of the original cost, not a fraction of the total business. Choice (C) is incorrect because it is a detail. The year that the company started business is not the main idea. Choice (D) is incorrect because it is a detail. The announcement does not discuss the importance of the brand name.

Skill Focus

The main idea of a reading passage is not always in the same place in a passage. Sometimes you can state the main idea exactly as it was stated in the passage. Other times, the main idea is best stated in slightly different words. But the main idea almost always appears early in the passage. Study the following clues for finding the main idea in passages. Notice that you may have to read several sentences before the main idea becomes clear.

CLUE 1 The main idea may be in the first sentence of the passage, so the reader can know immediately what the passage is about.

Example: It is important to know how to write a good résumé. A potential employer sees your résumé before he or she ever meets you. Therefore, you must make sure your résumé makes a good impression.

Main idea: It is important to know how to write a good résumé.

(Continued on next page)

CLUE 2	The main idea may present a contrast to a statement in the first sentence (or first few sentences) of the passage because the main idea is a reaction to the statement.
Example:	Many people think that business is a complicated field. However, the principles that guide successful businesses are actually quite simple.
Main idea:	Business principles are simple.
CLUE 3	The main idea may be a summary of details in the first sentence (or first few sentences) of a passage because putting the details first may capture the reader's interest.
Example:	The seats are comfortable, and the view outside the windows is lovely. The telephone, computer, printer, and fax machine are the latest models. It is obviously a luxury office. Like more and more offices these days, this one is in an automobile.
Main idea:	The changing workplace includes offices in automobiles.

Skill 2: Exercise

Each group of sentences consists of one main idea and three supporting details. Choose the main idea in each group.

1. (A) This year 250 billion dollars were spent on dogs and cats.
(B) Toys and clothes for pets are very popular with consumers.
(C) Pet owners spend a lot of time and money on their pets.
(D) There are doctors and even psychiatrists who specialize in pets.

2. (A) There have been many famous military leaders in history.
(B) Alexander the Great led his troops from Greece to India.
(C) Genghis Khan's empire stretched from Mongolia to Eastern Europe.
(D) General Eisenhower became president of the United States.

3. (A) The captain has to supervise the officers on the bridge.
(B) One of the functions of the captain is to perform marriages at sea.
(C) The captain is ultimately responsible for the safety of the passengers.
(D) The captain of a ship has many duties.

4. (A) The hotel has a large fitness center with an indoor pool.
(B) This hotel is the most luxurious in the city.
(C) There is a concierge on every floor.
(D) All rooms are suites with balconies.

5. (A) The modem transmits data at 56 kbps.
(B) It has no wireless capability.
(C) My old computer is not equipped with the latest technology.
(D) The software programs have not been upgraded.

TEST TIP

Don't mark a choice simply because it is true. The choice may be true, but it may not answer the question. Read the question carefully.

Skill 3: Understanding the Facts

In Part 7, you may be asked to find and determine the relationships among the facts in a reading passage. To answer factual questions, focus on the details in the passage. All factual statements are true and all are stated in the passage.

Sample TOEIC Test Question

Question 1 refers to the following news article.

> RSX said its second quarter net income doubled to $6 million, even though the company had labor problems. An RSX spokesperson said the improved results showed a greater demand for its products. In its 20-year history, this is the most significant jump in earnings.

1. What was the net income of RSX in the first quarter?
   (A) Three million dollars
   (B) Six million dollars
   (C) Twelve million dollars
   (D) Twenty million dollars

Answer

Choice (A) is the correct answer. This fact is noted in the first sentence. In the second quarter the net income was double what it was in the first quarter. *To be doubled* means *to be twice as much.* This simple math makes the first-quarter net income $3 million. Choice (B) is the net income in the second quarter. Choice (C) is the net income if you doubled the second-quarter income. Choice (D) is not mentioned as earnings, but *20* is mentioned as the number of years the company has been in business.

Skill Focus

Locating facts usually means paying attention to details. Although a fact may be clearly stated, it may also be hidden among other information or other words. You may also have to do some simple calculations. Study the following clues for locating important facts.

CLUE 1 The passage might state the fact explicitly.
Example: The company is 20 years old.
Fact: The company is 20 years old.

CLUE 2 A sentence might "hide" a fact in a subordinate clause.
Example: No one believed the company would succeed when it began 20 years ago in a small town.
Fact: The company is 20 years old.

CLUE 3 The same fact might be stated in different words in the passage.
Example: In the two decades since it opened its doors, the company has always been profitable.
Fact: The company is 20 years old. (*Two decades* means the same as *20 years*, and *opened its doors* means the same *as started.*)

Skill 3: Exercise

Find two supporting facts for each general statement. Write the letters under the appropriate statement.

General Statements

1. The ship's cabins are equipped for the passenger's safety and comfort.

   _____ _____

2. Electronic mail has improved communication.

   _____ _____

3. The weather is seasonably cold.

   _____ _____

4. Medical research is under attack from animal rights groups.

   _____ _____

5. Oil companies are investigating alternate sources of fuels.

   _____ _____

Supporting Facts

(A) It was below freezing this morning.
(B) Life jackets are stowed under each bed.
(C) People write more often when they use e-mail.
(D) Protesters want to stop experiments on animals.
(E) All cabins have their own water purification system.
(F) Thousands of animal rights activists blocked the entrances to six research facilities.
(G) Oil, coal, and gas are limited resources.
(H) Correspondents from all over the world can send letters instantaneously via their computers.
(I) We expect more snow and ice later today.
(J) Solar energy may be one substitute for petroleum-based fuels.

TEST TIP

Don't guess too quickly and mark the first recognizable answer. Some test takers see a word or number from the passage and assume it's the correct answer. Take time to analyze.

Skill 4: Making Inferences

In Part 7, you may be asked to make inferences about a reading passage. To make correct inferences, draw conclusions about what is likely or logical from information that is explicitly stated in the passage.

Sample TOEIC Test Question

This question refers to the following electronic index.

Where to GO		
Online Index		
Business Data Plus	GO	BUSDP
Business Demographics	GO	BUSDEM
Executive News Service	GO	ENS
Entrepreneur's Small Business Forum	GO	SMALLBIZ
International Trade Forum	GO	ITFORUM
PR and Marketing Archives	GO	PRSIG

1. Who would most likely use this index?
   (A) Hotel housekeepers
   (B) Oil engineers
   (C) Businesspeople
   (D) Airline pilots

Answer

Choice (C) is the correct answer. From the list of topics, you can infer that most of them concern business. In fact, the word *business* is in three of the six topics. Choices (A), (B), and (D) are incorrect. Although a hotel housekeeper, an oil engineer, or an airline pilot might use this index, none of them would be the most likely user.

Skill Focus

Many different kinds of information can be clues to inferences. Clues may be found in the words used, in the way that the information is presented, and in probable occurrences based on information given. Study how the following clues can help you make inferences.

CLUE 1 Clues to inferences may be found in words or terms that are repeated or in the use of multiple words that are related to each other.

Example: Everyone wants to be with their families. Employees are happier if they have family time to take their children for bike rides, spend time with their parents, and go out to dinner with their spouses.

Inference: *Families*, *family*, *children*, *parents*, and *spouses* suggest that the idea of family is important to the passage.

(*Continued on next page*)

CLUE 2	Clues to inferences may be found in the way that information is combined, especially when steps seem to be left out.
Example:	On the first day of work, new employees report to orientation. There will be sessions on company policy, employee benefits, and product history. On the fourth day, employees will be assigned to a trainer in their department.
Inference:	The orientation sessions will last three days.
CLUE 3	An inference may be the next logical outcome of a statement.
Example:	Everyone will want to buy the product.
Inference:	The manufacturer of the product will make a profit.

Skill 4: Exercise

Each statement is followed by three possible inferences. Choose the most logical inference about the statement.

1. The politician lost the election.
   (A) She was absentminded.
   (B) Her policies weren't popular with the voters.
   (C) She was elected on the first ballot.

2. It took over an hour to drive just five miles.
   (A) The traffic was very heavy.
   (B) The distance was very long.
   (C) Our car is very fast.

3. Mozart could play the violin and the harpsichord when he was only five.
   (A) He was taught by his father.
   (B) He didn't want to play the trombone.
   (C) He was very precocious.

4. A knowledgeable consumer waits until items go on sale.
   (A) Smart shoppers like to save money.
   (B) If you know you need something, buy it now.
   (C) The best items are never on sale.

5. Company earnings would have been higher had there been no strike.
   (A) The workers will not go on strike.
   (B) The striking workers reduced the profitability of the company.
   (C) Earnings are always higher in the last quarter.

TEST TIP

You won't find direct answers to inferential questions in the reading passage. You need to analyze the information and make conclusions.

Skill 5: Understanding the Purpose

In Part 7, you may be asked to determine the purpose of a reading passage. To answer these questions, you must decide whether the purpose of the passage is to inform, persuade, criticize, amuse, praise, or apologize.

The purpose is not directly stated in the passage; you have to infer the purpose from the context. As you read, ask yourself: Why was this passage written?

Sample TOEIC Test Question

Question 1 refers to the following notice.

> Here's an opportunity to put your sales ability to work as the owner of your own direct marketing agency. You'll sell ad services and have an international company behind you. Your income will increase, and you will have more time to spend with your family. You will be able to take your vacations when YOU want to take them. Why work for others when you can work for yourself?
>
> For more information, come to the Business Opportunity Show at the Carlton Hotel on July 23–24. No need to schedule an appointment. Just meet us at Booth 345.

1. What is the purpose of this notice?
   (A) To give employees more time with their families
   (B) To persuade you to come to the Business Opportunity Show
   (C) To strengthen your sales ability
   (D) To schedule an appointment

Answer

Choice (B) is the correct answer. The purpose of the notice is to persuade the reader to come to the Business Opportunity Show. If the person does come, he or she will be able to learn what is required to start a business in direct marketing. Choice (A) is incorrect because having more time with your family is a result of having your own business. Choice (C) is incorrect because the notice assumes the reader already has strong sales ability. Choice (D) is incorrect because appointments are not required.

Skill Focus

When the reading passage is a chart, or form, it is usually easy to determine the purpose. The purpose is usually found in the title or heading of the form. When the reading passage is made up of one or more paragraphs, you may have to consider the passage carefully to decide the purpose. Study the following clues and examples for determining the purpose of a reading passage.

CLUE 1 An **informative passage** may contain several facts or figures. Such passages may be in the form of charts, graphs, lists, or paragraphs. Information tends to be objective.

Example: The number of students seeking admission to the graduate business program has increased 20% over the past 18 months. Among the reasons for the increase are the opening of our new suburban classroom building last January and the 97% excellence rating awarded to us by the accreditation board.

Explanation: The passage contains several facts and figures: *increased 20%, past 18 months, 97% excellence rating.* The only two adjectives that are not part of common phrases (such as graduate *business program* and *last January*) are *new* and *suburban*. Both of these are objective.

CLUE 2 A **persuasive passage** usually recommends an action or a way of thinking. It typically gives the reasons for that position and the benefits of adopting it.

Example: The newly developed Warm'n' Soft fabric may be the most comfortable winter fabric you have ever worn. It is 20% warmer than plain wool. It's also lightweight, which means that you won't be weighed down by a heavy coat. Warm 'n' Soft is water-resistant, too, so wet snow rolls right off. If you want to laugh at the cold weather this winter, make sure you choose a coat made of Warm 'n' Soft.

Explanation: The action recommended is the purchase of a Warm 'n' Soft coat. The reasons for recommending the purchase are that Warm 'n' Soft is warmer than wool, lightweight, and water-resistant. The benefit of purchasing a Warm 'n' Soft coat is that this coat will keep you warm, dry, and comfortable in wintertime.

CLUE 3 A **critical passage** is usually a reaction to a stated idea or situation. It may present many contrasts and alternatives. It probably contains adjectives and other words that have both positive and negative meanings.

Example: The new Civic Center was a good idea for our city, but it has failed due to poor planning. Lack of parking and nearby restaurants have made the center a place that is difficult to get to and uncomfortable to spend time in.

Explanation: This passage is a reaction to the first line, *The new Civic Center was a good idea for our city*. Notice that this is quite a positive statement, compared to the rest of the paragraph. The passage contrasts this good idea with the bad way the idea was carried out. It specifically mentions the effects of lack of parking and absence of nearby restaurants. It has a few positive words, *new* and *good*, but several negative words, *failed, poor, lack of, difficult,* and *uncomfortable.*

CLUE 4 A **passage to amuse** the reader may contain imaginative ideas. It may describe a situation or present an image that makes the reader smile. The facts presented are usually simple, rather than complicated.

Example: The Tasty Bakery is famous for making cakes in any shape or size. Among their most popular styles are cakes that look like roses, baskets of flowers, or footballs. They also make cakes to order, and some of the customers' requests have been unusual. One customer wanted a cake that looked like a hamburger. Another wanted a cake that looked like his dog. But the strangest request came from a mayor who wanted a replica of his town in cake for the town's Founder's Day celebration.

Explanation: The imaginative ideas presented in this passage are the many different shapes mentioned for the cakes. The images of these cakes in your mind may make you smile. The facts mentioned are all quite simple and do not require you to make calculations or complicated associations. These facts are that the Tasty Bakery is famous, they make cakes in different shapes and sizes, and some customer requests are unusual.

CLUE 5 A **passage to praise** something usually has a lot of positive adjectives and words with positive connotations. It may show a positive result of a past action, or it may predict a positive outcome of a current or future action.

Example: The recently published *Guide to City Restaurants* will be a big help to visitors and residents who want to eat out. The guide is a source of clear, precise information about food, location, and prices. It is also well organized so that information can be located quickly and easily.

Explanation: The many positive adjectives and other words in this passage indicate that its purpose is to praise the restaurant guide. The positive terms include *big help, clear, precise information, well organized, quickly,* and *easily*. It predicts a positive outcome of a future action, *will be a big help to visitors and residents who want to eat out*.

CLUE 6 A **passage to apologize** for something acknowledges a mistake and expresses regret for the problems that the mistake might have caused. It also usually mentions some current or future action intended to correct the mistake.

Example: This newspaper would like to announce that the sale price of Grip-Tight tires that appeared yesterday in the ad for Johnson's Garage was misprinted. The correct sale price of each tire is $90, as printed in today's ad. We regret any inconvenience that this error has caused Johnson's Garage and its customers.

Explanation: The mistake that is acknowledged is *the sale price of Grip-Tight tires that appeared yesterday in the ad for Johnson's Garage was misprinted*. The announcement expresses regret in the line *we regret any inconvenience that this error has caused Johnson's Garage and its customers*. The action to correct the mistake is the explicit one that the newspaper has printed the ad with the correct price today and the assumed one that they are correcting this mistake by printing the apology in the newspaper.

Skill 5: Exercise

Choose the correct purpose of each statement.

> **TEST TIP**
>
> Keep the main idea in mind as you determine the purpose. Most passages have details of several types. For example, a passage can praise part of an idea but criticize most of the idea. Look for the overall purpose of the passage.

1. We want to congratulate Mr. Prahinski, who was responsible for the award-winning design of our new handheld personal communicator.
   (A) To criticize
   (B) To persuade
   (C) To inform
   (D) To praise

2. I would like you to meet our new Front Desk Manager, Ms. Tamayo, who has been with our sister hotel in Rio.
   (A) To amuse
   (B) To praise
   (C) To inform
   (D) To criticize

3. In the future, I hope that there will be more attention paid to our customers' needs and less time spent on your own personal affairs.
   (A) To apologize
   (B) To praise
   (C) To criticize
   (D) To inform

4. There are 365 days in a year except in a leap year, when there are 366.
   (A) To inform
   (B) To persuade
   (C) To apologize
   (D) To praise

5. We are sorry for the delay, but the severe weather patterns in the area have grounded all planes.
   (A) To persuade
   (B) To apologize
   (C) To amuse
   (D) To criticize

Part 7 Practice

Single Passages

The questions that follow are based on a variety of reading materials. Choose the best answer to each question.

Questions 1–5 refer to the following appointment calendar page.

MARCH

28 MONDAY

Meet train 6:42 at station

29 TUESDAY

6:00 Tennis w/ T. Kral

30 WEDNESDAY

12:00 p.m. Lunch at Elizabeth's Café w/ Ms. Welby

31 THURSDAY

4:00 p.m. Teleconference

APRIL

1 FRIDAY

10:00 Staff meeting

11:00 Mr. James Gonsalves

2 SATURDAY

7:30 a.m. John Ling–golf course

3 SUNDAY

1. What period of time does this page cover?
   (A) One week
   (B) Two weeks
   (C) One month
   (D) Two months

2. Where is the appointment with John Ling?
   (A) At the train station
   (B) At a café
   (C) On the golf course
   (D) On the telephone

3. What can be inferred from this page?
   (A) There will be a teleconference on Tuesday.
   (B) The staff meeting on Friday will not be longer than an hour.
   (C) There will be a tennis game on Thursday.
   (D) Ms. Welby is a vegetarian.

4. What will happen on Tuesday?
   (A) A train will arrive two minutes late.
   (B) There will be a tennis game.
   (C) Elizabeth will serve lunch.
   (D) A new month will begin.

5. What time is the appointment with Ms. Welby?
   (A) 6:00
   (B) 10:00
   (C) Noon
   (D) Midnight

Questions 6–8 refer to the following form.

Call 1-800-555-5459
to make a reservation

You have the opportunity to reserve these accommodations for next year. Send a non-refundable reservation fee (10%). The lease will be sent to you by November 15. Fill out this form and return it to our office as soon as possible.

Name & Address: ____________________

____

Phone: ____________________

Today's date: ____________________

Reservation date: ____________________

10% paid by: ____________________

Cash ☐ Traveler's Check ☐ Credit Card ☐

Reserved for office use:

Accommodations #: Rec'd by:

6. What is this type of form used for?
   (A) To obtain insurance
   (B) To reserve accommodations
   (C) To pay a bill
   (D) To pay an invoice

7. Which of the following information is filled in at the office?
   (A) Name and address
   (B) Today's date
   (C) Phone number
   (D) Received by

8. Which of the following can NOT be used for payment?
   (A) Cash
   (B) Credit card
   (C) Personal check
   (D) Traveler's check

Questions 9–12 refer to the following newspaper article.

RAISING RATES IN THE CITY—FOR THE TOURIST

WHEN TAXES ON hotel rooms in Washington, D.C. rise this summer, the city will go from having the 30th highest hotel taxes to having the 10th highest among the top tourist cities in the United States. This increase, from 11 percent to 13 percent, is a big one; however, the tax rate is much lower than hotel taxes charged in New York.

In addition to hotel taxes, there will be new restaurant taxes. Taxes at Washington restaurants will rise from 9 percent to 10 percent. This increase gives Washington the highest restaurant taxes in the country.

Although the new restaurant taxes will affect local citizens, the taxes will mostly affect tourists to the city. These tourists will pay both the new hotel taxes and the new restaurant taxes.

An organization based in San Francisco made a survey of "tourist taxes" in 50 most-visited cities. The study of hotel, restaurant, gasoline, car rental, and airfare taxes showed that the average family pays 14 percent of its vacation budget in taxes. "The tourist is the easiest target to tax because tourists don't vote where they spend," said the chairman of the organization.

9. What does this article primarily discuss?
(A) The result of a survey
(B) Tourist taxes
(C) Washington, D.C.
(D) Taxes in restaurants

10. Which taxes will increase by 2 percentage points?
(A) Tourist taxes in San Francisco
(B) Hotel taxes in Washington, D.C.
(C) Restaurant taxes in Washington, D.C.
(D) Tourist taxes in 50 most-visited cities

11. Which of the following is NOT true?
(A) Hotel taxes in New York are higher than those in Washington, D.C.
(B) Tourists and local citizens pay restaurant taxes.
(C) Taxes make up more than 10 percent of a family's vacation budget.
(D) New York has the highest restaurant taxes in the United States.

12. The word "average" in paragraph 4, line 6 is closest in meaning to
(A) normal
(B) traveling
(C) largest
(D) wealthy

Questions 13–16 refer to the following message.

To: *Mr. Ramen*

Date: *12/08* Time: *10:15* (AM)/PM

WHILE YOU WERE OUT

(Mr.)/Ms. *Sam Keng*

of *Hotel Service Corporation*

Phone *(202) 555-1234 x341*

Area Code Number Extension

☑ TELEPHONED ☑ PLEASE CALL

☐ RETURNED YOUR CALL ☐ WILL CALL

Message

Unable to make tomorrow's meeting; let's meet next Monday

Ms. Murohisa

13. Who made the phone call?
(A) Mr. Sam Keng
(B) Mr. Ramen
(C) Ms. Murohisa
(D) Hotel Service Corporation

14. Who took the message?
(A) Mr. Sam Keng
(B) Mr. Ramen
(C) Ms. Murohisa
(D) Hotel Service Corporation

15. Why was the call made?
(A) To cancel a meeting
(B) To verify a meeting
(C) To take a message
(D) To return a call

16. What will probably happen next?
(A) Mr. Keng will call Mr. Ramen.
(B) Mr. Keng and Mr. Ramen will meet on Monday.
(C) Mr. Ramen will telephone Mr. Keng.
(D) Ms. Murohisa will return Mr. Keng's call.

Questions 17–20 refer to the following form.

CompuSys Conference
Secretaria Executiva
Av. Francisco Jose de Camargo Andrade, 34
13040-221 – Campinas, SP
Brazil

Telephone: (55) (192) 41-3204
Fax: (55) (192) 41-5432

Name: ____
Last/Family First Middle
CompuSys Membership #: ______________________________
Company Name: ______________________________________
Mailing Address: _____________________________________
City/State/Zip/Country: _______________________________
Work Phone: ______________ Fax: ______________ E-mail: ______________

CONFERENCE: Please check appropriate fee(s).

Advance Reservation Fees Until July 10, 20___	CompuSys Member Advance/Late or On-site	Non-Member Advance/Late or On-site
Full Conference Registration	☐ $330/ $420	☐ $430/ $530
Opening Ceremony	☐ $30/ $40	☐ $100/ $120
Day One of Conference (Oct. 2)	☐ $100/ $120	☐ $110/ $135
Day Two of Conference (Oct. 3)	☐ $100/ $120	☐ $110/ $135
Day Three of Conference (Oct. 4)	☐ $100/ $120	☐ $110/ $135
Proceedings of the Conference	☐ $80/ $100	☐ $110/ $135

Total (in U.S. dollars): $__________
Methods of Payment

☐ Payment Order
PAY TO: Banco do Brasil S.A., New York (USA)
SWIFT CODE: BRASUS44
CHIPS ABA: 0344
FED WIRE: ABA 0371-1466-8
FOR ACCT.: 128.141-6

☐ Credit Card ______________
Cardholder Name ______________
Card Number ______________
Expiration Date ______________
Authorized
Signature ______________

17. Who should fill out this form?
(A) Conference organizers
(B) Conference attendees
(C) Conference presenters
(D) Conference assistants

18. What is the cost for non-members to register for the opening ceremony on-site?
(A) $30
(B) $40
(C) $100
(D) $120

19. Where does the conference take place?
(A) France
(B) Switzerland
(C) New York
(D) Brazil

20. To save money, registration must be received no later than
(A) July 10
(B) October 2
(C) October 3
(D) October 4

Questions 21–24 refer to the following fax.

SE
29 December 20__

Via Facsimile Number: 1-42-72-61-66

For the attention of: Mr. Armand Dubois

General Manager's Office
Grand Hotel Limited
Berkeley Square
London, W1A 2JQ
Telephone (0171) 518 7759
Telex 10761 Fax (0171) 518 1109

DUBOIS AND LEGER, L.L.P.
Attorneys at Law

Dear Mr. Dubois:

Thank you for your facsimile letter dated 28 December, addressed to Ms. Anna Wong, Assistant Sales Manager, for whom I am replying.

It is with great pleasure that I reconfirm we have now reserved your one-bedroom suite from Sunday, 20 January until departure on Monday, 28 January.

We will, of course, do our utmost to allocate your usual suite #301 for you. However, should this suite not be available, we will naturally provide a suitable alternative. I have noted that you require a non-smoking suite with a king-size bed with bed boards. This room will also be away from the room service waiter area or construction.

The daily rate for this accommodation is £500.00, inclusive of Service, excluding Value Added Tax at 17.5%.

I trust all is in order, and I look forward very much indeed to welcoming you back to the Grand. You may rest assured that we will do our utmost to ensure that your stay is as comfortable and as enjoyable as possible.

If you should feel I can be of any further assistance, please do not hesitate to contact me.

Yours sincerely,

Malcolm A. Ashton

Malcolm A. Ashton

General Manager

21. What is the purpose of the fax?
    (A) To promote the hotel
    (B) To confirm a reservation
    (C) To ask for legal advice
    (D) To change the arrival date

22. Who did Mr. Dubois originally write to?
    (A) Mr. Leger
    (B) The General Manager
    (C) Mr. Ashton
    (D) Ms. Wong

23. What can be said about Mr. Dubois?
    (A) He often stays at the Grand.
    (B) He likes to smoke.
    (C) He never stays longer than two nights.
    (D) He likes to be close to the waiter area.

24. What is included in the room rate?
    (A) Value Added Tax
    (B) Service
    (C) A private car
    (D) Airport transfers

Questions 25–28 refer to the following brochure.

Visitors who want to see the city's attractions have several transportation options. The use of private cars is discouraged, since parking is limited and the streets of the historical district are narrow. Fortunately, excellent alternatives are available. The subway system provides fast, inexpensive transportation to all areas of the city, from 6:00 A.M. to 12 midnight. Bus service operates 24 hours a day, for those who prefer to travel above ground and sneak in some extra sightseeing en route. Those of you who want to make sure that you see all the tourist attractions may be especially interested in our visitors' tour buses, which make stops at all points of interest throughout the city. For your convenience, special visitors' passes for all forms of public transportation are sold at hotels throughout the city, along with maps and schedules for transportation routes. Subway tickets may also be purchased at subway stops.

25. What is this announcement about?
    (A) Hotels
    (B) Visitors
    (C) Transportation
    (D) Attractions

26. What should visitors NOT do in the city?
    (A) Spend the night
    (B) Drive their cars
    (C) Walk alone
    (D) Travel at rush hour

27. Which service stops at midnight?
    (A) Bus service
    (B) Subway service
    (C) Tour service
    (D) Taxi service

28. Why may some visitors prefer traveling by bus?
    (A) People can see more of the city.
    (B) Buses are faster.
    (C) The subway is more expensive.
    (D) Bus routes are more convenient.

Double Passages

The questions that follow are based on a variety of reading materials. Choose the best answer to each question.

Questions 29–33 refer to the following notice and memo.

NOTICE TO ALL TENANTS:

Painting of the Park Side Towers office building will begin next month, according to the following schedule:

Week of

March 2—lobby and first-floor hallways
March 9—second-floor hallways
March 16—third-floor hallways
March 23—fourth-floor hallways
March 30—basement and cafeteria
April 6—begin repair on elevators

Elevator repair is scheduled for completion on April 15. Some elevators may be out of service at times during the repairs. We apologize for the inconvenience and thank you for your cooperation.

—Manager, Park Side Towers

Writex, Inc.
INTEROFFICE MEMO

TO: Office staff
FROM: Peter Chang, Office Manager
RE: Painting

By now you have all seen the notice regarding the painting to be done in the building next month. The board meeting, which was originally scheduled for March 25, has been postponed since that is the same week our floor will be painted. We decided that it is best to wait until all work on the building is completed. Therefore, the meeting has been rescheduled for the day after the elevator repair is finished. Please make a note of it. Please be aware that there may be times when the elevators will be out of service during the first part of April. Please contact me if you think this will cause you difficulties, and I will make arrangements with the maintenance supervisor to make sure you always have access to the office.

29. How many weeks will the painting take?
(A) Five
(B) Six
(C) Seven
(D) Eight

30. When will the cafeteria be painted?
(A) After the elevators are repaired
(B) At the same time as the basement
(C) During the week of April 6
(D) Before the fourth floor

31. On which floor is Writex, Inc. located?
(A) First
(B) Second
(C) Third
(D) Fourth

32. When will the board meeting take place?
(A) March 25
(B) April 6
(C) April 15
(D) April 16

33. Who should a Writex employee speak to about difficulties with the elevator?
(A) The building manager
(B) The maintenance supervisor
(C) The office manager
(D) The elevator operator

Questions 34–38 refer to the following two letters.

Leo Zimmerman
President
Beach Patio Restaurants
1226 Hanover Boulevard
Littleton, NY 10009

Dear Mr. Zimmerman:

I am writing to let you know about my recent experience at the Beach Patio Restaurant in Sandy Hill. I went there for dinner recently because friends had recommended it. I was very disappointed. I had to wait a long time for my order to be taken and then for my dinner to be served. When the waiter finally brought my food, he got my order wrong. He was not nice about this and implied that it was my fault. When dessert time came, the waiter gave me only two choices instead of the five promised by the menu (I had ordered the three-course dinner special). On top of the poor service, my tea was cold and the table was dirty. I was surprised by everything that happened that night because the Beach Patio Restaurants have such a good reputation. I was sure you would want to know about this.

Sincerely,

Eun Hwa Park

Eun Hwa Park
17 Maple Lane
Riverton, CT 06877

Beach Patio Restaurants
Corporate Headquarters
Littleton, NY 10009

Eun Hwa Park
17 Maple Lane
Riverton, CT 06877

Dear Ms. Park:

I was very sorry to hear about your recent unpleasant experience at a Beach Patio Restaurant. As you may know, customers can enjoy fine Beach Patio food and service at several locations, including Sunnydale, Merrifield, and Waterford. The branch you visited is our newest location, and that may be the source of the unpleasant experience you had. Please be assured that I will contact the manager of that branch and have the matter investigated. In the meantime, please accept the enclosed coupon. It entitles you to the same special you ordered on your recent visit, and I am sure that this time you will enjoy your food and your visit 100%. Thank you for bringing this matter to my attention.

Sincerely,

Leo Zimmerman

Leo Zimmerman
President

34. Why did Ms. Park write this letter?
(A) To recommend the restaurant
(B) To ask for a job at the restaurant
(C) To complain about the restaurant
(D) To ask for directions to the restaurant

35. Which Beach Patio location did Ms. Park visit?
(A) Sunnydale
(B) Riverton
(C) Littleton
(D) Sandy Hill

36. Which of the following best describes the waiter?
(A) Pleasant
(B) Rude
(C) Efficient
(D) Helpful

37. What will Mr. Zimmerman do?
(A) Contact the restaurant manager
(B) Have dinner with Ms. Park
(C) Visit the restaurant soon
(D) Open a new branch

38. What can Ms. Park get with the coupon?
(A) Two desserts
(B) Afternoon tea
(C) A three-course dinner
(D) A cleaner table

Questions 39–43 refer to the following train schedule and e-mail.

Eastern Railway
Timetable
Harford–Lakeville
Spring, 20__

Leave Harford	Arrive Lakeville
7:15 A.M.	10:25 A.M.
8:45 A.M.	11:55 A.M.
10:15 A.M.	1:25 P.M.
12:30 P.M.	3:45 P.M.
2:15 P.M.	5:25 P.M.

Leave Lakeville	Arrive Harford
6:55 A.M.	10:05 A.M.
8:05 A.M.	11:15 A.M.
9:45 A.M.	12:55 P.M.
11:15 A.M.	2:25 P.M.
1:45 P.M.	4:55 P.M.

Fare information
One way: $75
Round trip: $125
(Special round-trip fare is not available on weekends.)

To: **Lee Martin**
From: **Sylvia Elliott**
Subject: **trip plans**

Hi Lee,

It's time to get the tickets for my trip to Lakeville. I've been looking over the train schedule. I have a lunch meeting at 12:30, so I think the second morning train will be fine. I won't need hotel reservations since I will be staying with my sister, but I will need you to arrange a rental car for me. Also, do you remember the name of that new restaurant in Lakeville that everyone is talking about? Please try to find out because I'd like to take my sister there if we have time. Please get me a return ticket for Saturday. I am meeting a friend for dinner at the Harford Hotel at 6:00 Saturday evening, and I'd like to arrive at the station an hour or so ahead of time for that. We're going to the play at the Harford Theater afterward. Have you seen it? I hear it's wonderful. Thanks for your help.

Sylvia

39. What time will Sylvia leave for Lakeville?
(A) 7:15
(B) 8:45
(C) 10:15
(D) 12:30

40. How long is the train ride from Harford to Lakeville?
(A) one hour
(B) one and one-half hours
(C) three hours
(D) three hours and ten minutes

41. What does she want Lee to reserve for her?
(A) A hotel room
(B) A restaurant table
(C) A rental car
(D) A theater ticket

42. What time will Sylvia arrive in Harford?
(A) 2:25
(B) 4:55
(C) 5:00
(D) 6:00

43. How much will Sylvia's train ticket to Lakeville and back cost?
(A) $75
(B) $125
(C) $150
(D) $175

Questions 44–48 refer to the following memo and e-mail.

MEMO

To: All personnel
From: Suzan Reed, Human Resources Manager
RE: Insurance workshop
Date: May 15

On June 5, a workshop on health insurance options will be offered by insurance expert Rudy Shapiro. The workshop will take place in Conference Room 4 from 1:00–3:30. Refreshments will be served. This workshop is highly recommended to all staff members. If you are interested in attending, please let me know before May 20, and be sure you have permission from your department head to be away from your desk at this time. We hope to offer the workshop again in September and November so that everyone will have a chance to attend.

To: Suzan Reed
From: George Peters
Subject: Workshop

Hi Suzan,

In regard to the memo you sent out yesterday, I would like to attend the workshop on health insurance options next month. I will have to leave the workshop 20 minutes early because I have a meeting downtown at 3:45 that day that can't be changed. I hope that won't be a problem. Also, I'd like to make a suggestion. The room you have planned for the workshop is scheduled to be painted the day before the workshop. It will probably still be full of fumes on June 5. Would it be possible to have the workshop in Conference Room 3? The cafeteria might be even more suitable if you expect a large turnout. Let me know what you think.

George

44. Who can attend the workshop?
(A) Everyone who is interested
(B) Insurance agents only
(C) Doctors and nurses
(D) Department heads only

45. When did George Peters write his e-mail?
(A) May 15
(B) May 16
(C) May 20
(D) June 5

46. What time will George Peters leave the workshop?
(A) 3:00
(B) 3:10
(C) 3:30
(D) 3:45

47. Which room will be painted on June 4?
(A) George Peters' office
(B) Suzan Reed's office
(C) Conference Room 3
(D) Conference Room 4

48. What is probably true about the cafeteria?
(A) It is never used for workshops.
(B) It is near George Peters' office.
(C) It will be painted in early June.
(D) It is larger than the conference rooms.

III Speaking

OBJECTIVES

You can improve your score in Speaking by:

- developing business vocabulary
- using correct stress
- describing objects and actions in a photo
- talking about common activities and events
- finding and explaining information on a schedule
- finding a solution to a problem
- stating and explaining your opinion

The new TOEIC® Speaking Test is delivered through the Internet. It evaluates your ability to communicate in spoken English. The test involves a variety of speaking tasks, including reading aloud, answering questions, and expressing an opinion. You may be asked to read a text, look at a picture, or view some information before speaking or answering. For most of the tasks, you will be given time to prepare before you start speaking. For all tasks, you will be given a specific amount of time to perform the task. The test has a total of 11 questions and takes about 20 minutes to complete.

Types of Questions

There are several different types of questions in the new TOEIC Speaking Test.

Questions 1–2

For each question, you will see a text on the screen and read it aloud.

Question 3

You will describe a photo on the screen, including as many details as possible about the objects, people, and actions in the photo.

Questions 4–6

You will read three questions from an imaginary market research firm and answer them.

Questions 7–9

You will read a schedule or agenda. Then you will hear three questions about information on the schedule or agenda and answer them.

Question 10

You will hear a problem. Then you will give a solution to the problem.

Question 11

You will read a question and explain your opinion about it, giving reasons for your opinion.

Evaluation Criteria

When you take the test, you will need to understand what is required for each task, and you will need to speak clearly and correctly. The evaluation criteria are similar for most of the questions.

In all of the questions, you will be evaluated on

- pronunciation
- intonation and stress

In Questions 3–11, you will also be evaluated on

- grammar
- vocabulary
- cohesion of your ideas

In Questions 4–11, you will also be evaluated on

- appropriateness of content

Sample TOEIC® Speaking Test Questions

Questions 1–2: Read a text aloud

Read the text on the screen aloud. You will have 45 seconds to prepare and 45 seconds to read the text aloud.

Sample TOEIC Speaking Test Text

Bicycle riding is a wonderful way to get exercise. It is good for your mind as well as for your body. While you ride, you can enjoy beautiful scenery. It is easy to relax and forget your everyday worries. People with all levels of experience can enjoy bicycle riding. If you want a challenge, choose a route with many hills. If you want an easy ride, choose a flat road. Everyone can enjoy this sport.

Question 3: Describe a photo

Describe the photo in as much detail as you can. You will have 30 seconds to prepare your response and 45 seconds to speak.

Sample TOEIC Speaking Test Photo

Sample TOEIC Speaking Test Questions

Questions 4–6: Respond to questions

You will answer three questions. Begin responding as soon as you hear the beep for each question. You will have 15 seconds to respond to Questions 4 and 5. You will have 30 seconds to respond to Question 6. You will have no additional preparation time.

You will read:

Imagine that a marketing firm is doing research in your country. You have agreed to participate in a telephone interview about weekend activities.

Question 4

What is your favorite way to spend Saturday night?

Question 5

What did you do last Saturday night?

Question 6

What do you think is a good way for a family to spend Saturday night together and why?

Sample TOEIC Speaking Test Questions

Questions 7–9: Respond to questions using information provided

You will answer three questions based on information provided. You will have 30 seconds to read the information. You will have 15 seconds to respond to Questions 7 and 8. You will have 30 seconds to respond to Question 9. You will have no additional preparation time. Begin responding as soon as you hear the beep for each question.

You will read:

Train Schedule
Pinedale–Warwick

Leave Pinedale	Arrive Warwick
*7:15 A.M.	10:15 A.M.
8:45 A.M.	11:45 A.M.
10:15 A.M.	1:15 P.M.
12:30 P.M.	3:30 P.M.
2:15 P.M.	5:15 P.M.

*This train is Monday–Friday only.
Fare information
One way: $65
Round-trip: $120
Children under 12: half price

You will hear:

Question 7

Hello, I'm calling about trains between Pinedale and Warwick. I want to travel to Warwick on Saturday. What time does the first train leave Pinedale on Saturday, and how long does the trip last?

Question 8

Can you tell me how many trains travel between Pinedale and Warwick on Saturday?

Question 9

I would like to buy round-trip tickets for myself and my ten-year-old daughter. How much will each ticket cost?

Sample TOEIC Speaking Test Question

Question 10: Propose a solution

You will be presented with a problem and asked to propose a solution. You will have 30 seconds to prepare and 60 seconds to speak.

Your response should

- show that you understand the problem
- propose a solution to the problem

Question 10

Propose a solution to the following problem.

You will hear:

Hello, Cutting Edge Computers? This is Tom Andrews. I've brought my computer there for service in the past. I have a bit of an emergency today, and I was wondering if you would make a house call. I'm in the middle of a big project, and my computer just crashed. I have a deadline on this project. It's due in two days, so I can't afford to lose a lot of time here. I know you don't normally make house calls, but it would save me a lot of time if you would send a technician over this morning to get my computer running again. I really need to get back to work on this project by this afternoon. I would be happy to pay extra for the house call. I am a longtime customer of yours, so I hope you can do me this favor. Thanks. Call Tom Andrews at 577-555-9253.

Sample TOEIC Speaking Test Question

Question 11: Express an opinion

You will give your opinion about a specific topic. Say as much as you can in the time allowed. You will have 15 seconds to prepare and 60 seconds to speak.

Question 11

Is it better to have a few close friends whom you know well, or a lot of different friends with whom you can do a variety of things? Give reasons for your opinion.

Scoring Criteria

The TOEIC Speaking Test is evaluated based on the following criteria:

Criterion 1 The test taker can generate language intelligible to native and proficient non-native English speakers. This is evaluated in Questions 1–3.

Criterion 2 The test taker can select appropriate language to carry out routine social and occupational interactions (such as giving and receiving directions, asking for information, asking for clarification, making purchases, greetings and introductions, etc.). This is evaluated in Questions 4–9.

Criterion 3 The test taker can create connected, sustained discourse appropriate to the typical workplace. This is evaluated in Questions 10–11.

Skill 1: Developing Business Vocabulary

Exercise 1

Write the letter of the correct definition next to each word. Then complete the passage with the correct words.

Group A

____	**1.** assignment	**a.** a set of clothes
____	**2.** departs	**b.** a car used to take people to and from the airport
____	**3.** itinerary	**c.** a task or special job given to someone
____	**4.** limousine	**d.** a plan for a trip
____	**5.** outfit	**e.** leaves

To: Mary Smith
From: John Brown
Subject: Your trip
Attach: itinerary.doc

Hi Mary,
The plans for your business trip are all arranged. Please read the (6)____________ carefully so you will know exactly where you need to go and when. You will be happy to see that your plane (7)____________ at noon, so you won't have to get up early for your flight. We'll send the (8)____________ to take you to the airport so you won't need to take a taxi. Also note that you will need clothes for the party following the conference, so don't forget to pack a party (9)____________. I know you will work hard on this (10)____________. You always do a good job. Good luck!

John

Group B

____	**1.** casual	**a.** routine tasks
____	**2.** caterer	**b.** people who don't eat meat
____	**3.** chores	**c.** informal
____	**4.** impression	**d.** a company that prepares and serves food
____	**5.** vegetarians	**e.** impact; lasting effect

Healthy Gourmet, the city's most popular (6)____________, is looking for an assistant chef. Most of our clients are (7)____________, so we prefer someone with experience preparing a variety of vegetable dishes. Your (8)____________ will include helping in the preparation and serving of meals, as well as table setup and cleanup. We are a friendly company, but we want to give a professional (9)____________ to our clients. Therefore, dress should never be (10)____________. Please call Jim Morris at 532-555-7543 to apply.

Group C

____ 1. behave a. act

____ 2. confidence b. notice

____ 3. conservative c. in a nice way

____ 4. observe d. traditional

____ 5. pleasantly e. feeling sure

When you give a presentation at a meeting or conference, your clothes can be as important as the words you say. It is a good idea to dress in (6)____________ clothes instead of wearing something unusual. The way you (7)____________ is also important. During your presentation, speak slowly, clearly, and with (8)____________. All of this will make your presentation easier to follow. (9)____________ your audience carefully, and if people seem tired or bored, try to move ahead more quickly. Be sure to answer all questions (10)____________. Answering a lot of questions may be tiring, but you don't want your audience to know this.

Exercise 2

Complete the sentences with the correct word form.

confidence (*noun*) **confident** (*adjective*) **confidently** (*adverb*)

1. He was not afraid of the test and answered all the questions ____________.
2. If you feel ____________, you should not have any problems.
3. She knew she was doing a good job and spoke to her boss with ____________.

impression (*noun*) **impress** (*verb*) **impressive** (*adjective*)

4. If you turn in your work late, you will not make a good ____________ on your boss.
5. The number of famous paintings in the New York museums is ____________.
6. Some people try to ____________ their friends by driving expensive cars.

observers (*noun*) **observe** (*verb*) **observant** (*adjective*)

7. He is a very ____________ person and always notices details.
8. Many ____________ saw the event.
9. ____________ the audience carefully before you begin to speak.

Skill 2: Using Correct Stress

On Questions 1 and 2 on the new TOEIC Speaking Test, you will be asked to read a text aloud. When you read, you will have to pronounce the words with the correct stress. Practice reading the following paragraph aloud.

Sample TOEIC Speaking Test Text

> Haven Beach is a wonderful place for a family vacation. You can spend the entire day enjoying the sand and sea. Hotels line the beach and offer spectacular ocean views. Some families prefer to rent one of the many rustic cottages in town. The town offers a variety of restaurants, from casual to formal. It is easy to see why so many families return here year after year for their vacation.

Skill Focus

When reading words of more than one syllable, it is important to know which syllable to stress. The following list of words has been divided into syllables. The stressed syllable in each word is shown in bold. Practice reading the words aloud.

First syllable stressed	Second syllable stressed
rus tic	ho **tel**
for mal	en **joy**
cot tage	pre **fer**
of fer	re **turn**
ca ter er	va **ca** tion
fam i ly	spec **tac** u lar
ca su al	va **ri** e ty
res tau rant	

Skill 2: Exercise

Divide the words into syllables, and circle the stressed syllable. Use a dictionary if necessary. Then practice reading the words aloud.

1. Saturday ____(Sat)/ur/day____
2. bicycle ________
3. beautiful ________
4. scenery ________
5. relax ________
6. experience ________
7. challenge ________
8. ticket ________
9. computer ________
10. technician ________
11. customer ________
12. agenda ________
13. observe ________
14. important ________
15. dessert ________
16. tasty ________
17. agree ________
18. opinion ________
19. tourist ________
20. equipment ________

Skill 3: Describing Objects and Actions in a Photo

In Question 3 of the new TOEIC Speaking Test, you will be asked to describe a photo in as much detail as possible. Observing the objects and actions in a photo will help you describe the details.

Remember: For Question 3, you will have 30 seconds to prepare your response and 45 seconds to speak.

Sample TOEIC Speaking Test Photo

Sample Answer

"A large passenger jet is on the ground at an airport. Two baggage handlers are next to a conveyor belt that has several suitcases on it. One man in a safety vest is loading the bags onto a large baggage cart. Another man in a dark shirt is bending over next to the conveyor belt. We can only see his arm. There is one other person in the photo. He is getting off the plane, but we don't know whether he is a passenger or a worker. In the background, there are several pieces of equipment which are used to service the airplane."

Skill Focus

In Question 3 of the new TOEIC Speaking Test, you will see a photo of a person or people engaged in some sort of activity. The people may be at work, at school, or at home. They may be eating, working, traveling, or enjoying a free-time activity. Some photos may be just a scene. When you look at the photo, pay attention to the objects you see and the activities that are happening.

Skill 3: Exercise

List the objects and activities you see in each photo. Then write five sentences about each photo.

1.

Objects

____

____

____

____

____

Activities

____

____

____

____

____

> **TEST TIP**
>
> You can use *there is* or *there are* when describing objects and the present continuous tense when describing activities.

Sentences

1. ____
2. ____
3. ____
4. ____
5. ____

2.

Objects	**Activities**
plastic Gloves	Chemestry
glasses	Experiment
cylinder	taking notes
white coat / lab coat	protecting his eyes and hands
pen	Using acided

Sentences

1. ______________________________

2. ______________________________

3. ______________________________

4. ______________________________

5. ______________________________

3.

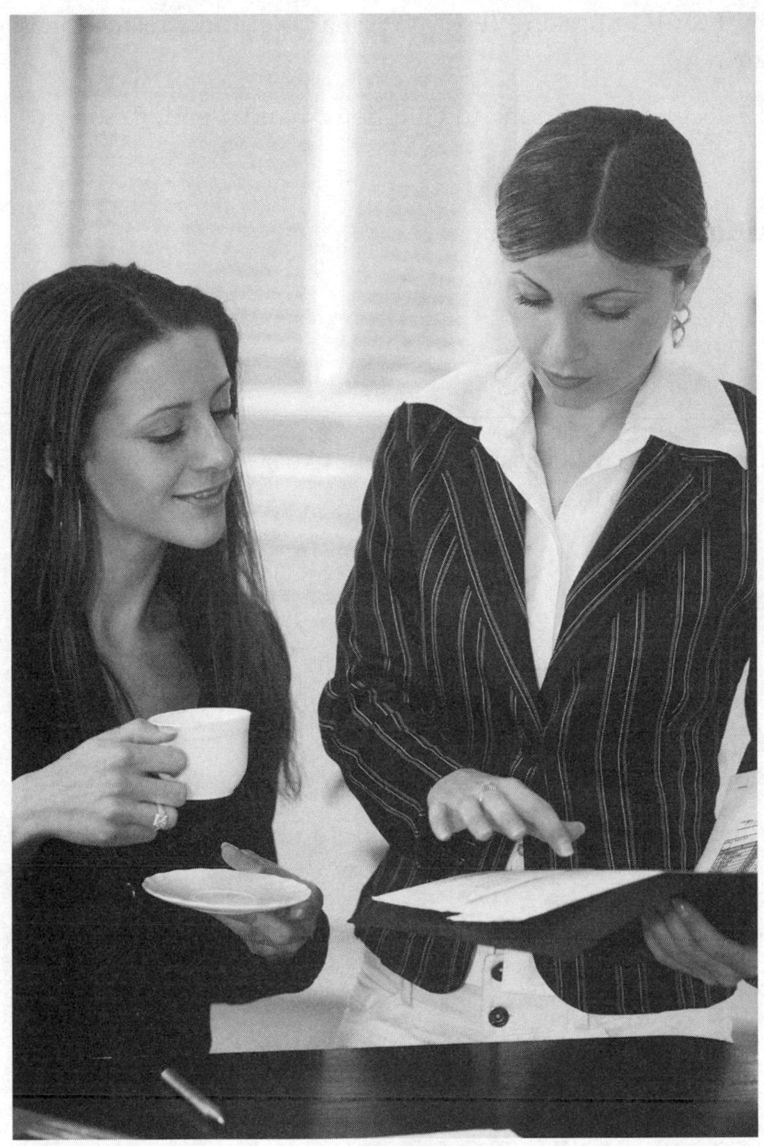

Objects

Mug
paper
Wedding ring
big earing
pen on the desk

Activities

talking
drinking tea
analazing something

Sentences

1. ______________________________
2. ______________________________
3. ______________________________
4. ______________________________
5. ______________________________

Skill 4: Talking About Common Activities and Events

In Questions 4–6 of the new TOEIC Speaking Test, you will answer three related questions about common activities and events.

Remember: You will have 15 seconds to respond to Questions 4 and 5 and 30 seconds to respond to Question 6.

Sample TOEIC Speaking Test Question

You will read:

What is your favorite sport and why?

Sample Answer

"My favorite sport is swimming. I enjoy being in the water. I like swimming because I can do it all year. When the weather is cold, I go to an indoor pool."

Skill Focus

In Questions 4–6 of the new TOEIC Speaking Test, you may be asked about things you usually do or what your preferences are, you may be asked about the last time you did something, and you may be asked for opinions, such as why you like something or what you think is the best way to do something.

When you answer these questions, be sure to answer with more than one or two words. Say several sentences about why this is your preference or why you think this is the best way to do something.

Question: What do you think is a good way to spend a vacation?

Incomplete answer: "Going to the beach."

Complete answer: "I think going to the beach is a good way to spend a vacation. Vacations are for relaxing. At the beach, you can lie on the sand all day and relax. If you get bored, you can go swimming. There are a lot of fun things to do at the beach, but it is also a good place to relax and do nothing."

TEST TIP

Practice by timing yourself as you answer each type of question. You will only have a few seconds to plan and answer questions, so you want to be comfortable with these time constraints before you take the test.

Skill 4: Exercise

Answer the questions. Write 4–5 sentences for each question.

1. What is your favorite holiday and why?

____
____
____
____
____

2. What did you do the last time you visited a friend?

____
____
____
____
____

3. What is your favorite free-time activity and why?

____
____
____
____
____

4. What is a good way for a family to spend free time together?

____
____
____
____
____

5. Where do people usually go for entertainment in your city?

____
____
____
____
____

6. What is a good way to look for a job?

____
____
____
____
____

Skill 5: Finding and Explaining Information on a Schedule

In Questions 7–9 of the new TOEIC Speaking Test, you will be asked to find and explain information on a schedule or agenda.

Remember: You will have 30 seconds to read the information. Then you will have 15 seconds to respond to Questions 7 and 8 and 30 seconds to respond to Question 9.

Sample TOEIC Speaking Test Question

You will read:

Passenger(s):

Julie Farmer

Itinerary:

Date	**Flight**	**Details**
Friday, June 2	823	Depart Baltimore at 7:35 A.M.
		Arrive in Manchester at 8:50 A.M.
Sunday, June 4	3812	Depart Manchester at 4:50 P.M.
		Arrive in Baltimore at 6:15 P.M.

You will hear:

Could you tell me how long the flight from Baltimore to Manchester is?

Sample Answer

"Let's see. It leaves at 7:35 and arrives at 8:50, so it takes one hour and 15 minutes."

Skill Focus

In Questions 7–9, you will be asked questions about a schedule or agenda. You will scan the schedule or agenda to find the right information and then explain it.

For Questions 7 and 8, you will be asked very specific questions, such as:

What time does it start?
How long will it last?
How often do the buses leave?
When does the first train arrive?
How much does it cost?
How many people will speak?
Does the price include meals?
Where does it take place?
Who will speak first?

For Question 9, you will be asked a question that requires a longer answer, such as:

What will happen after lunch?
What is she planning to do after the conference?
What other topics will be covered?
Will I have time to meet the presenters after the workshop?

Skill 5: Exercise

Imagine you work at Caldwell Language Center. Look at the schedule and answer the questions. Write two or three sentences for each question.

Caldwell Language Center—Spring Semester Class Schedule

Class	Day	Time	Instructor
French I	Mon., Wed.	9 A.M.–11 A.M.	Mr. Florian
French I	Mon., Wed.	7 P.M.–9 P.M.	Ms. Bennett
French II	Tues., Thurs.	9 A.M.–11 A.M.	Mr. Florian
Spanish I	Mon., Wed.	9 A.M.–11 A.M.	Ms. Montero
Spanish I	Tues., Thurs.	9 A.M.–11 A.M.	Ms. Montero
Spanish II	Tues., Thurs.	7 P.M.–9 P.M.	Mr. Florian

- All classes are $250 for the semester
- Books for each class are $35 and are available in the school bookstore
- Instructor office hours are Monday afternoons 12–3, or by appointment

1. Which classes is Mr. Florian teaching, and when are they?

____

____

2. How much does it cost to take a French class, including books?

____

____

3. I'd like to learn Spanish. Do you have any beginning level classes?

____

____

4. If I have questions about my assignments, is it possible to speak to the teacher outside of class hours?

____

____

5. I work during the day. Do you offer classes in the evening?

____

____

6. Who teaches the French classes, and when are the classes?

____

____

7. What classes are taught on Mondays?

____

____

TEST TIP

Practice writing and using the common contractions for words like *isn't/aren't* and *doesn't/don't*. This will make your speech sound more natural.

Skill 6: Finding a Solution to a Problem

In Question 10 of the new TOEIC Speaking Test, you will listen to a caller describing a problem. Then you will describe your solution to the problem.

Remember: For Question 10, you will have 30 seconds to prepare and 60 seconds to speak.

Sample TOEIC Speaking Test Question

You will hear:

> *Hello, Computer Training Center? I was wondering if it was too late to sign up for computer classes. I want to take Word Processing. I know your classes started last week, but I was sick, so I couldn't register. I really, really need to take this class now. I need it for my job, and my boss has been pressuring me a lot. I would really appreciate it if you would let me sign up for a class now, and I'll make up the class work I missed. I can send you a check right away. My name is Maya Ricard, and my number is 874-555-0422. Thank you so much.*

Sample Answer

"Hello, this is Peter Rosen from the Computer Training Center. I am calling to answer your question about the Word Processing class. I've spoken to the instructor for that class, and he says he would be happy to let you take the class even though you are starting late. However, you will have to be ready to start tonight. The class begins at seven o'clock. Please arrive early in order to register, and bring a check or credit card with you. You will also need to buy some books. You can get them at our school bookstore. Your instructor will explain the assignment you missed, and he will give you some homework to make it up. We look forward to seeing you tonight."

Skill Focus

In Question 10, you will listen to a phone message from a caller describing a problem. You will have to listen carefully to understand who the caller is and what he or she wants. Then you will give a solution to the problem described. Your solution may involve giving the caller what he or she asks for, or you may suggest alternatives.

You can use phrases such as:

> *I would be happy to . . .*
> *I'm sorry, but it won't be possible to . . .*
> *I suggest that you . . .*
> *I'm afraid that it isn't possible to . . .*
> *I will do my best to . . .*
> *If you . . . , then I will . . .*
> *Why don't you . . .?*
> *I would . . .*
> *You might try . . .*
> *Perhaps you could . . .*

Skill 6: Exercise

Read each situation. What do you say? Write a 2 or 3 sentence solution for each problem.

1. Imagine you are an auto mechanic. A customer says, "My car broke down, and I need to use it this afternoon." What do you say? (+) (−)

→ Bring our car today afternoon | → Full schedule
→ land another car | → make an appointment
→ recommend another garage | →

2. Imagine you are a tour operator. A customer says, "I lost my tickets for this morning's tour." What do you say? (+) (−)

→ I suggest you go to (going) the office | → Buy another ticket
→ If you show your ID we can replace | → We can't replace any tickets
→ I remember you, you don't need to buy another ticket. | → You can buy another ticket for 50% off

3. Imagine you own a painting company. A client says, "There is an important meeting tomorrow afternoon, and the conference room needs painting before then." What do you say?

→ prepare the Local for the painting | → You need to call 1 week before the day of the painting
→ You have to buy the paint | → Our workers aren't free tomorrow
→ | →

4. Imagine you are an office caterer. A client says, "You sent only roast beef sandwiches, but our most important seminar guest is a strict vegetarian." What do you say?

→ We can send vegetarian Sandwiches for free | → We just had roast beef
→ You get discount on your next order | → We don't work with vegetarian Sandwiches
→ | →

5. Imagine you are a hotel desk clerk. A guest says, "The airline lost my suitcase, and I don't have any clothes for my job interview tomorrow morning." What do you say?

→ You should ask the airline company to give you some money to buy clothes | → You should buy clothes
→ We can give you discount on the Hotel store | →
→ We can lend you some clothes. | →

Skill 7: Stating and Explaining Your Opinion

In Question 11 of the new TOEIC Speaking Test, you will be asked to state an opinion and give reasons for it.

Remember: For Question 11, you will have 15 seconds to prepare and 60 seconds to speak.

Sample TOEIC Speaking Test Question

You will read:

> Some people like to spend their vacation in one place. Other people like to visit several different places during one vacation. Which type of vacation do you prefer? Give reasons for your opinion.

Sample Answer

"I think it's better to spend a vacation in one place because it is much more relaxing. When you spend your vacation in one place, you know where you will sleep every night, and you know where you will eat every day. You become familiar with the place. You know where things are, and you know how to get places, so you don't have to worry about anything. You can spend your time visiting tourist attractions, or you can spend time just relaxing. Another reason is that you don't have to think about getting to another place. You don't have to spend all day on a train or plane just to get to the next place. I know that some people like to see a lot of different places in the world. I like to see different places, too. However, there is a more relaxing way to do this. If I spend each vacation in a different place, over time I'll be able to visit many different places. I think this is the best way to take vacations."

Skill Focus

In Question 11, you will be asked to state an opinion and support it with reasons and examples. You will have 15 seconds to prepare your response. Use this time to form a statement of your opinion in your mind and think of three or four ways to support your opinion. You will then have 60 seconds to give your response.

When you state your opinion, you can use phrases such as:

I believe	*I would rather*
I think	*It's better*
I feel	*I agree*
I prefer	*I disagree*

You can connect your reasons and examples with phrases such as:

in the first place	*another reason*
first of all	*I also think*
first	*in addition*
second	*furthermore*
also	

You can state opposing ideas with phrases such as:

however	*but*
on the other hand	*although*

Skill 7: Exercise 1

For each question, write a statement of your opinion. Then list at least three reasons or examples to support your opinion.

1. Would you rather live in a house or an apartment?

   Opinion: *I would rather live in a house than in an apartment*

   Reasons: *more room* | *a garden* | *privacy*

2. Is it better to use public transportation or your own car to get to work every day?

   Opinion: I belive that is better to use your own car to go to work

   Reasons: more pratical | convenient | comfarble.

3. Should children be given responsibility for household chores?

   Opinion: I think children should have responsibility in househeld chores

   Reasons: learn how to do for the future. | responsabilty | be helpful

4. Do you prefer to spend your free time alone or with other people?

   Opinion: I prefer to be alone on my free time

   Reasons: time to think | relax | do things that you want to do

5. Is it better to study at a small university or at a large one?

   Opinion: I belive that a large university is better.

   Reasons: high quality of education. | more unvestiments in school | more know than the smal one.

> **TEST TIP**
>
> The wording of the question should guide you in the wording of your opinion. By repeating key parts of the question in the first sentence of your response, you show that you have understood the question.

Skill 7: Exercise 2

Write a paragraph expressing your opinion about each statement in Exercise 1. Use a separate piece of paper.

Sample Answer

I would rather live in a house than in an apartment. In the first place, a house has much more room. I like to have a lot of space. Also, a house usually has a yard or a garden. I like to spend time outside, and I like to work in the garden. You can't do that if you live in an apartment. Another reason why I prefer a house is that it has more privacy. In an apartment, your neighbors are right next to you. Often you can hear them through the walls. In a house, on the other hand, your neighbors are farther away. You only hear or see them when they are outside. Overall, I think a house is much more comfortable than an apartment.

Speaking Practice

Questions 1–2: Read a text aloud

Read the text on the screen aloud. You will have 45 seconds to prepare and 45 seconds to read the text aloud.

Speaking

Question 1 of 11

When you go on a job interview, it is important to make a good impression. The first thing the interviewer will observe about you is your clothes, so dress in a neat, conservative outfit. Dark colors are best. Men should wear simple ties, and women should not wear short skirts. The way you behave is equally important. Enter the room with confidence. Look the interviewer in the eye while shaking hands. Don't forget to smile pleasantly at the same time. Introduce yourself in a clear voice.

Speaking

Question 2 of 11

Do you like seafood? The Ocean View Restaurant offers the tastiest seafood dishes in town. Relax in our spacious dining room while enjoying spectacular views of the beach and ocean. Choose from a large variety of seafood dishes on our menu or enjoy a little bit of everything at our Sunday evening buffet. At the end of your meal, be sure to try one of our famous desserts. The chocolate cake is simply scrumptious. For a relaxing, delicious meal, visit the Ocean View.

Question 3: Describe a photo

Describe the photo in as much detail as you can. You will have 30 seconds to prepare your response and 45 seconds to speak.

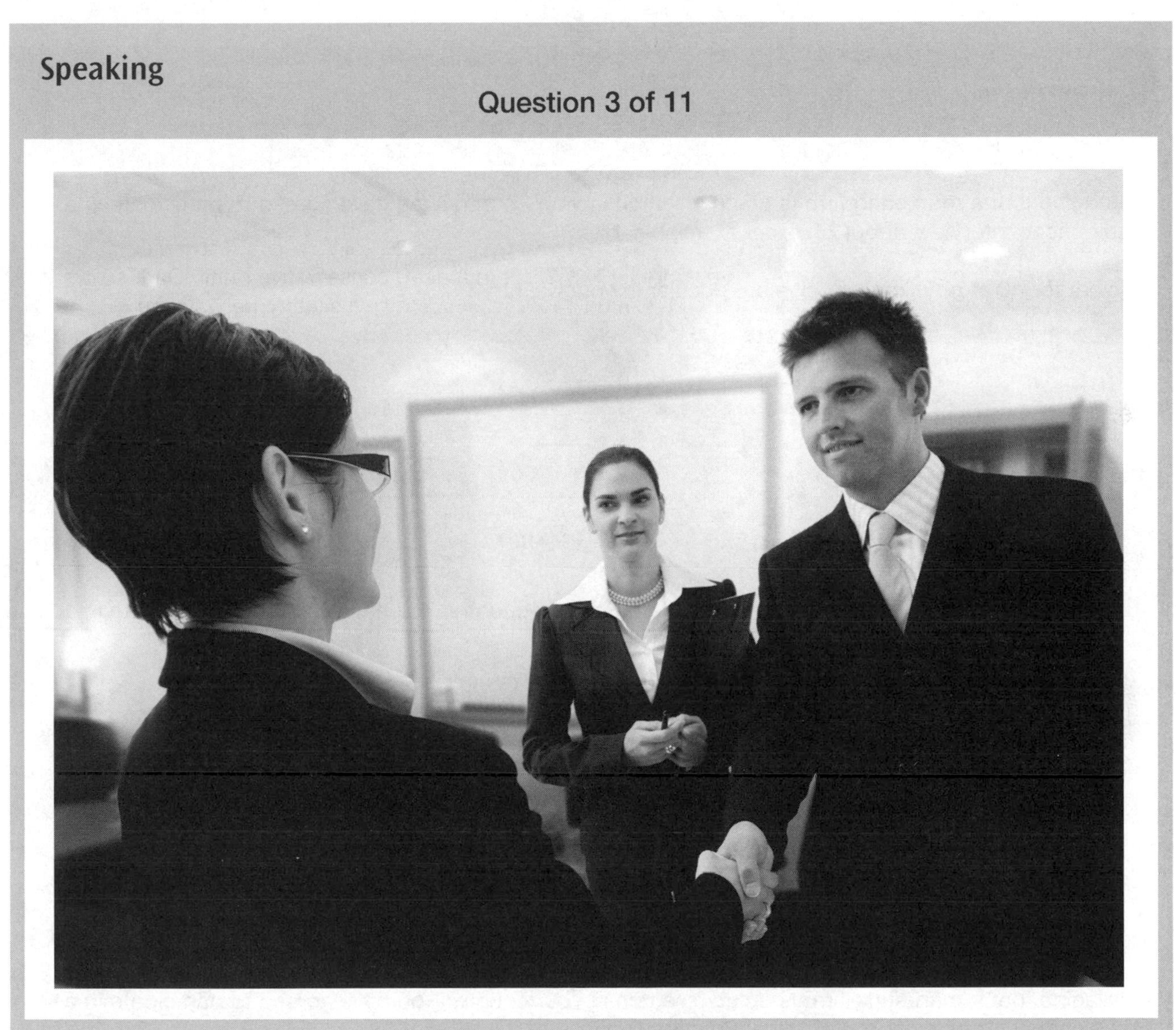

Questions 4–6: Respond to questions

You will answer three questions. Begin responding as soon as you hear the beep for each question. You will have 15 seconds to respond to Questions 4 and 5. You will have 30 seconds to respond to Question 6. You will have no additional preparation time.

Speaking

Question 4 of 11

Imagine that a marketing firm is doing research in your country. You have agreed to participate in a telephone interview about physical exercise habits.

What forms of physical exercise are popular in your country?

Speaking

Question 5 of 11

Imagine that a marketing firm is doing research in your country. You have agreed to participate in a telephone interview about physical exercise habits.

How do you normally get exercise?

Speaking

Question 6 of 11

Imagine that a marketing firm is doing research in your country. You have agreed to participate in a telephone interview about physical exercise habits.

How can people be encouraged to get enough physical exercise?

Questions 7–9: Respond to questions using information provided

You will answer three questions based on information provided. You will have 30 seconds to read the information. You will have 15 seconds to respond to Questions 7 and 8. You will have 30 seconds to respond to Question 9. You will have no additional preparation time. Begin responding as soon as you hear the beep for each question.

Speaking

Questions 7–9 of 11

Travel Itinerary
Sharon Rosen
April 12–13

April 12

9:00 A.M.—Flight 321 on Green Air to New York

12:00 P.M.—Arrive New York, taxi to Van Buren Hotel

2:00 P.M.—Meeting with Jonathan Stein and Marianne Brevoort, ExTime Office

4:00 P.M.—Meeting with ExTime Sales team

April 13

8:00 A.M.—Breakfast meeting with Bart Baines, ExTime Sales Manager, at the Van Buren Hotel

9:30 A.M.—Present quarterly plan to ExTime Board

12:00 P.M.—Lunch with ExTime Board members

1:30 P.M.—Limousine to airport

3:00 P.M.—Flight 765 on Green Air to Miami

Question 10: Propose a solution

You will be presented with a problem and asked to propose a solution. You will have 30 seconds to prepare and 60 seconds to speak.

Your response should

- show that you understand the problem
- propose a solution to the problem

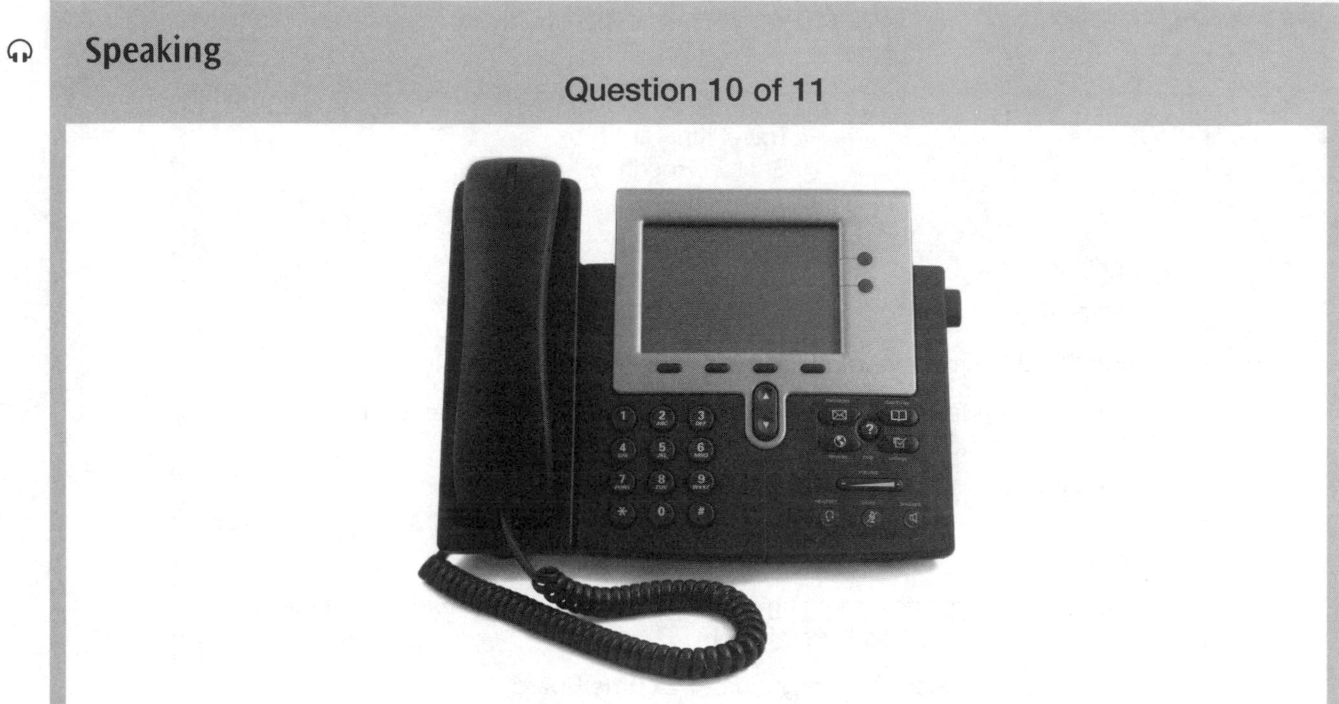

Question 11: Express an opinion

You will give your opinion about a specific topic. Say as much as you can in the time allowed. You will have 15 seconds to prepare and 60 seconds to speak.

Speaking

Question 11 of 11

Some people think that smoking should be banned in all public places. What is your opinion about smoking in public places? Give reasons for your opinion.

IV Writing

OBJECTIVES

You can improve your score in Writing by:

- developing business vocabulary
- using subordinating conjunctions
- making suggestions and requests
- explaining a problem
- supporting your opinion

The new TOEIC® Writing Test is delivered through the Internet. It evaluates your ability to communicate in written English. The test has three different question types and a total of eight questions. It requires you to perform a variety of writing tasks, including writing sentences about photos, responding to e-mails, and expressing an opinion. You will be given a specific amount of time to complete each task. The entire Writing Test has eight questions and takes about one hour to complete.

Types of Questions

There are several different types of questions in the new TOEIC Writing Test.

Questions 1–5

For each question, you will see a photo and two words or phrases. You will write one sentence about the photo using the words. You may change the word form or order, and you must use good grammar.

Questions 6–7

For each question, you will read an e-mail and write a response. In your response, you must write a variety of well-constructed, meaningful sentences, use correct and varied vocabulary, and organize your ideas well.

Question 8

You will read a question and write an essay expressing your opinion. In your essay, you must support your opinion with reasons and examples, use good grammar and vocabulary, and organize your ideas well.

When you take the test, it is important to understand the requirements for each task and to express your ideas clearly and correctly.

Scoring Criteria

The TOEIC Writing Test is evaluated based on the following criteria:

Criterion 1 The test taker can produce well-formed sentences (including subordination). This is evaluated in Questions 1–5.

Criterion 2 The test taker can produce multi-sentence-length text to convey straightforward information, questions, instructions, narratives, etc. This is evaluated in Questions 6–7.

Criterion 3 The test taker can produce multi-paragraph-length text to express complex ideas, using, as appropriate, reasons, evidence, and extended explanations. This is evaluated in Question 8.

Sample TOEIC® Writing Test Questions

Questions 1–5: Write a sentence based on a photo

You will write ONE sentence based on a photo. Each photo has TWO words that you must use in your sentence. You can use the words in any order, and you can change the word forms.

Your sentence will be scored on

- appropriate use of grammar
- relevance of the sentence to the photo

You have 8 minutes to write the sentences.

Sample TOEIC Writing Test Photo

passengers / as soon as

Sample Answer

The passengers got on as soon as the train arrived.

Questions 6–7: Respond to a written request

You will write responses to two e-mails.

Your response will be scored on

- quality and variety of sentences
- vocabulary
- organization

You have 10 minutes to read and answer each e-mail.

Sample TOEIC Writing Test Question

Read the e-mail.

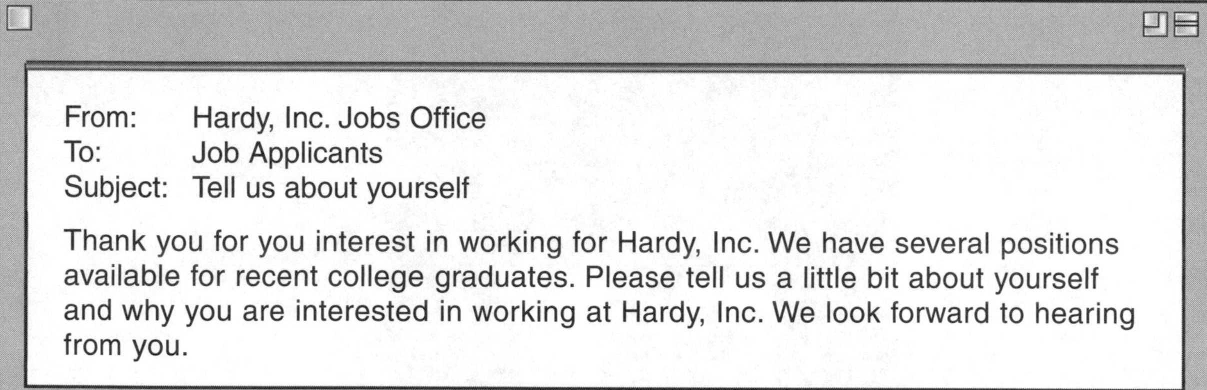

From: Hardy, Inc. Jobs Office
To: Job Applicants
Subject: Tell us about yourself

Thank you for you interest in working for Hardy, Inc. We have several positions available for recent college graduates. Please tell us a little bit about yourself and why you are interested in working at Hardy, Inc. We look forward to hearing from you.

Respond to the e-mail as if you are a recent college graduate looking for your first job. In your e-mail, give TWO pieces of information and ask ONE question.

Sample Answer

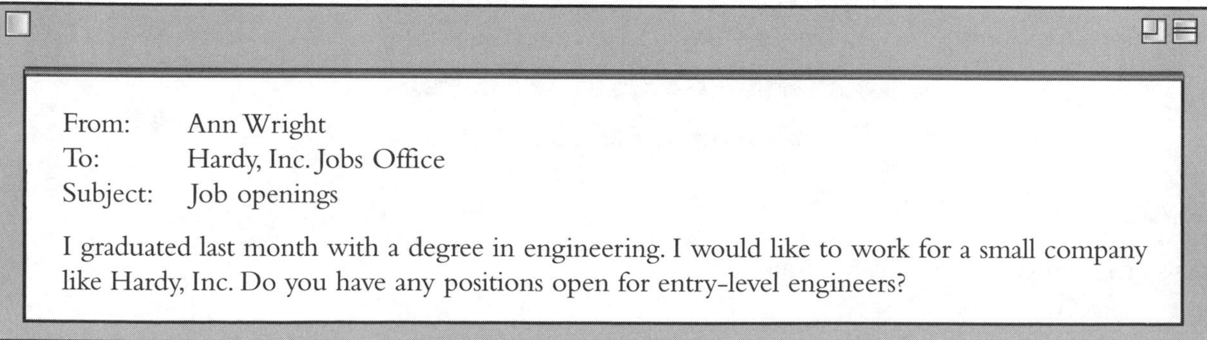

From: Ann Wright
To: Hardy, Inc. Jobs Office
Subject: Job openings

I graduated last month with a degree in engineering. I would like to work for a small company like Hardy, Inc. Do you have any positions open for entry-level engineers?

Question 8: Write an opinion essay

You will write an essay in response to a question about your opinion. Typically, an effective essay will have at least 300 words.

Your essay will be scored on

- supporting reasons and/or examples for your opinion
- grammar
- vocabulary
- organization

You have 30 minutes to plan, write, and revise your essay.

Sample TOEIC Writing Test Question

Some people enjoy spending their free time engaged in outdoor activities. Others like to spend their time indoors. What is your preference? Explain why.

Sample Answer

I prefer spending my free time outdoors. There is something to do and see outdoors during every season of the year, and all types of outdoor activities are good for your health.

Spring is my favorite season to spend time outdoors. After the long, gray winter, the warm spring days feel good and the colors of the flowers and new green leaves lift my spirit. I like to take long walks and look at the beautiful spring flowers. In my neighborhood park, there are several flowering cherry trees. In the early spring, pale pink blossoms completely cover the trees. Later, the petals fall and cover the ground. In the summer, my family and I often go to the zoo, the park, or the beach. The children play while I sit and read. The sun feels so good, but we are always careful not to get sunburned. When we go to the beach or a park, we usually take a picnic lunch with us and lots of cold drinks. In the fall, there is nothing more pleasant than a bike ride down a country road. The fall leaves in all their shades of red, yellow, and orange arch over my head as I ride. Fall is the time when the children play soccer on the weekends, and I like watching their games. It reminds me of my own childhood. Winter is also very special. A blanket of fresh white snow makes everything feel so quiet and peaceful.

There is nothing that I enjoy more than a walk to relax and wind down after a hard day at work or at school, and a walk is good exercise, too. Outdoor activities like baseball, soccer, and swimming are all good types of exercise, and you don't need to pay for a gym membership to take a walk or ride a bike.

Skill 1: Developing Business Vocabulary

Exercise 1

Write the letter of the correct definition next to each word. Then complete the passage with the correct words.

Group A

____	**1.** candidates	**a.**	coworkers
____	**2.** colleagues	**b.**	show or mention
____	**3.** indicate	**c.**	not long ago
____	**4.** prospective	**d.**	applicants for a position
____	**5.** recent	**e.**	probable; likely to become

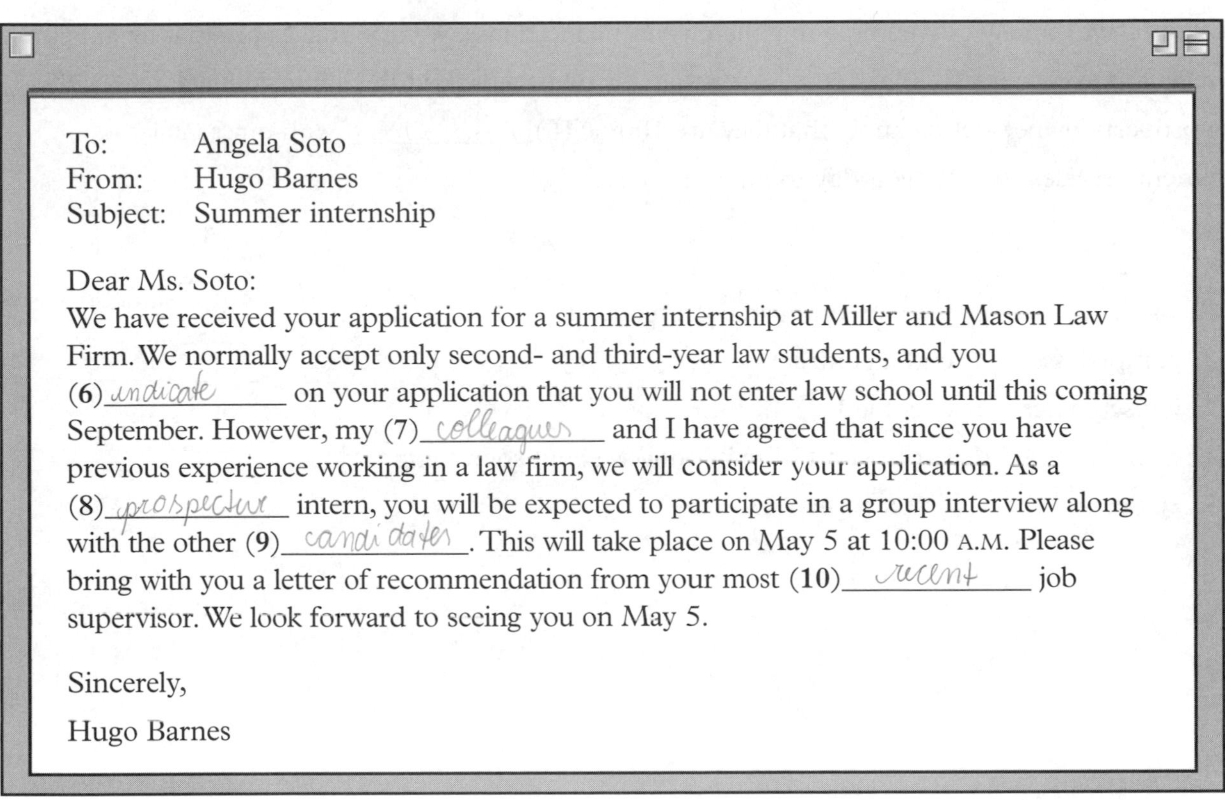

To: Angela Soto
From: Hugo Barnes
Subject: Summer internship

Dear Ms. Soto:

We have received your application for a summer internship at Miller and Mason Law Firm. We normally accept only second- and third-year law students, and you **(6)**__________ on your application that you will not enter law school until this coming September. However, my (7)__________ and I have agreed that since you have previous experience working in a law firm, we will consider your application. As a **(8)**__________ intern, you will be expected to participate in a group interview along with the other **(9)**__________. This will take place on May 5 at 10:00 A.M. Please bring with you a letter of recommendation from your most **(10)**__________ job supervisor. We look forward to seeing you on May 5.

Sincerely,

Hugo Barnes

Group B

C 1. advantage a. happy; pleased

E 2. condition b. individually owned apartment

B 3. condominium c. benefit; help

D 4. ensure d. make certain

A 5. satisfied e. state; order

If you are considering buying a new (6) condominium at Seaside Towers, keep the following in mind. Most of the apartment owners at Seaside Towers own their property as a vacation home and choose to rent it to other vacationers when they themselves aren't using it. This is a great (7) advantage as it lessens the cost of owning a second home. The management of Seaside Towers is ready to assist owners in renting out their property. We find suitable tenants for each apartment and (8) ensure that the owner receives timely payment so that there is no financial loss. We also make sure that tenants leave the property in excellent (9) condition, or that any damage is paid for. Time and again, Seaside Towers property owners let us know that they are 100% (10) satisfied with our rental management services. Talk to us today to find out more.

Group C

B 1. cancel a. take attention away from; disturb

D 2. complaints b. end a contract

E 3. consequence c. occupied

A 4. distract d. expressions of unhappiness about something

C 5. engaged e. direct result

Metro Health Club

Fitness Room Rules

In order to maintain a pleasant atmosphere and not **(6)**___distract___ other members who are using this room, please observe the following rules:

- Cell phone use is forbidden in the Fitness Room.
- Members are asked to keep their voices low when (7)___engaged___ in conversation with others.
- Members are asked to use equipment for no more than 30 minutes when others are waiting to use it.
- Please inform the management of any members breaking these rules.

There have been a number of problems with members ignoring the Fitness Room rules. As a **(8)**___consequence___, the club has formed the following policy: If several **(9)**___complants___ are made against any one member, the club reserves the right to **(10)**___cancel___ that person's membership.

Exercise 2

Complete the sentences with the correct word forms.

advantage (*noun*) **disadvantage** (*noun*) ✓ **advantageous** (*adjective*)

1. It is a big ___advantage___ to have a graduate school degree.
2. Many people find that it is ___advantageus___ to speak several languages.
3. The location of his home was a big ___disadvantage___; it took him close to an hour to get to work.

distraction (*noun*) **distract** (*verb*) **distractible** (*adjective*) ✓

4. Some people are very ___distractible___ and can't work if there is any noise around.
5. The ringing telephone was such a ____________ that we couldn't get the work finished.
6. Please don't talk loudly in the library; it will ____________ the other library users.

satisfaction (*noun*) **satisfy** (*verb*) **satisfied** (*adjective*)

7. We hope every customer leaves our store completely ____________.
8. There is nothing like the ____________ of a job well done.
9. This huge meal should ____________ our appetites.

Skill 2: Using Subordinating Conjunctions

In Questions 1–5 of the new TOEIC Writing Test, you will have to write a sentence about a photo using two words that you are given. Often, one of the words will be a subordinating conjunction. This means that you will have to write a sentence with a main clause and a subordinating clause.

Sample TOEIC Writing Test Photo

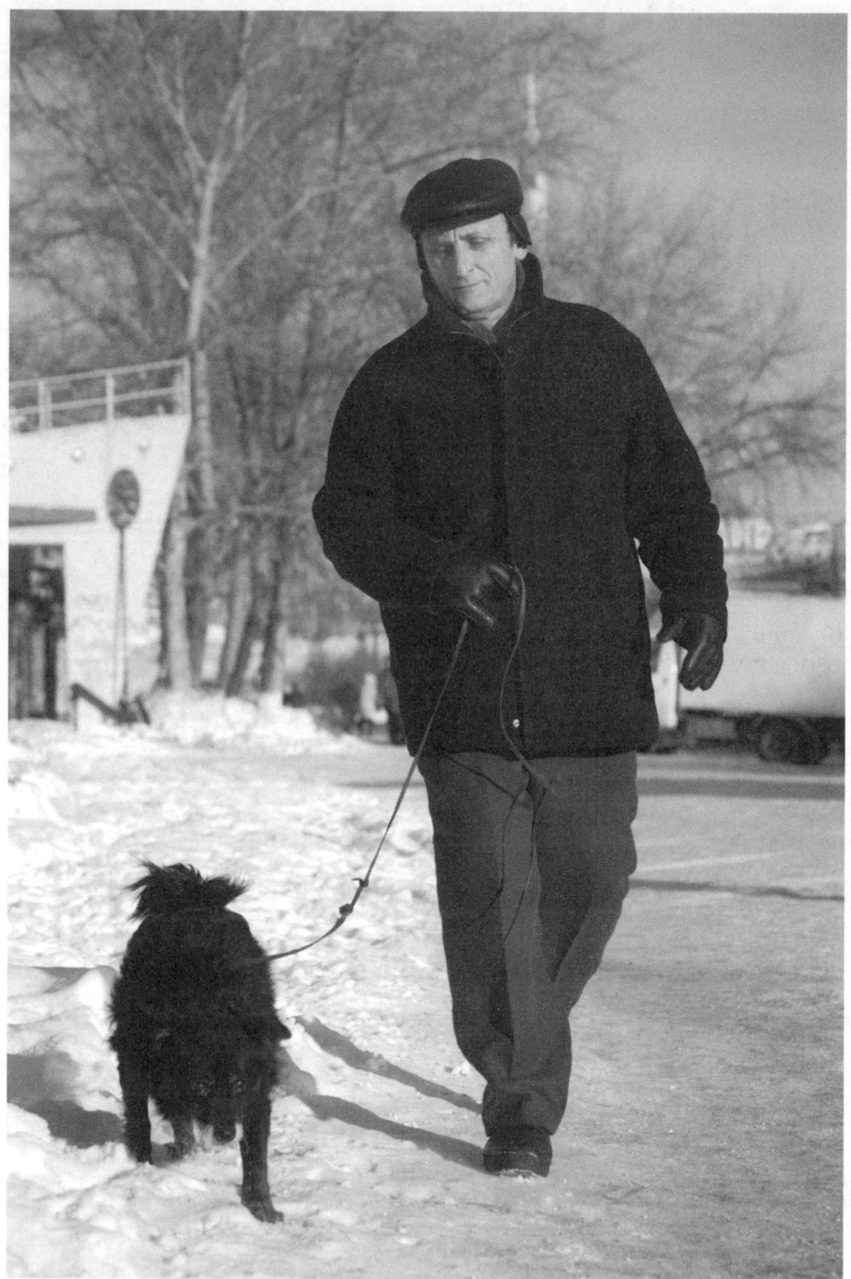

coat / because

Sample Answer

The man is wearing a warm coat because the weather is very cold.

Skill Focus

A main clause can be a complete sentence. A subordinate clause cannot be a complete sentence; it must be connected to a main clause. The subordinate conjunction at the beginning of the subordinate clause shows how the two clauses are related.

Examples:

1. Sylvia went home early *because* she was tired.
   (main clause) (subordinate clause)

   Because tells us the reason that Sylvia went home early.

2. Jack finished reading the newspaper *before* he went to bed.
   (main clause) (subordinate clause)

   Before tells us that the action in the main clause occurred before the action in the subordinate clause.

3. I'll go to the beach this weekend *if* it stops raining.
   (main clause) (subordinate clause)

   If tells us the condition under which I will go to the beach.

You can change the order of the clauses and have the same meaning.

Example:

They kept on walking even though they were tired.
(main clause) (subordinate clause)
Even though they were tired, they kept on walking.
(subordinate clause) (main clause)

When you begin a sentence with the subordinate clause, put a comma between the two clauses.

Specific subordinating conjunctions show the relationships between clauses. To understand these relationships, study the following chart.

Reason	Condition	Purpose	Time	Contrast
because	if	so that	before	although
as	unless	so	after	even though
since	Only if	In order that	when	though
for	dispite		as soon as	However
			while	

Skill 2: Exercise

Complete the sentences. Be sure to use subordinating conjunctions correctly.

1. The man is packing his suitcase because she has a party to go. To
2. The woman ate a big meal even though she was really fat
3. The man will get on the bus as soon as he gets out of this Job
4. The woman will get a better job if she does a major.
5. After they ate dinner, They went to a cinema
6. As today is a holiday, I will probabley sleep all day
7. Although it is very cold today, I ate a ice cream.
8. While Mary drives to work, her husband is sleeping
9. They want to arrive early so that They can enjoy more the party.
10. We won't call you unless we find a problem

> **TEST TIP**
>
> Be careful with *so*. It is a subordinating conjunction showing purpose, but it can also be a coordinating conjunction showing result. The test is whether *that* or *and* can be used with it. If *so that* fits the context, it is a subordinating conjunction showing purpose. If *and so* fits the context, it is a coordinating conjunction.

Skill 3: Making Suggestions and Requests

In Questions 6–7 of the new TOEIC Writing Test, you will be asked to read and respond to an e-mail. You may be asked to make a request or a suggestion in your response.

Sample TOEIC Writing Test Question

Read the e-mail.

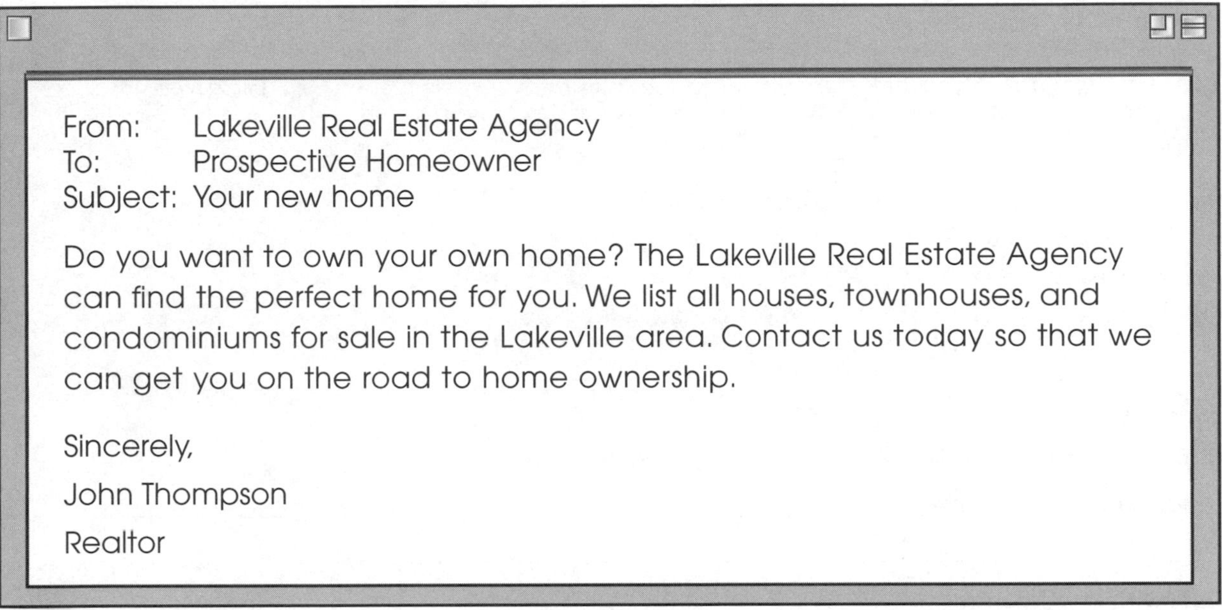

From: Lakeville Real Estate Agency
To: Prospective Homeowner
Subject: Your new home

Do you want to own your own home? The Lakeville Real Estate Agency can find the perfect home for you. We list all houses, townhouses, and condominiums for sale in the Lakeville area. Contact us today so that we can get you on the road to home ownership.

Sincerely,

John Thompson

Realtor

Respond to the e-mail as if you are looking for a house or apartment to buy. In your e-mail, ask TWO questions and make ONE request.

Sample Answer

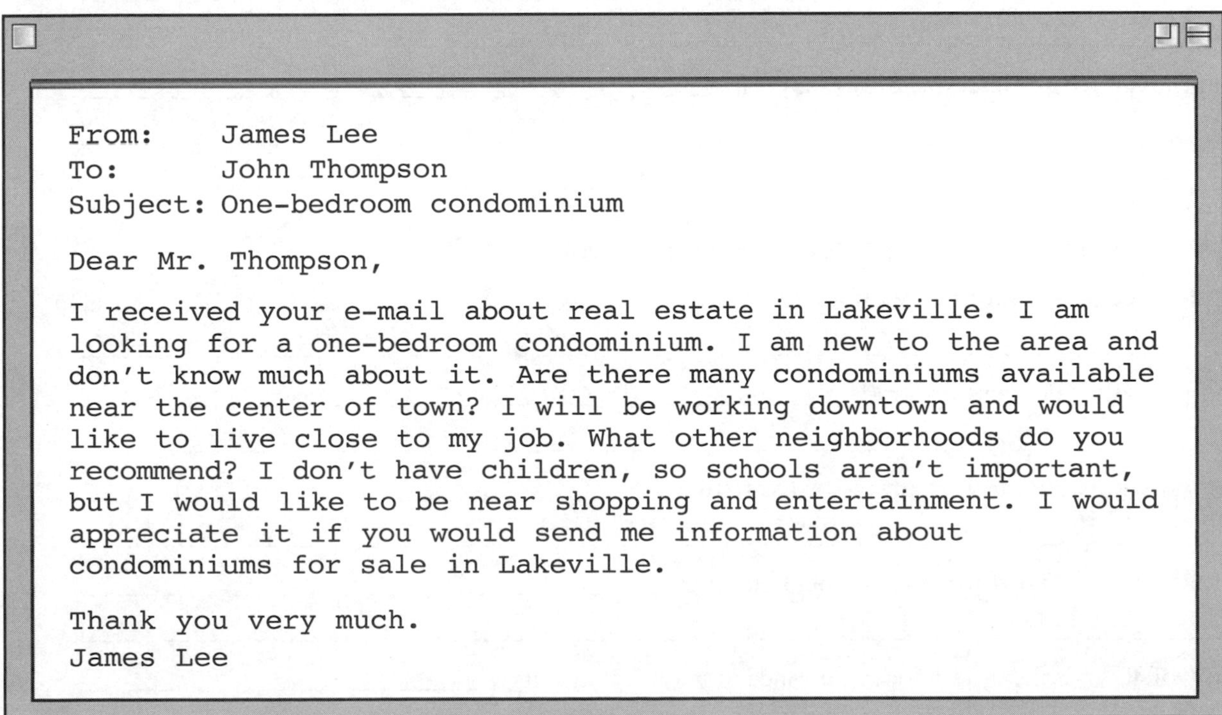

From: James Lee
To: John Thompson
Subject: One-bedroom condominium

Dear Mr. Thompson,

I received your e-mail about real estate in Lakeville. I am looking for a one-bedroom condominium. I am new to the area and don't know much about it. Are there many condominiums available near the center of town? I will be working downtown and would like to live close to my job. What other neighborhoods do you recommend? I don't have children, so schools aren't important, but I would like to be near shopping and entertainment. I would appreciate it if you would send me information about condominiums for sale in Lakeville.

Thank you very much.
James Lee

Skill Focus

Certain phrases are useful when making requests and suggestions. Study the following phrases and verb forms.

Requests

Would you please + (base form verb)
Could you please + (base form verb)
Would it be possible + (infinitive verb)
Would you mind + (gerund)
I would appreciate it if you would + (base form verb)

Suggestions

I suggest + (gerund)
I suggest that you + (base form verb)
You could + (base form verb)
It would be a good idea + (infinitive verb)
I think you should + (base form verb)

Examples

Would you please send me more information?
Would it be possible to change the time of my appointment?
I suggest revising the budget.
It would be a good idea to interview more candidates.

Skill 3: Exercise 1

Write one request to each person or company below.

1. an office supply company ______________________________
____
2. a client who owes you money ______________________________
____
3. a company where you would like to work ______________________________
____
4. a school where you would like to study ______________________________
____
5. an employee who is late submitting a project ______________________________
____

Skill 3: Exercise 2

Write one suggestion for each person or company below.

1. the manager of a restaurant with a rude waiter ______________________________
____
2. a company that delivers orders late ______________________________
____
3. a person who wants to hire an office assistant ______________________________
____
4. the manager of a store with long checkout lines ______________________________
____
5. an out-of-town colleague needing a place to stay in your city ______________________________
____

Skill 4: Explaining a Problem

In Questions 6–7 of the new TOEIC Writing Test, you will be asked to read and respond to an e-mail. The e-mail may mention a problem, and you may be asked to explain reasons for the problem in your response.

Sample TOEIC Writing Test Question

Read the e-mail.

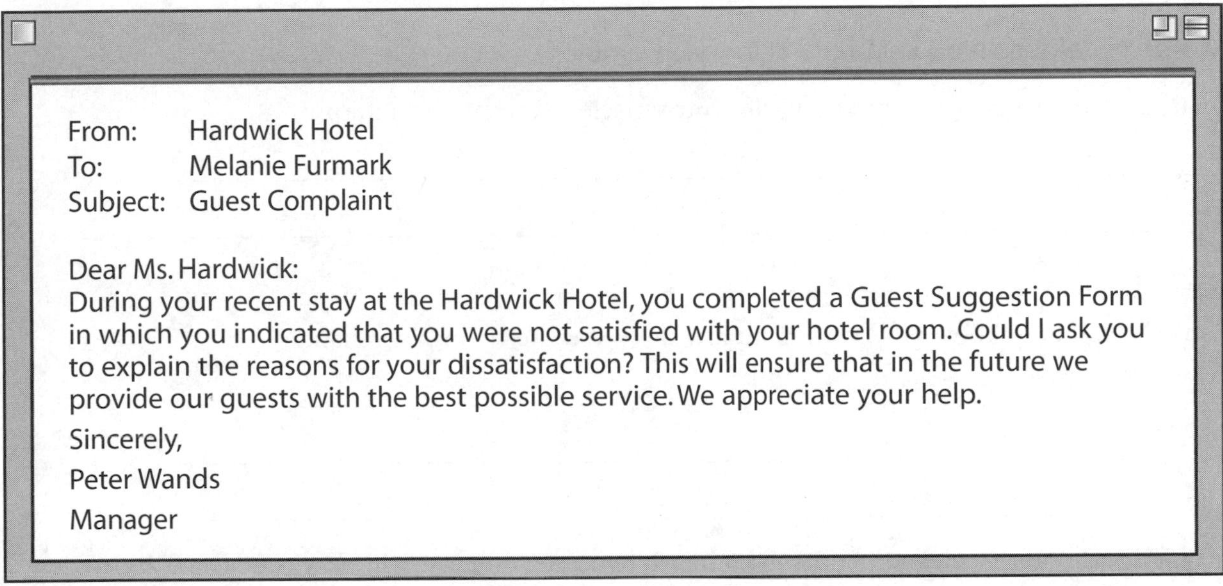

From: Hardwick Hotel
To: Melanie Furmark
Subject: Guest Complaint

Dear Ms. Hardwick:
During your recent stay at the Hardwick Hotel, you completed a Guest Suggestion Form in which you indicated that you were not satisfied with your hotel room. Could I ask you to explain the reasons for your dissatisfaction? This will ensure that in the future we provide our guests with the best possible service. We appreciate your help.

Sincerely,

Peter Wands

Manager

Respond to the e-mail as if you are Melanie Furmark, the recent guest at the Hardwick Hotel. In your e-mail, describe TWO problems and make ONE suggestion.

Sample Answer

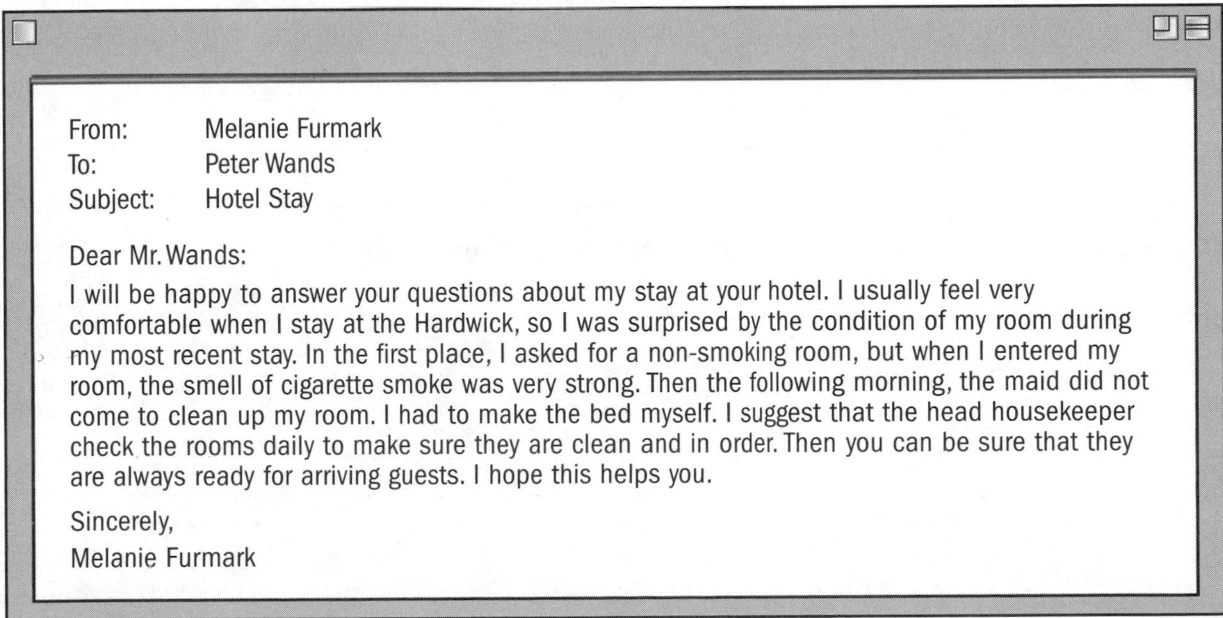

From: Melanie Furmark
To: Peter Wands
Subject: Hotel Stay

Dear Mr. Wands:
I will be happy to answer your questions about my stay at your hotel. I usually feel very comfortable when I stay at the Hardwick, so I was surprised by the condition of my room during my most recent stay. In the first place, I asked for a non-smoking room, but when I entered my room, the smell of cigarette smoke was very strong. Then the following morning, the maid did not come to clean up my room. I had to make the bed myself. I suggest that the head housekeeper check the rooms daily to make sure they are clean and in order. Then you can be sure that they are always ready for arriving guests. I hope this helps you.

Sincerely,
Melanie Furmark

Skill Focus

In Questions 6–7 you may be asked to describe or explain a problem in an e-mail. The problems may occur at a business, such as an office, a store, an airline, a restaurant, or a hotel. You will have to think of ideas that fit the situation presented. As you read, brainstorm ideas. There is no one right answer, but you need to make sure that your ideas fit the situation.

Skill 4: Exercise

Write two or three possible explanations for each problem.

1. A health club manager wants to know why you canceled your membership.

____

____

____

2. A customer wants to know why your company delivered the wrong merchandise.

____

____

____

3. Your neighborhood dry cleaner wants to know why you no longer use its services.

____

____

____

4. A painting company wants to know why you have not made the final payment for its services.

____

____

____

5. A job applicant wants to know why he has not received a response to his application.

____

____

____

Skill 5: Supporting Your Opinion

In Question 8 of the new TOEIC Writing Test, you will be asked to write an essay in response to a question. You will have to state your opinion and support it with reasons and examples.

Sample TOEIC Writing Test Question

Teenage drivers have more car accidents than older drivers. Because of this, many people believe that young people should not be allowed to drive until they are 21 years old. Do you agree or disagree with this idea? Give reasons or examples to support your opinion.

Sample Answer

I agree that young people should not be allowed to drive until they are 21 years old. Driving is a big responsibility, and most teenagers are not mature enough to handle it.

First, everyone knows that teenagers are vulnerable to peer pressure. They tend to do whatever their friends do or tell them to do. If a friend says, "Drive faster," a teen will drive faster without thinking about the consequences of this action. A teen might drive dangerously in order to impress his friends. More than anything else, teens want to be accepted by their peer group.

Furthermore, teens are easily distracted. A group of young friends riding in a car together will probably be laughing and talking. The driver naturally wants to be part of this and may easily pay more attention to what his friends are doing than to what is happening on the road. Teens are also easily distracted by listening to music or talking on the phone while driving.

Finally, it is a characteristic of youth to feel invincible. Teenagers feel safe no matter what they do. It is hard for a teenager to understand that he really could hurt someone else, be seriously injured himself, or even die.

A car is a dangerous machine. When a young, inexperienced person is in charge of such a machine, he puts not only himself in danger, but also other people. This is too much responsibility for a teenager. It is much safer for everyone to make people wait until they are 21 years old before they are allowed to drive.

Skill Focus

Your essay must contain a clearly stated opinion supported by reasons and/or examples. You will be able to make notes before you write the essay, but remember that you will have no more than 30 minutes to plan, write, and revise. Use the first few minutes to write a clear statement of your opinion, and then note down three or four reasons or examples that support your opinion. This gives you a quick outline for your essay. Then you can begin writing.

Example:

Opinion: I agree that young people should not be allowed to drive until they are 21 years old.

Reasons: Vulnerable to peer pressure, easily distracted, feel invincible.

Skill 5: Exercise 1

For each essay question, state your opinion and three supporting reasons or examples.

1. Art and music are an important part of many people's lives. Why do you think art and music are important to people? Support your opinion with specific reasons and examples.

   Opinion statement: ______________________________

   Supporting ideas: ______________________________

   ____

   ____

2. Many people believe that you have to earn a lot of money to be considered successful. What is your opinion of this idea of success? Support your opinion with specific reasons and examples.

   Opinion statement: ______________________________

   Supporting ideas: ______________________________

   ____

   ____

3. Some parents think it is better to bring up their children in the city. Other parents prefer to bring up their children in the countryside. Which is your preference? Support your opinion with specific reasons and examples.

   Opinion statement: ______________________________

   Supporting ideas: ______________________________

   ____

   ____

Skill 5: Exercise 2

Using the outlines from Exercise 1, write a 300-word response to each question on a separate piece of paper.

Writing Practice

Questions 1–5: Write a sentence based on a photo

You will write ONE sentence based on each photo. Each photo has TWO words that you must use in your sentence. You can use the words in any order, and you can change the word forms.

Your sentence will be scored on

- appropriate use of grammar
- relevance of the sentence to the photo

You have 8 minutes to complete this part of the test.

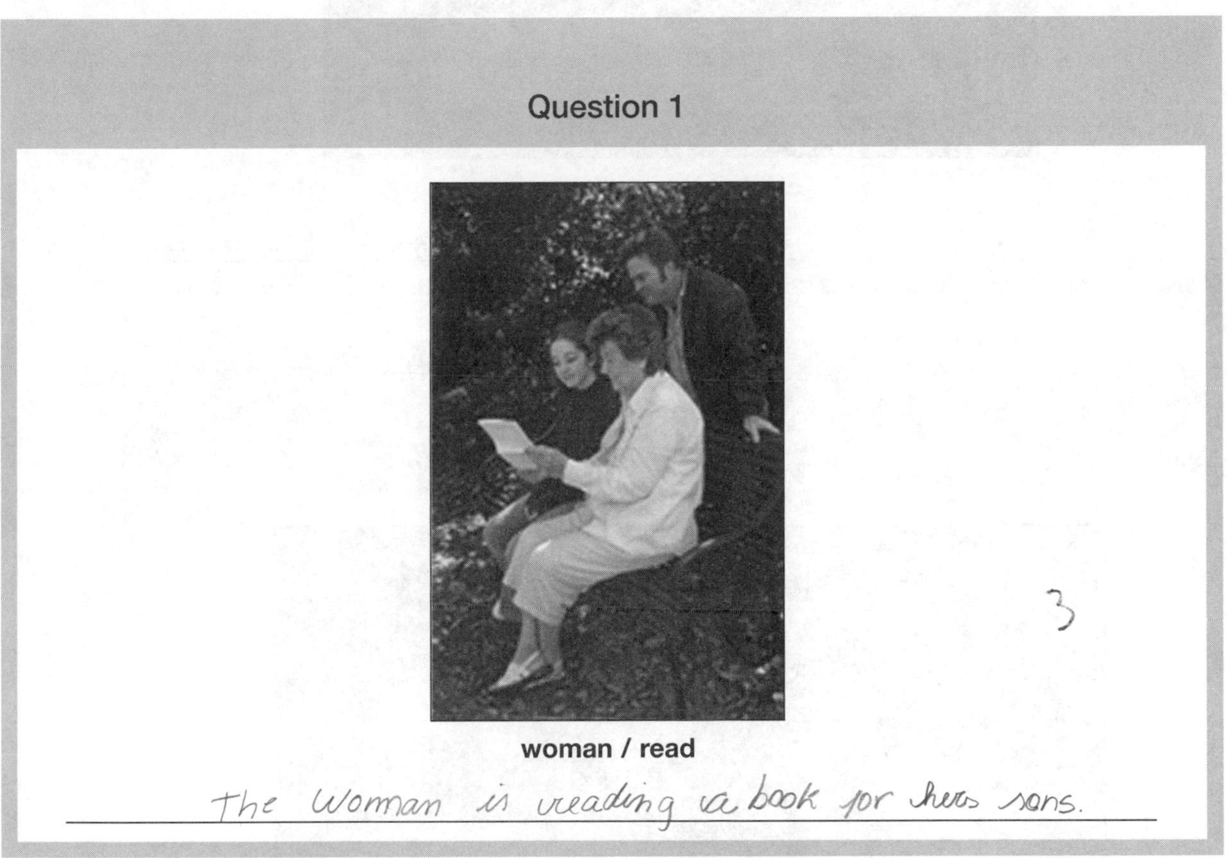

Question 1

woman / read

The Woman is reading a book for hers sons.

3

Question 2

children / together

The Children are organazing the backyard together

2.5

Question 3

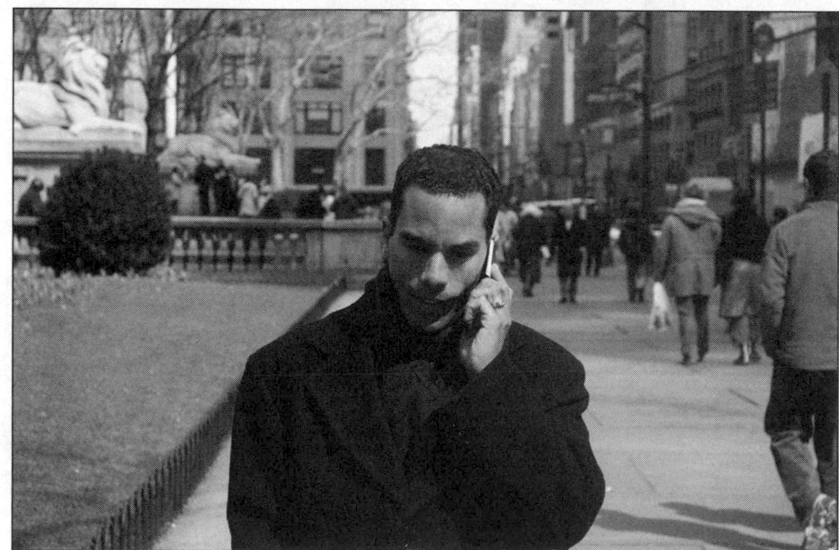

call / while

The man was calling his boss while he was going to work

3

Question 4

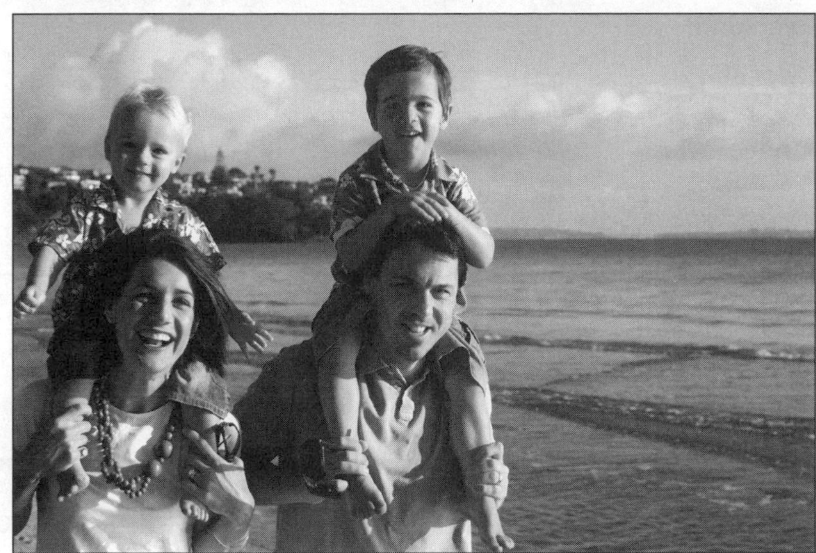

3

beach / because

The family went to the beach because It was a hot day

Question 5

2.5

wash / after

The man is washing the diches after the dinner

sh

Questions 6–7: Respond to a written request

You will write responses to two e-mails.

Your writing will be scored on

- quality and variety of sentences
- vocabulary
- organization

You have 10 minutes to read and answer each e-mail.

Question 6

Read the e-mail.

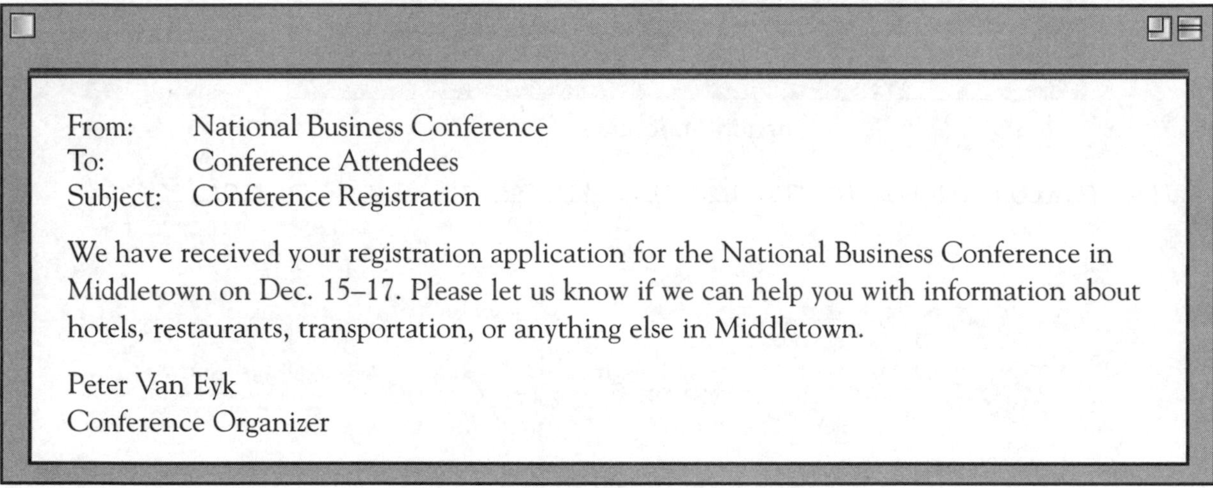

From: National Business Conference
To: Conference Attendees
Subject: Conference Registration

We have received your registration application for the National Business Conference in Middletown on Dec. 15–17. Please let us know if we can help you with information about hotels, restaurants, transportation, or anything else in Middletown.

Peter Van Eyk
Conference Organizer

Respond to the e-mail as if you are planning to attend a conference in a strange city. In your e-mail, ask THREE questions.

From:
To:
Subject:

Question 7

Read the e-mail.

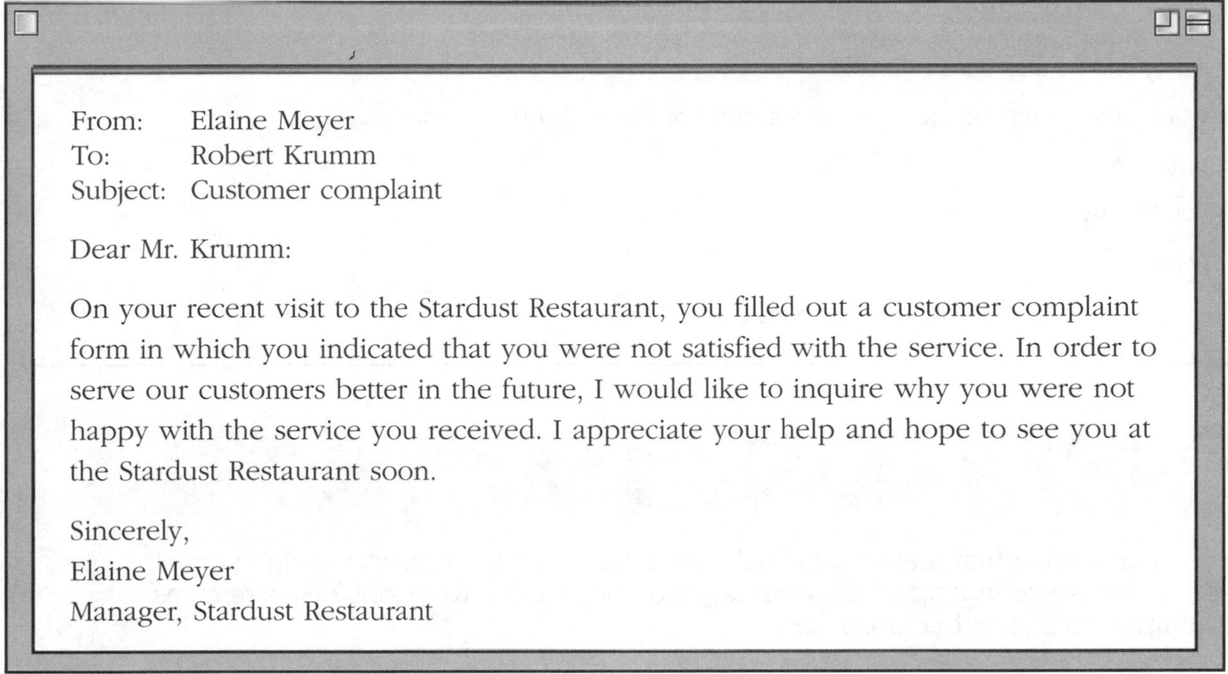

From: Elaine Meyer
To: Robert Krumm
Subject: Customer complaint

Dear Mr. Krumm:

On your recent visit to the Stardust Restaurant, you filled out a customer complaint form in which you indicated that you were not satisfied with the service. In order to serve our customers better in the future, I would like to inquire why you were not happy with the service you received. I appreciate your help and hope to see you at the Stardust Restaurant soon.

Sincerely,
Elaine Meyer
Manager, Stardust Restaurant

Respond to the e-mail as if you are Robert Krumm, a restaurant customer. In your e-mail, describe ONE problem and make TWO suggestions.

From:
To:
Subject:

Question 8: Write an opinion essay

You will write an essay in response to a question about your opinion. Typically, an effective essay will have at least 300 words.

Your essay will be scored on

- whether you give reasons and/or examples to support your opinion
- grammar
- vocabulary
- organization

You have 30 minutes to plan, write, and revise your essay.

Some people think that teenagers should have jobs while they are still in high school. What are the advantages and disadvantages of teenagers having jobs? Give reasons or examples to support your opinion.

Practice Tests

This section includes six tests: two complete **Practice TOEIC® Tests**, two **Practice TOEIC Speaking Tests**, and two **Practice TOEIC Writing Tests**.

Each **Practice TOEIC Test** includes the same sections and the same number of questions as the actual TOEIC Test. The Listening Comprehension section includes 100 questions and is to be completed in 45 minutes. You will need a CD player for the Listening Comprehension section. The Reading section includes 100 questions and is to be completed in one hour and 15 minutes.

Answer sheets in the back of the book are like the TOEIC test answer sheets. Use a dark pencil to mark your answers, and fill in each oval completely. If you change an answer, be sure to erase completely. Do not write on the test itself; write only on the answer sheet. Do not mark more than one answer for each question. If you do not know the right answer, you should guess. You can improve your score if you do not leave questions blank.

Each **Practice TOEIC Speaking Test** and each **Practice TOEIC Writing Test** includes the same numbers and types of questions as the actual tests. The Speaking Test has 11 questions and takes about 20 minutes to complete. For the Speaking Test, you will need a CD player. The Writing Test has eight questions and takes about one hour.

TOEIC® Test Scoring Guide

Overall Scores

The highest possible total score on the new TOEIC test is 990. Each of the two sections—Listening Comprehension and Reading—has a possible subscore of 5 to 495. The score on each section is combined to produce a total combined score ranging from 10 to 990. Each section of the TOEIC test has 100 test items, and the test score you receive for each section is a scaled score. This means that the raw score—the total correct—is converted to a scaled score using special scoring criteria.

Each section on the Practice Tests in this book has 100 items, as in the actual TOEIC test, so your score on the Practice Tests can be estimated using a sample conversion chart such as the one on page 174.

When you take the actual TOEIC test, you receive three separate scores: a score for Listening Comprehension, a score for Reading, and a combined total score. The actual interpretation of those scores is determined by the organization that receives and evaluates your scores.

Scoring the Practice Tests

Each of the two Listening Comprehension Practice Tests in this book has 100 items. The number of items among the four parts of Listening Comprehension and the total number of items for the section match the numbers in the actual TOEIC test.

Listening Comprehension Practice Test Results	
Part 1	______ out of 10
Part 2	______ out of 30
Part 3	______ out of 30
Part 4	______ out of 30
TOTAL	______ out of 100

You can find your estimated score in the conversion chart on page 174. Simply look for the number you got correct in Listening Comprehension. For example, if you got a total of 57 correct in the four parts of the Listening Comprehension Practice Test, your score on the sample conversion chart is 295. Remember that this is a subscore; the scores for the two sections are added together to produce a total score.

Each of the two Reading Practice Tests in this book has 100 items. The number of items among the three parts of Reading and the total number of items for the section match the numbers in the actual TOEIC test.

Reading Practice Test Results	
Part 5	______ out of 40
Part 6	______ out of 12
Part 7	______ out of 48
TOTAL	______ out of 100

If you got 73 correct in the Reading Practice Test, your score on the sample conversion chart is 355. Remember that this is a subscore; the scores for the two sections are added together to produce a total score.

To get your combined total, simply add your scores for the two sections together. The combined score using the above examples is as follows:

295 (Listening Comprehension score)
+ 355 (Reading score)

650 (Combined total)

Practice TOEIC® Test Estimated Conversion Chart

Number Correct	Listening	Reading
0	5	5
1	5	5
2	5	5
3	5	5
4	5	5
5	5	5
6	5	5
7	10	5
8	15	5
9	20	5
10	25	5
11	30	5
12	35	5
13	40	5
14	45	5
15	50	5
16	55	10
17	60	15
18	65	20
19	70	25
20	75	30
21	80	35
22	85	40
23	90	45
24	95	50
25	100	60
26	110	65
27	115	70
28	120	80
29	125	85
30	130	90
31	135	95
32	140	100
33	145	110
34	150	115
35	160	120
36	165	125
37	170	130
38	175	140
39	180	145
40	185	150
41	190	160
42	195	165
43	200	170
44	210	175
45	215	180
46	220	190
47	230	195
48	240	200
49	245	210
50	250	215
51	255	220
52	260	225
53	270	230
54	275	235
55	280	240
56	290	250
57	295	255
58	300	260
59	310	265
60	315	270
61	320	280
62	325	285
63	330	290
64	340	300
65	345	305
66	350	310
67	360	320
68	365	325
69	370	330
70	380	335
71	385	340
72	390	350
73	395	355
74	400	360
75	405	365
76	410	370
77	420	380
78	425	385
79	430	390
80	440	395
81	445	400
82	450	405
83	460	410
84	465	415
85	470	420
86	475	425
87	480	430
88	485	435
89	490	445
90	495	450
91	495	455
92	495	465
93	495	470
94	495	480
95	495	485
96	495	490
97	495	495
98	495	495
99	495	495
100	495	495

What the Scores Mean

The charts that follow show a breakdown of skills generally associated with the score ranges for both Listening Comprehension and Reading, the two sections in the new TOEIC test and the two sections for which practice tests are included in this book. Both the Listening Comprehension and Reading sections are multiple-choice, and both test receptive skills.

Each higher ability level on a chart assumes that the test taker is able to perform all of the lower-level tasks as well.

Chart 1. Listening Comprehension Subscores

Scores	Listening Comprehension Abilities
455–495	• Understands native English speakers in meetings • Performs all of the tasks below in professional and social settings with a grasp of both concrete and abstract subjects
395–450	• Follows most spoken communication in a business setting • Understands most English speakers in international meetings • Performs all of the tasks below with more accuracy and more ease
305–390	• Comprehends explanations of problems in a work setting • Understands and processes requests for products or information by phone
205–300	• Understands and follows one-to-one explanations of routine work tasks • Understands travel announcements • Participates in limited conversations in a social setting
130–200	• Understands and follows simple business or social exchanges with a native English speaker accustomed to communicating with non-native English speakers • Can take simple phone messages
5–125	• Understands basic survival topics such as directions, prices, and time • Understands simple questions in social settings

Chart 2. Reading Subscores

Scores	Reading Abilities
455–495	• Is able to read more abstract material and most materials for professional needs, including highly technical manuals in own area • Reads all of the materials below
395–450	• Reads technical documents and most other types of documents with little need for a dictionary • May experience some difficulty with more abstract writing
305–390	• Reads technical manuals, news articles, or popular novels with occasional dictionary use • Is able to find inconsistencies
205–300	• Understands basic simplified technical manuals • Is able to use a dictionary for more complex technical terms • Reads a meeting agenda
130–200	• Is able to use a directory or listing • Comprehends simple instructions • Understands simple business correspondence
5–125	• Understands uncommon names of people and businesses • Reads simple e-mails, memos, menus, schedules, and signs

Chart 3. Combined Total Scores

General Professional Proficiency	Advanced Working Proficiency	Basic Working Proficiency	Intermediate	Elementary	Novice
905–990 (Advanced 960–990)	785–900	605–780	405–600	255–400	10–250

The organization that receives the score decides how to interpret it. Generally speaking, organizations require higher scores for people who interact with native English speakers from other organizations at the management level. Managers who negotiate contracts, for example, might be expected to have General Professional Proficiency of between 905 and 990. Some organizations might even expect Advanced Proficiency of over 960. Managers who contribute to the process of negotiating contracts along with others in the organization might be expected to have Advanced Working Proficiency of between 785 and 900.

Organizations may decide to break down these broad categories and score ranges even further. An organization might decide that employees participating in international meetings in which English will be the medium for communication—even though participants may not be native speakers of English—should have a score of between 700 and 780. At the same time, an organization might decide that those in support roles for such meetings might have a score of 605 to 695. An employee who greets clients or who reads mail or e-mail in English might be in the 405 to 600, Intermediate, proficiency range.

It is important to remember that each organization will have its own interpretation of the scores.

TOEIC® Speaking Test Scoring Guide

The TOEIC Speaking Test is sent online to ETS®, where it is scored by at least three people. Each task receives a score of 0–3 or 0–5, depending on the task. The test taker receives a final scaled score ranging from 0 to 200, in increments of 10, with 200 the highest possible score. The test taker also receives a proficiency level ranking from 1 to 8.

The following chart shows scaled scores and proficiency levels in the left and middle columns. The right column describes the proficiency levels as they relate to a business environment.

Chart 4. Speaking Test Scaled Scores and Proficiency Levels

Scaled Scores	Proficiency Levels	Speaking Abilities
190–200	8	• Produces connected, sustained speech • Uses complex grammar and vocabulary accurately • Pronunciation, intonation, and stress are highly intelligible
160–180	7	• Produces connected, sustained speech • Some difficulties with complex grammar or vocabulary • Some difficulties with pronunciation, intonation, or stress
130–150	6	• Able to produce an appropriate response, but reasons or explanations may be unclear • Mistakes in grammar or limited vocabulary • Difficulties with pronunciation, intonation, or stress
110–120	5	• Difficulties providing explanations, and responses may be difficult to understand • Mistakes in grammar; limited vocabulary and awareness of audience • Difficulties with pronunciation, intonation, or stress
80–100	4	• Generally unable to explain an opinion; responses limited • Severe limits in language and vocabulary and little awareness of audience • Consistent difficulties with pronunciation, intonation, or stress
60–70	3	• Can provide an opinion but without support • Insufficient language and vocabulary and little awareness of audience • Difficult to understand when reading aloud

Scaled Scores	Proficiency Levels	Speaking Abilities
40–50	2	• Cannot provide an opinion • Difficulty producing intelligble answers or providing basic information • Difficult to understand when reading aloud
0–30	1	• Test taker left tasks unanswered • Has difficulty reading or understanding spoken language

Chart 5 shows the tasks and scoring scales for the TOEIC Speaking test questions.

Chart 5. Speaking Tasks and Scoring Scales

Question	Task	Scale	
1–2	Read a text aloud	0–3	(also includes separate ratings for pronunciation and for intonation and stress)
3	Describe a photo	0–3	
4–6	Respond to questions	0–3	
7–9	Respond to questions using information provided	0–3	
10	Propose a solution	0–5	
11	Express an opinion	0–5	

Using and Scoring the Speaking Tests

Students can record their responses in the Practice TOEIC Speaking Tests by using audio cassettes, audio CDs, digital files, or online audio files. Teachers can then listen to the recordings and use the information in Charts 4 and 5 to evaluate and score the tests.

TOEIC® Writing Test Scoring Guide

The new TOEIC Writing Test is sent online to ETS®, where it is scored by at least three people. Each task receives a score of 0–3, 0–4, or 0–5, depending on the task. The test taker receives a final scaled score ranging from 0–200, with 200 the highest possible score. The test taker also receives a proficiency level ranking from 1 to 9.

Chart 6 shows scaled scores and proficiency levels in the left and middle columns. The right column describes the proficiency levels as they relate to a business environment.

Chart 6. Writing Test Scaled Score and Proficiency Levels

Scaled Scores	Proficiency Levels	Writing Test Abilities
200	9	• Writing is effective, clear, coherent, and grammatically correct • Uses reasons, examples, and explanations
170–190	8	• Uses reasons, examples, and explanations to support answers • Minor grammatical errors or word choice problems
140–160	7	• Presents relevant ideas and some support • Some grammatical errors or word choice problems
110–130	6	• Somewhat successful using reasons and explanations to support answers • Grammatical errors or word choice problems
90–100	5	• Difficulty using reasons and explanations to support answers • Serious grammatical errors or word choice problems
70–80	4	• Some ability to organize and develop ideas • Some ability to produce grammatical sentences
50–60	3	• Disorganized or underdeveloped ideas • Inconsistent ability to produce grammatical sentences
40	2	• Disorganized or underdeveloped ideas • Unable to produce grammatical sentences
0–30	1	• Test taker left tasks unanswered • Has difficulty reading and understanding the directions

Chart 7. Writing Tasks and Scoring Scales

Questions	Task	Scale
1–5	Write a sentence based on a photo	0–3
6–7	Respond to a written request	0–4
8	Write an opinion essay	0–5

Using and Scoring the Writing Tests

Students can write their responses in the Practice TOEIC Writing Tests by typing on the computer and printing out or e-mailing the tasks to the teacher. They can also submit handwritten responses. Teachers can use the information in Charts 6 and 7 to evaluate the writing tasks in the Practice TOEIC Writing Tests.

Practice TOEIC® Test 1

This is a test of your ability to use the English language. The total time for the test is approximately two hours. The test is divided into seven parts. Each part begins with a set of specific directions. Be sure you understand what you are to do before you begin work on a part.

You will find that some of the questions are harder than others, but you should try to answer all of them. There is no penalty for guessing. Do not be concerned if you cannot answer all of the questions.

Do not mark your answers in the test book. You must put all of your answers on a separate answer sheet. Be sure to fill out the answer space corresponding to the letter of your choice. Fill in the space so that the letter inside the oval cannot be seen, as shown in the following example.

Sample Answer

Mr. Jones ______ to his accountant yesterday.

Ⓐ Ⓑ ● Ⓓ

(A) talk
(B) talking
(C) talked
(D) to talk

The sentence should read, *Mr. Jones talked to his accountant yesterday.* Therefore, you should choose answer (C). Notice how this has been done in the example given.

Mark only *one* answer for each question. If you change your mind about an answer after you have marked it on your answer sheet, completely erase your old answer and then mark your new answer. You must mark the answer sheet carefully so that the test-scoring machine can accurately record your test score.

You will find the answer sheet for Practice TOEIC Test 1 on page 347. Detach it from the book and use it to record your answers. Play the audio CD for Practice TOEIC Test 1 when you are ready to begin.

Listening Test

In the Listening test, you will demonstrate how well you understand spoken English. The entire Listening test lasts approximately 45 minutes. There are four parts to the Listening test. The directions are given for each part. You must mark your answers on the separate answer sheet. Do not write your answers in the test book.

Part 1

You will hear four statements about a photo in your test book. Choose the statement that best describes the photo. Mark the answer on your answer sheet. The statements are not printed in your test book. You will hear the statements only once.

1. (A) (B) (C) (D)

2. (A) (B) (C) (D)

3. (A) (B) (C) (D)

4. (A) (B) (C) (D)

5. (A) (B) (C) (D)

6. (A) (B) (C) (D)

7. (A) (B) (C) (D)

8. (A) (B) (C) (D)

9. (A) (B) (C) (D)

10. (A) (B) (C) (D)

Part 2

You will hear a question or statement and three responses. You will hear them only once, and they are not printed in your test book. Mark the letter of the best response on your answer sheet.

Example

<u>You will hear</u>: Where is the conference room?

<u>You will also hear</u>: (A) To meet the new manager.
(B) It's the second room on the left.
(C) Yes, at four o'clock.

The best response to the question *Where is the conference room?* is choice (B), *It's the second room on the left*, so (B) is the correct answer. You should mark (B) on your answer sheet.

11. Mark your answer on your answer sheet.
12. Mark your answer on your answer sheet.
13. Mark your answer on your answer sheet.
14. Mark your answer on your answer sheet.
15. Mark your answer on your answer sheet.
16. Mark your answer on your answer sheet.
17. Mark your answer on your answer sheet.
18. Mark your answer on your answer sheet.
19. Mark your answer on your answer sheet.
20. Mark your answer on your answer sheet.
21. Mark your answer on your answer sheet.
22. Mark your answer on your answer sheet.
23. Mark your answer on your answer sheet.
24. Mark your answer on your answer sheet.
25. Mark your answer on your answer sheet.
26. Mark your answer on your answer sheet.
27. Mark your answer on your answer sheet.
28. Mark your answer on your answer sheet.
29. Mark your answer on your answer sheet.
30. Mark your answer on your answer sheet.
31. Mark your answer on your answer sheet.
32. Mark your answer on your answer sheet.
33. Mark your answer on your answer sheet.
34. Mark your answer on your answer sheet.
35. Mark your answer on your answer sheet.
36. Mark your answer on your answer sheet.
37. Mark your answer on your answer sheet.
38. Mark your answer on your answer sheet.
39. Mark your answer on your answer sheet.
40. Mark your answer on your answer sheet.

Part 3

You will hear conversations between two people. You will answer three questions about each conversation. Mark the letter of the best answer on your answer sheet. You will hear the conversations only once, and they are not printed in your test book.

41. What do the speakers need to talk about?
(A) Police service.
(B) The hiring policy.
(C) Planning a lunch.
(D) A conference.

42. When will they meet?
(A) Today.
(B) In two days.
(C) On Tuesday.
(D) On Wednesday.

43. Where will they meet?
(A) Downtown.
(B) In the conference room.
(C) In the woman's office.
(D) In the man's office.

44. Where does this conversation take place?
(A) At a store.
(B) At the woman's home.
(C) At the post office.
(D) At an employment office.

45. What does the man want the woman to do?
(A) Go to work.
(B) Sign a card.
(C) Write a letter.
(D) Fill out a form.

46. What will the woman receive in the mail?
(A) Bills.
(B) Notices.
(C) A newsletter.
(D) A credit card.

47. What will the man have?
(A) A roll.
(B) Pastry.
(C) Coffee.
(D) Some cream.

48. How much does it cost?
(A) \$1.00.
(B) \$1.17.
(C) \$1.75.
(D) \$2.00.

49. How does he pay?
(A) Cash.
(B) Check.
(C) Credit card.
(D) Money order.

50. What does the woman want the man to do?
(A) Wait for the client.
(B) Send the client up.
(C) Call her.
(D) Ask the client inside.

51. What time is the client expected?
(A) 5:00.
(B) 7:30.
(C) 11:00.
(D) 11:30.

52. What does the woman want to give the client?
(A) A tour.
(B) A call.
(C) Some mail.
(D) Some messages.

GO ON TO THE NEXT PAGE

53. What is the problem with the meeting?
(A) There is no time for it.
(B) Everyone is too busy for it.
(C) The conference room isn't available for it.
(D) No one has prepared for it.

54. How many people are expected for the meeting?
(A) 10.
(B) 20.
(C) 25.
(D) 30.

55. What will they do?
(A) Have the meeting at another time.
(B) Use the conference room this morning.
(C) Find a larger room.
(D) Cancel the meeting.

56. How long does it take the man to get to work?
(A) A little less than one hour.
(B) Exactly one hour.
(C) A little more than one hour.
(D) About two hours.

57. How does the man get to work?
(A) Walking.
(B) By subway.
(C) By taxi.
(D) By car.

58. What does the man do on the way to work?
(A) He stops to buy clothes.
(B) He thinks about work.
(C) He makes phone calls.
(D) He relaxes.

59. What is the woman's profession?
(A) Doctor.
(B) Pharmacist.
(C) Nurse.
(D) Clerk.

60. How long will the man have to wait?
(A) Two minutes.
(B) Eight minutes.
(C) Nine minutes.
(D) Ten minutes.

61. How will he pay?
(A) He'll pay with cash.
(B) He'll write a check.
(C) He'll use a credit card.
(D) He'll charge it to his account.

62. What is the man expecting?
(A) A letter.
(B) Some pills.
(C) A package.
(D) Some checks.

63. When is the mail usually delivered?
(A) By 5:00.
(B) At 7:00.
(C) Before 11:00.
(D) Around noon.

64. What does the woman want the man to do?
(A) Cook something.
(B) Go downtown.
(C) Look for the mail.
(D) Read a book.

65. Where does this conversation take place?
(A) At a restaurant.
(B) At a furniture store.
(C) At the woman's home.
(D) At a school.

66. What time is it?
(A) 4:15.
(B) 4:45.
(C) 5:00.
(D) 5:15.

67. Why shouldn't the woman worry?
(A) There's not enough time.
(B) The man is helping her.
(C) He can stay late.
(D) The clock is wrong.

68. Where is the man going?
(A) Downtown.
(B) To a fair.
(C) To the university.
(D) To the bank.

69. How much does the bus cost?
(A) 19 cents.
(B) 90 cents.
(C) 95 cents.
(D) One dollar.

70. Why is the man disappointed?
(A) The driver doesn't make change.
(B) He will have to change buses.
(C) The driver will send him a bill.
(D) He will be late for class.

GO ON TO THE NEXT PAGE

Part 4

You will hear talks given by one speaker. You will answer three questions about each talk. Mark the letter of the best answer on your answer sheet. You will hear the talks only once, and they are not printed in your test book.

71. When should passengers approach the gate?
    (A) When their names are called.
    (B) When their boarding passes are ready.
    (C) When their bags are on board.
    (D) When their row number is called.

72. When can first-class passengers board?
    (A) Before everyone else.
    (B) After everyone else.
    (C) Any time.
    (D) During first-class boarding.

73. What should passengers give the flight attendants?
    (A) Their names.
    (B) Their passports.
    (C) Their boarding passes.
    (D) Their extra carry-on items.

---

74. Why should people leave the building?
    (A) There will be a safety inspection.
    (B) The building is closing.
    (C) There's a meeting outside.
    (D) There is a fire.

75. What should people NOT do?
    (A) Gather their personal belongings.
    (B) Move quickly to the exits.
    (C) Call the fire department.
    (D) Notify others.

76. How should people leave the building?
    (A) On the elevators.
    (B) By the stairways.
    (C) Through the windows.
    (D) At the back door.

---

77. What service does this provide information about?
    (A) Restaurants.
    (B) Theaters.
    (C) Tours.
    (D) Shopping.

78. Which tour is NOT mentioned?
    (A) Museum.
    (B) Candlelight.
    (C) Walking.
    (D) Guided.

79. What can you get if you stay on the line?
    (A) Seats on a bus tour.
    (B) Some maps of downtown.
    (C) A special tour book.
    (D) A personal guide.

---

80. What business is advertised?
    (A) Cleaning services.
    (B) Delivery services.
    (C) Accounting services.
    (D) Printing services.

81. If customers place a large order, what will they get?
    (A) Special low rates.
    (B) Extra stationery.
    (C) Free advertising.
    (D) Guaranteed work.

82. How many branches does this business have?
    (A) Five.
    (B) Seven.
    (C) Nine.
    (D) Eleven.

83. What kind of weather is predicted for the next twenty-four hours?
(A) Sunny.
(B) Cloudy.
(C) Mild.
(D) Warm.

84. How will the wind change during the night?
(A) It will increase.
(B) It will decrease.
(C) It will become dangerous.
(D) It will become constant.

85. When is rain expected?
(A) Late tonight.
(B) Early tomorrow.
(C) Around noon.
(D) Late tomorrow.

---

86. Where is this mailroom probably located?
(A) The post office.
(B) A large company.
(C) A neighborhood.
(D) The government.

87. What is NOT mentioned as a function of the mailroom?
(A) Sorting mail.
(B) Delivering mail.
(C) Selling stamps.
(D) Wrapping packages.

88. What kind of package should employees let the mailroom prepare?
(A) Fragile packages.
(B) Expensive packages.
(C) Heavy packages.
(D) Sturdy packages.

---

89. What is Dr. Yung's profession?
(A) Scientist.
(B) Medical doctor.
(C) Professor.
(D) Psychologist.

90. Where is this introduction most likely given?
(A) In a classroom.
(B) In a hospital.
(C) At a banquet.
(D) At a conference.

91. What will happen right after Dr. Yung's presentation?
(A) Everyone will go to lunch.
(B) People will ask questions.
(C) There will be another speaker.
(D) It will be time to go home.

---

92. What does the news item discuss?
(A) Banking practices.
(B) The economy.
(C) New car sales.
(D) Automobile exports.

93. What is an explanation for the increase?
(A) Old cars are wearing out.
(B) It's easier to get a car loan.
(C) Traffic is less congested.
(D) People own more than one car.

94. What prompted more safety features on new cars?
(A) The number of accidents.
(B) Injuries to passengers.
(C) Government regulations.
(D) Consumer demand.

GO ON TO THE NEXT PAGE

95. Who is the person addressing?
(A) A theater audience.
(B) Television viewers.
(C) School children.
(D) A group of actors.

96. What does he ask people to do?
(A) Serve snacks.
(B) Take pictures.
(C) Turn off their phones.
(D) Apply for a permit.

97. When will drinks be served?
(A) At the end of the program.
(B) In an hour.
(C) During the performance.
(D) Now.

98. How is the weather today?
(A) Rainy.
(B) Sunny.
(C) Windy.
(D) Snowy.

99. What happened in the first accident?
(A) A bus collided with a truck.
(B) Two trucks slid off the road.
(C) A car hit a bus.
(D) The driver fell asleep in his truck.

100. What time did the second accident occur?
(A) 12:00.
(B) 1:00.
(C) 1:30.
(D) 2:00.

This is the end of the Listening Comprehension section of the test. Turn to Part 5 in your test book.

Reading Test

In the Reading test, you will read a variety of texts and answer several different types of reading comprehension questions. The entire Reading test lasts 75 minutes, and there are four parts. The directions are given for each part. Try to answer as many questions as possible in the time allowed. You must mark your answers on the separate answer sheet. Do not write your answers in the test book.

Part 5

A word or phrase is missing in each sentence. Mark the letter of the best answer on your answer sheet.

101. People _______ always willing to switch to a better product.
(A) is
(B) are
(C) be
(D) being

102. Our new computer program is _______ selling software on the market.
(A) the fast
(B) fastest
(C) faster
(D) the fastest

103. Many companies hire consultants to give _______ on special projects.
(A) advise
(B) advertise
(C) advice
(D) adventure

104. Mr. Lee _______ his vacation after the project is completed.
(A) will take
(B) took
(C) has taken
(D) taking

105. Business travelers usually do paperwork _______ their flights.
(A) during
(B) while
(C) when
(D) as

106. The person _______ prepared this report has a real talent for writing.
(A) which
(B) who
(C) whose
(D) she

107. The restaurant will prepare any dish without salt if a guest _______ it.
(A) will request
(B) requests
(C) requested
(D) request

108. The Jones Company has a reputation for quality _______ service.
(A) nor
(B) but
(C) and
(D) or

GO ON TO THE NEXT PAGE

109. The pharmacist needed the doctor ______ the prescription before she filled it.
(A) verifying
(B) verified
(C) verifies
(D) to verify

110. The radio advertisements will start airing ______ Friday.
(A) of
(B) in
(C) on
(D) at

111. Effective staff members ______ to instructions.
(A) always listen carefully
(B) carefully always listen
(C) carefully listen always
(D) listen always carefully

112. Mr. Golino has been worrying too much and ______.
(A) works too hard
(B) worked too hard
(C) working too hard
(D) to work too hard

113. Both ______ must be on my desk by 3:00 this afternoon.
(A) reporter
(B) reports
(C) reporting
(D) report

114. ______ her innovative advertising ideas, she was not promoted.
(A) Because of
(B) Even though
(C) Although
(D) Despite

115. The offices in the Pacific region ______ their meeting for next month.
(A) have scheduled
(B) has scheduled
(C) is scheduling
(D) schedules

116. The ______ participants wanted the meeting to end soon.
(A) boring
(B) bores
(C) bored
(D) is boring

117. Ms. Wei returns all her phone calls ______.
(A) rarely
(B) every day
(C) never
(D) always

118. The only room that is large enough is ______ large conference room.
(A) the
(B) a
(C) an
(D) it

119. The food must be served ______ it is prepared.
(A) as soon
(B) as soon as
(C) soon as
(D) sooner than

120. Mr. Stein ______ for the day when the phone call came.
(A) has already left
(B) already leaves
(C) already left
(D) had already left

121. The restaurant ______ overlooks the river is very popular.
(A) it
(B) that
(C) whose
(D) who

122. Please take extra soap and towels ______ Room 312.
(A) at
(B) of
(C) to
(D) in

123. The waitress suggested that we _______ the spicy chicken.
(A) order
(B) ordered
(C) to order
(D) ordering

124. The _______ argument caused everyone to vote in favor of the proposal.
(A) convinced
(B) convince
(C) convincing
(D) to convince

125. Although it seems unlikely, _______ sometimes influences business decisions.
(A) politicians
(B) politics
(C) political
(D) politicize

126. This long letter will require three _______.
(A) paper
(B) papers
(C) sheets of paper
(D) sheet of paper

127. The hotel tries to have fresh flowers _______ the lobby.
(A) out
(B) of
(C) to
(D) in

128. Ms. Dubois is the head of our department of research and _______.
(A) developed
(B) developing
(C) development
(D) develops

129. Both the TV ads _______ the newspaper ads will be withdrawn.
(A) and
(B) also
(C) but also
(D) nor

130. A company cannot survive if losses are always _______ profits.
(A) great as
(B) greater than
(C) great than
(D) the greatest

131. Guests may select a single room _______ a suite with a bedroom and office.
(A) but
(B) and
(C) or
(D) nor

132. Ms. Ajai can probably _______ a way for the computer to run the program.
(A) devote
(B) desire
(C) device
(D) devise

133. The new desk, _______ was delivered yesterday, looks wonderful in the reception area.
(A) that
(B) which
(C) it
(D) whose

134. If Mr. Chi _______ the project, it will be finished on schedule.
(A) had managed
(B) has managed
(C) managing
(D) manages

135. The chairwoman urged that we _______ a deal with the competitors.
(A) making
(B) to make
(C) make
(D) will make

136. The _______ highways in the area make commuting difficult.
(A) crowded
(B) crowding
(C) crowds
(D) crowd

GO ON TO THE NEXT PAGE

137. The passengers ______ for a long time before they could be seated.
(A) wished
(B) wanted
(C) waited
(D) went

138. Ms. Barrios ______ to the convention if she can get time off.
(A) has gone
(B) had gone
(C) will go
(D) was going

139. The manager made his employees ______ the computer training classes.
(A) attending
(B) attend
(C) to attend
(D) attendance

140. The meeting will take place ______ 11:00.
(A) in
(B) on
(C) for
(D) at

Part 6

Read the texts that follow. A word or phrase is missing in some sentences. Mark the letter of the best answer on your answer sheet.

Questions 141–143 refer to the following letter.

National Bank of Fernwood
1001 Putnam Avenue
Fernwood, ND 70802

Dear Ms. Kim:

As a valued National Bank of Fernwood customer, you are eligible to apply for the Fernwood Signature credit card. This credit card is available to only a few select customers like you. This credit card has a low ________ rate of only

141. (A) interest
(B) interests
(C) interested
(D) interesting

12 percent and has no annual fee. You cannot afford not to have this card. To apply for the Fernwood Signature credit card, simply fill ________ the

142. (A) over
(B) up
(C) out
(D) through

enclosed form and bring it into any National Bank of Fernwood branch office. A bank officer will be happy to assist you and start you on the way to using your Fernwood Signature credit card. Or, for an instant over-the-phone decision, call our special line at 888-555-1234. You will find out right away whether your application ________, as well as the size of your credit line.

143. (A) approves
(B) approved
(C) is approved
(D) is approving

Whether in person or over the phone, we at the National Bank of Fernwood are always ready to offer you superior service with a friendly smile. Contact us today!

Sincerely,

Miranda Mendez

President, National Bank of Fernwood

GO ON TO THE NEXT PAGE

Questions 144–146 refer to the following e-mail.

To: Peter Marks
From: Maya Cho
Subject: Meeting

Hi Peter,

We have finally decided on a date and time for the meeting. It will be next Thursday afternoon at 2:00 in conference room 4. Please be on time. We plan _________ a number of

144. (A) discuss
(B) to discuss
(C) discussing
(D) discussion

items and would like to finish by 5:00. My assistant will fax you a copy of the agenda by Tuesday afternoon at the latest. That way you'll have a _________ to look it over. Please let

145. (A) change
(B) charge
(C) chart
(D) chance

me know if you have any questions or if you would like to make additions to the agenda. I know the process of organizing this meeting has been somewhat complicated, and I appreciate _________ patience. Next time, I hope the arrangements go more smoothly!

146. (A) you
(B) your
(C) you're
(D) you've

In any case, I look forward to meeting with you next week.

Maya

Questions 147–149 refer to the following advertisement.

Now Renting

Global Office Towers on Park Boulevard now has several offices _________ for rent. Building amenities include a café, post office, and

147. (A) available
(B) awardable
(C) avertable
(D) avoidable

office supply store on the ground floor, as well as a health club with membership discounts for building tenants. We also offer parking for your staff and clients in the garage at low daily and monthly rates. All vacant offices are _________ and sunny and have views of the park.

148. (A) space
(B) spaced
(C) spacious
(D) spaciously

With advantages like these, why rent anywhere else?

_________ this opportunity to locate your business at one of the most

149. (A) Miss
(B) Missing
(C) Not to miss
(D) Don't miss

exclusive addresses in the city. It's more affordable than you think! Call Mark Wotherspoon, building manager, for an appointment today.

GO ON TO THE NEXT PAGE

Questions 150–152 refer to the following article.

Clothing Store to Reopen

Francine's Fashions, which closed its doors last September, announced that it will reopen early next month. The store will host a grand opening on March 5. There will be music and refreshments and a special sale on casual clothing. Store owner Francine Bernard says the newly reopened store will have a totally new look. "We _________ redesigned the entire interior," she explained. "We have a more

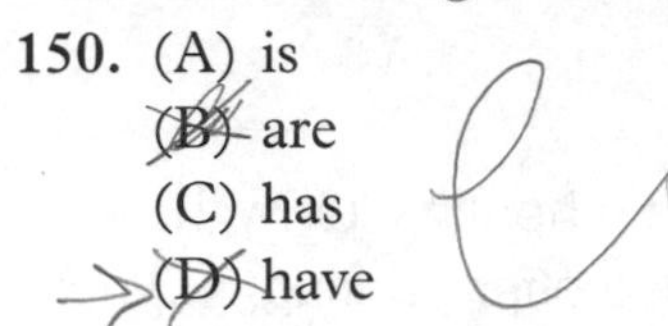

150. (A) is
(B) are
(C) has
(D) have

up-to-date look now that matches the clothing styles we sell." Ms. Bernard says she hopes to attract more professional women to her store. To this end, she will be stocking business _________ as well as evening and weekend wear.

151. (A) attire
(B) partner
(C) associate
(D) equipment

By _________ professional women, Ms. Bernard hopes to bring in a clientele

152. (A) target
(B) to target
(C) targeting
(D) will target

that typically is more willing to spend money on clothes. "We want to be seen as a high-end clothing store," she says.

Part 7

In this part, you will read a variety of texts, such as magazine and newspaper articles, e-mail messages, letters, and advertisements. Several questions follow each text. Mark the letter of the best answer for each question on your answer sheet.

Questions 153–156 refer to the following memo.

MEMO
TO: All employees
FROM: Ron Starsky, Accounting
DATE: March 15, 20 ___

There has been an unprecedented increase in the amount of taxi fare indicated on the expense accounts of our business travelers. To help keep costs under control, please remember the following guidelines when using taxicabs in an unfamiliar city.

Be sure that the meter is turned on after, not before, you sit down in the cab. Request that you take the most direct route to your destination. Establish an approximate fare to your destination before the driver moves the cab. Always ask the taxicab driver for a receipt showing the driver's name, I.D. number, name of the cab company, destination, and the amount paid for the fare. This will enable us to verify the trip should the fare be disputed.

153. What is this memo about?
(A) Filling out travel vouchers
(B) Learning your way around a city
(C) Traveling safely
(D) Saving cab costs

154. Who should pay attention to this memo?
(A) Company employees
(B) Taxi drivers
(C) Accountants
(D) Cab companies

155. When should the driver turn on the meter?
(A) When you hail the cab
(B) Before you get in the cab
(C) After you are in the taxi
(D) After the driver puts bags in the trunk

156. Why should employees get a receipt from the driver?
(A) To prove why they went
(B) To verify the trip
(C) To give to the cab company
(D) To obtain the driver's signature

GO ON TO THE NEXT PAGE

Questions 157–159 refer to the following article.

Busy executives are always looking for more ways to squeeze time into their day. This effort has led them to start work even before they get to their offices at nine with what has become known as the power breakfast. The power breakfast is essentially a meeting between two or more powerful executives who consider themselves too busy to get together at any other time. Restaurants—particularly the ones at large hotels in large cities—go out of their way to accommodate these meetings. Some start serving full breakfasts in their most elegant dining rooms as early as 6:30 A.M., and most require reservations before 9:00 A.M.

157. What is one way business people get more work out of their day?
- (A) Have breakfast meetings
- (B) Work late
- (C) Hire more assistants
- (D) Move closer to the office

158. Who started this trend?
- (A) People who leave work early
- (B) People who can't cook
- (C) People who had to get to work early
- (D) People who are too busy to meet at other times

159. What is one sign that this has become common?
- (A) Restaurants have begun to serve breakfast.
- (B) Restaurants require reservations for breakfast.
- (C) Restaurants have hired more waiters to serve breakfast.
- (D) Restaurants give wake-up calls.

Questions 160–162 refer to the following article.

> Companies that are looking to establish a new headquarters or other facility must consider location very carefully. The match, or lack of it, between the company's requirements and the available human and natural resources in the area can be crucial. A company's future growth and prosperity depends on a successful match of needs and resources.
>
> Different companies, of course, have different needs. Some are looking for a good climate and sound infrastructure, like public transportation, schools, and other facilities for their employees. Others are seeking affordable office space and a large workforce. Still others want a low cost of living and access to cultural or outdoor activities to keep their employees happy. But the one common denominator must be a pro-business attitude in the community. If the citizens do not want commercial enterprises in their neighborhood, a company should consider another location.

160. What must companies look for when choosing a location?
- (A) Abundant natural resources
- (B) The desires of the board
- (C) A match between needs and resources
- (D) A range of different needs

161. What possible requirement is NOT mentioned in the article?
- (A) Affordable office space
- (B) Tax advantages
- (C) Sound infrastructure
- (D) Climate

162. What is essential for success in all cases?
- (A) Low cost of living
- (B) Access to cultural activities
- (C) A large workforce
- (D) A pro-business attitude

GO ON TO THE NEXT PAGE

Questions 163–165 refer to the following letter.

Maria Gomez
408 Republic Avenue
Nogales, Mexico

Clothes by Mail Catalog
10 Lake Street
Springfield, Wisconsin 67032
January 12, 20 ___

To Whom It May Concern:

I am returning a pair of pants, item number 7042, because they did not fit. I would like my credit card, which was used for the original purchase, to be credited with the amount of the sale. I have enclosed the sales slip and credit receipt.

Thank you for your attention.

Sincerely,

Maria Gomez

Maria Gomez

163. How was the original purchase made?
- (A) By credit card
- (B) By check
- (C) In cash
- (D) As a gift

164. What does she request that the company do?
- (A) Deliver the pants
- (B) Refund her money
- (C) Exchange the pants
- (D) Credit her credit card

165. The word "slip" in line 4 of the letter is closest in meaning to
- (A) fall
- (B) mistake
- (C) piece of paper
- (D) wrapping material

Questions 166–169 refer to the following advertisement.

If you plan your visit in October, don't miss the Harvest Festival. The festival offers a variety of activities for all age groups and interests. Children will enjoy listening to traditional stories and learning folk dances. Adults will enjoy the antique show and the crafts fair. Other attractions include a celebration of musical heritage and demonstrations of traditional skills such as candle making, butter churning, and bee keeping. The festival is held at the County Fairgrounds, 10 miles outside of town on Highway 64 West. Space is available for you to park your car at the festival at no extra charge. The admission fee of $2 for adults and $1 for children 6 and younger is donated to the Preserve Our History Fund.

166. What does this ad describe?
(A) A lecture
(B) A parade
(C) A school
(D) A festival

167. What activity is available for children?
(A) Dancing
(B) Painting
(C) Ball playing
(D) Singing

168. How does the advertisement assume that people get to the fairgrounds?
(A) Walking
(B) Flying
(C) Taking the subway
(D) Driving a car

169. What happens to the admissions fee?
(A) It is used to rent the fairgrounds.
(B) It pays the performers.
(C) It is donated to charity.
(D) It pays for supplies.

GO ON TO THE NEXT PAGE

Questions 170–173 refer to the following article.

Most people give little thought to the pens they write with, especially since the printers in modern homes and offices mean that very few items are handwritten. All too often, people buy a pen based only on looks and wonder why they are not satisfied once they begin to use it. However, buying a pen that you will enjoy is not difficult if you keep a few simple tips in mind.

First of all, a pen should fit comfortably in your hand and be easy to manipulate. The thickness of the pen is the most important characteristic when determining comfort. If you have a small hand and thick fingers, you may be comfortable with a slender pen. If you have a larger hand and thicker fingers, you may prefer a fatter pen. The length of a pen can also influence comfort. A pen that is too long can easily feel top-heavy and unstable as you write.

Next, the writing point of the pen (called a nib on fountain pens) should allow the ink to flow evenly while the pen remains in contact with the paper. This will create a smooth line of writing, with no skips or gaps that indicate an irregular flow of ink within the pen. The point should also be sensitive enough to prevent ink from flowing when the pen is lifted from the paper. A point that does not seal off the flow may leave blots of ink at the end and beginning of each word, as you pick the pen up and put it down again.

Finally, the pen should make a bold, dark line. Fine-line pens may compensate for bad handwriting, but fine, delicate lines do not command attention next to printed text, as, for example, a signature on a printed letter. A broader line, by contrast, gives an impression of confidence and authority.

170. What does this article encourage people to do?
(A) Write more legibly
(B) Purchase better printers
(C) Write more things by hand
(D) Pay more attention to their pens

171. What is the most important characteristic to consider when determining the comfort of a pen?
(A) Thickness
(B) Length
(C) Weight
(D) Size

172. What might an irregular flow of ink cause?
(A) Smears
(B) Skips
(C) Blots
(D) Smudges

173. What is an advantage of fine-line pens?
(A) They are easier to write with.
(B) They convey confidence and authority.
(C) They can compensate for bad handwriting.
(D) They command attention.

GO ON TO THE NEXT PAGE

Questions 174–177 refer to the following announcement.

> The Organization of Responsible Executives was founded five years ago to provide support and assistance for member executives who are looking for better ways to solve their problems. ORE concentrates on finding solutions that are environmentally and socially responsible. "If you need suggestions on non-polluting alternatives to chemicals, or want to know the pros and cons of setting up a day care center for your working parent, then we are the group to call," says director David Anderson. "If we don't have the information on hand, we'll find it for you." It is this kind of responsiveness that has made ORE the fastest-growing business organization to come along in years. It provides a one-source solution for executives who are trying help the company without hurting the world.

174. Who belongs to ORE?
(A) Secretaries
(B) Executives
(C) Parents
(D) Researchers

175. What is the purpose of ORE?
(A) To provide responsible solutions
(B) To introduce executives to each other
(C) To make money for executives
(D) To arrange mergers

176. How long has ORE been operating?
(A) For one year
(B) For two years
(C) For four years
(D) For five years

177. What shows that ORE is successful?
(A) It has large offices.
(B) It has high profits.
(C) It has grown fast.
(D) It has a good director.

Questions 178–180 refer to the following news item.

News Flash	News Flash	News Flash
Devastating floods along the coast have left many people homeless. People are asked to help by donating food, clothes, furniture, and other supplies to the Assistance Fund. Donations of bottled water are especially needed, since the floods have disrupted the local water supply. In addition, volunteers are needed to travel to the flooded area to help distribute the donations.		

178. What does this news item concern?
   (A) Hazardous roads
   (B) Safety precautions
   (C) Help for flood victims
   (D) Warnings about weather

179. What kinds of supplies are NOT mentioned?
   (A) Medical supplies
   (B) Food
   (C) Clothing
   (D) Furniture

180. In addition to supplies, what is needed?
   (A) Teachers
   (B) New bridges
   (C) Places to stay
   (D) Volunteers

GO ON TO THE NEXT PAGE

Questions 181–185 refer to the following two letters.

Radka Stuchlik
Westmore Corporation
1568 East Binney Drive, Suite 100
Northland, NY 10001

Dear Ms. Stuchlik:

In response to your ad in last Sunday's newspaper, I am interested in applying for the position of office manager at the Westmore Corporation. I am a recent graduate of Northland College, where I majored in business. I plan to continue my studies in the future to get a Master of Business Administration degree, but first I would like to have several years of work experience. While I was a college student, I spent my summer vacations working as an office assistant at the Weston and Smith law firm in Northland. During that time I learned a great deal about how offices are run. I believe my job at Weston and Smith gave me the experience I need to be a top-notch office manager.

I am enclosing my résumé and a letter of reference. I look forward to hearing from you.

Sincerely,

Alex Hayes

Alex Hayes

Weston and Smith
Attorneys-at-Law
January 17, 20___

Radka Stuchlik
Westmore Corporation
1568 East Binney Drive, Suite 100
Northland, NY 10001

Dear Ms. Stuchlik:

This is a letter of reference for Mr. Alex Hayes. Mr. Hayes worked for our firm during the summers while he was a business student at Northland College. He carried out a variety of office duties, including answering the phones, making appointments for clients, photocopying, and keeping track of and ordering supplies. Mr. Hayes brought to this job good organizational skills and an eagerness to learn. He is a responsible and reliable worker. Unfortunately, now that he is ready to work full time, we do not currently have any full-time positions that would suit his skills and goals. We enjoyed having him work here. He would make a fine addition to the staff of any place of business. Please feel free to contact me if you have any questions about Mr. Hayes's work with our firm.

Sincerely,

Georgina Smith

Georgina Smith

181. Who is Alex Hayes?
- (A) A recent college graduate
- (B) An assistant professor
- (C) A current business student
- (D) An attorney

182. Why did Alex Hayes write the letter to Ms. Stuchlik?
- (A) He plans to get a master's degree.
- (B) He has to order office supplies.
- (C) He needs an attorney.
- (D) He wants a job.

183. What did Alex Hayes send with his letter to Ms. Stuchlik?
- (A) A business plan
- (B) A letter from Ms. Smith
- (C) An application form
- (D) A copy of his college degree

184. Who is Georgina Smith?
- (A) An employee of the Westmore Corporation
- (B) A professor at Northland College
- (C) Alex's former employer
- (D) A friend of Ms. Stuchlik

185. What is Ms. Smith's opinion of Alex Hayes?
- (A) He is a good worker.
- (B) He is a top-notch manager.
- (C) He shouldn't work full time.
- (D) He takes too many vacations.

Questions 186–190 refer to the following itinerary and e-mail.

Travel Itinerary
For: Ms. Mai Chan

July 7
1:15 P.M.—leave New York on Sky Blue Airways flight 210, in-flight lunch and movie
4:30 P.M.—arrive San Francisco

July 7–July 9
Hotel Hacienda, San Francisco

July 10
9:30 A.M.—leave San Francisco on Sky Blue Airways flight 34
11:10 A.M.—arrive Los Angeles

July 10–13
Hightowers Hotel, Los Angeles

July 11
3:30–6:00—Hollywood sightseeing tour with LA Tour Company

July 14
8:45 A.M.—leave Los Angeles on Sky Blue Airways flight 567, in-flight lunch and movie
4:14 P.M.—arrive New York

To: Paul Sommers
From: Mai Chan
Subject: Itinerary

Hi Paul,

I just received the itinerary. Thanks for getting me a room at the Hotel Hacienda. I know how difficult it can be to book rooms there. It's such a popular place. Last time, I had to stay at the Woodrow Suites, and it was very inconvenient. I need to make one change to the itinerary. I have a meeting in San Francisco at 5:00 on the day of my arrival, so I really think I should arrive at least an hour and a half earlier than you have me scheduled for. So please see if you can get me on the next earlier flight. Also, I would like to stay one more day in LA. My work will be done, but I have friends there I would like to visit. So I guess you'll have to change my flight back and reserve my room for another night at the hotel. I appreciate it. Also, please don't forget that Mr. Young Kim from the Seoul office will be here the day after I return from Los Angeles. Please get him a room at the Radcliff Inn for two nights, and arrange for a car for him, too.

Thanks,

Mai

186. What time does Ms. Chan want to arrive in San Francisco?
(A) 1:15
(B) 3:00
(C) 4:30
(D) 5:00

187. What will she do in San Francisco?
(A) Attend a meeting
(B) Take a tour
(C) Read a book
(D) Visit friends

188. Where will Ms. Chan stay in Los Angeles?
(A) Hotel Hacienda
(B) Woodrow Suites
(C) Hightowers Hotel
(D) Radcliff Inn

189. How many nights will she stay in Los Angeles?
(A) Two
(B) Three
(C) Four
(D) Five

190. When will Mr. Kim arrive in New York?
(A) July 11
(B) July 14
(C) July 15
(D) July 16

GO ON TO THE NEXT PAGE

Questions 191–195 refer to the following agenda and e-mail.

Meeting Agenda
Monday, March 15
Conference Room 3
(draft)

9:00–9:30	Marketing goals for the next year	Roberta Giuliani
9:30–10:00	New strategies for the new millennium	Rita Mendes
10:00–10:30	Product development	Tami Tabaku
10:30–10:45	Break	
10:45–11:15	Employee training	Peter Clark
11:15–11:45	Financial outlook	Ivan Sokolov

Immediately following the meeting, lunch will be served in the company cafeteria, catered by The Ivy Pot Restaurant.

To: Peter Clark
From: Maria Petras
Subject: Meeting next week

Hi Peter,

Attached is a draft of the agenda for next week's meeting. I'd like to make a few small changes. First, Roberta won't be available since she's leaving for an extended trip to the West Coast day after tomorrow. I was hoping you could take her spot since you know a lot about the subject. I also thought that Ivan should be given a little more time since he will probably have a lot of information to present. I thought we should give him 45 minutes to talk. Then we could still break for lunch at a reasonable hour. I hope these changes meet with your approval. Oh, one more thing: Conference Room 3 won't be available as it turns out, so I've reserved the Board Room instead. I don't think anyone will object to that! I think that's all.

Maria

191. What does Maria want Peter to do?
(A) Reserve another room
(B) Talk about marketing goals
(C) Take a trip to the West Coast
(D) Help Roberta prepare her presentation

192. What will Tami talk about?
(A) Financial outlook
(B) Employee training
(C) Product development
(D) New strategies

193. What time does Maria want the meeting to end?
(A) 11:15
(B) 11:45
(C) 12:00
(D) 12:45

194. Where will the meeting take place?
(A) Conference Room 3
(B) The company cafeteria
(C) A restaurant
(D) The Board Room

195. What did Maria send to Peter?
(A) A draft of the meeting agenda
(B) The lunch menu
(C) A trip itinerary
(D) Ivan's presentation

Questions 196–200 refer to the following article and letter.

Development Proposal Accepted

The City Planning Board voted yesterday to approve the proposal by the Windsor Development Corporation to revitalize the downtown business district. This proposal has been the subject of a great deal of controversy over the past several years. "Despite the great disagreement the original proposals excited, I feel we have finally come to a decision that everyone can be happy with," said Shirley Johnson, a long-time member of the Planning Board. According to Ms. Johnson, once the revitalization of the district is completed, more customers will be attracted to downtown stores and higher-paying tenants will occupy the office buildings. "It's a win-win situation," she says. "We will have better places to shop, and retailers and landlords will be able to earn higher profits."

April 15, 20 ___

Editor
City Times
198 State Street
Riverdale, IN 73407

To the editor:

As a concerned citizen, it was with great dismay that I read in yesterday's City Times about the approval of the proposal by the Windsor Development Corporation to revitalize the downtown business district. While I agree that the business district is in desperate need of revitalization, I cannot agree that the proposal of the Windsor Development Corporation is the best route to take. We have only to look at other examples of its work to understand that this company cares little for anything but profit. The Riverdale Shopping Mall, Windsor's most recent project which opened last October 12, is just one example. It is a terrible eyesore. Our downtown has several beautiful old buildings which the Windsor Corporation proposes to destroy and replace with modern concrete and steel. This will not be a benefit to anyone. I suggest that the City Planning Board seek another development company for this job, one that is willing to preserve historic buildings. This has been done successfully in other cities, which we should look to as examples.

Sincerely yours,

Jules Rothman

Jules Rothman

196. When did the article appear in the newspaper?
(A) April 14
(B) April 15
(C) October 11
(D) October 12

197. Who is Shirley Johnson?
(A) A concerned citizen
(B) The editor of the City Times
(C) A member of the City Planning Board
(D) The director of the Windsor Development Corporation

198. Why does Ms. Johnson like the proposal?
(A) It will be completed quickly.
(B) Office space will be less expensive.
(C) Building owners will earn more money.
(D) The Windsor Corporation will make a huge profit.

199. Why did Jules Rothman write the letter?
(A) He doesn't approve of the proposal.
(B) He wants to help the Windsor Corporation.
(C) He is interested in the City Shopping Mall.
(D) He doesn't want the downtown to be revitalized.

200. What does Jules Rothman like?
(A) Modern offices
(B) Old buildings
(C) Shopping malls
(D) Concrete buildings

This is the end of the test. If you finish early, you may check your work in Parts 5, 6, and 7.

Practice TOEIC® Test 2

This is a test of your ability to use the English language. The total time for the test is approximately two hours. The test is divided into seven parts. Each part begins with a set of specific directions. Be sure you understand what you are to do before you begin work on a part.

You will find that some of the questions are harder than others, but you should try to answer all of them. There is no penalty for guessing. Do not be concerned if you cannot answer all of the questions.

Do not mark your answers in the test book. You must put all of your answers on a separate answer sheet. Be sure to fill out the answer space corresponding to the letter of your choice. Fill in the space so that the letter inside the oval cannot be seen, as shown in the following example.

Sample Answer

Ⓐ Ⓑ ● Ⓓ

Mr. Jones ______ to his accountant yesterday.

(A) talk
(B) talking
(C) talked
(D) to talk

The sentence should read, *Mr. Jones talked to his accountant yesterday.* Therefore, you should choose answer (C). Notice how this has been done in the example given.

Mark only *one* answer for each question. If you change your mind about an answer after you have marked it on your answer sheet, completely erase your old answer and then mark your new answer. You must mark the answer sheet carefully so that the test-scoring machine can accurately record your test score.

You will find the answer sheet for Practice TOEIC Test 2 on page 349. Detach it from the book and use it to record your answers. Play the audio CD for Practice TOEIC Test 1 when you are ready to begin.

Listening Test

In the Listening test, you will demonstrate how well you understand spoken English. The entire Listening test lasts approximately 45 minutes. There are four parts to the Listening test. The directions are given for each part. You must mark your answers on the separate answer sheet. Do not write your answers in the test book.

Part 1

You will hear four statements about a photo in your test book. Choose the statement that best describes the photo. Mark the answer on your answer sheet. The statements are not printed in your test book. You will hear the statements only once.

1. (A) (B) (C) (D)

2. (A) (B) (C) (D)

3. (A) (B) (C) (D)

4. (A) (B) (C) (D)

5. (A) (B) (C) (D)

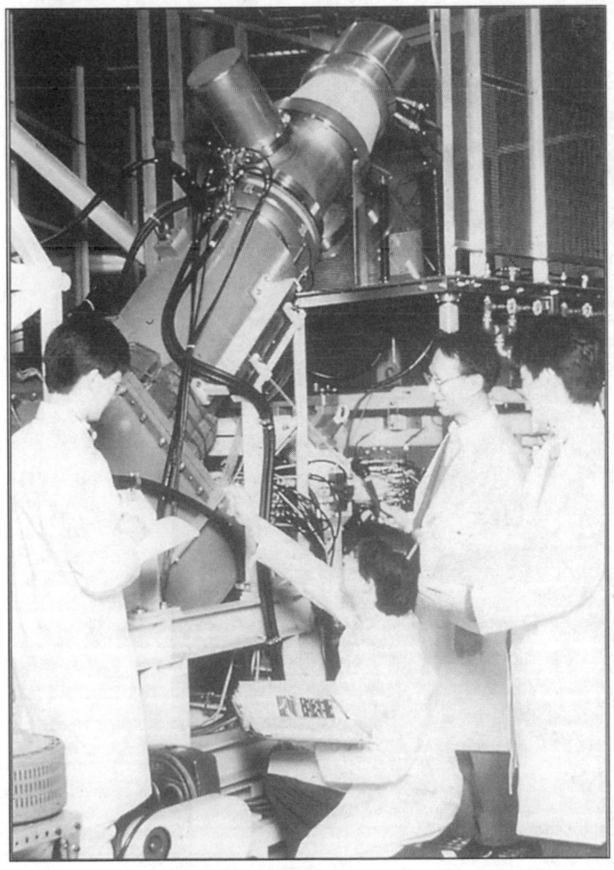

6. (A) (B) (C) (D)

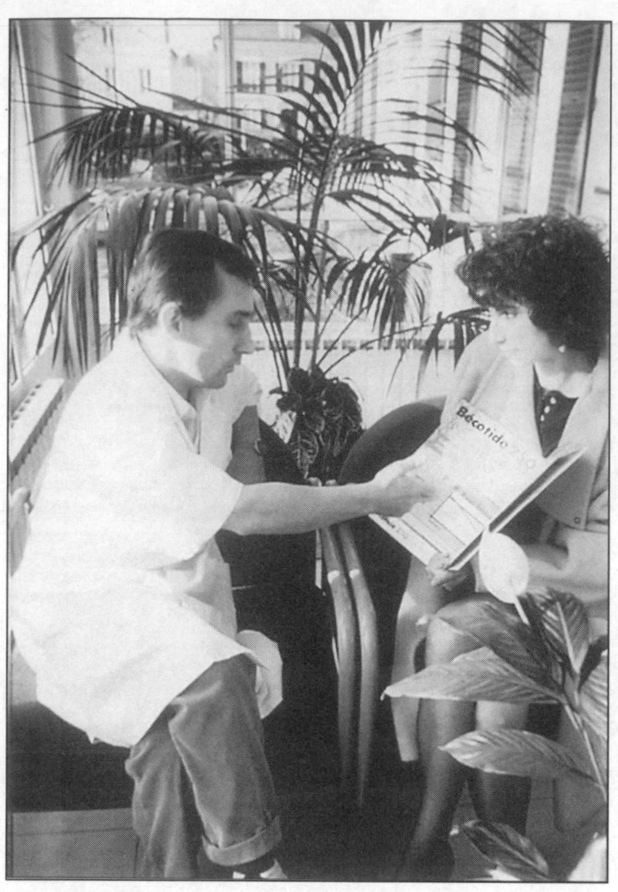

7. (A) (B) (C) (D)

8. (A) (B) (C) (D)

9. (A) (B) (C) (D)

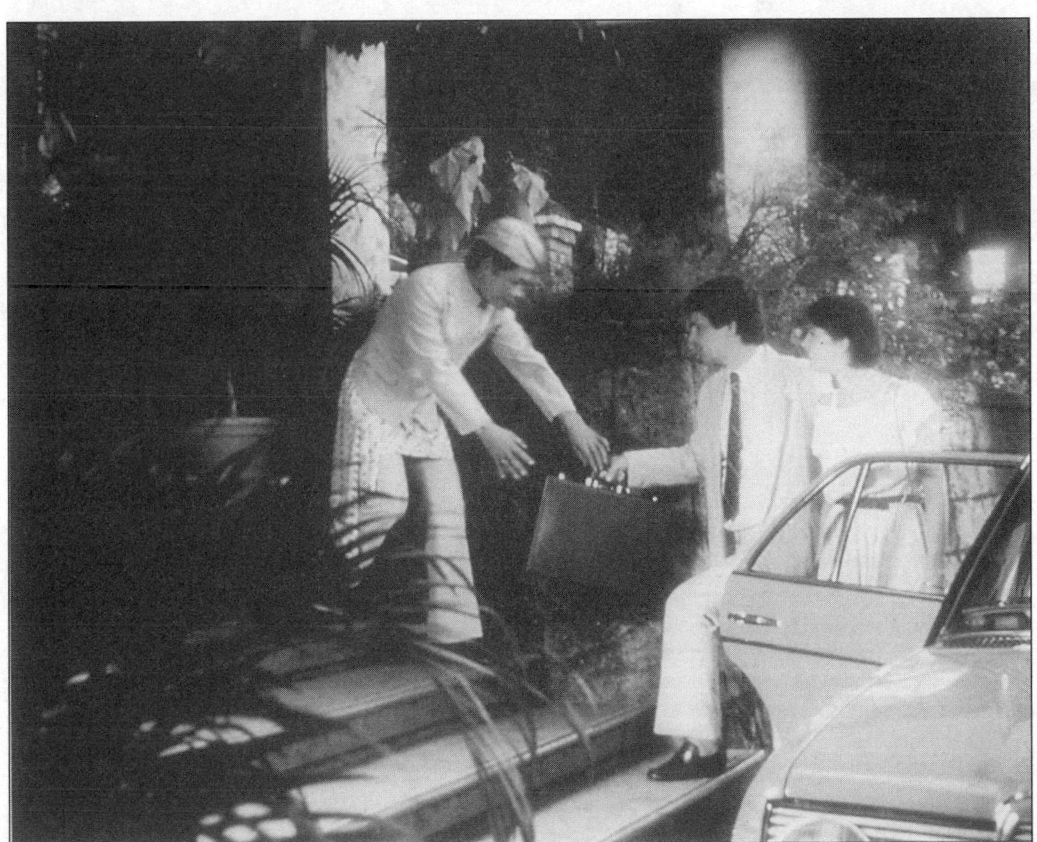

10. (A) (B) (C) (D)

Part 2

You will hear a question or statement and three responses. You will hear them only once, and they are not printed in your test book. Mark the letter of the best response on your answer sheet.

Example

<u>You will hear</u>: Where is the conference room?

<u>You will also hear</u>: (A) To meet the new manager.
(B) It's the second room on the left.
(C) Yes, at four o'clock.

The best response to the question *Where is the conference room?* is choice (B), *It's the second room on the left*, so (B) is the correct answer. You should mark (B) on your answer sheet.

11. Mark your answer on your answer sheet.
12. Mark your answer on your answer sheet.
13. Mark your answer on your answer sheet.
14. Mark your answer on your answer sheet.
15. Mark your answer on your answer sheet.
16. Mark your answer on your answer sheet.
17. Mark your answer on your answer sheet.
18. Mark your answer on your answer sheet.
19. Mark your answer on your answer sheet.
20. Mark your answer on your answer sheet.
21. Mark your answer on your answer sheet.
22. Mark your answer on your answer sheet.
23. Mark your answer on your answer sheet.
24. Mark your answer on your answer sheet.
25. Mark your answer on your answer sheet.
26. Mark your answer on your answer sheet.
27. Mark your answer on your answer sheet.
28. Mark your answer on your answer sheet.
29. Mark your answer on your answer sheet.
30. Mark your answer on your answer sheet.
31. Mark your answer on your answer sheet.
32. Mark your answer on your answer sheet.
33. Mark your answer on your answer sheet.
34. Mark your answer on your answer sheet.
35. Mark your answer on your answer sheet.
36. Mark your answer on your answer sheet.
37. Mark your answer on your answer sheet.
38. Mark your answer on your answer sheet.
39. Mark your answer on your answer sheet.
40. Mark your answer on your answer sheet.

Part 3

You will hear conversations between two people. You will answer three questions about each conversation. Mark the letter of the best answer on your answer sheet. You will hear the conversations only once, and they are not printed in your test book.

41. What will the man do for the woman?
(A) Take notes.
(B) Copy his notes.
(C) Go to the meeting.
(D) Help her search.

42. When was the meeting?
(A) Today.
(B) On Tuesday.
(C) Two days ago.
(D) Yesterday afternoon.

43. What will the woman do next Monday?
(A) Give a presentation.
(B) Do some reading.
(C) Take notes at a meeting.
(D) Get notes from the man.

---

44. When did the air conditioner break again?
(A) Last week.
(B) Yesterday.
(C) This morning.
(D) This afternoon.

45. What does the woman think they should do?
(A) Open windows.
(B) Fix the old air conditioner.
(C) Get a new air conditioner.
(D) Turn on some fans.

46. What will the man do?
(A) Concentrate harder.
(B) Turn down the air conditioner.
(C) Order a new air conditioner.
(D) Speak to the manager.

---

47. Where is the woman going?
(A) To the park.
(B) To the police station.
(C) To the courthouse.
(D) To work.

48. How will she get there?
(A) By walking.
(B) By car.
(C) By train.
(D) By bike.

49. How long will it take her to get there?
(A) Four minutes.
(B) Six minutes.
(C) Eight minutes.
(D) Ten minutes.

---

50. What is the problem with the paper?
(A) It should be in rolls.
(B) It is covered with jam.
(C) It is too thin.
(D) It is too thick.

51. When does the man need the copies finished?
(A) By 2:00.
(B) By 3:00.
(C) By 8:00.
(D) By 10:00.

52. What will the woman do?
(A) Staple the copies.
(B) Buy thicker paper.
(C) Plan a new program with the man.
(D) Show the man how to use the machine.

GO ON TO THE NEXT PAGE

53. How does the man feel?
(A) Sad.
(B) Angry.
(C) Happy.
(D) Relaxed.

54. What does the woman say about the jacket?
(A) It was very expensive.
(B) It is good for the rain.
(C) The cleaners can't fix it.
(D) The stain will come out.

55. How much did the man pay for the jacket?
(A) About $200.
(B) About $400.
(C) About $500.
(D) About $900.

---

56. What kind of trip is the man planning?
(A) Bike.
(B) School.
(C) Camping.
(D) Business.

57. Why does the woman say he should cancel the trip?
(A) Because the weather is bad.
(B) Because it will be too long.
(C) Because he'll be away overnight.
(D) Because he didn't invite her.

58. When will the man decide about canceling the trip?
(A) Before 8:00.
(B) Tonight.
(C) Tomorrow.
(D) On the weekend.

---

59. Where does this conversation take place?
(A) At home.
(B) At a picnic.
(C) On an airplane.
(D) At a restaurant.

60. What is the problem?
(A) The fork is dirty.
(B) The food isn't good.
(C) There isn't any silverware.
(D) Everything is out of order.

61. What does the man want to eat?
(A) Steak.
(B) Chicken.
(C) Fish.
(D) Ice cream.

---

62. Who is the woman planning to see?
(A) A dentist.
(B) A painter.
(C) A horse trainer.
(D) A hairdresser.

63. How often does she get an appointment?
(A) Every month.
(B) Twice a year.
(C) Six times a year.
(D) Every 16 months.

64. When is her next appointment?
(A) June 5th.
(B) June 6th.
(C) June 15th.
(D) June 16th.

---

65. What will they do for Mrs. Green?
(A) Send flowers.
(B) Give her a card.
(C) Order balloons.
(D) Call her.

66. Why will they do this?
(A) It's her birthday.
(B) She bought a new home.
(C) She had a baby.
(D) She had surgery.

67. When will they do this?
(A) At 4:00.
(B) At 10:00.
(C) This evening.
(D) On Tuesday.

68. What is the man complaining about?
(A) A late train.
(B) The rain.
(C) The dirty stations.
(D) His work.

69. What does the man think that tourists should do?
(A) Drive into town.
(B) Avoid rush hour.
(C) Stop visiting the city.
(D) Take the bus.

70. What time does the woman say they'll be home?
(A) Before 7:00.
(B) Just after 7:00.
(C) Before 11:00.
(D) At 11:00.

GO ON TO THE NEXT PAGE

Part 4

You will hear talks given by one speaker. You will answer three questions about each talk. Mark the letter of the best answer on your answer sheet. You will hear the talks only once, and they are not printed in your test book.

71. What is different about this sidewalk?
    (A) It is well built.
    (B) It moves.
    (C) It is indoors.
    (D) It is crowded.

72. Where would this sidewalk most likely be found?
    (A) At a store.
    (B) In front of a building.
    (C) At a shopping mall.
    (D) In an airport.

73. What are sidewalk users asked NOT to do?
    (A) Run.
    (B) Do exercises.
    (C) Hold the handrails.
    (D) Stand to the right.

---

74. When can members of the audience ask questions?
    (A) When the moderator says so.
    (B) After each speech is given.
    (C) When all speakers have finished.
    (D) After they submit written questions.

75. Where should they ask the questions?
    (A) From the speaker's platform.
    (B) From the center of the room.
    (C) From where they are sitting.
    (D) At the microphone.

76. How much time will be left for questions?
    (A) 15 minutes.
    (B) 30 minutes.
    (C) 45 minutes.
    (D) 60 minutes.

---

77. What is being advertised?
    (A) Dishes.
    (B) Forks.
    (C) Glasses.
    (D) Bowls.

78. What can people NOT do with these products?
    (A) Cook in them.
    (B) Serve in them.
    (C) Freeze food in them.
    (D) Refrigerate food in them.

79. How can people buy these products?
    (A) On line.
    (B) At a store.
    (C) From a catalog.
    (D) Over the telephone.

---

80. Why is this road important?
    (A) It doesn't need repairs.
    (B) It has nice scenery.
    (C) It leads into the city.
    (D) It goes to the business district.

81. How long will the construction take?
    (A) 24 hours.
    (B) A week.
    (C) A month.
    (D) A year.

82. What should drivers do to get into the business district?
    (A) Find another route.
    (B) Use the subway.
    (C) Ride with a friend.
    (D) Take the bus.

83. How is Madison House different from other houses on the tour?
(A) It is newer and larger.
(B) It is older and smaller.
(C) It is more expensive.
(D) It is more beautiful.

84. Why does Madison House have historical importance?
(A) A famous crime took place there.
(B) Famous people lived there.
(C) It is the oldest house in town.
(D) It shows the best design of its time.

85. What feature in particular is pointed out?
(A) Interesting gardens.
(B) Beautiful rugs.
(C) Carved ceilings.
(D) Spacious rooms.

---

86. What can people look forward to this weekend?
(A) A long holiday.
(B) Good weather.
(C) A city celebration.
(D) Time at the beach.

87. When will it get colder?
(A) At night.
(B) In the winter.
(C) In November.
(D) Next spring.

88. What does the speaker suggest that people carry?
(A) A hat.
(B) A scarf.
(C) A light.
(D) A jacket.

---

89. Where is this announcement probably heard?
(A) In a cafeteria.
(B) At an office.
(C) On a train.
(D) In a restaurant.

90. What is the announcement about?
(A) Ticket sales.
(B) Observation windows.
(C) Station stops.
(D) Seatings for dinner.

91. How many seatings are held?
(A) None.
(B) One.
(C) Two.
(D) Three.

---

92. What does this presentation discuss?
(A) Retailers' plans.
(B) Results of a survey.
(C) Technological advances.
(D) Salesclerk training.

93. What is the focus of the advertisements of most electronics stores?
(A) Efficiency.
(B) Quality.
(C) Convenience.
(D) Price.

94. What is more important to consumers than price?
(A) Repair service.
(B) Politeness.
(C) Store location.
(D) Type of advertisement.

GO ON TO THE NEXT PAGE

95. What will tour participants do at the museum?
(A) Take photographs.
(B) Look at buildings.
(C) Have lunch.
(D) Spend money.

96. What will they do right after visiting the museum?
(A) Eat pastries.
(B) Look at gardens.
(C) Visit a park.
(D) Go shopping.

97. What time will the tour end?
(A) 7:00.
(B) 9:00.
(C) 10:00.
(D) 11:00.

98. What day is the store closed?
(A) Sunday.
(B) Monday.
(C) Tuesday.
(D) Wednesday.

99. What will you hear when you press 2?
(A) Store hours.
(B) A list of events.
(C) Directions to the store.
(D) Instructions for ordering books.

100. How can you find book reviews?
(A) Visit the café.
(B) Press 1.
(C) Speak to a customer service specialist.
(D) Go to the website.

This is the end of the Listening Comprehension section of the test. Turn to Part 5 in your test book.

Reading Test

In the Reading test, you will read a variety of texts and answer several different types of reading comprehension questions. The entire Reading test lasts 75 minutes, and there are four parts. The directions are given for each part. Try to answer as many questions as possible in the time allowed. You must mark your answers on the separate answer sheet. Do not write your answers in the test book.

Part 5

A word or phrase is missing in each sentence. Mark the letter of the best answer on your answer sheet.

101. The housekeeping department needs to give ______ uniform to any new employee.
(A) an
(B) a
(C) the
(D) some

102. The director ______ for his vacation and will not return until next week.
(A) leaving
(B) had left
(C) has left
(D) will have left

103. The ______ document describes the new regulations.
(A) enclosed
(B) enclose
(C) enclosing
(D) to enclose

104. The receptionist refused to ______ the package.
(A) except
(B) exception
(C) affect
(D) accept

105. The man ______ hat blew off in the wind chased it across the park.
(A) his
(B) whose
(C) who
(D) that

106. The solution they suggested requires ______ the entire department.
(A) reorganization
(B) reorganize
(C) to reorganize
(D) rcorganizing

107. Ms. Sirichanya ______ the package when she discovered the address was wrong.
(A) had mailed
(B) has mailed
(C) will mail
(D) would mail

108. The captain's solutions are usually quite ______.
(A) sensitive
(B) sense
(C) sensible
(D) senses

GO ON TO THE NEXT PAGE

109. The convention is being held _______ the Greenwood Conference Center.
(A) on
(B) in
(C) of
(D) at

110. If Mr. Hu does not arrive soon, we _______ without him.
(A) left
(B) is leaving
(C) will leave
(D) had left

111. People in urban areas _______ credit cards for major purchases.
(A) uses
(B) use
(C) to use
(D) using

112. Ms. Quistorf felt hungry, _______ there was nothing at the snack bar she wanted to eat.
(A) for
(B) or
(C) nor
(D) but

113. The chef greets each of his cooks _______.
(A) every day
(B) always
(C) rarely
(D) never

114. She is a good manager _______ biggest asset is her ability to organize a project.
(A) who
(B) her
(C) whose
(D) it

115. The driver decided to take a detour _______ there was an accident on the highway.
(A) whether
(B) because
(C) although
(D) where

116. The research division announced it has made _______ toward an effective vaccine.
(A) progress
(B) a progress
(C) the progress
(D) one progress

117. Trying to cut costs by 8 percent may be _______ task the team has faced yet.
(A) a hard
(B) as hard as
(C) the hardest
(D) harder than

118. Ms. Rios is interested in learning about the company and _______ her business skills.
(A) to improve
(B) improving
(C) improve
(D) improved

119. The engineer _______ can devise a way to overcome this problem will receive a bonus.
(A) he
(B) she
(C) who
(D) whom

120. The _______ statement shocked the board members.
(A) surprising
(B) surprised
(C) surprises
(D) had surprised

121. Television advertising costs _______ print advertising.
(A) most than
(B) as much
(C) more as
(D) more than

122. Consumers' desire for low-fat foods _______ the current health trend in the food industry.
(A) influence
(B) has influenced
(C) had influenced
(D) is influenced

123. The new design failed because it was not _______ the original one.
(A) as convenient as
(B) more convenient
(C) convenient than
(D) most convenient

124. Mr. Atari was getting ready to leave the hotel when he _______ a phone call.
(A) receives
(B) had received
(C) is receiving
(D) received

125. Unless the factory can increase _______, headquarters will consider closing it.
(A) produce
(B) producing
(C) production
(D) productive

126. Because traffic is heavy, I suggest _______ for the airport early.
(A) leaving
(B) to leave
(C) will leave
(D) am going to leave

127. Mr. Kam _______ night classes for the past three months.
(A) is attending
(B) has been attending
(C) will attend
(D) had attended

128. Limited space forced the writer _______ his article shorter.
(A) making
(B) make
(C) makes
(D) to make

129. The manager will have a meeting _______ the client this afternoon to discuss the problem.
(A) for
(B) to
(C) with
(D) as

130. The scientist will postpone the test if he _______ any problems.
(A) anticipates
(B) anticipated
(C) will anticipate
(D) has anticipated

131. The board _______ about the merger by the time the new president takes over.
(A) decides
(B) decided
(C) has decided
(D) will have decided

132. Bags checked by a passenger _______ sent to security.
(A) is
(B) are
(C) was
(D) am

133. Ms. Ni always arrives early _______ her long commute.
(A) because of
(B) because
(C) in spite of
(D) since

134. The copy machine was reduced to even _______ last week's sale price.
(A) less than
(B) more than
(C) as much as
(D) least as

135. The passengers were not allowed to board _______ the crew was cleaning the cabin.
(A) during
(B) while
(C) for
(D) whether

136. Ms. Kezmarsky is known not only for her intelligence _______ for her efficiency.
(A) but also
(B) also
(C) and
(D) so

GO ON TO THE NEXT PAGE

137. The hole in the side indicated that the crate had been _______ during shipment.
(A) hurt
(B) injured
(C) damaged
(D) wounded

138. I _______ her for help whenever my department is understaffed.
(A) ask
(B) asks
(C) asked
(D) had asked

139. Mr. Nakara added the figures quickly _______ accurately.
(A) and
(B) but
(C) or
(D) nor

140. _______ the chairman gets his exercise by walking to work.
(A) Rarely
(B) Each morning
(C) Never
(D) Always

Part 6

Read the texts that follow. A word or phrase is missing in some sentences. Mark the letter of the best answer on your answer sheet.

Questions 141–143 refer to the following letter.

23 Butterworth Avenue
Apt. 564
Chesterton, VT 05888

Dear Mr. Simms:

I am responding _______ your ad in last Sunday's Chesterton Times for a paralegal to work at your

141. (A) to
(B) at
(C) by
(D) for

law firm. I have just completed a paralegal certification course at Chester Community College and am now seeking my first job in the field. I have worked as an administrative _______ for the

142. (A) assist
(B) assisted
(C) assistant
(D) assistance

past six years. Two of those years were at a law office. I believe I have a lot to offer your firm. I am responsible, hardworking, and well organized. I am not afraid to work extra hours to get a job done.

I am enclosing my résumé and two letters of _______. Please don't hesitate to contact me if

143. (A) referee
(B) reference
(C) refurbish
(D) refreshment

you have any questions. I look forward to hearing from you.

Sincerely,

Lucy Ling

Lucy Ling

GO ON TO THE NEXT PAGE

Questions 144–146 refer to the following notice.

The Middletown Area Chamber of Commerce, the Small Business Assistance Office, and the Business Owners Association of Middletown ______ you to a Small Business

144. (A) invite
(B) invites
(C) is inviting
(D) has invited

Day next April 12 at the Hardwick Hotel in Middletown Center. Middletown Mayor Elizabeth Wilson will give the keynote address. She will talk about recent efforts made by the city to support the continued success of local small businesses. Local business leaders will lead a panel discussion on a ______ of small business issues, including health insurance

145. (A) vanity
(B) vacuity
(C) variety
(D) validity

choices, employee training programs,and finding an affordable space for your business in a climate of ______ rising rents. The event begins at 8:00 and runs until 3:30.

146. (A) rapid
(B) rapidity
(C) rabidly
(D) rapidly

Tickets are $45 for members of the Business Owners Association and $55 for non-members. The price includes a luncheon catered by the Hardwick Hotel. Call the Chamber of Commerce for reservations.

Questions 147–149 refer to the following article.

The Interstate Railroad has announced the inauguration of its new business class service. This is an effort to attract travelers who would normally take a plane for middle distance business trips. Business class travelers on Interstate will ride in luxury in special cars that have _______ seats than economy class cars. Each seat will be equipped with electrical

147. (A) comfortable
(B) more comfortable
(C) most comfortable
(D) the most comfortable

outlets for laptop computers. Coffee, tea, and bottled water _______ free of charge. In

148. (A) provide
(B) are providing
(C) will provide
(D) will be provided

addition to the comfort and services of its business class cars, Interstate is advertising the _______ of train travel, pointing out that train stations are usually conveniently situated

149. (A) ease
(B) easy
(C) easily
(D) easement

in downtown areas, while airports are not. Interstate plans to launch a large advertising campaign next month throughout the eastern region. Television and radio commercials as well as billboard ads are planned as part of the campaign.

GO ON TO THE NEXT PAGE

Questions 150–152 refer to the following e-mail.

To: Will Smith
From: Lee Chang
Subject: Singapore conference

Hi, Will.

I hear you'll be going to the conference in Singapore next month. I look forward to seeing you there. Do you know where you'll be staying? I have reservations at the Holton Hotel. I highly recommend it. I always stay there when I'm in Singapore. The downtown _______ is great; it's close to everything. The rooms aren't so big, but

150. (A) staff
(B) service
(C) quality
(D) location

they're quite comfortable. Anyhow, you probably won't be spending much time in your room. A group of us from our company will be hosting a party the last night of the conference. I hope you and your colleagues can come. I'm not sure where _______, but I can let you know when I see you at the conference.

151. (A) is
(B) will be
(C) it will be
(D) will it be

By the way, when do you plan to arrive? I'll get there the Wednesday before the conference because I want a little time for sightseeing. Maybe you _______ like to join me. Let me know.

152. (A) have
(B) must
(C) would
(D) should

Lee

Part 7

In this part you will read a variety of texts, such as magazine and newspaper articles, e-mail messages, letters, and advertisements. Several questions follow each text. Mark the letter of the best answer for each question on your answer sheet.

Questions 153–154 refer to the following instructions.

To open the child-resistant cap on this medicine bottle, match the arrow on the cap with the arrow on the bottle. Press down to release. Then twist cap to the right to open bottle.

153. What kind of cap is on the bottle?
   (A) Easy-open
   (B) Child-resistant
   (C) Waterproof
   (D) Metal cap

154. What does a person have to do before twisting the cap off?
   (A) Turn upside down.
   (B) Twist to the left.
   (C) Press downward.
   (D) Lift upward.

GO ON TO THE NEXT PAGE

Questions 155–157 refer to the following letter.

Davis & Reeves
16 Salisbury Road
Tsinshatsui Kowloon
Hong Kong, China
Tel: (852) 03 721 1121
Fax: (852) 03 739-4466

Dr. Li Han
Enviro-Chemicals, Inc.
7499 Hannam-dong
Yongsan-ku
Seoul, Korea

Dear Dr. Han:

We have received your registration for our annual conference. Information about hotels and transportation are found in the enclosed conference brochure.

If you need further assistance in arranging your trip, please call our conference coordinator in Hong Kong at (852) 03 721 1121.

We look forward to seeing you at the conference.

Sincerely,

Le Zhaolie

Conference Registration

155. What is the purpose of this letter?
(A) To get money for the conference
(B) To invite speakers to the conference
(C) To acknowledge conference registration
(D) To make travel arrangements

156. What is enclosed with the letter?
(A) A registration form
(B) A brochure about the conference
(C) Tickets for the conference
(D) An invitation to the conference

157. Who should Dr. Han contact if she has other questions?
(A) The conference coordinator
(B) Le Zhaolie
(C) Davis & Reeves
(D) A ticket agent

Questions 158–160 refer to the following notice.

> **NOTICE:**
>
> To make your shopping at Harold's as easy as possible, you are invited to use our concierge services at the Concierge Desk. The Concierge Desk is located on the main level, beside the Gourmet Food Shop. We offer a range of shopper services, including public transportation schedules, direct lines to taxi services, and package mailing. We also have a complete database of merchandise in our stores, so that we can direct you to the store that will best suit your needs. You may visit the Concierge Desk in person, or you may call from the direct-line telephone at any of the lighted directory maps in the mall.

158. What does the Concierge Desk provide?
(A) Directions to tourist attractions
(B) Advice on fashion
(C) Information for the hotel guest
(D) Services for the shopper

159. Where is the Concierge Desk located?
(A) In a hotel
(B) By the Gourmet Food Shop
(C) At the tourist bureau
(D) In an airport

160. What is one way to get in touch with the Concierge Desk?
(A) Stop one of their representatives
(B) Page them from a store
(C) Write a letter
(D) Use the direct phone

GO ON TO THE NEXT PAGE

Questions 161–164 refer to the following article.

YEARS AGO WHEN THE PERSONAL computer hit the business world, experts predicted the advent of the paperless office. But time has proved them wrong. Offices have more paper than ever. People can easily print out a personal copy of a document for anyone who needs to see it. Programs such as spelling and grammar checkers, as well as improved computer graphics, have led people to expect perfection in their documents, and to keep printing copies until they get it. The simple truth is that most people simply prefer paper. Scientific studies have shown that paper copies are easier for people to read and to edit than text on a screen. And many people are still nervous about documents being accidentally deleted from a computer—if not through their own fault, through a computer system failure or a power outage. In short, although office paper may be significantly reduced, the paperless office is unlikely to become a reality.

161. The word "advent" in line 2 is closest in meaning to
(A) success
(B) failure
(C) arrival
(D) popularity

162. When was the paperless office first predicted?
(A) When office computers became common
(B) When people realized the need to recycle
(C) When paper became too expensive
(D) When printers failed to work as advertised

163. How have computer programs generated more paper?
(A) They use lots of paper.
(B) They print multiple copies.
(C) They make documents easy to prepare.
(D) They connect easily to printers.

164. Why will offices probably always use paper?
(A) Paper can be signed.
(B) Paper is traditional.
(C) Paper is easier to mail.
(D) Many people prefer paper.

Questions 165–167 refer to the following graph.

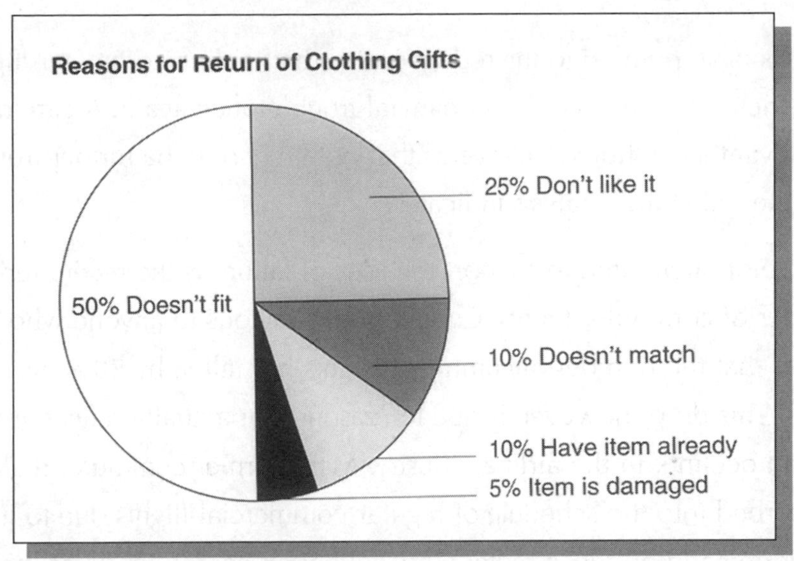

165. Why are most clothing gifts returned?
(A) They do not match other clothes.
(B) They are too expensive.
(C) They do not fit.
(D) They are ugly.

166. What percentage of people do NOT like the gift they received?
(A) 15%
(B) 20%
(C) 25%
(D) 50%

167. What is the least common reason for clothing to be returned?
(A) It is not expensive enough.
(B) There is something wrong with it.
(C) The quality is poor.
(D) It did not arrive on time.

GO ON TO THE NEXT PAGE

Questions 168–172 refer to the following article.

Economists have pointed to the reduction in small airline commuter flights as a sign that the airline industry is in financial trouble once again. A careful review of the relevant facts, however, reveals that nothing could be further from the truth, as the following analysis indicates.

The first point often cited to support the idea of failure is the recent reduction in the number of commuter flights. Certainly it is obvious to anyone who looks at the figures that the number of commuter flights has fallen by 20% over the past five years. This drop, however, is due to reasons that actually reflect growth, rather than decline, in the airline industry. Many former commuter flights have been absorbed into the schedule of regular commercial flights due to increased passenger demand on those routes. Thus, although commuter flights have decreased, non-commuter flights have increased, reflecting an overall increase in passengers.

Second, some former commuter routes were designated as such only because the smaller airports at the destination could not accommodate larger planes. But many growing cities have improved and expanded their airport facilities in recent years to encourage business and tourism in their regions. These physical improvements to the airports have eliminated the need for all flights in these areas to be made in small commuter planes. It is questionable whether such flights should ever have been described as commuter flights, since in these cases the label applied to airport restriction, rather than flight distance or passenger demand.

Finally, increased numbers of passengers for short flights have made flying larger planes more economical for the airlines, which means that due to plane size alone these flights are no longer officially considered commuters. Thus, the commuter flight is alive and well, and bigger than it has ever been before.

168. Why do some economists think the airline industry may be in trouble?
(A) Commuter flights have decreased.
(B) The number of passengers is down.
(C) The rate of complaints is higher.
(D) Many pilots have resigned.

169. Why has the number of commuter flights fallen recently?
(A) Fewer people want to fly them.
(B) They have been merged with regular flights.
(C) Commuter planes are not safe.
(D) There are not enough planes.

170. How have improvements at airports influenced commuter flights?
(A) They have made passengers more comfortable.
(B) They can handle many more flights.
(C) There are now more airports.
(D) They can accommodate larger planes.

171. Why are airlines flying larger planes on these routes?
(A) It is more economical.
(B) It is easier.
(C) It is safer.
(D) It is faster.

172. What does this say about commuter flights?
(A) They have increased.
(B) They have changed.
(C) They are more expensive.
(D) They are quicker.

Questions 173–176 refer to the following article.

People's concern about keeping their diets healthy has reached a peak in recent years. Everyone is trying to eat foods that are low in fat and high in fiber. They watch their intake of salt, sugar, and calories. They shun food additives and shop for organic fruits and vegetables. It should not be surprising, then, that these health concerns have now been extended to the diets of their pets. In the past, owners simply gave their pets leftover food from family meals or bought whatever dog food was on sale. Now, these choices are considered to be lacking in necessary nutrients for proper animal growth and development. The emphasis has shifted to health and nutritional value.

Gourmet stores that have traditionally sold rare and imported foods are beginning to sell gourmet dog and cat foods alongside their "people" food. Specialty pet shops are opening, offering foods with healthier ingredients such as rice and lamb, even though such ingredients are not traditionally considered suitable for pets. There are even specific lines of food for pets with special needs. Some lines are based on the age of the pet. These include high-energy varieties for puppies or kittens, vitamin-enriched styles for adult animals, and low-calorie and high-fiber food for elderly animals.

Other lines of pet food are designed in consideration of the health problems of the animals (or health concerns of their owners). Brands may be salt-free to combat high blood pressure, additive-free to fight allergies, and fat-free to prevent excessive weight gain. There are even animal drinks for pets in special circumstances. For example, drinks containing electrolytes, which help the body maintain a proper balance of fluids, can be helpful for animals that live in hot, dry climates where dehydration is a potential problem. All of these new pet foods claim to be recommended by veterinarians and scientifically developed to address the nutrition and health needs of that special pet.

173. What did people feed their pets in the past?
(A) Organic food
(B) Low-fat diets
(C) Leftovers
(D) Special drinks

174. Where can pet owners find special new pet foods?
(A) Cookbooks
(B) Gourmet food stores
(C) Grocery stores
(D) Catalogs

175. Why are the new foods supposed to be better?
(A) They are healthier.
(B) They taste better.
(C) Pets like them better.
(D) Owners have confidence in them.

176. What special line of food is NOT mentioned?
(A) Salt-free
(B) Puppy food
(C) Additive-free
(D) Vegetarian

Questions 177–180 refer to the following article.

Almost every office is looking for additional space. One easy way to get it is to use moveable partitions instead of, or in conjunction with, the solid interior walls of your existing office space. These walls provide several important benefits. First, they let you take maximum advantage of existing space. No more conflicts where one office is just a little too small and another is just a little too big—just move the partition over a foot to adjust the space for everyone. Second, you can change the positions of the partitions as your business needs change. If one project ends and another begins, you can easily change the office space to accommodate project needs. Finally, new materials make these walls both sound-absorbent and lightweight, so they provide the privacy of built-in walls with the advantages of flexible space.

177. The word "interior" in line 3 is closest in meaning to
   (A) less good
   (B) inside
   (C) more expensive
   (D) permanent

178. Why do partitions create space?
   (A) They are cheaper than real walls.
   (B) They are narrower than real walls.
   (C) You can move them where you need them.
   (D) They have shelves on them.

179. Why are partitions a good choice for businesses with different projects?
   (A) They can be easily stored.
   (B) They make the office look different.
   (C) They help you organize information.
   (D) You can change the space for different projects.

180. How do the partitions provide privacy?
   (A) They absorb sound.
   (B) They reach the ceiling.
   (C) They do not have windows.
   (D) They do not have doors.

Questions 181–185 refer to the following schedule and e-mail.

Business Association of Hartland
Spring Conference
Hartland Hotel

8:00–9:00	Registration and coffee hour	Front Lobby
9:00–9:45	Keynote address	Main Hall
10:00–11:00	Workshop Session 1 (choose one):	
	Starting a Small Business	Room 3
	Marketing Strategies	Room 5
	Revitalize Your Web Page	Room 7
11:15–12:15	Workshop Session 2 (choose one)	
	Using the Internet to Grow Your Business	Room 5
	Accounting for Small Businesses	Room 7
	Options for Health Insurance	Room 9
12:30–1:00	Lunch	Fountain Room Restaurant
1:15–2:15	The Future of Small Businesses	Main Hall

To: Rick Hong
From: Louise Sibiu
Subject: Spring Conference

Hi Rick,

I'm looking forward to seeing you at the conference next week. Have you seen the schedule yet? I am really excited about the Marketing Strategies workshop. I hear that it will be given by Maxine King, so I definitely plan to attend that one. Why don't we get together at lunch? That seems the easiest thing to do. I'll meet you at the restaurant, and I promise to be on time. I'll be giving a presentation in Room 9 right before lunch. That's quite near the restaurant, so I shouldn't have any problem meeting you on time. To tell you the truth, I'm sorry they chose this restaurant for the conference lunch. It really isn't the best one around. There's another restaurant in the hotel, The Garden View, which has much better food. Oh, well. Are you planning to stay after lunch? I am. I think the 1:15 lecture will be good. See you soon.

Louise

181. Who would be most interested in attending this conference?
(A) An insurance agent
(B) A small business owner
(C) An Internet service provider
(D) An employee of a large corporation

182. Where will Louise be at 10:00?
(A) Room 3
(B) Room 5
(C) Room 7
(D) Room 9

183. What is the topic of Louise's presentation?
(A) Marketing strategies
(B) Web pages
(C) Accounting
(D) Health insurance

184. What time does Louise want to meet Rick?
(A) 12:15
(B) 12:30
(C) 1:00
(D) 1:15

185. What is Louise's opinion of The Fountain Room Restaurant?
(A) It's better than The Garden View Restaurant.
(B) It's the best restaurant in town.
(C) It's not very good.
(D) It's too far away.

GO ON TO THE NEXT PAGE

Questions 186–190 refer to the following advertisement and letter.

Marketing assistant sought to work in busy, fast-paced office. We are a cutting-edge fashion company seeking a creative, energetic person to work in our Marketing Department. Assist in the planning of marketing strategies, promotional events, and special advertising. Knowledge of fashion is a must. Degree in business or marketing and five years relevant work experience are required. We offer a competitive salary, health and life insurance, and paid vacation and sick days. Send résumé before September 30 to: Mija Kim, Human Resources Director, Box 45, Springdale, OH 40441.

September 22, 20 ___
10 Frontage Rd.
Parma, OH 40424

Mija Kim
Human Resources Director
Box 45
Springdale, OH 40441

Dear Ms. Kim:

I am interested in applying for the position of marketing assistant as advertised in yesterday's paper. I received a business degree from Clifton College five years ago. I have three years experience working in the Marketing Department at River Run Publishers, where I worked on developing marketing strategies and planning publicity events. I have a great interest in fashion and have taken several courses in fashion marketing as well as in fashion design. For this reason, I am currently seeking a position with a fashion company such as yours.

I am enclosing my résumé and a letter of reference from my supervisor at River Run. Thank you for your attention, and I look forward to hearing from you.

Sincerely,

Josefa Silva

Josefa Silva

186. Who would most likely qualify for this job?
(A) A fashion model
(B) A book publisher
(C) A fashion designer
(D) A marketing major

187. When did the advertisement appear in the newspaper?
(A) September 21
(B) September 22
(C) September 29
(D) September 30

188. What is Mija Kim's job?
(A) Marketing assistant
(B) Marketing director
(C) Human resources director
(D) Fashion designer

189. Where did Josefa Silva work before?
(A) At a college
(B) At a marketing firm
(C) At a fashion company
(D) At a publishing company

190. What is one requirement of the job that Ms. Silva does NOT meet?
(A) College degree
(B) Competitive spirit
(C) Knowledge of fashion
(D) Number of years of experience

Questions 191–195 refer to the following letter and form.

City Health and Fitness Center
Your health is our priority!
May 6, 20 ___

Jonathan Siebold
84 Rockingham Lane
Portland, MA 01972

Dear Mr. Siebold:

Thank you for your interest in the City Health and Fitness Center. As you may be aware, we are the largest fitness center in Portland, with two Olympic-size pools, three squash courts, one indoor tennis court, an exercise room with state-of-the-art exercise equipment, and an indoor running track. We also have a full schedule of swimming, tennis, and exercise classes, as well as personal trainers ready to assist you at your convenience. In addition, our club store provides you with all the equipment you need to participate in these sports at reasonable prices.

We have both six-month and one-year memberships available. Right now we have a special promotion. If we receive your membership application before May 25, you will receive a 15% discount off the regular fee of $500 for a one-year individual membership. A six-month membership is $300, and there is no special discount on that at this time. One-year members are entitled to their own locker, free of charge, but availability is limited. If you want a locker, you will need to call the membership office to find out if there are any lockers available at this time.

I am enclosing a membership application for your convenience. Please feel free to call me if you have any questions. Thank you.

Elvira Montague

Elvira Montague
Membership Director

City Health and Fitness Center
Your health is our priority!

Application for Membership

Name: *Jonathan Siebold* Date: *May 27, 20* ___

Address: *84 Rockingham Lane*

Portland, MA 01972

Occupation: *Accountant*

Membership type: _X_ individual __ family

__ six months _X_ one year

What classes are you interested in?

__ swimming _X_ tennis __ squash __ fitness training

Do you want a locker? _X_ yes __ no

Please enclose your check, made payable to CHFC.

191. What is one thing you cannot do at the City Health and Fitness Center?
(A) Have lunch
(B) Go running
(C) Learn to swim
(D) Buy a tennis racket

192. How much will Jonathan Siebold pay for his membership?
(A) $255
(B) $300
(C) $425
(D) $500

193. What class does Jonathan Siebold want to take?
(A) Swimming
(B) Tennis
(C) Squash
(D) Fitness Training

194. What is Jonathan Siebold's job?
(A) Fitness trainer
(B) Accountant
(C) Health club director
(D) Professional athlete

195. Why will Jonathan Siebold have to call the health club?
(A) To sign up for a class
(B) To request an application
(C) To find out about lockers
(D) To get the discount

GO ON TO THE NEXT PAGE

Questions 196–200 refer to the following two e-mails.

To: Tamara Burke
From: Jamal Watson
Subject: placing orders

I recently discovered your website and am very interested in ordering supplies from you for our office. Your products are stylish and environmentally friendly at the same time. That's a hard combination to find! Currently, I am interested in ordering the energy-saving desk lamps and the desktop organizers. In the near future I will also need some of the recycled photocopier paper and envelopes. While you have a detailed price list, your website did not have any information on volume discounts. I make frequent large orders of supplies such as paper and printer ink for my office, and I would like to order from your company if you offer volume discounts.

For right now, I would like to order five desk lamps and five desktop organizers. Please let me know the total cost, including shipping. Thank you for your help.

Jamal Watson

To: Jamal Watson
From: Tamara Burke
Subject: re: placing orders

Dear Mr. Watson:

Thank you for your interest in Office Things. We appreciate your business. In answer to your question, we do offer volume discounts on certain items. For example, photocopier paper is normally $5 a package. If you order a small box of paper (10 packages), the price is $40 a box. Large boxes (25 packages) are $75 each. Shipping is free on all orders over $200. For smaller orders, shipping costs 10% of the total price of the order. Unfortunately, we do not offer discounts on office furniture, such as the lamps and organizers you mentioned. As noted on our website, the lamps are $10 each, and the organizers are $8 each. You may also be interested in our line of desks and desk chairs since they are made out of 100% recycled materials. Visit our website for more information. Please let me know if you have any further questions.

Sincerely,

Tamara Burke

196. What is the information that Mr. Watson could not find on the website?
(A) Price list
(B) Discounts on large orders
(C) How to order paper and envelopes
(D) E-mail address of the sales department

197. If Mr. Watson orders three large boxes of paper, what will he pay for shipping?
(A) $0
(B) $7.50
(C) $12.00
(D) $22.50

198. What will he pay for his lamps and organizers, with shipping?
(A) $44
(B) $55
(C) $90
(D) $99

199. What is true about the desk lamps?
(A) They don't have a discount.
(B) They use a lot of electricity.
(C) They are made of recycled materials.
(D) They are cheaper than the organizers.

200. Why does Ms. Burke think Mr. Watson will like the desks and desk chairs?
(A) They are stylish.
(B) They have free shipping.
(C) They have a 10% discount.
(D) They are environmentally friendly.

This is the end of the test. If you finish early, you may check your work in Parts 5, 6, and 7.

Practice TOEIC® Speaking Test 1

Speaking

Questions 1–2: Read a text aloud

Directions: Read the text on the screen aloud. You will have 45 seconds to prepare and 45 seconds to read the text aloud.

Speaking

Question 1 of 11

Wonderland Mall is the largest shopping mall in the city, with over one hundred stores on three levels. Wonderland Mall is conveniently located near all major bus lines, and we offer free parking in our garage. Everything you need to buy is here—clothes, shoes, books, sports equipment, furniture, and much more. After shopping, you can enjoy a tasty snack, lunch, or dinner. We have seven restaurants and three cafés. Then, relax with a movie at our fifteen-screen movie theater. Wonderland Mall is a great place for the whole family.

Speaking

Question 2 of 11

Tourist agencies often offer sightseeing tours by bus. Many tourists, however, prefer to sightsee on foot. A walk through the streets of an unfamiliar city brings you closer to the people and activities around you. On foot, you can really hear the sounds, smell the smells, and see the sights of the city. If you see an interesting store, you can pay it a quick visit. You can stop at a café to try out some local dishes. Or you can take a shortcut through a pretty park. It's fun to take a sightseeing tour on foot.

Speaking

Question 3: Describe a photo

Directions: Describe the photo in as much detail as you can. You will have 30 seconds to prepare your response and 45 seconds to speak about the photo.

Speaking

Question 3 of 11

GO ON TO THE NEXT PAGE

Speaking

Questions 4–6: Respond to questions

Directions: You will answer three questions. Begin responding as soon as you hear the beep for each question. You will have 15 seconds to respond to Questions 4 and 5. You will have 30 seconds to respond to Question 6. You will have no additional preparation time.

Speaking

Question 4 of 11

Imagine that a marketing firm is doing research in your country. You have agreed to participate in a telephone interview about eating at restaurants.

Do you prefer to eat at home or at a restaurant?

Speaking

Question 5 of 11

Imagine that a marketing firm is doing research in your country. You have agreed to participate in a telephone interview about eating at restaurants.

What types of restaurants do you like?

Speaking

Question 6 of 11

Imagine that a marketing firm is doing research in your country. You have agreed to participate in a telephone interview about eating at restaurants.

Describe your favorite restaurant and say why you like it.

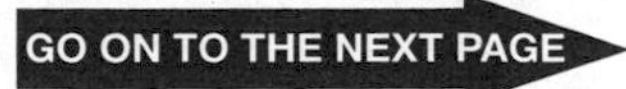

Speaking

Questions 7–9: Respond to questions using information provided

Directions: You will answer three questions based on information provided. You will have 30 seconds to read the information. You will have 15 seconds to respond to Questions 7 and 8. You will have 30 seconds to respond to Question 9. You will have no additional preparation time. Begin responding as soon as you hear the beep for each question.

Speaking

Question 7 of 11

Computer Training Center

Class	Days	Hours
Word Processing (beginning)	Monday and Wednesday	5:00–6:30 or 7:00–8:30
Web Design	Tuesday and Thursday	5:00–7:00
Using the Internet (for adults)	Saturday	9:00–12:00
Using the Internet (for children)	Saturday	10:30–12:00
Word Processing (advanced)	Saturday	1:00–4:00

Tuition: All classes are $250 for an eight-week session. Books and materials for each class cost $50.

Speaking

Question 8 of 11

Computer Training Center		
Class	**Days**	**Hours**
Word Processing (beginning)	Monday and Wednesday	5:00–6:30 or 7:00–8:30
Web Design	Tuesday and Thursday	5:00–7:00
Using the Internet (for adults)	Saturday	9:00–12:00
Using the Internet (for children)	Saturday	10:30–12:00
Word Processing (advanced)	Saturday	1:00–4:00

Tuition: All classes are $250 for an eight-week session. Books and materials for each class cost $50.

Speaking

Question 9 of 11

Computer Training Center		
Class	**Days**	**Hours**
Word Processing (beginning)	Monday and Wednesday	5:00–6:30 or 7:00–8:30
Web Design	Tuesday and Thursday	5:00–7:00
Using the Internet (for adults)	Saturday	9:00–12:00
Using the Internet (for children)	Saturday	10:30–12:00
Word Processing (advanced)	Saturday	1:00–4:00

Tuition: All classes are $250 for an eight-week session. Books and materials for each class cost $50.

GO ON TO THE NEXT PAGE

Speaking

Question 10: Propose a solution

Directions: You will be presented with a problem and asked to propose a solution. You will have 30 seconds to prepare and 60 seconds to speak.

Your response should

- show that you understand the problem
- propose a solution to the problem

Speaking

Question 10 of 11

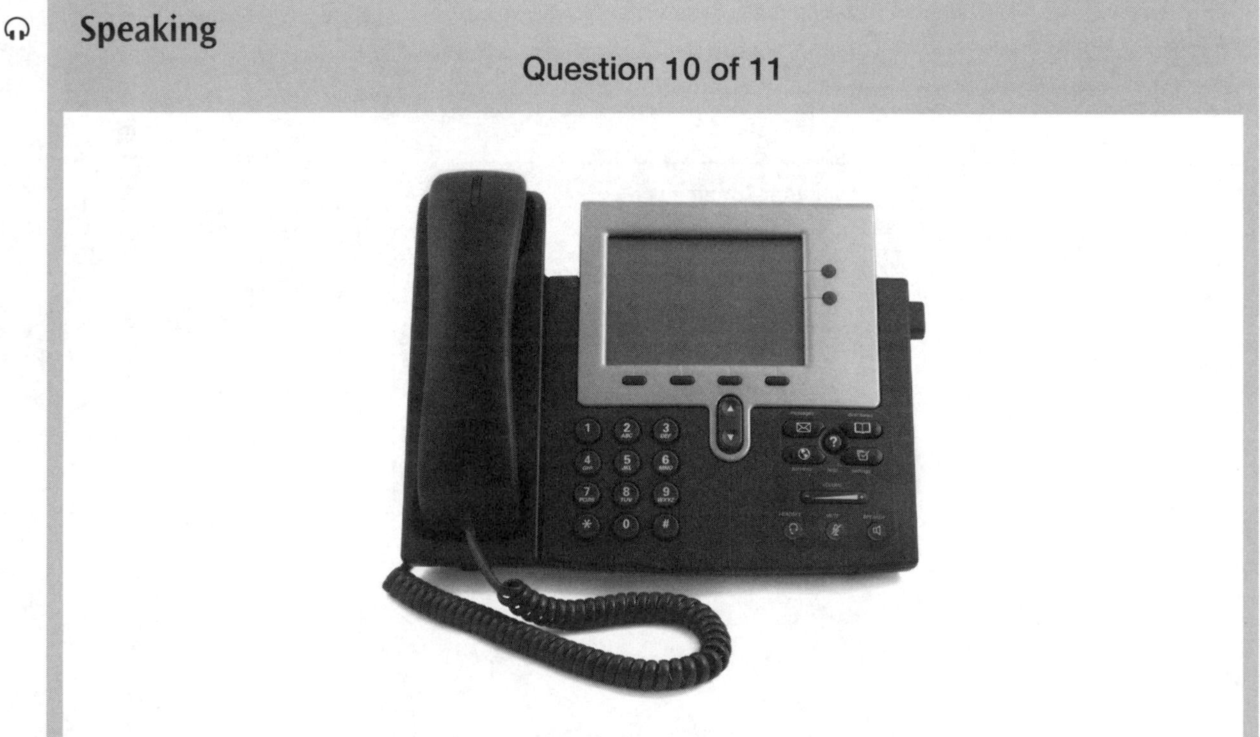

Speaking

Question 11: Express an opinion

Directions: You will give your opinion about a specific topic. Say as much as you can in the time allowed. You will have 15 seconds to prepare and 60 seconds to speak.

Speaking

Question 11 of 11

Many people prefer to live in a city, but other people believe that the countryside is a better place to live. What is your opinion about living in a city or the countryside? Give reasons for your opinion.

This is the end of the Speaking Test.

Practice TOEIC® Speaking Test 2

Speaking

Questions 1–2: Read a text aloud

Directions: Read the text on the screen aloud. You will have 45 seconds to prepare and 45 seconds to read the text aloud.

Speaking

Question 1 of 11

When looking for a place to live, most people think about convenience. If they are parents with children, they want to live near the best schools. They want to have public transportation or good roads available to them. They don't want to have to travel far for shopping and entertainment. People also enjoy living near a park or gym so that they have easy access to recreation. And, of course, for the majority of people the most important thing is to live in close proximity to their jobs.

Speaking

Question 2 of 11

Whether you're visiting the city for business or pleasure, High Towers Hotel is the place to stay. All our rooms are clean and spacious with comfortable beds and pleasant views of the city. We are conveniently located in the center of the city, near stores, museums, and offices. For the enjoyment of our guests, we have a swimming pool and exercise room. The hotel restaurant is one of the best in the city. Tourists and businesspeople alike choose the High Towers Hotel time after time.

Speaking

Question 3: Describe a photo

Directions: Describe the photo in as much detail as you can. You will have 30 seconds to prepare your response and 45 seconds to speak.

Speaking

Question 3 of 11

GO ON TO THE NEXT PAGE

Speaking

Questions 4–6: Respond to questions

Directions: You will answer three questions. Begin responding as soon as you hear the beep for each question. You will have 15 seconds to respond to Questions 4 and 5. You will have 30 seconds to respond to Question 6. You will have no additional preparation time.

Speaking

Question 4 of 11

Imagine that a marketing firm is doing research in your country. You have agreed to participate in a telephone interview about birthday celebrations.

Are birthday celebrations important in your country?

Speaking

Question 5 of 11

Imagine that a marketing firm is doing research in your country. You have agreed to participate in a telephone interview about birthday celebrations.

How do people in your country celebrate birthdays?

Speaking

Question 6 of 11

Imagine that a marketing firm is doing research in your country. You have agreed to participate in a telephone interview about birthday celebrations.

How do people in your country generally feel about getting older?

Speaking

Questions 7–9: Respond to questions using information provided

Directions: You will answer three questions based on information provided. You will have 30 seconds to read the information. You will have 15 seconds to respond to Questions 7 and 8. You will have 30 seconds to respond to Question 9. You will have no additional preparation time. Begin responding as soon as you hear the beep for each question.

Speaking

Question 7 of 11

Meeting Agenda
Thursday, May 15
Conference Room 1

9:15–9:45	Marketing Strategies (Martin Brown)
9:45–10:30	Sales Report, Part 1 (Martha Warren)
10:30–11:00	Sales Report, Part 2 (Robert Jones)
11:00–12:00	Product Development (Sally Simmons)
12:00–1:00	Lunch in the Board Room
1:00–3:00	Planning Discussion (everybody)
3:00–3:30	Video: *The Creation of a Company*
3:30–4:00	Coffee and snacks in the Board Room

Speaking

Question 8 of 11

Meeting Agenda
Thursday, May 15
Conference Room 1

Time	Item
9:15–9:45	Marketing Strategies (Martin Brown)
9:45–10:30	Sales Report, Part 1 (Martha Warren)
10:30–11:00	Sales Report, Part 2 (Robert Jones)
11:00–12:00	Product Development (Sally Simmons)
12:00–1:00	Lunch in the Board Room
1:00–3:00	Planning Discussion (everybody)
3:00–3:30	Video: *The Creation of a Company*
3:30–4:00	Coffee and snacks in the Board Room

Speaking

Question 9 of 11

Meeting Agenda
Thursday, May 15
Conference Room 1

Time	Item
9:15–9:45	Marketing Strategies (Martin Brown)
9:45–10:30	Sales Report, Part 1 (Martha Warren)
10:30–11:00	Sales Report, Part 2 (Robert Jones)
11:00–12:00	Product Development (Sally Simmons)
12:00–1:00	Lunch in the Board Room
1:00–3:00	Planning Discussion (everybody)
3:00–3:30	Video: *The Creation of a Company*
3:30–4:00	Coffee and snacks in the Board Room

Speaking

Question 10: Propose a solution

Directions: You will be presented with a problem and asked to propose a solution. You will have 30 seconds to prepare and 60 seconds to speak.

Your response should

- show that you understand the problem
- propose a solution to the problem

Speaking

Question 10 of 11

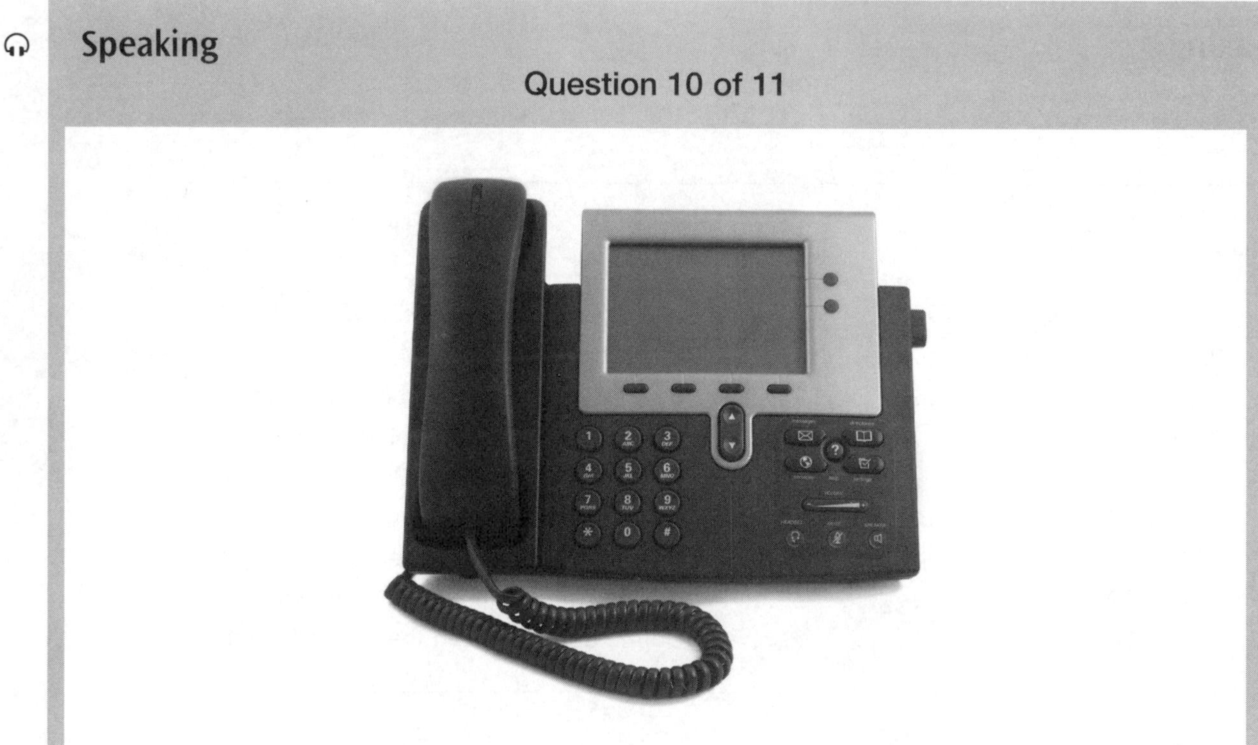

Speaking

Question 11: Express an opinion

Directions: You will give your opinion about a specific topic. Say as much as you can in the time allowed. You will have 15 seconds to prepare and 60 seconds to speak.

Speaking

Question 11 of 11

Some people prefer to take a job that pays a high salary even if they don't like the job. What is your opinion about accepting a job you don't like because it pays a high salary? Give reasons for your opinion.

This is the end of the Speaking Test.

Practice TOEIC® Writing Test 1

Writing

Questions 1–5: Write a sentence based on a photo

Directions: You will write ONE sentence based on each photo. Each photo has TWO words that you must use in your sentence. You can use the words in any order, and you can change the word forms.

Your sentence will be scored on

- appropriate use of grammar
- relevance of the sentence to the photo

You have 8 minutes to complete this part of the test.

Writing

Question 1 of 8

man / bicycle

GO ON TO THE NEXT PAGE

Writing

Question 2 of 8

food / very

Writing

Question 3 of 8

tickets / so

Writing

Question 4 of 8

while / lunch

____

Writing

Question 5 of 8

when / arrive

____

GO ON TO THE NEXT PAGE

Questions 6–7: Respond to a written request

Directions: You will write responses to two e-mails.

Your writing will be scored on

- quality and variety of sentences
- vocabulary
- organization

You have 10 minutes to read and answer each e-mail.

Writing

Question 6 of 8

Read the e-mail.

From: City Sports and Fitness Club
To: New Members
Subject: Welcome to the club

We are happy to have you as a new member of our club. We offer facilities for all kinds of sports and fitness activities, and we have classes for all ability levels. Please let us know if you have any questions.

Phyllis Rich
Manager

Writing

Directions: Respond to the e-mail as a new member of the sports and fitness club. In your e-mail, ask THREE questions.

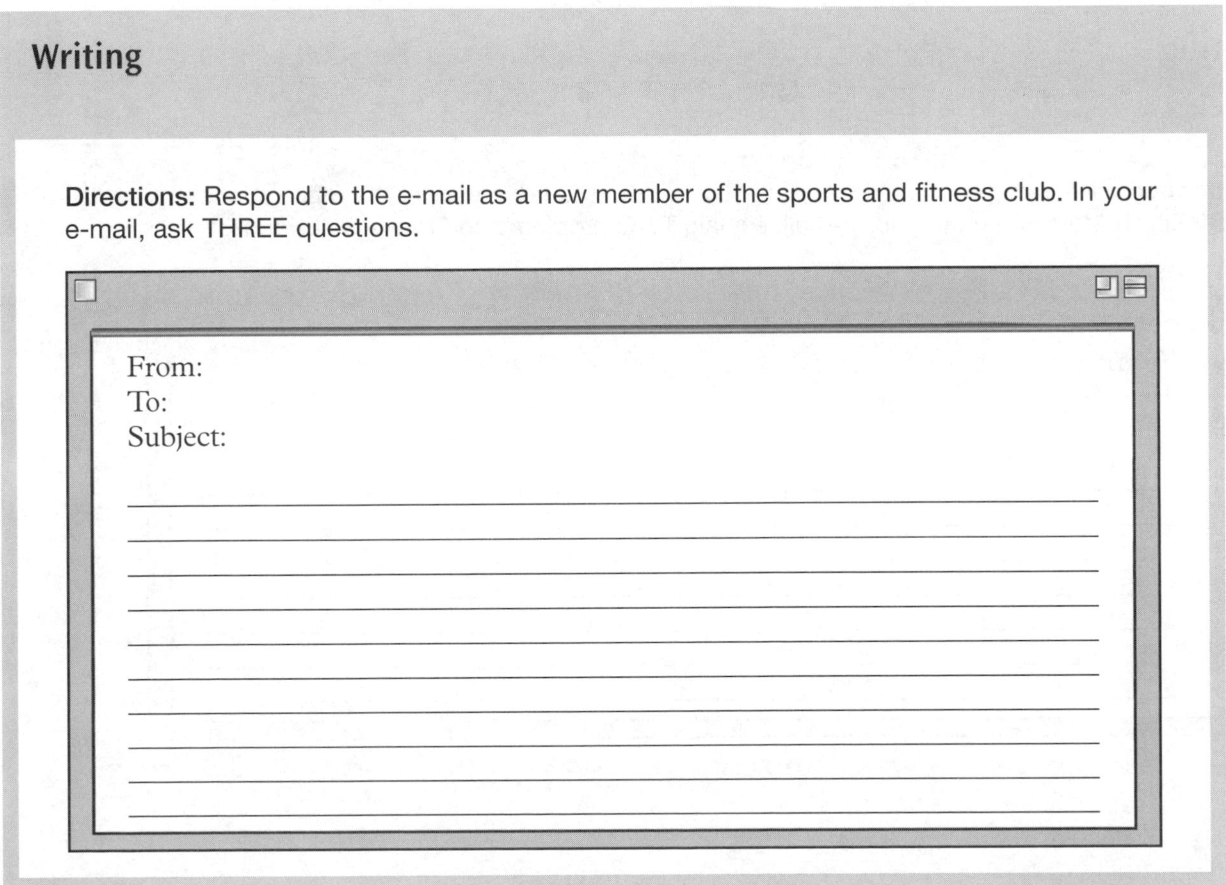

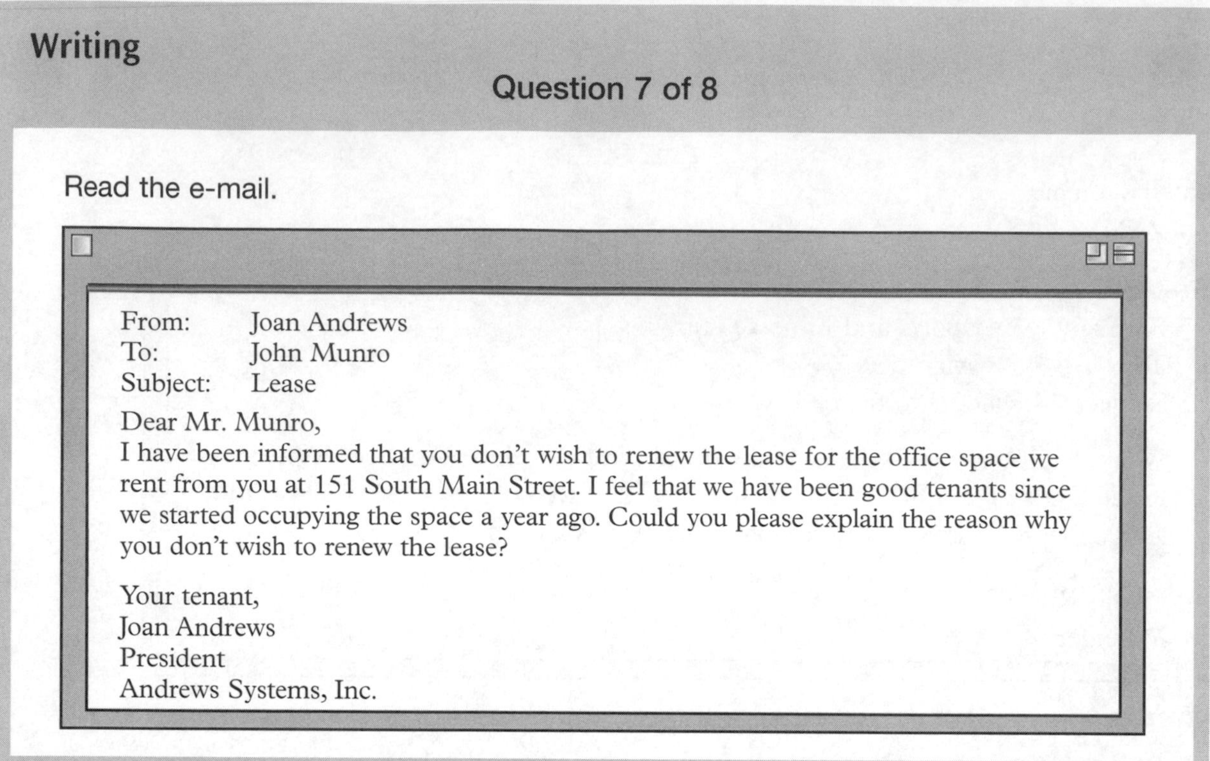

Writing

Question 7 of 8

Read the e-mail.

From: Joan Andrews
To: John Munro
Subject: Lease

Dear Mr. Munro,

I have been informed that you don't wish to renew the lease for the office space we rent from you at 151 South Main Street. I feel that we have been good tenants since we started occupying the space a year ago. Could you please explain the reason why you don't wish to renew the lease?

Your tenant,
Joan Andrews
President
Andrews Systems, Inc.

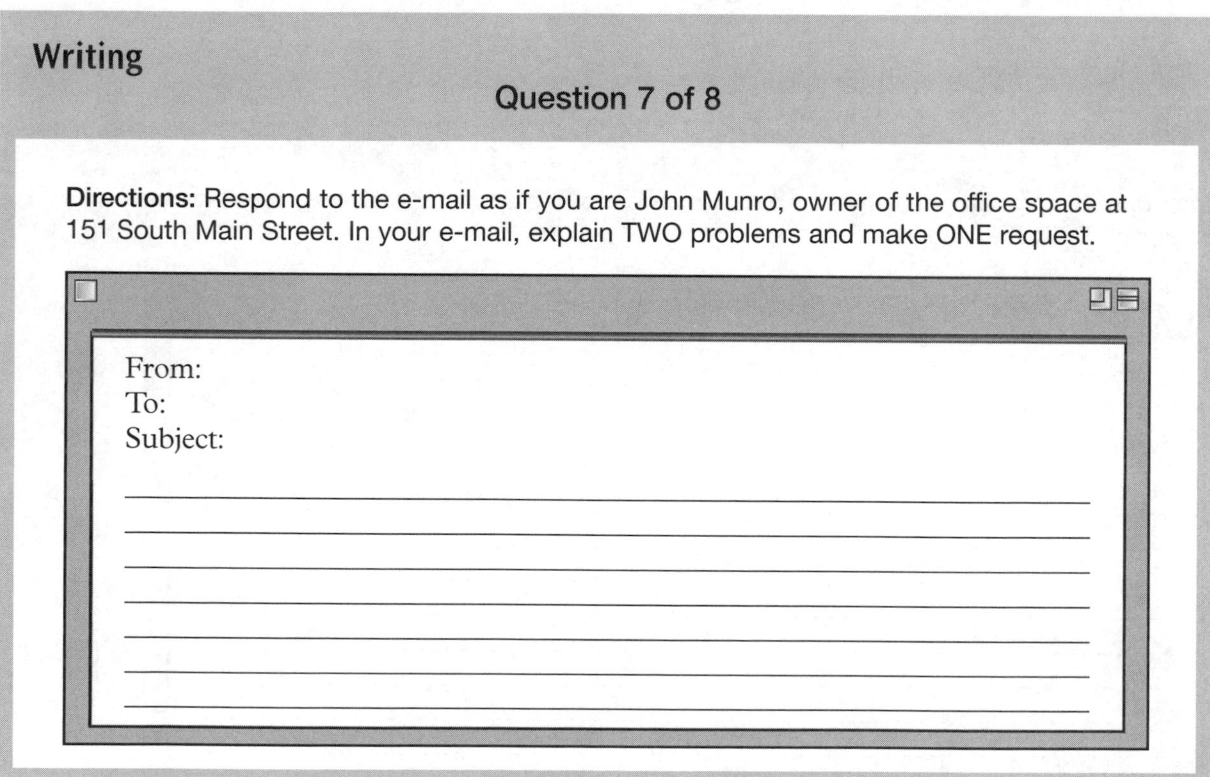

Writing

Question 7 of 8

Directions: Respond to the e-mail as if you are John Munro, owner of the office space at 151 South Main Street. In your e-mail, explain TWO problems and make ONE request.

From:
To:
Subject:

Writing

Question 8: Write an opinion essay

Directions: You will write an essay in response to a question about your opinion. Typically, an effective essay will have at least 300 words.

Your essay will be scored on

- whether you give reasons and/or examples to support your opinion
- grammar
- vocabulary
- organization

You have 30 minutes to plan, write, and revise your essay.

Writing

Question 8 of 8

Some people enjoy working alone. Others would rather work in a group. What is your preference? Explain why.

GO ON TO THE NEXT PAGE

Writing

Question 8 of 8 *(continued)*

This is the end of the Writing Test.

Practice TOEIC® Writing Test 2

Writing

Questions 1–5: Write a sentence based on a photo

Directions: You will write ONE sentence based on each photo. Each photo has TWO words that you must use in your sentence. You can use the words in any order, and you can change the word forms.

Your sentence will be scored on

- appropriate use of grammar
- relevance of the sentence to the photo

You will have 8 minutes to complete this part of the test.

Writing

Question 1 of 8

woman / open

GO ON TO THE NEXT PAGE

Writing

Question 2 of 8

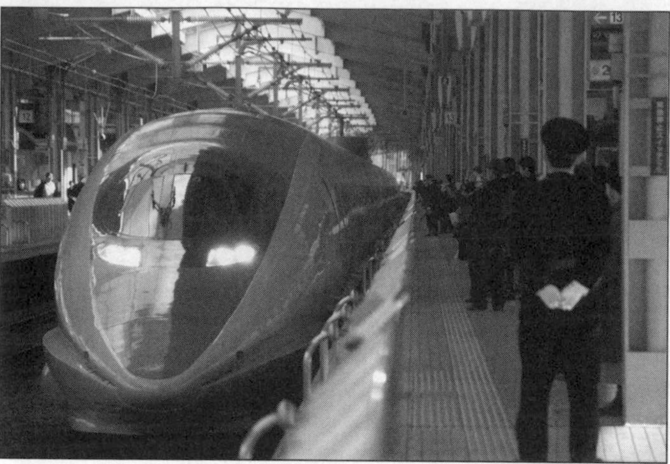

a lot of / station

Writing

Question 3 of 8

umbrellas / because

Writing

Question 4 of 8

so / heavy

Writing

Question 5 of 8

pour / so that

Writing

Questions 6–7: Respond to a written request

Directions: You will write responses to two e-mails.

Your writing will be scored on

- quality and variety of sentences
- vocabulary
- organization

You have 10 minutes to read and answer each e-mail.

Writing

Question 6 of 8

Read the e-mail.

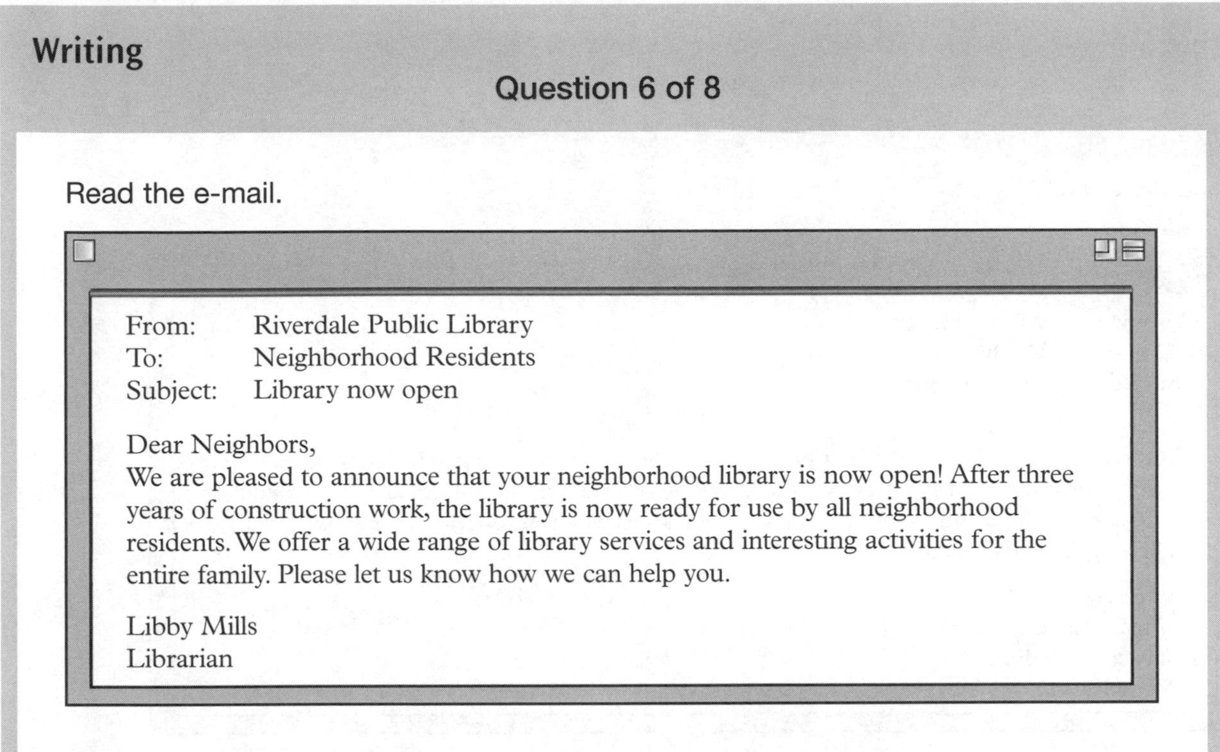

From: Riverdale Public Library
To: Neighborhood Residents
Subject: Library now open

Dear Neighbors,
We are pleased to announce that your neighborhood library is now open! After three years of construction work, the library is now ready for use by all neighborhood residents. We offer a wide range of library services and interesting activities for the entire family. Please let us know how we can help you.

Libby Mills
Librarian

Writing

Directions: Respond to the e-mail as a local resident who wants to use the library. In your e-mail, ask TWO questions and make ONE request.

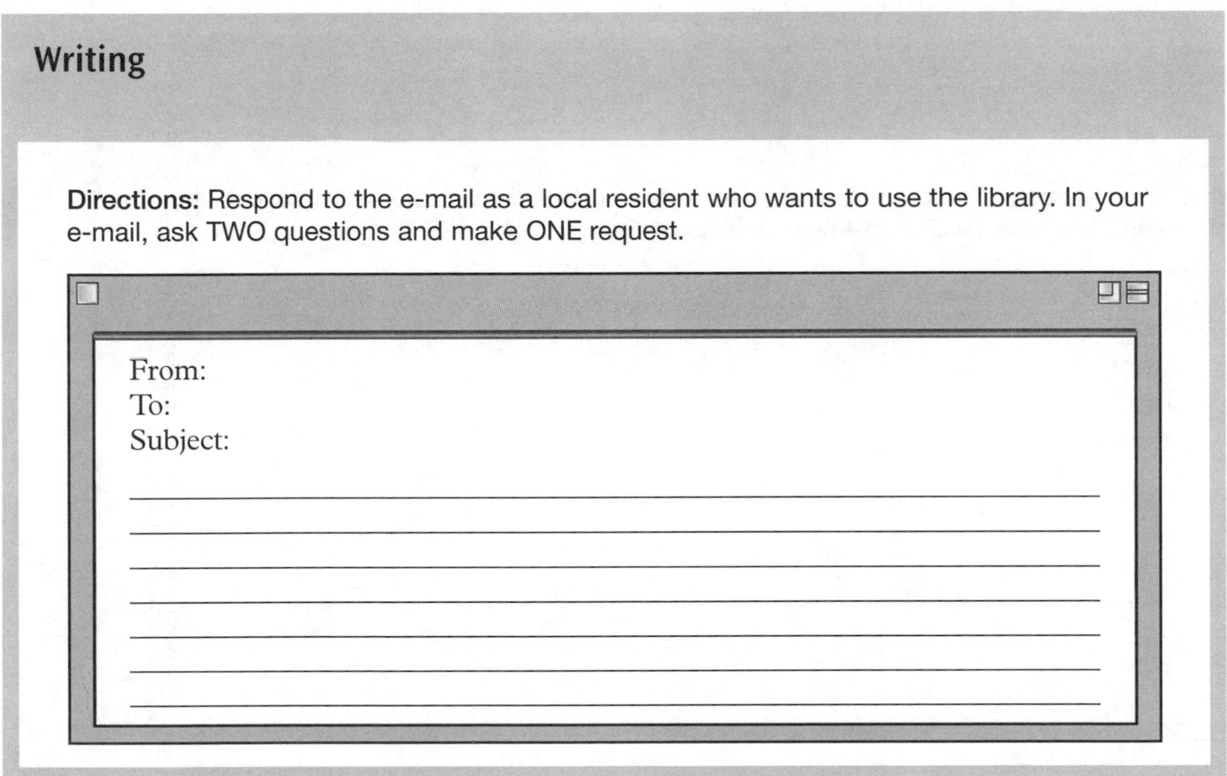

From:
To:
Subject:

GO ON TO THE NEXT PAGE

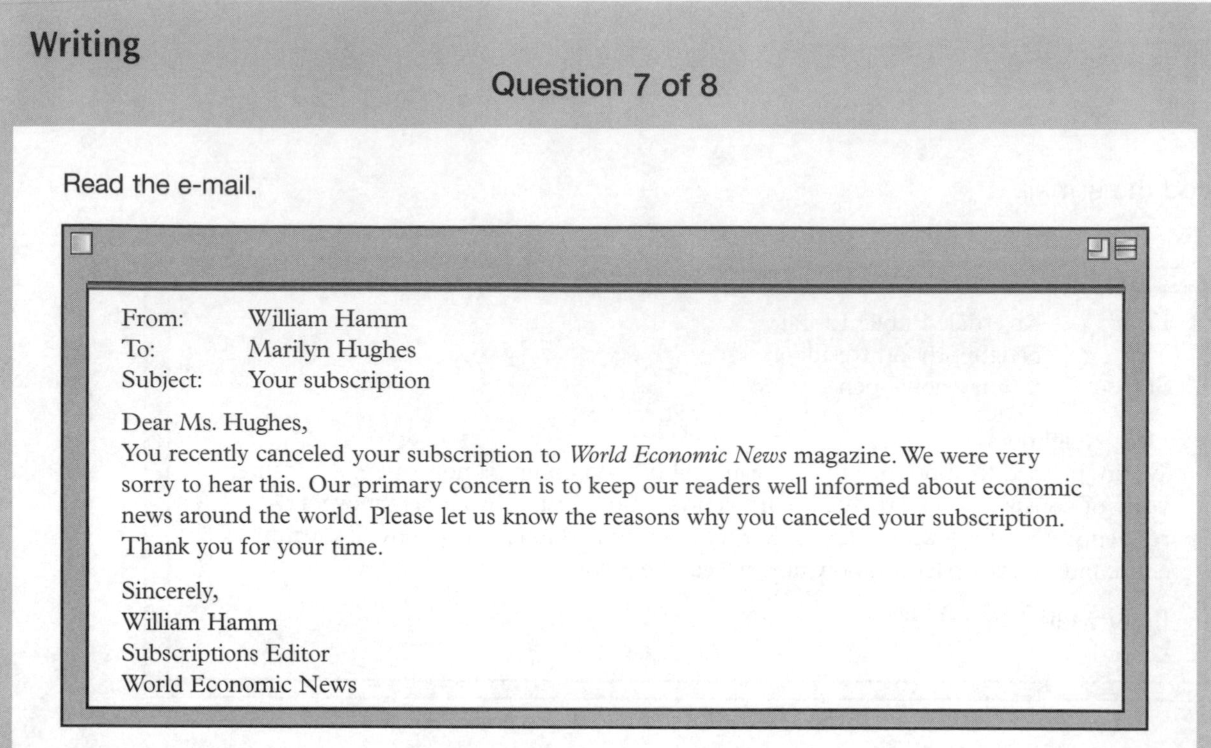

Writing

Question 7 of 8

Read the e-mail.

From: William Hamm
To: Marilyn Hughes
Subject: Your subscription

Dear Ms. Hughes,

You recently canceled your subscription to *World Economic News* magazine. We were very sorry to hear this. Our primary concern is to keep our readers well informed about economic news around the world. Please let us know the reasons why you canceled your subscription. Thank you for your time.

Sincerely,
William Hamm
Subscriptions Editor
World Economic News

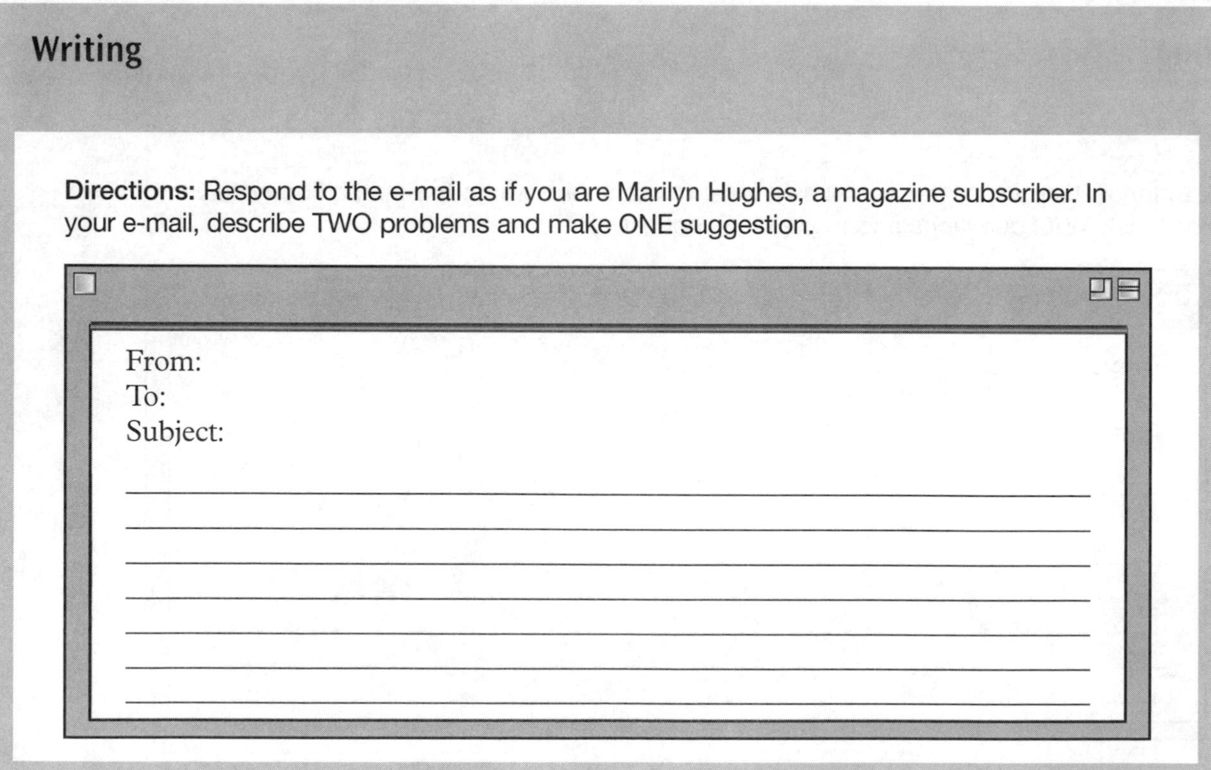

Writing

Directions: Respond to the e-mail as if you are Marilyn Hughes, a magazine subscriber. In your e-mail, describe TWO problems and make ONE suggestion.

From:
To:
Subject:

Writing

Question 8: Write an opinion essay

Directions: You will write an essay in response to a question about your opinion. Typically, an effective essay will have at least 300 words.

Your essay will be scored on

- supporting reasons and/or examples for your opinion
- grammar
- vocabulary
- organization

You have 30 minutes to plan, write, and revise your essay.

Writing

Question 8 of 8

Many people enjoy watching or playing sports. Why do you think sports are important to people? Use specific reasons and examples to explain your answer.

____

____

____

____

____

____

____

____

____

____

____

____

GO ON TO THE NEXT PAGE

Writing

Question 8 of 8 *(continued)*

This is the end of the Writing Test.

Audioscript

I Listening Comprehension

Part 1 Practice (page 15)

1. (A) He's working at his desk.
   (B) He's asleep.
   (C) He's answering his mail.
   (D) He's talking on the telephone.
2. (A) One woman is giving her address.
   (B) They're discussing a dress.
   (C) A woman is addressing the group.
   (D) They're hairdressers.
3. (A) A man is buying a book.
   (B) They're talking about the equipment.
   (C) The workers are having lunch.
   (D) A man is pointing to the book.
4. (A) They're cleaning the tables.
   (B) They're washing the glasses.
   (C) They're serving dinner.
   (D) They're eating lunch.
5. (A) He's repairing his car.
   (B) He's watching the clock.
   (C) He's standing by the door.
   (D) He's wearing a mask.
6. (A) The men are carrying pearls.
   (B) Two women are talking.
   (C) The scientists are doing experiments.
   (D) The engineers are on the train.

Part 2 Practice (page 28)

1. Where are you going?
   (A) Yes, we are.
   (B) We're going to lunch.
   (C) It's time to go.
2. Didn't your friends leave late?
   (A) To the meeting.
   (B) No, they ate at noon.
   (C) Yes, but they still arrived on time.
3. Where did you leave the car?
   (A) Sometimes.
   (B) In the parking lot.
   (C) This morning.
4. Have you calculated the ad revenue for this quarter?
   (A) Yes, here is the total.
   (B) No, we need to subtract.
   (C) Because we needed the sum.
5. On what date was the invoice sent?
   (A) My voice is too weak.
   (B) The boys arrived yesterday.
   (C) The tenth.
6. Was it difficult to contact the reservation department?
   (A) A round-trip ticket.
   (B) No, not really.
   (C) Hardly ever.
7. Did you forget to weigh the shipment?
   (A) No, the weight is listed here.
   (B) I don't know the way.
   (C) It's too long to wait.
8. Can I help you?
   (A) No, thank you.
   (B) Please don't do that.
   (C) Downtown.
9. When will Mr. Yoshimura arrive?
   (A) In two weeks.
   (B) Yes, it's possible.
   (C) Last month.
10. Could you give me your account number, please?
   (A) We've counted 150.
   (B) Certainly.
   (C) Yes, I'm pleased.

Part 3 Practice (page 40)

Questions 1 through 3 refer to the following conversation.

MAN: Do you have an appointment Wednesday morning?

WOMAN: Why? Do you want to meet about the overseas project?

MAN: No, I want to show you the new employee work schedule. I wondered if you'd have some free time before lunch, say, eleven thirty?

WOMAN: That would be fine. I'll be between appointments then. I'll look for you in the conference room.

Questions 4 through 6 refer to the following conversation.

WOMAN: I'm Sarah Parker. Ms. Salam is expecting me.

MAN: Oh, yes, you're the three o'clock appointment. I'll have to ask you to sign the visitor's book first. And here is your visitor's pass.

WOMAN: Thank you. Which office is hers?

MAN: It's right down the hall, second door on the left.

Questions 7 through 9 refer to the following conversation.

WOMAN: Your presentation was very well received.

MAN: Thank you. I feel that way, too. I was worried there would be no interest, but then there were more than a dozen questions.
WOMAN: And you weren't nervous at all. You looked so calm and cool.
MAN: I'm glad to hear that. And I'm glad it went well and is over with now so I can relax.

Questions 10 through 12 refer to the following conversation.
WOMAN: Have you had any news from Mr. Ling?
MAN: He sent a fax this morning. He feels very positive about the deal.
WOMAN: I certainly hope he's not mistaken.
MAN: I doubt that he is. He's been doing this sort of thing for a long time. He's been with this company for fifteen years, after all.

Part 4 Practice (page 52)

Questions 1 through 3 refer to the following advertisement.
Your company's computer keyboard, monitor, and mouse could cause problems and injuries. Make some changes in work habits and avoid wrist injuries and other computer-related stresses. Computer Accessories has produced the most up-to-date designs for compatible computer keyboards, monitors, and mouse units. Call now to receive information and a catalog of products.

Questions 4 through 6 refer to the following advertisement.
Timeshares go on sale at the annual meeting scheduled for September 28th in Palm Springs. Interested buyers can participate in person, online, or by fax. Last year, 90 timeshares sold at prices as low as five hundred dollars for one week in Rio de Janeiro to ten thousand dollars for two weeks in Hawaii. The sponsors of the event say resales come in at approximately fifty percent of the original price. Call the Timeshares International office in Los Angeles at 800-555-7866 for an advance copy of the listings.

III Speaking

Practice (pages 145–146)

7. Hi, Samuel, this is Sharon Rosen. I understand you are arranging the plans for my trip to New York next week. I'd like you to tell me a few details, if you would. Will there be a limousine to pick me up at the airport in New York?
8. How many meetings are scheduled for the day that I arrive?
9. What am I scheduled to do on April 13th?
10. Hello, this is Barbara Peters. I'm a patient of Dr. Warren. I have a dental emergency, I mean, I think it's an emergency. Anyhow, my tooth has been bothering me since yesterday. It started to ache a little in the afternoon, then the pain got so bad at night that I didn't sleep well. Would the doctor have time to see me today? I have an important meeting this afternoon, so I would really like to see him this morning if possible. The pain is really bad. It's bothering me a lot and just keeps getting worse. My job is not too far from your office. I can be there in fifteen minutes if I take a cab. Here's my cell phone number: 342-555-0965. Again, my name is Barbara Peters. I know the doctor's schedule is usually full, but I really hope he can help me this morning. Thanks.

Practice TOEIC Test 1

Part 1 (page 184)

1. (A) They're looking for books.
(B) The library is closed today.
(C) The shelves have everything but books.
(D) The men are writing a story.
2. (A) They're taking a nap.
(B) The light show is very beautiful.
(C) The trees lose their leaves in winter.
(D) The skiers are sitting on the snow.
3. (A) All of the chairs are occupied.
(B) The people are eating lunch.
(C) The label is long.
(D) They're having a meeting.
4. (A) The rain is coming down quickly.
(B) The swimmers are in training.
(C) The bridge crosses the water.
(D) The plane goes to Cambridge.
5. (A) The cooks are preparing a meal.
(B) The farmers are growing vegetables.
(C) The waiter is serving the customer.
(D) The menu is in French.
6. (A) They're playing volleyball.
(B) Beyond the valley are tall hills.
(C) The fish are caught in the net.
(D) The players are looking for a match.
7. (A) The sheep are ready for market.
(B) The ship is being loaded.
(C) The containers are made of paper.
(D) The doctor is busy.
8. (A) The door to the plane is closed.
(B) The men are carrying a box.
(C) The helicopter is in the air.
(D) The pilot light is on.

9. (A) The workers are on strike.
(B) The artist is drawing a straight line.
(C) The men are assembling an engine.
(D) Everyone is wearing a coat and tie.

10. (A) The windows are cleaned automatically.
(B) They're washing their car.
(C) The car is made by hand.
(D) They're taking a bath.

Part 2 (page 190)

11. Where do you live?
(A) I live on Church Street.
(B) My parents are still alive.
(C) You're in Room C.

12. Can we reschedule our meeting for Friday?
(A) Here's the plane schedule.
(B) No, I didn't eat meat on Friday.
(C) No, I'm busy then.

13. Who are you sending this memo to?
(A) I'll send both memos.
(B) To the housekeeping staff.
(C) My secretary sent it.

14. What do you think of her idea?
(A) I didn't do it.
(B) He's very clever.
(C) I wasn't impressed.

15. Has this product been tested yet?
(A) It's being tested now.
(B) He failed the class.
(C) She won't pass the exam.

16. When will the weather get warmer?
(A) Not until July.
(B) Her sweater is very warm.
(C) December isn't very warm.

17. How long have you been working here?
(A) I'm busy.
(B) Not until five.
(C) For three months now.

18. Would you like more coffee?
(A) The coffee is very good.
(B) Yes, thank you.
(C) You like coffee, don't you?

19. When are you leaving?
(A) At six tonight.
(B) To San Francisco.
(C) By plane.

20. I can return this if it doesn't match, can't I?
(A) Sorry. I don't have a match.
(B) Yes, we have a return policy.
(C) It's not too much.

21. How fast can you read?
(A) I learned in school.
(B) I write fast, too.
(C) Only 90 words a minute.

22. Why don't we plan a picnic for Sunday?
(A) I've lost the map.
(B) Use a blanket instead.
(C) Sure. That sounds fun.

23. Does every employee have to fill out this form?
(A) Sign your name here.
(B) Your interview is at one.
(C) Yes. It's required by law.

24. What's good at this restaurant?
(A) We're ready to order.
(B) I recommend the grilled fish.
(C) The check, please.

25. Can you pick up the package when you go?
(A) I'm sorry. I won't have time.
(B) It's too heavy for her.
(C) I'm going to the park soon.

26. Why didn't you call the repairperson earlier?
(A) He couldn't hear me.
(B) I didn't know there was a problem.
(C) She's always late.

27. Do you know her?
(A) Yes, but not well.
(B) I'll show up on time.
(C) She won't say no.

28. I think it's a big risk, don't you?
(A) I ruined the disk.
(B) It's too small.
(C) I certainly agree.

29. When will the speeches be over?
(A) The president is speaking.
(B) Probably about ten o'clock.
(C) They'll come over after lunch.

30. Why aren't they taking the subway?
(A) There's a delay on the tracks.
(B) I took the pictures on the way.
(C) We should stop for the day.

31. Do you bring lunch from home every day?
(A) I commute by car.
(B) No. It's too cold at noon.
(C) Yes. It's expensive to eat out.

32. May I help you?
(A) She doesn't know where.
(B) I'll help you into the car.
(C) Yes, I'm looking for the shoe department.

33. I can't find my briefcase.
(A) I like short speeches.
(B) Did you leave it in the conference room?
(C) He's doing fine, thank you.

34. Is that coat comfortable?
(A) Yes, he was able to afford a coat.
(B) I could do it.
(C) No, it's tight in the shoulders.

35. Who are they talking about?
    (A) Because they're both cooks.
    (B) His latest game.
    (C) The new assistant manager.

36. How does the camera work?
    (A) Just push the button on top.
    (B) I need to get it fixed.
    (C) She works very quickly.

37. Are you the head of security?
    (A) Yes, she will.
    (B) No, he can't.
    (C) Yes, I am.

38. What's wrong with the fax machine?
    (A) The room was very clean.
    (B) It won't send documents.
    (C) It's too long.

39. Will you be able to attend the reception?
    (A) No, I'll be out of town.
    (B) The reservations clerk is on duty.
    (C) She likes to stay home.

40. Do we have enough time?
    (A) There are always too many limes.
    (B) Stay until six thirty.
    (C) No, we'll have to finish tomorrow.

Part 3 (page 191)

Questions 41 through 43 refer to the following conversation.

MAN: We need to discuss the new hiring policy. Can we meet next Tuesday after lunch?
WOMAN: I can't. I'm all tied up on Tuesday. I have a conference downtown.
MAN: We'll have to make it Wednesday then. Can you come to my office at one?
WOMAN: One o'clock is fine, but you'll have to come here.

Questions 44 through 46 refer to the following conversation.

MAN: Would you like to fill out a card for our store's mailing list?
WOMAN: What kind of mail will I receive? I don't want to get any newsletters or anything like that.
MAN: No, no, nothing like that. You'll just get notices about upcoming sales.
WOMAN: Well, all right. But I don't want to give you my home address. I'll put down my work address.

Questions 47 through 49 refer to the following conversation.

WOMAN: Would you like something with your coffee? A roll? A pastry?
MAN: Just the coffee, please. No cream, but a drop of milk if you have it.
WOMAN: Let me check. Yes, there's milk. That'll be a dollar seventy-five. You can pick up your order over there.
MAN: Thanks. Here are two dollars. Keep the change.

Questions 50 through 52 refer to the following conversation.

MAN: There aren't any messages for you, but here's your mail.
WOMAN: Thanks. Oh, by the way, I'm expecting a new client this morning at around 11:30—Frank Evans.
MAN: Do you want me to send him up when he arrives?
WOMAN: No, call me instead, and I'll come and get him. I want to give him a tour of the new office.

Questions 53 through 55 refer to the following conversation.

MAN: We need to book the conference room for our ten-thirty meeting this morning.
WOMAN: The conference room is being used every morning this week.
MAN: But no other room is large enough for our group. There will be 25 people there, and we can't cancel now.
WOMAN: I don't think we'll have to cancel. The conference room is free this afternoon. We'll just change the time of the meeting.

Questions 56 through 58 refer to the following conversation.

MAN: I commute from the suburbs every morning. It takes me close to an hour.
WOMAN: Doesn't the long drive bother you?
MAN: Not at all. I use the time to think about work. I can solve a lot of problems while I'm driving.
WOMAN: That doesn't sound relaxing at all. It just sounds like an extension of your work day.

Questions 59 through 61 refer to the following conversation.

WOMAN: I'll be happy to fill this prescription for you. We have the medicine in stock, and I can do it right away.
MAN: Fine. Thanks. I'll wait.
WOMAN: It'll only take me ten minutes. Will you be paying cash, or by check? We also take credit cards.
MAN: Just charge it to my account, if you would. That would be the easiest way.

Questions 62 through 64 refer to the following conversation.

MAN: Has the mail arrived yet?
WOMAN: Not yet. I just checked. Are you expecting something besides bills?

MAN: I'm supposed to get an important package. The mail should be here soon. It almost always arrives by eleven.

WOMAN: Yes, it does. Calm down. It'll be here. Why don't you go find something else to do? Go read a book.

Questions 65 through 67 refer to the following conversation.

WOMAN: Look how late it is! It's five o'clock already, and we haven't even set the tables.

MAN: Don't worry. Relax. That clock is fifteen minutes fast.

WOMAN: Well, that's a relief. We still have time to finish then.

MAN: While you're setting the tables, I'll get the menus ready and write the specials on the board.

Questions 68 through 70 refer to the following conversation.

MAN: What's the fare to the university?

WOMAN: Well, it's outside of the downtown zone, so 95 cents. And the driver doesn't make change.

MAN: Now what? I only have a dollar bill.

WOMAN: So? Give him the dollar. You can afford an extra five cents, can't you?

Part 4 (page 194)

Questions 71 through 73 refer to the following announcement.

We are now boarding Flight 357 to Tokyo. Please have your boarding passes ready to show the gate attendant and wait until your row number is called to approach the gate. First-class passengers may board at their convenience. Each passenger is allowed only one small carry-on item. Please give any extra carry-on items to a flight attendant before boarding the plane. We appreciate your cooperation. Have a pleasant flight and thank you for flying Clear Skies Airways.

Questions 74 through 76 refer to the following announcement.

Attention, please! Attention! A fire has been reported in the building. The fire department has been notified and is on the way. Please exit the building immediately. Move quickly. Do not stop for personal belongings. Exit using the stairways. Do not use the elevators. Once you are outside, move away from the building as quickly as possible. Do not stand close to the building, and do not go back inside. This is for your safety. I repeat: Exit the building now. Move outside and away from the building as quickly as possible.

Questions 77 through 79 refer to the following recording.

Thank you for calling the Tour Service Line. If you would like to book a guided tour of the city, press 1. If you would like maps for the walking tour, press 2. If you would like personal tours of the city's museums, press 3. If you would like information about special tours not listed, press 4. There are still seats available on the downtown city bus tour for tomorrow, May 5th. To book seats for this tour, please stay on the line and an agent will be with you shortly.

Questions 80 through 82 refer to the following advertisement.

Call Business Printing Services for all your printing needs. Our design specialists will create unique stationery and brochures for your company that convey your professional image, and we print them for you in the quantities you need. We can accommodate all orders, large or small, and we offer special low rates for large-volume orders. For your convenience, we're open seven days a week. Visit us soon at one of our five convenient locations throughout the city, or online.

Questions 83 through 85 refer to the following weather report.

Tonight we expect partly cloudy conditions and colder temperatures with lows around 40 degrees. The wind will be picking up, too, with gusts to 25 miles an hour. Tomorrow morning the skies will be mostly cloudy, developing into rain by late afternoon.

Questions 86 through 88 refer to the following explanation.

In the mailroom, we sort the incoming mail for employees and deliver it to their office mailboxes. We also help employees with their outgoing mail. We ask them to bring all fragile packages to us for wrapping. We have envelopes, boxes, and special packing materials so nothing will get broken in the mail.

Questions 89 through 91 refer to the following introduction.

Our next speaker is Dr. Anna Yung. Dr. Yung is well known for her research on new techniques for increasing the strength of metals used in industrial machinery. She is here today to bring us up to date on her latest research findings. Dr. Yung promises to be brief in order to leave time for a question-and-answer session immediately following her presentation, as I am sure you will have a lot of questions for her. We'll try to end the question-and-answer session by 12:15 so that we can all get to lunch on time. I know that no one will want to miss our lunchtime speaker or the delicious meal that has been planned.

Questions 92 through 94 refer to the following news item.

New car sales have risen by nearly 2.2 percent over the same period last year. Economists attribute the rise to the increase in loans available for new car purchases. Auto experts, however, say that the increase is due to the innovative safety features on new car models. These features are the result of consumer demand for safer, more reliable cars.

Questions 95 through 97 refer to the following announcement.

Welcome. Tonight you'll be watching the hit comedy, *Laugh Out Loud*. We hope that you enjoy the show. In order to ensure everyone's comfort, we have a few rules. First, we do not permit taking pictures or using cell phones. We don't want to distract our actors. Please take out your cell phone and turn it off now. Also, no talking is allowed during the performance. But you may, of course, talk to your friends during intermission. That will be in about one hour. At that time we will also serve drinks and snacks in the lobby. Enjoy the show!

Questions 98 through 100 refer to the following report.

Our first heavy rainfall of the season has arrived, and with it some very wet roads and low visibility conditions. The driving out there is dangerous today, folks, and already we have some traffic accidents to report. A car collided with a bus at the corner of Belmont Avenue and Walker Road around noon today. No injuries were reported. A second accident occurred at Keller Street and Kings Lane at 1:30. Two cars and a truck slid off the road. The truck driver has been taken to the hospital. We're expecting the rain to continue all day, but things are looking up. Sunny weather will arrive Wednesday and should stay with us the rest of the week. Meanwhile, drive safely.

Practice TOEIC Test 2

Part 1 (page 224)

1. (A) The mountain climbers are at the summit.
   (B) The family is taking a walk.
   (C) The mother is carrying her child.
   (D) The talk is very familiar.
2. (A) The bureau chief is out to lunch.
   (B) The tomato sauce is spicy.
   (C) The chef is holding a basket of tomatoes.
   (D) The cook is chopping vegetables.
3. (A) There are flags over the counter.
   (B) The arrival hall is empty.
   (C) The tickets to the fair are free.
   (D) They will pass the port after dinner.
4. (A) The players are on the field.
   (B) The man is shooting wild game.
   (C) There is a pool in Bill's yard.
   (D) The woman is watching the man.
5. (A) His hobby is collecting stamps.
   (B) The visiting team will rest tonight.
   (C) She guessed the answer.
   (D) The couple are talking in the lobby.
6. (A) The doctors are performing an operation.
   (B) The men are playing golf.
   (C) The lazy workers are taking a nap.
   (D) The technicians are discussing the equipment.
7. (A) The man is pointing to the book.
   (B) They're sitting in the forest.
   (C) The pharmacist is dispensing medicine.
   (D) They're buying flowers.
8. (A) The drummer is beating the drum.
   (B) The drum is in the window.
   (C) They're listening to music on the radio.
   (D) Prisoners would like freedom.
9. (A) He's talking on the phone.
   (B) There's no lamp on the table.
   (C) The journalist is reporting the news.
   (D) The man is reading the paper.
10. (A) The bellhop is reaching for the bag.
    (B) The couple is driving away.
    (C) They fell down the stairs.
    (D) The car door is locked.

Part 2 (page 230)

11. May I borrow your dictionary?
    (A) Sure. I never use it.
    (B) I know how to spell that.
    (C) You have too many books.
12. Do you know when she's scheduled to lecture?
    (A) The plane left on schedule.
    (B) I don't like to speak in public.
    (C) No, I haven't seen the agenda.
13. Better staff training would solve the problem, don't you think?
    (A) The train service is really bad here.
    (B) It would certainly help.
    (C) No, I'm afraid I can't.
14. Who opened the window?
    (A) It always stays closed.
    (B) I did; it was stuffy in here.
    (C) No, I'm comfortable, thanks.
15. When will we hear from the client?
    (A) He's fine, thank you.
    (B) By telephone.
    (C) After their board meeting next week.
16. Do you think print advertising reaches the right market?
    (A) It depends which magazines run our ads.
    (B) The fish is always fresh there.
    (C) Yes, turn right at Market Street.
17. Who was on the phone?
    (A) I loaned them my skis.
    (B) She didn't hear it ringing.
    (C) It was our supplier.
18. Did you see the accident happen?
    (A) No. I heard the crash and then looked up.
    (B) No one was hurt.
    (C) Nobody called the police.

19. What did you think of the movie?
(A) Those movers were very efficient.
(B) The actors were wonderful.
(C) We do need more ink.

20. Have you ever been to Paris?
(A) No, I want a pair of those.
(B) You always seem to arrive late.
(C) Actually, we went there on our honeymoon.

21. Is it snowing yet?
(A) No, he won't be here until four.
(B) No, but it could start any minute.
(C) Yes, they finished last week.

22. May I speak to someone in your billing department, please?
(A) I'll connect you with Ms. Smith.
(B) We never get letters, just bills.
(C) I told him to pay it already.

23. Do you know of a way to increase our efficiency?
(A) Faster computers would be a start.
(B) We can place an order for more.
(C) It takes longer to get there.

24. You've worked with this director before, haven't you?
(A) Yes, I worked overtime yesterday.
(B) No, I remember him.
(C) Yes, many years ago.

25. Is someone sitting here?
(A) We have to stand.
(B) Yes, I'm sorry.
(C) The seats are too hard.

26. At what time did the call come in?
(A) At two-ten exactly.
(B) Into the lobby.
(C) It was cold outside.

27. How about working late tonight?
(A) You always get up early.
(B) I can't. I have plans.
(C) I'll go later.

28. Didn't you remind her about her appointment?
(A) I did, but she forgot.
(B) She left an hour ago.
(C) It's on the corner.

29. Do you want fresh pepper on your salad?
(A) My salary is high.
(B) The salad is served before the soup.
(C) Yes, thank you.

30. Do you take the bus?
(A) Only 75 cents.
(B) No, the subway.
(C) I can't find a parking space.

31. Are you going out for lunch?
(A) They're predicting rain.
(B) Only long enough to get a sandwich.
(C) No, a bunch of grapes.

32. When do you open on Sundays?
(A) Not until one o'clock.
(B) Be sure to close it tightly.
(C) I opened the present this morning.

33. Do you know if the order was placed?
(A) Yes, I placed it myself.
(B) He's always losing things.
(C) I'll have the chicken.

34. Whose notebook is this?
(A) The musicians read sheet music.
(B) I can't read my handwriting.
(C) It looks like mine.

35. Can I have her return your call?
(A) She'll be back on Wednesday.
(B) No, I won't be near a phone.
(C) Yes, I'd like a refund.

36. Where will you go on your vacation?
(A) We don't have any vacancies.
(B) He's leaving next week.
(C) I'm going to the beach.

37. Can I help you with that report?
(A) That broadcast has the best reporters.
(B) Thanks, but I just finished it.
(C) I'm too busy right now.

38. The new ship will have more deck space, won't it?
(A) Yes, that should attract more passengers.
(B) No, I can't race.
(C) We need to redecorate.

39. Are the new cabin assignments posted yet?
(A) Thanks, I already have a cab.
(B) Yes, they're posting them right now.
(C) The fence needs to be repaired.

40. How much is the full fare?
(A) It lasts until five.
(B) Five hundred dollars each way.
(C) It's already empty.

Part 3 (page 231)

Questions 41 through 43 refer to the following conversation.

MAN: What's wrong?
WOMAN: I can't find my notes from Tuesday's meeting.
MAN: I've got mine. I'll copy them for you. I'll have them for you this afternoon.
WOMAN: Thanks so much. You've saved my life. I need those notes to prepare for my presentation next Monday.

Questions 44 through 46 refer to the following conversation.

WOMAN: It's so hot in this room I can't concentrate. I can't spend another afternoon working in here.

MAN: The air conditioner broke down again this morning.

WOMAN: Again? Didn't we just have it fixed last week? We should buy a new one.

MAN: I think you're right. I'll speak to the manager about it today. Maybe I can persuade him to order a new one.

Questions 47 through 49 refer to the following conversation.

WOMAN: How far away is the courthouse from here?

MAN: Not far. It's just by the police station.

WOMAN: Great. I know where that is. I can walk from here, then I won't have to park my car again.

MAN: You're right. It's just a short hike from here. It shouldn't take you more than six minutes or so to get there.

Questions 50 through 52 refer to the following conversation.

MAN: The paper jams in this copier.

WOMAN: The problem is your paper. The sheets are too thin to go through the rollers.

MAN: I'll try this thicker paper then. I need to hurry. I have to have these copies done by three o'clock.

WOMAN: It won't take you long with this machine. It staples and collates and everything. Here, I'll show you how to program it. It's easy.

Questions 53 through 55 refer to the following conversation.

MAN: Look! You've spilled coffee all over my jacket! Look at that big stain!

WOMAN: Oh, don't be mad. I'm sure the stain will come out if you take it to the cleaners right away.

MAN: It had better come out. This is a brand-new jacket, and it was expensive, too. I paid more than 500 dollars for it.

WOMAN: Relax. It'll be fine. I'll take it to the cleaners myself if that will make you happy.

Questions 56 through 58 refer to the following conversation.

WOMAN: It's raining again. This is turning into a long wet spell.

MAN: I don't like hearing that. I've planned a camping trip for this weekend.

WOMAN: I know it's none of my business, but I'd cancel the trip if I were you. All this rain! And the air is so cool.

MAN: I think I'll wait another day before I decide. It could clear up overnight.

Questions 59 through 61 refer to the following conversation.

MAN: Excuse me. This fork appears to be dirty.

WOMAN: I'm so sorry, sir. Here is a new set of silverware.

MAN: Thank you. I'm ready to order now. I'll take the chicken and rice casserole.

WOMAN: That's a good choice, sir. It's our most popular dish.

Questions 62 through 64 refer to the following conversation.

WOMAN: I'd like to make an appointment, please.

MAN: Of course. Are you having any pain or discomfort?

WOMAN: No, no trouble. I just need to have my teeth cleaned. I do it every six months like I'm supposed to.

MAN: Great. OK, let's see. We're full this month, but I can give you something in June. I'll put you down for the sixteenth.

Questions 65 through 67 refer to the following conversation.

MAN: Mrs. Green had surgery today, didn't she?

WOMAN: Yes, and everything went well, I hear. Maybe we should send her flowers and a card.

MAN: I think we should order balloons instead. She's allergic to flowers.

WOMAN: You're right. Balloons are better. We can call the store before we go home this evening.

Questions 68 through 70 refer to the following conversation.

MAN: The subway train is late again. I'm really getting tired of this.

WOMAN: The trains are often late during tourist season. The tourists are slow getting on and off at the stations.

MAN: Then they ought to wait until after rush hour to take the trains. Why do they have to get on the trains at five just when the rest of us are leaving work?

WOMAN: Well, a lot of people like to visit this city. Anyhow, we'll be home by seven, so don't worry.

Part 4 (page 234)

Questions 71 through 73 refer to the following announcement.

For your safety, please exercise caution when using the moving sidewalk. Please stand to the right and hold onto the handrails. Place your luggage in front of you so it will not obstruct the sidewalk. If you prefer to walk, please use the left-hand side. Do not run, and be careful when stepping off the sidewalk. Please be considerate of the safety of others and move away from the sidewalk quickly as soon as you have stepped off.

Questions 74 through 76 refer to the following announcement.
Welcome to the seminar. Before we begin our presentations, let me say that we welcome questions from the audience. But in the interest of time, we ask that you hold your questions until all speakers have finished their presentations. Then, please step to the center of the room so that everyone may hear your question. We hope to leave half an hour for questions so that everyone who wants to ask a question will have a chance. We plan to break for lunch at twelve fifteen and return no later than one forty-five for the afternoon session.

Questions 77 through 79 refer to the following advertisement.
This set of everyday cookware is the most convenient thing in your kitchen. Mix the ingredients in the dish, and put it directly into the oven. Our cookware is made to withstand even the hottest oven temperatures. When your food is done, take the dish out of the oven and put it on the table. Our cookware is so pretty you can serve directly from it. Even leftovers are not a problem. Just snap on our convenient plastic lids, and refrigerate them for later use. Freezing is not recommended. How much do you think this beautiful line of cookware should cost? It is not available in any store or catalog. We are offering this exclusive line to you for just one hundred and fifty dollars if you call us today. Call now, 800-555-6295—to order your cookware today.

Questions 80 through 82 refer to the following announcement.
Construction crews are getting ready to start improvement on River Parkway into the city. Because this road is a vital artery into the business district, a series of construction crews will work around the clock for the next four weeks to finish the repairs as quickly as possible. One lane each way will be kept open during the morning and evening rush hours, but motorists are advised to find alternate routes into the city for the next month.

Questions 83 through 85 refer to the following announcement.
One of the most charming houses to visit while in town is Madison House, on Broad Street in the old downtown district. Built in 1780, it is not as large as the newer houses on the tour. But Madison House is far more valuable historically for the care and detail that went into building it. Everything in the house, from the woodwork to the custom furniture, represents the highest quality available at that time. Be sure to notice the intricate carved ceilings throughout the house, specially designed for the house and carved by an unknown artisan.

Questions 86 through 88 refer to the following weather report.
We can expect another unseasonably warm weekend. Usually the beginning of November feels as if it's already winter. But not this weekend. We can look forward to sunny skies both Saturday and Sunday, with the temperature at a very comfortable seventy degrees. It will get chilly after the sun goes down, though, so be sure to carry a light jacket if you plan to be out after dark. At least you won't be needing an umbrella for a while as we have several days of clear weather ahead of us. And if this warm weather stays with us, you can put away those hats and scarves, too.

Questions 89 through 91 refer to the following announcement.
Your attention, please. We invite our Vista-Rail passengers to relax with a gourmet meal while enjoying the beautiful countryside from our observation windows. The first seating for dinner will begin at six o'clock. If you have tickets for the first seating, you may take your place in the dining car at that time. Those passengers who hold tickets for the second seating will be served in the dining car at 8:30. There will be an announcement for the second seating at that time.

Questions 92 through 94 refer to the following report.
Most retailers of electronic goods concentrate on price and count on bringing customers into their stores by advertising the lowest prices. But our survey shows that potential buyers have some surprising preferences about how they shop. They acknowledge that price is important but say it is not the determining factor in their purchases. Equally important is the quality of service they can expect from the store if something goes wrong with their purchase. Consumers also say they appreciate a knowledgeable sales staff that keeps up with the rapid advances in technology.

Questions 95 through 97 refer to the following announcement.
Welcome to City Lights Bus Tours. We will begin our tour today by heading to the City Museum of Art. Our route to the museum will take us by some of the city's most beautiful historic buildings, and we'll stop on the way so that you can take photographs. We'll spend two hours enjoying the museum. Please remember that taking photographs is not allowed inside the museum building. We'll have lunch at the museum café. Then, before an afternoon snack at the famous Gretel's Pastry Shop, we'll take a quick ride around the City Gardens located next to City Park. Following our snack break, we'll leave some time for shopping at City Mall. Then we'll have you back at the hotel at seven, just in time for the buffet dinner at the hotel restaurant.

Questions 98 through 100 refer to the following recording.
Thank you for calling Biddeford Bookstore. Our regular hours are 9 A.M. to 9 P.M. Tuesday through Sunday. When you're in the store, enjoy a cup of coffee and a tasty pastry at our café. To hear a list of our upcoming events, press 1. To hear directions to the store, press 2. To check on an order, press 3. To speak to a customer service specialist, press 4. Book reviews,

a calendar of events, and staff recommendations are also available on our website.

away, I would really appreciate it. Call me as soon as possible, Robert Jones, in Room 125. Thanks.

Practice TOEIC® Speaking Test 1

(pages 268–269)

7. Hello. I'm calling about your computer classes. I'm interested in word processing. When can I take a word processing class for beginners?
8. How much does it cost to take a word processing class?
9. I may not have time to take a class during the week. Can you tell me about classes that you offer on Saturdays?

(page 270)

10. Hi, this is Robert Jones in Room 125. I just had a little accident and spilled coffee all over my suit. Does the hotel have a cleaning service, or know of one, that's open in the evening? I have an important meeting first thing tomorrow morning, and I really can't go to the meeting dressed in a stained suit. This is the only suit I brought with me because I only plan to be here for a short time. I've never been in this city before, and I don't know where anything is. If someone here at the hotel can help me figure out how to get my suit cleaned right

Practice TOEIC® Speaking Test 2

(pages 278–279)

7. Hello, Sue, I'm preparing for the meeting next Thursday, and I need some information about it. Can you tell me who will speak first and for how long?
8. Who is going to give the sales report?
9. I may have to leave the meeting early. Could you tell me what will happen after lunch?

(page 280)

10. Hello, is this the karate school? I would like some information about karate lessons for my son. I know you give classes for children, but I think they're group classes. My son is very shy, and he doesn't do well in groups. Also, I noticed in your ad that your classes started last week. My son really wants to take karate lessons this semester, and the only reason we didn't sign up earlier is because we were away on vacation. Do you have a class my son can take? He's ten years old, and he has never taken karate lessons before. He has time in the afternoons after school and on Saturdays. My name is Sam Lee, and my number is 876-555-9876. Thank you.

Answer Key

I Listening Comprehension

Part 1: Photos

Skill 1 (page 5)

Exercise 1

Group A

1. d	6. station
2. b	7. delayed
3. a	8. change
4. e	9. discussion
5. c	10. board

Group B

1. c	6. check in
2. d	7. jam
3. a	8. attendant
4. e	9. hairdresser
5. b	10. fashion

Group C

1. b	6. puddles
2. e	7. windshield
3. c	8. address
4. d	9. experiment
5. a	10. elevator

Exercise 2

1. attend	6. discuss
2. attendance	7. experiment
3. attendant	8. experiment
4. discussant	9. experimental
5. discussion	

Skill 2 (page 8)

1. (A)	4. (C)	7. (B)
2. (C)	5. (D)	8. (D)
3. (A)	6. (A)	

Skill 3 (page 11)

1. pipe	6. glib
2. high	7. cost
3. show	8. choose
4. smokes	9. bin
5. trunk	10. lame

Skill 4 (page 13)

1. **(B)** If the sky is cloudy, it probably means it is going to rain. Choice (A) is incorrect because it could be cloudy for days. Choice (C) is incorrect because a cloudy sky does not mean that stars will come out. Choice (D) is incorrect because it confuses the similar-sounding *cloud in the sky* with *cloudy sky.*
2. **(C)** If the cars are in a traffic jam, the cars wouldn't be able to move forward and people might be late. Choice (A) is the opposite situation to a traffic jam. Choice (B) is incorrect because drivers may not be patient in a traffic jam. Choice (D) is incorrect because *no one is driving slowly* means everyone is driving fast.
3. **(A)** If people are lined up at an airport gate, they are probably boarding a plane. Choice (B) is incorrect because the description of the picture suggests that their flight is ready now. Choice (C) is incorrect because some passengers may be beginning trips, not ending trips. Choice (D) might be true, but it is an assumption that cannot be made from the description of the photograph.
4. **(C)** Since the housekeeper is entering a messy room, the housekeeper is probably going to clean it. Choice (A) is incorrect because a housekeeper cleans hotel rooms, not checks into them. Choice (B) is incorrect because housekeepers would receive tips, not give tips. Choice (D) is incorrect; since the room is messy, the housekeeper is probably going to clean it, not sleep in it.
5. **(B)** Since the person is carrying a package, he is probably going to take it somewhere. Choice (A) is incorrect because he may open the package, but he needs to put it down or deliver it first. Choice (C) is incorrect because he is holding the package and there is no way of knowing if he will drop it. Choice (D) might be true but cannot be determined from the description of the photo.
6. **(A)** A woman who is running after a bus probably missed the bus and is trying to catch it. Choice (B) is incorrect because people do not usually like to chase buses. Choice (C) is incorrect because chasing buses is not a normal type of exercise. Choice (D) is incorrect because we do not know where she was planning to go.
7. **(D)** A man who is carrying a shopping bag probably bought something, so this is the most logical choice. Choice (A) is incorrect because even though a thief might steal a shopping bag from someone, we cannot assume that this is the case. Choice (B) is incorrect because we do not know what the man is planning to do. Choice (C) is incorrect because being an accountant has nothing to do with shopping bags.
8. **(B)** A man would probably be wearing a heavy coat because it is cold outside. Choice (A) is incorrect because we do not normally associate swimming with heavy coats. Choice (C) is incorrect because we do not usually associate summer with heavy coats. Choice (D) is incorrect

because even though the man might be walking after his car broke down, we cannot assume that this is the case.

Part 1 Practice (page 15)

1. **(D)** The man is holding the telephone receiver and probably having a conversation with a person on the other end. Choice (A) is incorrect because the man may be working, but he is not sitting at his desk. Choice (B) is incorrect because the man is lying down, but there are no other signs that he is sleeping. Choice (C) is incorrect because the man is talking on the phone, not answering his mail.
2. **(C)** *A woman is addressing the group* is the statement that best describes the photo. Be aware of the meaning of the verb *address*. Choice (A) is incorrect because it confuses the verb *address* with the noun *address* (a home address or a business address). Choice (B) is incorrect because it confuses the similar-sounding *address* with *dress*. Choice (D) is incorrect because it confuses the similar-sounding *address* with *hairdressers*.
3. **(B)** One man is pointing with a pencil at a machine; they seem to be discussing the equipment. Choice (A) incorrectly identifies the action. One man is *holding* a book. Choice (C) is not represented in the photo. Choice (D) incorrectly identifies what the man is pointing to.
4. **(A)** Two workers are wiping the tables. Choice (B) uses the related word *washing*, but they are not washing glasses. Choice (C) uses the related words *serving* and *dinner*. Choice (D) also uses the related words *eating* and *lunch*.
5. **(D)** The man is wearing protective clothing: a mask, gloves, suit, and boots. Choice (A) incorrectly identifies the action. Choice (B) incorrectly identifies what he is watching. Choice (C) incorrectly identifies the action; he is kneeling on the floor.
6. **(B)** *Two women are talking* is the statement that best describes the photo. Choice (A) confuses the similar-sounding *women wearing* and *men carrying*; the picture shows women wearing pearls, not men carrying pearls. Choice (C) confuses the related word *science* with *scientists* doing experiments. Choice (D) confuses *engineering* with *train engineers*.

Part 2: Question-Response

Skill 1 (page 19)

Exercise 1

Group A

1. a
2. c
3. e
4. d
5. b
6. shipment
7. invoice
8. revenue
9. subtract
10. loyal

Group B

1. b
2. a
3. e
4. d
5. c
6. agency
7. raze
8. reservation
9. aisle
10. calculate

Group C

1. c
2. d
3. e
4. b
5. a
6. functioning
7. contact
8. microphone
9. omit
10. recognize

Exercise 2

1. calculator
2. calculate
3. calculation
4. recognizable
5. recognize
6. recognition
7. shippable
8. shipment
9. ship

Skill 2 (page 22)

1. (A)
2. (B)
3. (A)
4. (B)
5. (A)
6. (B)
7. (B)
8. (A)
9. (A)
10. (B)

Skill 3 (page 25)

1. **(A)** The homophones are *where* and *wear*. A second pair of homophones is *meet* and *meat*.
2. **(B)** The homophones are *hire* and *higher* (related word *lower*).
3. **(A)** The homophones are *sum* and *some* (related word *any*).
4. **(A)** The homophones are *fare* and *fair*. A second pair of homophones is *raise* and *raze*.
5. **(C)** The homophones are *aisle* and *I'll*. A second pair of homophones is *guest* and *guessed*.
6. **(C)** The homophones are *wait* and *weight*.

Skill 4 (page 27)

1. (B)
2. (A)
3. (A)
4. (B)
5. (A)
6. (A)
7. (B)
8. (A)

Part 2 Practice (page 28)

1. **(B)** *We're going to lunch* is the only response that answers the question *where*. Choice (A) is incorrect because it answers the question *Are*

you going to lunch? Choice (C) is incorrect because it answers *when.*

2. (C) This is the only response that logically answers the Yes/No question. Choice (A) is incorrect because it answers the question *where.* Choice (B) confuses the similar-sounding *ate* with *late.*
3. (B) This is the only response that answers the question *where.* Choice (A) is not a logical response. Choice (C) is incorrect because it does not answer the question *where.*
4. (A) *Yes, here is the total* answers the Yes/No question by offering the total of the ad revenue. Choice (B) is incorrect because although it answers a Yes/No question, it confuses the related word *subtract* with the incorrect homophone *add.* Choice (C) is incorrect because it confuses the related word *sum* with the incorrect homophone *add*; it also answers the question *why*, not a Yes/No question.
5. (C) *The tenth* is the only response that gives a specific date. Choice (A) confuses the homophone *weak* with *week.* Choice (B) is incorrect because the question asks when the invoice was sent, not when the boys arrived.
6. (B) *No, not really* is the best response to the question. Choice (A) is incorrect because it confuses the related word *reservation* with *round-trip ticket.* Choice (C) would answer a habitual question.
7. (A) *No, the weight is listed here* is the only Yes/No response to this Yes/No question. Choice (B) is incorrect because it confuses the homophones *way* and *weigh.* Choice (C) is incorrect because it confuses the homophones *wait* and *weight.*
8. (A) *No, thank you* is a polite response to the question. Choice (B) confuses *please don't do that* with *please help me.* Choice (C) is incorrect because it gives a location.
9. (A) *In two weeks* answers *when will.* Choice (B) is incorrect because the question is not a Yes/No question. Choice (C) is incorrect because it refers to the past.
10. (B) *Certainly* is a polite answer to the question. Choice (A) confuses the related words *count(ed)* and *account.* Choice (C) is incorrect because it answers a Yes/No question and confuses *pleased* with *please.*

Part 3: Conversations

Skill 1 (page 31)

Exercise 1

Group A

1. a	3. e
2. b	4. c
5. d	8. recommend
6. appetizers	9. illustrated
7. check	10. numerous

Group B

1. c	6. presentation
2. e	7. proposal
3. b	8. researched
4. a	9. graphics
5. d	10. submit

Group C

1. c	6. employee
2. d	7. contract
3. b	8. inquire
4. e	9. postpone
5. a	10. promotion

Exercise 2

1. employer	6. illustrator
2. employee	7. presenter
3. employ	8. present
4. illustrate	9. presentation
5. illustration	

Skill 2 (page 34)

1. (B) Main idea: check a late order
2. (A) Main idea: making a presentation
3. (A) Main idea: offer her a job
4. (B) Main idea: negotiating a contract
5. (A) Main idea: finding exercise facilities

Skill 3 (page 36)

1. (B) 2. (A) 3. (A) 4. (B) 5. (B)

Skill 4 (page 38)

1. (C) 2. (B) 3. (C) 4. (D) 5. (A)

Part 3 Practice (page 40)

1. (A) The man is asking the woman if she is free on Wednesday morning because he wants to meet with her then. Choice (B) repeats the word *lunch*—the man wants to meet before lunch. Choice (C) repeats the word *conference*—the woman suggests meeting in the conference room. Choice (D) repeats the word *employee*—they will discuss employee work schedules.
2. (D) The man says he wants to show the woman the new employee work schedule. Choice (A) repeats the word *overseas*—the woman guesses the man wants to talk about the overseas project. Choice (B) confuses *apartment* with the similar-sounding *appointment.* Choice (C) repeats the word *project* from the phrase *overseas project.*

3. **(D)** This is the time the man suggests, and the woman agrees. Choice (A) confuses *nine* with the similar-sounding *fine*. Choice (B) confuses *fifteen* with the similar-sounding *between*. Choice (C) sounds similar to the correct answer.

4. **(B)** The woman has arrived for an appointment, and the man is a receptionist. Choice (A) associates *elevator* with *office* and *down*. Choice (C) is incorrect because the first woman's introduction is often heard on the telephone, but other clues help you understand this is not a telephone conversation. Choice (D) is not possible.

5. **(C)** The man gives the woman a visitor's pass. Choice (A) confuses the meaning of the word *sign*—the man asks the woman to sign the book. Choice (B) repeats the word *book*. Choice (D) is incorrect because the woman had already made the appointment.

6. **(B)** The man says that the office is *right down the hall, second door on the left*. Choice (A) confuses the meaning of the word *right*. Choice (C) confuses *downstairs* with *down*. Choice (D) confuses *next door* with *door*.

7. **(D)** The woman says, *Your presentation was very well received*. Choices (A) and (B) confuse *pool* and *school* with the similar-sounding word *cool*. Choice (C) confuses *present* with the similar-sounding word *presentation* and associates it with *received*.

8. **(D)** *Over twelve* means the same as *more than a dozen*. Choice (A) confuses *two* with *too*. Choice (B) confuses *four* with the similar-sounding word *more*. Choice (C) confuses *ten* with the similar-sounding word *then*.

9. **(A)** The man is happy that the presentation went well. Choice (B) is how he felt before the presentation. Choice (C) confuses *mad* with the similar-sounding word *glad*. Choice (D) repeats the word *nervous*.

10. **(B)** The man says that Mr. Ling sent a fax this morning. Choice (A) confuses *tax* with the similar-sounding word *fax*. Choice (C) confuses *taxi* with the similar-sounding word *fax*. Choice (D) confuses *shoes* with the similar-sounding word *news*.

11. **(C)** The man says that Mr. Ling feels positive. Choice (A) is the opposite of the correct answer. Choice (B) confuses *uncertain* with the related word *certainly*. Choice (D) repeats the word *mistaken*.

12. **(C)** The man states that Mr. Ling has been with the company for fifteen years. Choice (A) confuses *four* with *for*. Choice (B) confuses *nine* with the similar-sounding word *time*. Choice (D) sounds similar to the correct answer.

Part 4: Talks

Skill 1 (page 43)

Exercise 1

Group A

1. d	6. increase
2. b	7. rate
3. e	8. commuters
4. a	9. construction
5. c	10. location

Group B

1. d	6. century
2. a	7. existence
3. e	8. approximately
4. b	9. injury
5. c	10. demonstrates

Group C

1. e	6. investments
2. c	7. seminar
3. a	8. advisors
4. b	9. majority
5. d	10. personnel

Exercise 2

1. invest	6. advice
2. investor	7. advise
3. investment	8. injurious
4. advisor	9. injury
5. advisable	10. injure

Skill 2 (page 46)

1. (A) 2. (D) 3. (D) 4. (A) 5. (C) 6. (C)

Skill 3 (page 48)

1. (A) 2. (A) 3. (B) 4. (C) 5. (D) 6. (B)

Skill 4 (page 51)

1. (A) 2. (B) 3. (D) 4. (A) 5. (A) 6. (B)

Part 4 Practice (page 52)

1. **(A)** The injury is mentioned in the second sentence, *. . . avoid wrist injuries*. Choice (B) confuses *injuries to the mouse* with *injuries to the wrist*. Choice (C) confuses *keyboard injuries* with *wrist injuries*. Choice (D) is not mentioned.

2. **(C)** The answer is in the name of the company *Computer Accessories*. Choice (A) confuses *computer operators* with *computer accessories*. Choices (B) and (D) are not mentioned.

3. **(A)** The words *computer, keyboard, mouse, monitor, products* should help you make the correct inference that the advertisement is meant for people who use computers. Choices (B), (C), and (D) are not necessarily people who would face these problems.
4. **(A)** The location of the meeting is stated in the first sentence. Choices (B) and (C) are mentioned as places where timeshares were sold. Choice (D) is the location of the office.
5. **(B)** This answer is stated in the third sentence. Choice (A) is confused with *fifty percent of the original price*. Choices (C) and (D) are confused with prices at which timeshares have been sold.
6. **(D)** It is stated in the last sentence that *an advance copy of the listings* can be had by calling the office. Choice (A) repeats the word *event,* but no tickets are mentioned in the talk. Choice (B) repeats *fifty percent,* which refers to prices at which timeshares have sold. Choice (C) repeats the word *sponsors,* but a list of their names is not offered.

Part 5: Incomplete Sentences

Skill 1 (page 55)

Exercise 1

Group A

1. a
2. c
3. e
4. d
5. b
6. appreciate
7. handle
8. fill in
9. theft
10. invented

Group B

1. c
2. a
3. d
4. e
5. b
6. applicant
7. supervisor
8. judge
9. verify
10. previous

Group C

1. d
2. e
3. b
4. a
5. c
6. reminder
7. proposal
8. translator
9. eliminate
10. negotiations

Exercise 2

1. apply
2. application
3. applicant
4. invention
5. invent
6. inventor
7. negotiator
8. negotiable
9. negotiations

Skill 2 (page 59)

1. anti-, contra-, counter-, dis-, il-, in-, ir-, mal-, mis-
2. bene-, pro-
3. bi-, multi-, hyper-, hypo-, poly-
4. after-, ante-, post-, pre-

Skill 3 (page 61)

1. -ance, -ancy, -ary, -ation/-tion, -ency, -hood, -ity, -ment, -ness, -ship
2. -al, -ary, -ic, -ly, -ous
3. -ly
4. -ate, -en, -fy, -ize

Skill 4 (page 63)

1. (B) 2. (A) 3. (A) 4. (B) 5. (A)

Skill 5 (page 65)

1. (A) 2. (B) 3. (A) 4. (B) 5. (A)

Skill 6 (page 67)

1. in (at)
2. in
3. at
4. until
5. since
6. at
7. from
8. for

Skill 7 (page 69)

1. (A)
2. (B)
3. (A)
4. (B)
5. (B)
6. (B)
7. (A)
8. (A)
9. (B)
10. (A)

Part 5 Practice (page 70)

1. **(D)** The sentence should read, *The restaurant that has just opened has a famous chef.* The sentence requires a relative pronoun to refer to *the restaurant*. The relative pronoun *that* can refer to things, so it is the correct answer. Choice (A) can refer to things, but it indicates possession. Choice (B) refers to people. Choice (C) is not a relative pronoun.
2. **(B)** The sentence should read, *Negotiations will take place in London.* Notice that you need a preposition to introduce a phrase showing place (*London*). Choice (A), *at,* is not used with cities. Choice (C), *by,* is not used with cities. Choice (D), *to,* is used with the meaning of destination.
3. **(C)** The sentence should read, *We were in agreement with our supplier.* Notice the preposition *in.* You need to follow the preposition with a noun. Choice (A) is incorrect because *agree* is the verb form. Choice (B) is incorrect because *agreeing* is the present participle. Choice (D) is incorrect because *agreed* is the past verb form.

4. **(A)** The sentence should read, *Mrs. Dubois is a confident supervisor.* You need an adjective to modify the noun *supervisor*. Choice (B) is incorrect because *confidence* is a noun form. Choice (C) is incorrect because *confidentially* is an adverb. Choice (D) is incorrect because *confidently* is also an adverb.

5. **(D)** The sentence should read, *Our store gets more business in our new location.* Choice (A) is incorrect because *of* suggests possession. Choice (B) is incorrect because *to* is used with destinations. Choice (C) is incorrect because *from* means direction away.

6. **(C)** The sentence should read, *The proposals are delivered by messenger.* The preposition *by* introduces the agent in a passive voice construction. This lets you know to choose a passive verb form. Choices (A), (B), and (D) are all incorrect because they are active verb forms.

7. **(C)** The sentence should read, *On what date did you receive the shipment?* Use your knowledge of prefixes to choose the best answer. Choice (A) is incorrect because *per-* means *through.* Choice (B) is incorrect because *de-* means *away from.* Choice (D) is incorrect because *recede* has a different root and, therefore, a different meaning.

8. **(C)** The sentence should read, *Two weeks ago, Mr. Uto made his reservations.* Notice the doer of the action is important, so you need the active voice. Notice also the tense marker *ago*, which indicates the past tense. Choice (A) is incorrect because *makes* is present tense. Choice (B) is incorrect because *was made* is the passive voice. Choice (D) is incorrect because *has made* is not used with *ago*.

9. **(D)** The sentence should read, *All the members have arrived except Mr. Sampson.* Notice that you need a preposition in this sentence. Choice (A) is incorrect because it confuses the similar-sounding words *accept* and *except*. Choice (B) is incorrect because it confuses the similar-sounding words *expect* and *except*. Choice (C) is incorrect because *not* is not a preposition.

10. **(C)** The sentence should read, *She expressed her appreciation.* The sentence requires a noun as the object of *expressed*. Choice (A) is incorrect because *appreciate* is a verb. Choice (B) is incorrect because *appreciative* is an adjective. Choice (D) is incorrect because *appreciated* is in the past tense.

11. **(C)** The sentence should read, *Eliza Donato will be promoted to vice president in January.* Notice that *Eliza Donato* is the receiver of the action, so you need to use the passive voice. Choices (A), (B), and (D) are all incorrect because they are active voice.

12. **(D)** The sentence should read, *Mr. Yung sent a reminder to customers who didn't pay their bills.* You need a relative pronoun that can refer to people. Choice (A) is incorrect because *what* is not a relative pronoun. Choice (B) is incorrect because *whom* is a relative pronoun that is used as an object. Choice (C) is incorrect because *which* is a relative pronoun used for things.

13. **(D)** The sentence should read, *Mr. Weber hired a new assistant.* You need a noun that is a person. Choice (A) is incorrect because *assist* is a verb. Choice (B) is incorrect because although *assistance* is a noun it is a thing. Choice (C) is incorrect because *assisted* is the past verb.

14. **(B)** The sentence should read, *Send a fax to verify the prices.* You need a verb; notice the infinitive signal, *to*, which is followed by the base form of the verb. Choice (A) is incorrect because *verily* is an adverb with a different meaning. Choice (C) is incorrect because *verifying* is the present participle. Choice (D) is incorrect because *verified* is the past verb.

15. **(A)** The sentence should read, *That product wasn't invented until recently.* Someone else invented the product, so you need to use the passive voice. Choices (B), (C), and (D) are all incorrect because they are active voice.

16. **(D)** The sentence should read, *We're sending Mary Sula to participate in the seminar.* Choice (A) is incorrect because *at* indicates general location. Choice (B) is incorrect because *to* indicates destination. Choice (C) is incorrect because *from* means direction away.

17. **(C)** The sentence should read, *The employees are asked by the director to give suggestions.* Notice that the *by* phrase signals the passive form, so you need to use the passive voice. Choice (A) is incorrect because *are asking* is active voice. Choice (B) is incorrect because *asking* is the present participle and cannot stand alone here. Choice (D) is incorrect because *be asked* is the base form of the passive voice.

18. **(D)** The sentence should read, *Mr. Caputo usually travels with a translator.* Notice the tense marker, *usually*, which indicates the present tense. Choice (A) is incorrect because *is traveled* is passive voice. Choice (B) is incorrect because *travel* cannot be used with a singular subject. Choice (C) is incorrect because *is traveling* is the present continuous, and it cannot be used with the tense marker, *usually*.

19. **(D)** The sentence should read, *Her previous employer gave her a good recommendation. Previous* means *the one before.* All choices have the prefix *pre-*, so

you must pay attention to the root. Choice (A) means *appears often.* Choice (B) means *keep from happening.* Choice (C) means *look at something before (someone else does).*

20. **(B)** The sentence should read, *Flight 201 will be arriving at Gate 7B on time*. Notice that you need a preposition to introduce a phrase of time, with the meaning of being punctual. Choice (A) is incorrect because *by* is used with a limit in time. Choice (C) is incorrect because *at* is used with specific hours but not with unspecified time. Choice (D) is incorrect because *within* is used with a limit in time.

Part 6: Text Completion

Skill 1 (page 74)

Exercise 1

Group A

1. c	6. renovations
2. e	7. display
3. a	8. merchandise
4. b	9. bulk
5. d	10. convenience

Group B

1. c	6. mood
2. b	7. temporary
3. d	8. valid
4. e	9. desire
5. a	10. properly

Group C

1. d	6. agenda
2. a	7. degree
3. e	8. extensive
4. c	9. published
5. b	10. finalized

Exercise 2

1. publish	6. extend
2. publisher	7. properly
3. publication	8. proper
4. extension	9. propriety
5. extensive	

Skill 2 (page 77)

1. (C) 2. (D) 3. (B) 4. (A) 5. (B)

Skill 3 (page 79)

1. (B) 2. (C) 3. (C) 4. (A) 5. (D)

Skill 4 (page 81)

1. temperature	4. temptation
2. temporary	5. tempo
3. temperament	

Skill 5 (page 83)

1. enjoyment, enjoy, enjoyable, enjoyably
2. nation, nationalize, national, nationally
3. brightness, brighten, bright, brightly
4. simplicity, simplify, simple, simply
5. politics, politicize, political, politically
6. activation, activate, active, actively
7. confidence, confide, confident, confidently
8. purity, purify, pure, purely
9. conclusion, conclude, conclusive, conclusively
10. theory, theorize, theoretical, theoretically

Skill 6 (page 85)

1. (C) 2. (B) 3. (D) 4. (A) 5. (C)

Part 6 Practice (page 86)

1. **(D)** A passive voice verb is required here since the subject, *contract*, is not an agent. Choices (A), (B), and (C) are all active voice.
2. **(A)** *Tear down* a building means *raze* it or *completely destroy* it. Choice (B) would mean *destroy a piece of paper*, but not a building. Choice (C) would mean *take a piece of paper from a notepad.* Choice (D) is not used with *tear.*
3. **(B)** The contract was signed only last night, so the renovations, and therefore their result, will occur in the future. Choice (A) is present tense. Choice (C) is past tense. Choice (D) is present perfect tense.
4. **(C)** Prepositions, in this case *of*, can be followed by gerunds, which are nouns. Choice (A) is the base form of the verb. Choice (B) is the infinitive. Choice (D) is present perfect tense.
5. **(A)** *Whether* introduces alternatives. Choice (B) is similar in meaning to *in spite of.* Choice (C) introduces a time clause and is similar in meaning to *before.* Choice (D) is similar in meaning to *except.*
6. **(D)** *Neighborhood* is a noun that refers to a place. Choice (A) is a noun that refers to a person. Choices (B) and (C) are adjectives.
7. **(A)** *Since* in this context means *because.* Choices (B), (C), and (D) do not make sense in this context.
8. **(B)** *Prepared* is used as an adjective in this sentence. Choice (A) is a verb. Choices (C) and (D) are nouns.
9. **(C)** *Received* means *accepted*; Cynthia feels sure that the board members will like the project. Choices (A), (B), and (D) look similar to the correct answer but have very different meanings and do not make sense in this context.

10. **(B)** *Bulk* means *large.* This notice describes an opportunity to have large items removed by a trash pickup team. Choice (A) does not make sense since the pickup is described as *annual,* meaning *yearly.* Choice (C) does not make sense because all trash could be described as dirty. Choice (D) describes a type of trash, but it is not the type that is the subject of this notice.
11. **(D)** This is a second person possessive adjective. It describes the house that belongs to the person to whom the notice is addressed, or *you.* Choices (A), (B), and (C) are not logical.
12. **(C)** *Properly* is an adverb modifying the verb *placed.* Choice (A) is an adjective. Choice (B) looks similar to the correct answer but has a very different meaning. Choice (D) is a noun.

Part 7: Reading Comprehension

Skill 1 (page 93)

Exercise 1

Group A

1. c	6. survey
2. d	7. accommodations
3. e	8. options
4. a	9. investigate
5. b	10. consumers

Group B

1. d	6. suitable
2. e	7. discourage
3. b	8. reputation
4. c	9. access
5. a	10. equip

Group C

1. c	6. budget
2. e	7. cooperation
3. a	8. apologize
4. d	9. source
5. b	10. entitle

Exercise 2

1. apology	6. cooperate
2. apologize	7. opt
3. apologetic	8. optional
4. cooperative	9. option
5. cooperation	

Skill 2 (page 96)

1. (C) 2. (A) 3. (D) 4. (B) 5. (C)

Skill 3 (page 98)

1. (B) and (E)
2. (C) and (H)
3. (A) and (I)
4. (D) and (F)
5. (G) and (J)

Skill 4 (page 100)

1. (B) 2. (A) 3. (C) 4. (A) 5. (B)

Skill 5 (page 104)

1. (D) 2. (C) 3. (C) 4. (A) 5. (B)

Part 7 Practice (page 105)

1. **(A)** This page covers the time from Monday to Sunday. Choice (B) is not mentioned. Choices (C) and (D) confuse the fact that a new month begins on Friday of the week covered.
2. **(C)** The appointment with John Ling is on Saturday on the golf course. Choice (A) is confused with the appointment on Monday. Choice (B) is confused with the appointment on Wednesday. Choice (D) is confused with the appointment on Thursday.
3. **(B)** On Friday there is a 10:00 A.M. staff meeting followed by an 11:00 A.M. meeting with Mr. Gonsalves; therefore, we can assume the staff meeting will be over before the next meeting is scheduled, which is an hour later. Choice (A) is incorrect because it confuses *tennis with T. Kral* with *teleconference* and *Tuesday* with *Thursday.* Choice (C) is incorrect because it confuses *Thursday* with *Tuesday.* Choice (D) is incorrect because this information is not given on the calendar.
4. **(B)** On Tuesday there is an appointment to play tennis. Choice (A) is confused with the time the train will arrive on Monday. Choice (C) is confused with the place for the appointment on Wednesday. Choice (D) is what will happen on Friday.
5. **(C)** The appointment is at 12:00 P.M, which means *noon.* Choice (A) is the time of the appointment with T. Kral. Choice (B) is the time of the staff meeting. Choice (D) is the same as 12:00 A.M., not 12:00 P.M.
6. **(B)** The first part of the form specifies that the form is for reserving accommodations for next year. Choices (A), (C), and (D) are not indicated, although they might use similar forms.
7. **(D)** *Rec'd by,* short for *received by,* is found under the heading *reserved for office use* on the form. Choices (A), (B), and (C) are items to be filled in by the person reserving the accommodations.
8. **(C)** There is no space given for personal check information, so you can assume that you cannot pay by personal check. Choices (A), (B), and (D) are options of payment given on the form.

9. **(B)** The article is about increases in tourist taxes in Washington, D.C. Choice (A) is incorrect because the article mentions the survey, but that is not the main idea of the article. Choice (C) is incorrect because the article is about tourist taxes in Washington, D.C., not about Washington, D.C. in general. Choice (D) is incorrect because the article is about more than just taxes in restaurants.

10. **(B)** Hotel taxes in Washington, D.C. will increase from 11 to 13 percent, which is an increase of 2 percentage points. Choice (A) confuses the location of the organization that conducted the survey (San Francisco) with the city that is raising hotel tax rates (Washington, D.C.). Choice (C) confuses restaurant tax increases of 1 percent with hotel tax increases of 2 percent. Choice (D) is incorrect: the article mentions the average tourist taxes in the 50 most-visited cities but does not mention how much the taxes have increased.

11. **(D)** The article states that the increase gives Washington the highest restaurant taxes in the country, although New York has higher hotel taxes than Washington. Choices (A), (B), and (C) are all true.

12. **(A)** The word *average* means *normal.* Choices (B), (C), and (D) are words that could be used to describe a family, but they do not have the correct meaning.

13. **(A)** Mr. Keng had telephoned. Choice (B) is incorrect because the call was made *to* Mr. Ramen, not *by* Mr. Ramen. Choice (C) is incorrect because Ms. Murohisa is the operator, the person who took the call and the message. Choice (D) is incorrect because the call was made by Mr. Keng, who works for the Hotel Service Corporation.

14. **(C)** Ms. Murohisa, the operator, is the person who took the message. Choice (A) is the person who called and left the message. Choice (B) is the person for whom the message was taken. Choice (D) is the organization for which Mr. Keng works.

15. **(A)** The message on the form states that Mr. Keng cannot make the meeting. Choice (B) is incorrect because Mr. Keng is canceling the meeting, not verifying it. Choice (C) is incorrect because he left a message. Choice (D) is incorrect because *telephoned* and *please call* are checked on the form, but *returned your call* is not checked.

16. **(C)** The message indicates that Mr. Keng wants Mr. Ramen to call him. Choice (A) is incorrect because *please call* is checked, but *will call* is not. Choice (B) is incorrect because there may not be a meeting on Monday; Mr. Ramen has not confirmed it. Choice (D) confuses the operator and the recipient of the message.

17. **(B)** This is a registration form for people who plan to attend a conference. Choices (A), (C), and (D) are all people who are associated with a conference, but they would not fill out a registration form.

18. **(D)** The answer is in the last column of the Opening Ceremony row. Choice (A) is the cost for members registering in advance. Choice (B) is the cost for members registering on-site. Choice (C) is the cost for non-members registering in advance.

19. **(D)** Since the form is to be sent to Brazil, the conference is probably to take place there. Choices (A) and (B) are not mentioned or indicated by this form. Choice (C) is the location of the bank branch where conference payments should be sent.

20. **(A)** If you pay by July 10, you pay advance registration fees, which are less expensive than on-site fees. Choices (B), (C), and (D) are the dates of the conference.

21. **(B)** The purpose of the faxed letter, *to confirm a reservation,* is stated in the second paragraph. Choice (A) is incorrect because there is a reference to the hotel, but hotel promotion is not the purpose of the letter. Choice (C) is incorrect because Mr. Dubois works for a law firm, but the letter does not concern legal advice. Choice (D) is incorrect because there is no mention of a change in the arrival date.

22. **(D)** The first paragraph states that the letter was addressed to Ms. Wong. Choice (A) is incorrect because it confuses *Mr. Leger* with *Dubois and Leger, L.L.P.* Choice (B) is incorrect because he originally wrote to the *Assistant Sales Manager,* not the *General Manager.* Choice (C) is incorrect because Mr. Dubois originally wrote to Ms. Wong; Mr. Ashton responded on behalf of Ms. Wong.

23. **(A)** Since the letter mentions that his *usual* suite may be unavailable, he is probably a frequent guest of the hotel. Choice (B) is incorrect because he has asked for a non-smoking room. Choice (C) is incorrect because the reservations are from January 20 to January 28, a total of eight nights; therefore, he does stay more than two nights. Choice (D) is incorrect because he has asked NOT to be near the waiter area.

24. **(B)** *Inclusive* means the same as *included in.* Choice (A) is incorrect because Value Added Tax is *excluded* from the daily rate. Choices (C) and (D) are not mentioned.

25. **(C)** The announcement is about the public transportation available in the city. Choice (A) is incorrect because although hotels are mentioned, and are certainly places that visitors stay, they are not the main idea of the passage. Choice (B) is incorrect because visitors are the audience for the announcement, not the subject. Choice (D) is incorrect because tourist attractions are mentioned but not described or enumerated.

26. **(B)** The announcement clearly states that the use of private cars is discouraged. This means that visitors should not drive their cars in the city. Choice (A) is not logical; hotels are mentioned and presumably visitors would stay overnight in the city. Choice (C) may or may not be a good idea, but it is not discussed in the announcement. Choice (D) is incorrect because the hours during which visitors might travel are not discussed.

27. **(B)** The announcement gives the hours of subway service as 6:00 in the morning until 12 midnight. Choice (A) is incorrect because the announcement states that buses run 24 hours a day, which means that they operate after midnight. Choice (C) is incorrect because the hours for tour service are not discussed in the announcement. Choice (D) is incorrect because taxi service is not mentioned and its hours are not discussed.

28. **(A)** The announcement says that buses may appeal to people who want to sneak in extra sightseeing. This suggests they can see more of the city. Choice (B) is incorrect because speed is not mentioned in connection with the bus service. Choice (C) is incorrect because the cost of the buses is not mentioned, but the article does say that the subway is inexpensive. This could mean that the subway is less expensive than the buses. Choice (D) is incorrect because the convenience of routes for different forms of transportation is not discussed.

29. **(A)** The work will begin on March 2 and be completed at the end of the week of March 30, which is a period of five weeks. The dates in April refer to the elevator repair, not to the painting. Choices (B), (C), and (D) are not correct.

30. **(B)** According to the schedule, the cafeteria and the basement will both be painted during the week of March 30. Choice (A) is incorrect because the elevators are scheduled to be repaired the following week. Choice (C) is incorrect because that is the week the elevators are scheduled to be repaired. Choice (D) is incorrect because the cafeteria will be painted the week after the fourth floor.

31. **(D)** The Writex board meeting, scheduled for March 25, has been postponed because the floor on which Writex is located will be painted that week. According to the painting schedule, this is the fourth floor. Choices (A), (B), and (C) are incorrect because those floors are scheduled to be painted during other weeks.

32. **(D)** The elevator repair work will be completed on April 15, and the board meeting will take place the following day. Choice (A) is the original meeting date. Choice (B) is the date elevator repair work will begin. Choice (C) is the day elevator repair work will end.

33. **(C)** The memo states *Please contact me*, and it was written by the office manager. Choice (A) is the person who wrote the notice about the painting schedule. Choice (B) is who the office manager will speak with. Choice (D) repeats the word *elevator*.

34. **(C)** Ms. Park wrote the letter to describe her recent bad experience at the restaurant. Choices (A), (B), and (D) are plausible reasons to write a letter about a restaurant but are not the main idea of this letter.

35. **(D)** Ms. Park states in her letter that she visited the restaurant in Sandy Hill. Choice (A) is another Beach Patio location. Choice (B) is Ms. Park's address. Choice (C) is Mr. Zimmerman's address.

36. **(B)** The waiter was slow in serving Ms. Park and implied that the wrong order was her mistake, not his. Choices (A), (C) and (D) are the opposite of the correct answer.

37. **(A)** Mr. Zimmerman writes *Please be assured that I will contact the manager of that branch. . . .* Choices (B), (C), and (D) are related to the topic of a restaurant but are not the correct answer.

38. **(C)** Mr. Zimmerman says that the coupon *entitles you to the same special you ordered on your recent visit*, and Ms. Park stated in her letter that she *had ordered the three-course dinner special*. Choices (A), (B), and (D) are all mentioned in the letters but are not the correct answer.

39. **(B)** Sylvia plans to leave on the second morning train. Choice (A) is the first train, choice (C) is the third train, and choice (D) is the fourth train.

40. **(D)** Counting the time between any of the scheduled departure times and its corresponding arrival time shows that all trips take three hours and ten minutes. Choices (A), (B), and (C) are not correct.

41. **(C)** Sylvia tells Lee that she will need a rental car. Choice (A) is what she says she will not need. Choice (B) is confused with the fact that she asks about a restaurant, but she does not ask for reservations there. Choice (D) is incorrect because she implies that she already has the ticket.

42. **(B)** Sylvia states that she wants to arrive in Harford about an hour ahead of her 6:00 dinner date. The closest arrival to that time is 4:55. Choice (A) is another arrival time, but it does not meet Sylvia's criterion. Choice (C) is when she says she wants to arrive, but there is no train at that exact time. Choice (D) is the time of her dinner date, and she wants to arrive before then.

43. **(C)** The train ticket costs $75 each way. Sylvia is not eligible for the special round-trip fare because she will be returning on the weekend. Choice (A) is the cost of a one-way ticket. Choice (B) is the round-trip fare that Sylvia is not eligible for. Choice (D) looks similar to the cost of a one-way ticket.

44. **(A)** The memo is addressed to *All personnel* and states that the *workshop is highly recommended to all staff members*. Choices (B) and (C) are confused with the topic of the workshop, health insurance. Choice (D) is confused with asking department heads for permission to attend the workshop.

45. **(B)** George Peters mentions *the memo you sent out yesterday* and the memo is dated May 15. Choice (A) is the date of Suzan Reed's memo. Choice (C) is the last date to sign up for the workshop. Choice (D) is the date of the workshop.

46. **(B)** The workshop will end at 3:30, and George Peters will leave 20 minutes early. Choice (A) is 30 minutes early. Choice (C) is the time the workshop will end. Choice (D) is the time of George Peters' meeting.

47. **(D)** This is the room planned for the workshop, and George reminds Suzan, *The room you have planned for the workshop is scheduled to be painted the day before the workshop.* Choices (A) and (B) are confused with the people involved in this correspondence. Choice (C) is one of the alternatives that George suggests.

48. **(D)** George suggests that the cafeteria would be a good place for the workshop *if you expect a large turnout*, that is, a large attendance. Therefore we can assume that it is larger than the other rooms. Choice (A) is not correct because George suggests it as a good place for the workshop. Choice (B) is not mentioned. Choice (C) is not correct because George seems to be looking for a room that will not be painted.

III Speaking

Skill 1 (page 127)

Exercise 1

Group A

1. c	6. itinerary
2. e	7. departs
3. d	8. limousine
4. b	9. outfit
5. a	10. assignment

Group B

1. c	6. caterer
2. d	7. vegetarians
3. a	8. chores
4. e	9. impression
5. b	10. casual

Group C

1. a	6. conservative
2. e	7. behave
3. d	8. confidence
4. b	9. Observe
5. c	10. pleasantly

Exercise 2

1. confidently	6. impress
2. confident	7. observant
3. confidence	8. observers
4. impression	9. Observe
5. impressive	

Skill 2 (page 129)

1. Sat ur day	11. cus to mer
2. bi cy cle	12. a gen da
3. beau ti ful	13. ob serve
4. scen er y	14. im por tant
5. re lax	15. des sert
6. ex pe ri ence	16. tast y
7. chal lenge	17. a gree
8. tick et	18. o pin ion
9. com pu ter	19. tour ist
10. tech ni cian	20. e quip ment

Skill 3 (page 131)

Sample answers

1. **Objects:** an outdoor automated ticket machine, instructions, buttons, a screen, coins, blue jeans, baseball cap, hooded sweatshirt

Activities: buying a ticket for a train, reading the instructions, taking the ticket, inserting a coin, looking at the money

Sentences:

1. There is a large automated ticket machine.
2. The machine is outdoors and is probably for a train.
3. A man is buying a ticket.
4. The man is wearing blue jeans, a hooded sweatshirt, and a baseball cap.
5. The man is inserting a coin.

2. **Objects:** glass beakers, safety goggles, white lab coats, tubes, rubber gloves

Activities: performing an experiment, doing research, pouring liquids, wearing gloves, watching the other person

Sentences:

1. A man and a woman are in a science lab.
2. The man is pouring a liquid from one glass beaker into another.
3. The woman is watching him.
4. Both people are wearing lab coats.
5. The man is wearing safety goggles.

3. **Objects:** cup, saucer, open folder with papers, striped jacket, white blouse, table

Activities: holding a cup and saucer, holding an open folder, pointing to some papers, smiling, discussing something

Sentences:

1. There are two women in the photo.
2. One woman is smiling and holding a cup and saucer.
3. The other woman is holding an open folder.
4. She is pointing to a paper in the folder.
5. That woman is wearing a striped jacket and a white blouse.

Skill 4 (page 135)

Sample answers

1. My favorite holiday is Valentine's Day. Maybe this isn't a very important holiday, but I like it. I am very romantic. I like to see all the beautiful, romantic gifts for sale. I love to receive gifts of flowers on Valentine's Day.
2. The last time I visited a friend, we had a quiet time. The weather was nice, so we sat on the balcony and talked. After a while, we decided to go out for something to eat at a neighborhood café. I like spending time talking with my friends.
3. In my free time, I enjoy watching movies. I know a lot about movies, especially old classics. I own a lot of DVDs. I also like to go to the movie theater with friends. We always like to analyze the movies we see together.
4. I think it is very nice for a family to make a little trip together on a weekend, maybe to a park, the zoo, or a museum. They can play games together or learn something new together. It's a way of sharing fun and interesting experiences. It's a way that both the parents and the children can enjoy themselves.
5. I live in a small town, and there aren't many things to do. Sometimes we go to the movies. Sometimes we meet our friends at a café. If we want to do something more interesting, like go to a concert or see a play or go to a club, we have to drive to a bigger town, about 25 miles away.
6. There are several ways to look for a job. One way is to look at ads on the Internet or in the newspaper. Another way is to look for companies that you are interested in and send them your résumé. It is also good to tell all your friends that you are looking. You never know who will have information about a job opening.

Skill 5 (page 137)

Sample answers

1. He's teaching both French and Spanish. He is teaching French I on Monday and Wednesday mornings and French II on Tuesday and Thursday mornings. He has one Spanish class—Spanish II, on Tuesday and Thursday evenings.
2. All our classes cost $250 for the semester. You can buy the books in the school bookstore for $35.
3. Yes, we have Spanish I. You can take it on Monday and Wednesday mornings from 9:00 to 11:00 or on Tuesday and Thursday evenings from 7:00 to 9:00.
4. You can talk to instructors during instructor office hours, which are on Monday from 12:00 to 3:00. Or you can make an appointment with the instructor for another time.
5. Yes, we have French I on Monday and Wednesday evening and Spanish I on Tuesday and Thursday evening. Classes are from 7:00 to 9:00.
6. Mr. Florian and Ms. Bennet both teach French. Mr. Florian teaches French I on Monday and Wednesday morning and French II on Tuesday and Thursday morning. Ms. Bennet teaches French I on Monday and Wednesday evening.
7. On Monday morning you can take French I or Spanish I. Those classes also meet on Wednesday morning. On Monday and Wednesday evening you can take French I.

Skill 6 (page 139)

Sample answers

1. I'm afraid we are very busy today and won't have time to fix your car. We would be happy to fix it tomorrow. In the meantime, I suggest that you rent a car from us.

2. That won't be a problem. Bring your identification card to the tourist office before the tour starts. We will be happy to give you new tickets.
3. I can send some painters over this afternoon. They will do their best to finish painting the room before tomorrow. However, the paint will still be drying tomorrow and may have a strong smell.
4. I would be very happy to send over some vegetarian sandwiches right away. My assistant will bring them in half an hour. We will just add this to your bill.
5. I'm sorry. It won't be possible to solve this problem tonight because it is very late. However, if you will be ready to go shopping early in the morning, I will give you the addresses of some nearby clothing stores.

Skill 7 (page 141)

Exercise 1

Sample answers

1. **Opinion:** I would rather live in a house than in an apartment.
   Reasons: more room, a garden, privacy

   I would rather live in a house than in an apartment. In the first place, a house has much more room. I like to have a lot of space. Also, a house usually has a yard or a garden. I like to spend time outside, and I like to work in the garden. You can't do that if you live in an apartment. Another reason why I prefer a house is that it has more privacy. In an apartment, your neighbors are right next to you. Often you can hear them through the walls. In a house, on the other hand, your neighbors are farther away. You only hear or see them when they are outside. Overall, I think a house is much more comfortable than an apartment.
2. **Opinion:** It is better to drive your own car to work than to take public transportation.
   Reasons: more convenient, faster, more comfortable

   I think it is better to drive your own car to work than to take public transportation. First, a car is much more convenient that public transportation. You can leave any time you want. You don't have to stand outside waiting for the bus. You don't have to follow a bus or train schedule. Because of this, a car is faster. You don't have to count the time it takes to wait for the bus or get to the train station. You just get in your car and you are on your way. In addition, a car is comfortable. You always have a place to sit. You never have to stand like you do on a crowded bus.
3. **Opinion:** Children should not be given responsibility for household chores.
   Reasons: need time to play, need time for homework, chores are too difficult

   I don't agree that children should be given responsibility for household chores. Children spend all day in school. When they come home, they need some time to play. That is what childhood is for. They also need time to do their homework after school. After they play and do homework, how will they find time to do chores, too? I also think that most household chores are too difficult for children. Children are small. It is hard for them to use a broom or a mop well enough to really get something clean. When they grow up, they can do household chores, but while they are small they need time to play, study, and grow.
4. **Opinion:** I prefer to spend my free time alone rather than with other people.
   Reasons: I am with people at work, I like to read, I like quiet time

   I prefer to spend my free time alone rather than with other people. In the first place, I am with other people at work all week. My free time on the weekend is my time to be away from other people. My favorite way to spend my free time is reading. That is something you have to do alone. In addition, I like quiet time. During the week, my life is very busy. The weekend is my time to be quiet and relax. Although I like to spend some of my free time with friends and family, my favorite way to spend it is in peace and quiet, and that means alone.
5. **Opinion:** It is better to study at a large university than at a small one.
   Reasons: more options for classes, more activities, can meet more people

   I believe it is better to study at a large university than at a small one. First of all, at a large university you have more options for classes to take—small universities don't offer all the classes that large universities offer. So you have more opportunities for your education. Another reason is that there are more activities at a large university. There are more student clubs, more movies and dances, more trips, and things like that. These things improve your education, and they are fun, too. Finally, you can meet more people at a large university. A small university doesn't have the same variety of people that a large university has. In general, you can get a better education at a large university, and life is more interesting there.

Exercise 2

Answers will vary.

Speaking Practice (page 143)

Sample answers

3. There are two women and one man in the photo. One of the women is shaking hands with the man. The other woman is standing in the background holding a pen and a clipboard. They are probably business people because they are all dressed in suits. All three people are about the same age, perhaps mid-30s.

4. People in my country like to get exercise in many ways. When the weather is warm, you can see a lot of people outside running or bike riding. A lot of people like to walk, too. And many people exercise at a gym.
5. My favorite way to get exercise is walking. I like it because you can do it anywhere. Also, you don't need to buy any expensive equipment. For me, walking is a very peaceful and relaxing way to start the day.
6. First, we need good physical education classes in schools. That way, children will learn from a young age that exercise is important, and it is fun, too. Also, cities should have parks with good exercise facilities such as tennis courts, swimming pools, and running tracks. If the city provides these things, then everyone can afford to get exercise.
7. No, I'm sorry there won't be a limousine. You are scheduled to take a taxi to the Van Buren Hotel.
8. You will have two meetings that day. The first will be with Jonathan Stein and Marianne Brevoort, at the ExTime Office. Then you will have a meeting with the ExTime Sales team at 4:00.
9. On April 13, you have a breakfast meeting at 8 with Bart Baines, the ExTime Sales Manager. Then you will present the quarterly plan to the ExTime board at 9:30. At 12, you'll have lunch with the ExTime Board members. You'll take a limousine to the airport at 1:30. Your flight home to Miami leaves at 3:00.
10. Hello, this is a message for Ms. Peters. I'm calling from Dr. Warren's office. You asked for an emergency appointment this morning, but I'm afraid that the doctor is completely booked. He has a very full schedule this morning. However, it would be possible for him to see you later this afternoon. Could you be here at 4:30? Please call back as soon as possible to let me know. If that time isn't good for you, the doctor can see you at 5:30 this afternoon, or I can give you an appointment early tomorrow morning. Please let me know which would work best for you. The doctor can also give you a prescription for pain. If you let me know the name of your pharmacy, we can give the prescription over the phone. Then you can pick it up this morning.
11. I agree that smoking should be banned in public places. In the first place, smoking is a very dangerous habit. It harms the health of both the smoker and the people nearby. A person smoking in a public place harms the health of other people, and that is not right. Second, smoking makes a place unpleasant. It leaves a bad smell, and many people are bothered by this smell. Smoking can also make people's eyes itch. In general, it makes a place uncomfortable to be in. So smokers ruin places for other people. Another reason is that there are children in public places. It is not good for children to see adults smoking. It sets a bad example for them. It lets them think that smoking is not a problem, and maybe they will start smoking, too. For all these reasons, I think that smoking should not be allowed in public places.

IV Writing

Skill 1 (page 153)

Exercise 1

Group A

1. d	6. indicate
2. a	7. colleagues
3. b	8. prospective
4. e	9. candidates
5. c	10. recent

Group B

1. c	6. condominium
2. e	7. advantage
3. b	8. ensure
4. d	9. condition
5. a	10. satisfied

Group C

1. b	6. distract
2. d	7. engaged
3. e	8. consequence
4. a	9. complaints
5. c	10. cancel

Exercise 2

1. advantage	6. distract
2. advantageous	7. satisfied
3. disadvantage	8. satisfaction
4. distractible	9. satisfy
5. distraction	

Skill 2 (page 158)

Sample answers

1. The man is packing his suitcase because he is leaving for a trip tomorrow.
2. The woman ate a big meal even though she wasn't very hungry.
3. The man will get on the bus as soon as it arrives.
4. The woman will get a better job if she gets a college degree.

5. After they ate dinner, they went for a walk.
6. As today is a holiday, all the stores are closed.
7. Although it is very cold today, it isn't snowing.
8. While Mary drives to work, she listens to the radio.
9. They want to arrive early so that they can get good seats.
10. We won't call you unless we have to cancel the meeting.

Skill 3 (page 160)

Sample answers

Exercise 1

1. Would it be possible to send me a price list?
2. I would appreciate it if you would send me a check before the end of the week.
3. Would you please let me know if you have any positions available?
4. Would you mind sending me a course catalog and an application form?
5. Would it be possible to complete the work by Friday?

Exercise 2

1. I suggest training your waiters in good customer relations.
2. I suggest that you reorganize your shipping department.
3. I think you should advertise the job opening on the Internet.
4. It would be a good idea to hire more cashiers.
5. You could stay at the Hillside Hotel.

Skill 4 (page 162)

Sample answers

1. I don't have time to use the club.
   There isn't enough equipment in the exercise room.
   It's too expensive.
2. We had an unusual number of orders last week and were very busy.
   We have a new shipping clerk who is still learning his job.
   Our shipping supervisor was out sick last week.
3. Your company damaged my coat.
   I moved to another neighborhood.
   A cleaners with lower prices opened down the street.
4. You haven't completed the job; there is still one room unpainted.
   Your painters spilled paint and damaged our carpet.
   I'm sorry, I forget to mail the check.
5. We only contact people who will be offered a position.
   Your application is incomplete; please send a college transcript.
   A large number of people have applied, and it will take a long time to contact everyone.

Skill 5 (page 164)

Exercise 1

Sample answers

1. **Opinion statement:**
   Art and music add value to everybody's life.
   Supporting ideas:
   They bring beauty to our lives.
   They give us a way to express ourselves.
   They help us understand our emotions.
2. **Opinion statement:**
   I think that success means reaching your goals, and these are different for everyone.
   Supporting ideas:
   People have different kinds of goals.
   Money can help people reach their goals, but it isn't a goal itself.
   There are some people whose most important goal is to make a lot of money.
3. **Opinion statement:**
   I believe the countryside is a much better place than the city to bring up children.
   Supporting ideas:
   The countryside is safer than the city.
   People in the countryside are friendlier.
   Life in the countryside is healthier.

Exercise 2

Sample answers

1. Art and music are important to artists and musicians, but they are important to other people as well. Art and music add value to everybody's life.

   Art and music bring beauty to our lives. An ordinary day can become a little bit special if you begin it by listening to your favorite music. An ordinary house is made a little bit more interesting when you hang a few paintings on the walls. A weekend is made more exciting by a trip to a concert or a museum. Without art and music to brighten our daily lives, the world would be a very dull place indeed.

   Art and music give us a way to express ourselves. It doesn't matter whether or not we are talented artists or musicians. Almost anyone can play a few notes on a piano or draw a simple picture or even write a short poem. The point is not necessarily to create a great work of art, but to give expression to something that matters to us. Little children understand this very well and do it all the time.

Art and music help us understand our emotions. Music reflects our feelings of joy or sorrow, of fear or longing. Painters show us their expressions of wonder, happiness, or sadness, and in doing so, touch those emotions inside each of us. We spend a lot of our time thinking about ordinary cares such as getting to work on time or cleaning the house or picking up the children at school. Art and music take us out of our everyday world and remind us of other, deeper parts of ourselves.

Some people think art and music are only for artists and musicians or that they are a luxury that only a few people can afford. I believe, however, that art and music are important for everyone. We should all find a place for these things in our lives.

2. Many people believe that money equals success, but I don't agree with this. I think that success means reaching your goals, and these are different for everyone.

People have different kinds of goals. For one person, getting a college degree may be the most important goal, while for another person the most important thing may be raising a happy family. Another person might want to learn how to do something very well. He may want to become an all-star athlete, for example, or a talented painter, or an accomplished musician.

Money can help people reach their goals, even if money itself is not the goal. The person who wants to get a college degree needs money to pay for school. The person who wants to raise a happy family needs money to buy things for the children. The aspiring athlete needs money for training and equipment. The would-be artist or musician needs money for lessons. In these cases, it is not the money that equals success, but the way in which each person uses the money to reach his goals.

There are some people whose most important goal is to make a lot of money. They may want money in order to feel secure, or they may imagine that money will make them look better in the eyes of the world. For these people, we can say that money equals success because money is their goal. But this is not the case for everyone.

Everyone has different goals. People may need money to reach their goals, but that doesn't mean that money equals success for them. The world may see a rich person as successful, but, to me, the successful person is the one who is able to reach the goals that he has set for himself.

3. I believe the countryside is a much better place than the city to bring up children. The countryside is a safer, friendlier, and healthier place to live. Children have a better life there.

Cities can be very dangerous places. There is a lot of crime in cities. People can be attacked while walking in the park or waiting for the bus. Their homes might be burglarized. In addition to crime, there is a lot of traffic. People can be hit by cars while crossing the street, and it is difficult to ride a bicycle safely on the crowded streets of a city. In the countryside, on the other hand, there is very little crime and very little traffic. A child can grow up feeling safe in the countryside.

City people are not usually very friendly. When you walk down the street in the city, you rarely see people that you know and nobody greets you. In the countryside, however, everybody knows everybody else. Even people who don't know you greet you when they see you. People are interested in each other. In the countryside, a child can grow up feeling surrounded by friends.

Life in the city isn't very healthy. The air is polluted by cars and factories. The water isn't very clean either. It is difficult to buy fresh fruit and vegetables. It is hard to find safe, clean places where children can play outside. The countryside, on the other hand, is very healthy. The air is clean and fresh. Children can play outside in the sunshine all day long. It is easy to buy fresh fruit and vegetables right from the farm. A child can grow up healthy in the countryside.

There are few advantages for a child in the city, but there are many in the countryside. I think the countryside is the best kind of place for a child to grow up.

Writing Practice (page 165)

Sample answers

1. The woman is reading a letter.
2. The children are playing together outside.
3. The man is making a phone call while he takes a walk.
4. They went to the beach because the weather is nice.
5. After the man washes the dishes, he will sweep the floor.
6. Dear Mr. Van Eyk:

   I am looking forward to attending the National Business Conference in December. I have never been to Middletown before, so I have some questions for you. First, are there any inexpensive hotels near the conference? I would like a comfortable place, but I would prefer not to spend too much money. Also, could you recommend some restaurants? I hear that Middletown has some very good restaurants, and I would like to try some while I am there. One more thing I would like to know about is the weather in Middletown. Is it very cold there in December? I need to know what kind of clothes to pack and if I need to bring a heavy coat.

Thank you very much for your help. I look forward to meeting you at the conference.

7. Dear Ms. Meyer:

I received your e-mail about my visit to the Stardust Restaurant. That was my first visit there, and I am not sure whether I will return. The service was very, very slow. It took a long time for the waitress to take our order, and then we waited almost half an hour to get our food. I don't know whether this was a problem with the waitress or with the kitchen. In any case, I think it would be a good idea to offer free appetizers to customers who have to wait a long time for their meal. This would go a long way toward eliminating bad feelings. You could also let the head waitress know about this problem. Maybe she can work with the staff to improve the situation.

Sincerely,
Robert Krumm

8. There are both advantages and disadvantages to teenagers having jobs while they are still in high school. Overall, I think the advantages outweigh the disadvantages.

In the first place, teenagers are almost grown-ups, and they need to have the opportunity to learn adult responsibilities. Having a job is the best way to do this. A teenager with a job will learn to go to work every day and on time, even when she doesn't feel like it. She will learn to work hard to do as good a job as possible.

Furthermore, teenagers like to feel independent. Earning money gives a teenager a certain amount of independence. She doesn't have to ask her parents for money, and she has her own money to spend as she likes. She can decide to spend it on immediate things like clothes and entertainment, or she can decide to save it toward a future goal such as owning a car or going to college. These are decisions that the working teenager can make on her own, independently, if she earns her own money.

It is true that there are certain disadvantages to teenagers having jobs while they are still in school. A job takes time and energy away from school work. A night job may mean that the teenager gets less sleep. A job gives a teenager less time to relax and have fun with friends. However, I don't believe these things mean that a teenager shouldn't have a job at all. A job with limited hours and a good schedule will give a teenager time to do all the other things she needs to do and at the same time offer her the advantages of working.

A job teaches a teenager responsibility and helps her learn how to act independently. These things are as important a part of education as school. I think it is a very good idea for teenagers to have jobs.

Practice TOEIC Test 1

Part 1 (page 184)

1. **(A)** The people are in a bookstore looking at books. Choice (B) confuses the word *library* with *bookstore*. Choice (C) is incorrect because there are only books on the shelves. Choice (D) confuses the word *writing* with *reading* and uses the related word *story*.
2. **(D)** The people are surrounded by skis and poles and are wearing ski clothes. They are probably skiers. The skiers are sitting on the snow. Choice (A) incorrectly identifies the action of the skiers; they are *resting*, not *sleeping*. Choice (B) confuses the similar-sounding *light snow* with *light show*. Choice (C) is a correct statement for deciduous trees, but these trees are not shown in the picture.
3. **(D)** The people seem to be discussing something. They are probably having a meeting. Choice (A) is incorrect because only four of the chairs are occupied. Choice (B) is incorrect because the people are reading, talking, or discussing, but not eating. Choice (C) confuses the similar-sounding *label* with *table*.
4. **(C)** A train is on the bridge going over the water. Choice (A) confuses the similar-sounding *rain* with *train*; the train is moving quickly, not the rain. Choice (B) is incorrect because it confuses *train* with *swimmers in training*. Choice (D) confuses the similar-sounding *plane* with *train* and *Cambridge* with *bridge*.
5. **(A)** The two men are preparing food. They are probably chefs. Choice (B) incorrectly identifies the activity of the people; they are preparing vegetables, not growing them. Choice (C) uses words related to a restaurant but describes an incorrect action. Choice (D) uses other related words, *menu* and *French*, but there is no menu in the picture.
6. **(A)** They are playing volleyball. Choice (B) confuses the similar-sounding *valley* with *volley* and *tall* with *ball*. Choice (C) confuses *fishing net* with *volleyball net*. Choice (D) incorrectly identifies the action; the players are playing a *match* (game), not looking for a *match* (to light a cigarette or a game).
7. **(B)** A ship is at a loading dock. Choice (A) confuses the similar-sounding *sheep* with *ship* and contains the related word *market*. Choice (C) is incorrect because the containers are made of metal, not paper. Choice (D) confuses the similar-sounding *doctor* with *dock*.

8. (B) Two men wearing hard hats are loading a box onto a helicopter. Choice (A) is incorrect because the door to the aircraft is open, not closed; it also confuses the related word *plane* with *helicopter*. Choice (C) incorrectly identifies the location of the helicopter, which is on the landing pad, not in the air. Choice (D) confuses *pilot light* (flame on a stove) with *pilot* (person who flies aircraft).

9. (C) The men are assembling engines at a factory. Choice (A) incorrectly identifies the action; the men are working, not striking. Choice (B) incorrectly identifies the actors and action and confuses the similar-sounding *line* with *assembly line*. Choice (D) is incorrect because no one in the picture is wearing a coat and tie.

10. (B) They are washing their car. Choice (A) is incorrect because the people are *manually* washing the car; it also confuses the related words *windows* and *cleaned*. Choice (C) identifies an incorrect action; the car is *cleaned* by hand, not *made* by hand. Choice (D) incorrectly describes the action and uses the related words *taking a bath*.

Part 2 (page 190)

11. (A) *I live on Church Street* answers the question *where do you live*. Choice (B) is incorrect because it confuses *alive* with *live*. Choice (C) confuses the similar-sounding *you're* and *you*, and it is incorrect because, although it answers *where*, it is the wrong context.

12. (C) *No, I'm busy then* is a logical response. Choice (A) confuses the related word *schedule* (n.) with *reschedule* (v.). Choice (B) confuses the similar-sounding *meat* with *meeting*.

13. (B) *To the housekeeping staff* answers the question *who*. Choice (A) confuses *to* with *two* (both) and confuses the verb tense *will send* with *are sending*. Choice (C) uses the related word *secretary* and incorrectly answers the question *who* sent it.

14. (C) *I wasn't impressed* is a logical answer. Choice (A) confuses the similar-sounding *I didn't* with *idea* and confuses the verb tense *didn't do* (past) with *do* (present). Choice (B) confuses the pronoun *he* with *her*.

15. (A) This statement indicates that the product (*it*) is currently being tested. Choice (B) confuses *class* with *test*. Choice (C) is incorrect because the question asks if the product *has been tested*, not if the girl *passed the exam*.

16. (A) *Not until July* answers the question *when*. Choice (B) confuses the related words *warm(er)* with *her*, *worn* with *warm*, and *sweater* with *weather*. Choice (C) repeats the word *warm* but confuses the similar ending sounds of *December* and *warmer*.

17. (C) This statement uses *for* to show duration and is the best response. Choice (A) confuses the related word *busy* with *work*. Choice (B) is not logical.

18. (B) *Yes, thank you* is a polite response to the question. Choice (A) is an incorrect response to the offer. Choice (C) repeats the word *you* but does not answer the question.

19. (A) This statement uses *at* to express a time and answers the question *when*. Choice (B) does not answer *when*, but *where*. Choice (C) does not answer *when*, but *how*.

20. (B) This statement answers the question *can't I* and mentions that there is a return policy. Choice (A) confuses *match* (v.) with *match* (n.), meaning *something to produce a flame*. Choice (C) confuses the similar-sounding *match* and *much*.

21. (C) The question asks for speed, which is usually given in numerical terms. Choice (A) incorrectly responds with a location. Choice (B) confuses *write* with *read*.

22. (C) *Sure. That sounds fun* is the best response to the suggestion *why don't we*. Choice (A) confuses *map* with *plan*. Choice (B) confuses *blanket* with *picnic*.

23. (C) This is the only choice that responds to the question *does*. Choice (A) confuses *sign* with *form*. Choice (B) confuses *interview* with *employee*.

24. (B) From the question you can assume the person is asking for a recommendation for what to order; (B) proposes a dish. Choice (A) uses the related word *order*. Choice (C) has the related word *check*.

25. (A) *I'm sorry. I won't have time* is the best response to *can you*. Choice (B) confuses *heavy* with *package*. Choice (C) confuses the similar-sounding *park* with *package* and does not answer the question *when*.

26. (B) *I didn't know there was a problem* gives a reason for not calling the repairperson. Choice (A) is the wrong context. Choice (C) is incorrect because it confuses *arriving late* with *calling earlier*.

27. (A) *I* is the understood subject; *yes, but not well* is the best response to the question. Choice (B) confuses the similar-sounding *show* with *know*. Choice (C) confuses *no* with *know*.

28. **(C)** *I certainly agree* is the best response to the question. Choice (A) confuses the similar-sounding *disk* and *risk*. Choice (B) confuses the antonym *small* with *big*.

29. **(B)** *Probably about ten o'clock* answers the question *when will the speeches be over*. Choice (A) confuses *speaking* with *speeches*. Choice (C) is incorrect because the question asks when the *speeches* will be over, not when *they* (people) are coming over.

30. **(A)** *A delay on the tracks* is a possible reason for not taking the subway. Choice (B) confuses *taking pictures* with *taking the subway*. Choice (C) confuses the similar-sounding *day* with *subway*.

31. **(C)** *Yes. It's expensive to eat out* answers the question and gives a reason. Choice (A) incorrectly relates *from home every day* with *commute*. Choice (B) confuses *noon* with *lunch*.

32. **(C)** *Yes, I'm looking for the shoe department* is the only possible response to *may I help you*. Choice (A) is an illogical response. Choice (B) repeats the word *help* but does not logically answer the question.

33. **(B)** This statement offers a suggestion about where the briefcase might be. Choice (A) confuses *short* with *brief*(case). Choice (C) confuses the similar-sounding *fine* with *find*.

34. **(C)** If it is tight in the shoulders, we can assume *it* refers to the coat and that it is not comfortable. Choice (A) confuses the similar-sounding *able* and comfort(*able*). Choice (B) confuses the similar-sounding *could* with *coat* and *confident* with *comfortable*.

35. **(C)** The new assistant manager answers the question *who*. Choice (A) is incorrect because it does not answer *who*, but *why*. Choice (B) is incorrect because it does not answer *who*, but *what*.

36. **(A)** This statement provides instructions for using the camera. Choice (B) does not answer the question. Choice (C) confuses the meaning of *work* and *she* with *it*.

37. **(C)** The question asks about *you* and requires an *I* response. Choice (A) answers in the incorrect pronoun and tense. Choice (B) uses an incorrect pronoun.

38. **(B)** *It won't send documents* tells *what's wrong*. Choice (A) confuses the similar-sounding *clean* with *machine*. Choice (C) confuses the similar-sounding *long* with *wrong*.

39. **(A)** This statement gives an answer and an excuse. Choice (B) confuses *reservations* with *reception*. Choice (C) uses *she*, which is the incorrect pronoun for the response.

40. **(C)** *No, we'll have to finish tomorrow* is the best response to the question. Choice (A) confuses the similar-sounding *limes* with *time*. Choice (B) gives a time, *six thirty*, but does not answer the question.

Part 3 (page 191)

41. **(B)** The man says, *We need to discuss the new hiring policy*. Choice (A) confuses the similar-sounding words *police* and *policy*. Choice (C) repeats the word *lunch*—the man says he wants to meet after lunch. Choice (D) repeats the word *conference*—the woman will be at a conference on Tuesday.

42. **(D)** They finally agree to meet on Wednesday. Choices (A) and (B) sound similar to Tuesday, the day the man suggests meeting. Choice (C) is the first day the man suggests.

43. **(C)** The woman says *you'll have to come here*, meaning to her office. Choice (A) is where the woman will be on Tuesday. Choice (B) repeats the word *conference*. Choice (D) is where the man suggests meeting, but the woman doesn't agree.

44. **(A)** The man mentions *our store's mailing list*, and says the woman can receive notices about sales. Choice (B) repeats the word *home*. Choice (C) associates *post office* with *mail*. Choice (D) associates *employment* with *work*.

45. **(D)** The man wants the woman to *fill out a card*, or form, for the store's mailing list. Choice (A) repeats the word *work*. Choice (B) repeats the word *card*. Choice (C) confuses *letter* with *newsletter*.

46. **(B)** The man tells the woman she will receive *notices about upcoming sales*. Choice (A) associates *bills* with *store*. Choice (C) repeats the word *newsletter*, which is what the woman says she doesn't want to receive. Choice (D) repeats the word *card*.

47. **(C)** The man says he'll just have coffee. Choices (A) and (B) are what the woman offers him. Choice (D) repeats the word *cream* out of context.

48. **(C)** The woman says, *That'll be a dollar seventy-five*. Choices (A) and (B) sound similar to the correct answer. Choice (D) is the amount of money the man gives the woman.

49. **(A)** The man hands the woman two dollars. Choice (B) uses the word *check* out of

context (*Let me check*). Choice (C) is not mentioned. Choice (D) uses the word *order* out of context (*You can pick up your order*).

50. **(C)** The woman asks the man to call her when the client arrives. Choice (A) is not mentioned. Choice (B) is what the man suggests. Choice (D) confuses *inside* with the similar-sounding word *instead.*

51. **(D)** This is the time the woman mentions. Choice (A) confuses *five* with the similar-sounding word *arrive.* Choices (B) and (C) sound similar to the correct answer.

52. **(A)** The woman says she wants to give the client a tour of the new office. Choice (B) is what the woman wants. Choice (C) is what the man gave the woman. Choice (D) repeats the word *messages.*

53. **(C)** The man planned the meeting for this morning, but the conference room isn't free. Choice (A) is related to the discussion of what time the meeting will take place. Choices (B) and (D) are not mentioned.

54. **(C)** The man says that he expects 25 people. Choices (A) and (D) sound similar to the original time of the meeting, *10:30.* Choice (B) sounds similar to the correct answer.

55. **(A)** The woman says that they will change the time of the meeting. Choice (B) is what they want to do but can't. Choice (C) is related to the discussion of the need for a large room. Choice (D) is what the man says they can't do.

56. **(A)** The man says *It takes me close to an hour*, meaning *a little less than an hour.* Choices (B) and (C) confuse the meaning of *close to.* Choice (D) confuses *two* with *to.*

57. **(D)** Both the man and the woman mention driving. Choice (A) confuses *walk* with the similar-sounding word *work.* Choice (B) confuses *subway* with the similar-sounding word *suburb.* Choice (C) confuses *taxi* with the similar-sounding word *relaxing.*

58. **(B)** The man tells the woman that he thinks about work. Choice (A) confuses *close* with the similar-sounding word *clothes.* Choice (C) confuses *call* with the similar-sounding word *all.* Choice (D) repeats the word *relax.*

59. **(B)** The woman is filling a prescription for the man, so she is a pharmacist. Choices (A) and (C) are related to the topic of medicine and prescriptions. Choice (D) is related to the situation of buying something.

60. **(D)** The woman says it will take her ten minutes to fill the prescription. Choice (A) confuses the similar-sounding *two* and *do*. Choice (B) confuses the similar-sounding *eight* and *wait.* Choice (C) confuses the similar-sounding *nine* and *fine.*

61. **(D)** The man asks the woman to charge it to his account. Choices (A), (B), and (C) are what the woman suggests.

62. **(C)** The man says that he is expecting an important package. Choice (A) is associated with *mail.* Choice (B) confuses the similar-sounding words *pills* and *bills.* Choice (D) uses the word *checks* out of context.

63. **(C)** The man and the woman agree that the mail usually arrives by 11:00. Choice (A) confuses the similar-sounding *five* and *arrive.* Choice (B) sounds similar to the correct answer. Choice (D) confuses the similar-sounding *noon* and *soon.*

64. **(D)** The woman tells the man to calm down and read a book. Choices (A) and (C) confuse the similar-sounding *cook* and *look* with *book.* Choice (B) confuses *downtown* with *down.*

65. **(A)** The woman is setting tables and the man is preparing menus, so they are at a restaurant. Choice (B) associates *furniture store* with *tables.* Choice (C) is a place where one might set tables, but it isn't a place where menus are found. Choice (D) associates *school* with *blackboard.*

66. **(B)** The clock says 5:00, and the man says that it is fifteen minutes fast, so the time is fifteen minutes before 5:00. Choices (A) and (D) repeat *fifteen.* Choice (C) is the time the clock wrongly says.

67. **(D)** The woman is worried about the time, but it is actually earlier than the clock says. Choice (A) is what the woman thinks, but it is not actually true. Choice (B) is true but is not what the woman is worried about. Choice (C) repeats the word *late.*

68. **(C)** The man asks about the fare to the university, so we can assume that is where he is going. Choice (A) repeats the word *downtown.* Choice (B) confuses *fair* with *fare.* Choice (D) associates *bank* with the discussion of money.

69. **(C)** The woman tells the man that the fare is 95 cents. Choices (A) and (B) sound similar to the correct answer. Choice (D) is the money that the man has.

70. **(A)** The man only has a dollar bill to pay the 95-cent fare. Choice (B) uses the word *change* in a different context. Choice (C) uses the word *bill* in a different context. Choice (D) associates *class* with *university.*

Part 4 (page 194)

71. **(D)** They should approach when *their row number is called.* Choices (A) and (C) are not mentioned. Choice (B) is contradicted by *when their row number is called.*

72. **(C)** *At their convenience* means *any time.* Choices (A), (B), and (D) are contradicted by *at their convenience.*

73. **(D)** Passengers are allowed only one carry-on item each and are asked to give any extras to the flight attendants. Choice (A) confuses *names* with the similar-sounding word *plane.* Choice (B) confuses *passports* with *boarding passes.* Choice (C) is what passengers should show the gate attendants.

74. **(D)** The announcer says that a fire has been reported in the building and the fire department is on the way. Choice (A) repeats the word *safety.* Choice (B) confuses *close* (shut) with *close* (near). Choice (C) repeats the word *outside* but in a different context.

75. **(A)** It says *do NOT stop for personal belongings.* Choice (B) is contradicted by *move quickly.* Choice (C) is contradicted by *the fire department is on the way.* Choice (D) is not mentioned—the announcement notifies everyone.

76. **(B)** It says *exit using the stairways.* Choice (A) is contradicted by *do not use the elevators.* Choices (C) and (D) are not mentioned.

77. **(C)** A Tour Service Line has information about *tours.* Choices (A), (B), and (D) are not mentioned.

78. **(B)** A *candlelight tour* is not mentioned. Choices (A), (C), and (D) are types of tours that are explicitly mentioned.

79. **(A)** Callers are asked to stay on the line to book seats on the bus tour. Choice (B) repeats the words *maps* and *downtown.* Choice (C) uses the word *book* in a different context. Choice (D) repeats the words *personal* and *guide.*

80. **(D)** *Printing services* are advertised. Choices (A), (B), and (C) are not consistent with the information in the advertisement.

81. **(A)** They offer *special low rates for large-volume orders.* Choices (B), (C), and (D) are contradicted by *special low rates.*

82. **(A)** The speaker says that there are five locations. Choice (B) is the number of days a week the business is open. Choice (C) confuses the similar-sounding *nine* and *line.* Choice (D) confuses the similar-sounding *eleven* and *seven.*

83. **(B)** They expect it to be *partly cloudy tonight* and *mostly cloudy tomorrow.* Choice (A) is contradicted by *cloudy.* Choices (C) and (D) are contradicted by *colder temperatures.*

84. **(A)** The *wind will pick up.* Choice (B) is contradicted by *pick up.* Choice (C) is not mentioned. Choice (D) is contradicted by *gusts to 25 miles an hour.*

85. **(D)** Rain is expected *late tomorrow afternoon.* Choices (A), (B), and (C) are all contradicted by *late tomorrow afternoon.*

86. **(B)** *Employees* and *office mailboxes* suggest a large company. Choices (A), (C), and (D) are not consistent with the information given.

87. **(C)** *Selling stamps* is not mentioned. Choices (A), (B), and (D) are all explicitly mentioned.

88. **(A)** Employees should bring *fragile* packages to the mail room. Choices (B), (C), and (D) are not mentioned.

89. **(A)** She is probably a *scientist.* Choices (B), (C), and (D) would not research the strength of industrial metals.

90. **(D)** It is probably given *at a conference.* Choices (A), (B), and (C) are not consistent with the information given.

91. **(B)** The speaker says that there will be a question-and-answer session. Choice (A) will happen after the question-and-answer session. Choice (C) will happen during lunch. Choice (D) is a plausible answer but is not mentioned.

92. **(C)** It discusses *new car sales.* Choices (A) and (B) are not mentioned. Choice (D) confuses the similar-sounding *export* and *expert.*

93. **(B)** Economists attribute it to the increase in *loans* for new car purchases. Choices (A), (C), and (D) are not mentioned.

94. **(D)** The new safety features are the result of *consumer demand.* Choices (A), (B), and (C) are not mentioned.

95. **(A)** The speaker mentions actors and an intermission, so they are in a theater. Choice (B) is associated with actors and a performance, but there is no intermission and there are no rules about cell phone use for television viewers. Choice (C) is not mentioned. Choice (D) repeats the word *actors.*

96. **(C)** The speaker asks listeners to turn off their cell phones in order not to distract the actors. Choice (A) will be done during intermission, presumably by the theater staff. Choice (B) is something the speaker asks

people not to do. Choice (D) uses the word *permit* out of context.

97. **(B)** Drinks will be served during intermission, which will occur in an hour. Choice (A) is contradicted by the correct answer. Choice (C) repeats the word *performance*. Choice (D) repeats the word *now*.

98. **(A)** The reporter says that a heavy rainfall has arrived. Choice (B) is how the weather will be on Wednesday. Choice (C) confuses the similar-sounding words *windy* and *Wednesday*. Choice (D) confuses the similar-sounding words *snow* and *low*.

99. **(C)** A car *collided with*, or hit, a bus. Choices (A), (B), and (D) repeat other words used in the descriptions of the accidents but in a different context.

100. **(C)** The second accident occurred at 1:30. Choice (A) is the time of the first accident. Choice (B) sounds similar to the correct answer. Choice (D) repeats the word *two*, which is the number of cars involved in the second accident.

Part 5 (page 197)

101. **(B)** *People* requires a plural verb. Choice (A) is the singular form. Choice (C) is the simple form. Choice (D) is the gerund or present participle form.

102. **(D)** Superlative comparisons require *the* and the superlative form of the adjective. Choice (A) has the simple form of the adjective. Choice (B) requires *the*. Choice (C) is the comparative form.

103. **(C)** The noun *advice* means *recommendations*. Choices (A) and (B) are verbs. Choice (D) is a noun, but it means *exciting experience*.

104. **(A)** The main verb *is completed* requires a future or present tense verb as the secondary verb. Choice (B) is the past tense. Choice (C) is the present perfect. Choice (D) is the gerund or the present participle form.

105. **(A)** *During* is a preposition and is followed by a noun phrase. Choices (B), (C), and (D) are conjunctions that introduce a clause.

106. **(B)** An adjective or restrictive clause referring to a person begins with *who*. Choice (A) is a relative pronoun but refers to things. Choice (C) is a relative pronoun but indicates possession. Choice (D) is not a relative pronoun.

107. **(B)** The future tense in a real condition requires the present tense in the *if* clause. Choice (A) is the future tense. Choice (C) is the past tense. Choice (D) is the present tense, but for a plural subject.

108. **(C)** *And* is a coordinating conjunction used to join items. Choice (A) excludes all items. Choice (B) contrasts items. Choice (D) indicates a choice among items.

109. **(D)** Causative *need* requires the infinitive. Choice (A) is the gerund or the present participle form. Choice (B) is the past tense. Choice (C) is the present tense.

110. **(C)** *On* is a preposition that can be used with days of the week. Choice (A) indicates possession. Choice (B) indicates location. Choice (D) indicates time.

111. **(A)** An adverb of indefinite frequency may come before the verb. Choice (B) incorrectly places *carefully* before the verb it modifies. Choices (C) and (D) have *always* after the verb.

112. **(C)** Items linked by *and* must have the same form. In this case, the second verb must be the participle form to match *worrying*. Choice (A) is the present tense. Choice (B) is the past tense. Choice (D) is an infinitive.

113. **(B)** *Reports* is a plural noun that is the subject of the sentence and that agrees with the plural adjective *both*. Choice (A) is a noun, but a person is not likely to be placed on a desk. Choice (C) is the gerund or the present participle form. Choice (D) is a singular noun.

114. **(D)** *Despite* is logical and can be followed by a noun phrase. Choice (A) is not logical. Choices (B) and (C) are usually followed by a clause.

115. **(A)** The subject *offices* requires a plural verb. Choices (B), (C), and (D) are singular.

116. **(C)** The participants are affected by the meeting. They are bored. Therefore, the past participle is required. Choice (A) is the present participle. Choice (B) is the present tense. Choice (D) is the present continuous.

117. **(B)** An adverb of definite frequency can appear at the end of a sentence. Choices (A), (C), and (D) are adverbs of indefinite frequency and appear within the sentence.

118. **(A)** A noun that is specified usually requires *the*. Choices (B) and (C) are indefinite articles. Choice (D) is a pronoun.

119. **(B)** Equal comparisons require *as* on both sides of the adverb. Choices (A) and (C) use *as* only once. Choice (D) is the comparative form.

120. (D) A past action that occurs before another past action requires the past perfect. Choice (A) is the present perfect. Choice (B) is the present tense. Choice (C) is the past tense.

121. (B) *That* can introduce relative clauses referring to things. Choice (A) is not a relative pronoun. Choice (C) is a possessive relative pronoun. Choice (D) is a relative pronoun that refers to people.

122. (C) *To* indicates direction toward a place. Choices (A) and (D) indicate location. Choice (B) indicates possession.

123. (A) *Suggest* requires the base form (subjunctive form) when it indicates that someone else will do something. Choice (B) is the past tense. Choice (C) is the infinitive. Choice (D) is a gerund or present participle form.

124. (C) When *the argument* is the cause (not the effect), use the present participle *convincing*. Choice (A) is the past tense. Choice (B) is the present tense. Choice (D) is the infinitive.

125. (B) The sentence requires a singular noun. Choice (A) is a plural noun. Choice (C) is an adjective. Choice (D) is a verb.

126. (C) A countable term (such as *sheet*) is added to a non-count noun (such as *paper*) to use it in a countable sense. Choice (A) is non-count. Choice (B) is only possible when it means *kinds of paper*. Choice (D) is not plural (*three sheets*).

127. (D) The preposition *in* indicates location within a place. Choice (A) indicates location outside of a place. Choice (B) indicates possession. Choice (C) indicates direction toward a place.

128. (C) Since *and* connects two similar items and since *research* is a noun, you need the noun *development*. Choice (A) is the past tense or the past participle form. Choice (B) is the gerund or the present participle form. Choice (D) is the present tense.

129. (A) *Both* is often paired with *and*. Choices (B), (C), and (D) are not paired with *both*.

130. (B) A comparison between two things requires the comparative form. Choice (A) is an incorrect equal comparison. Choice (C) is an incorrect comparative. Choice (D) is the superlative.

131. (C) *Or* indicates a choice between two items: a *room* or a *suite*. Choice (A) indicates a contrast. Choice (B) joins the items. Choice (D) eliminates both items.

132. (D) *Devise* is a verb meaning *develop or invent a method of doing something*. Choice (A) is a verb meaning *dedicate*. Choice (B) is a verb meaning *want something*. Choice (C) is a noun meaning *machine* (usually a small one).

133. (B) Non-restrictive relative clauses referring to things are introduced by *which*. Choice (A) is a relative pronoun referring to things but cannot be used in a non-restrictive clause. Choice (C) is not a relative pronoun. Choice (D) is a relative pronoun indicating possession.

134. (D) A future tense verb in the main clause of an *if* sentence requires a simple present tense verb in the *if* clause. Choice (A) is the past perfect. Choice (B) is the future perfect. Choice (C) is a continuous verb form that must be used with a form of *be*.

135. (C) The causative verb *urge* followed by a noun clause requires the base verb form. Choice (A) is a participle. Choice (B) is the infinitive. Choice (D) is the future.

136. (A) Since *the highways* are affected by the crowds (they are made crowded), use the past participle. Choice (B) is the present participle. Choices (C) and (D) are the present tense or nouns.

137. (C) In this context, only *waited* is the appropriate past tense verb. Choices (A), (B), and (D) are not logical.

138. (C) The present tense in the *if* clause of a real condition requires a present or future form in the remaining clause. Choice (A) is the present perfect. Choice (B) is the past perfect. Choice (D) is the past continuous.

139. (B) The causative verb *make* requires the base form of the verb. Choice (A) is the gerund or present participle form. Choice (C) is the infinitive. Choice (D) is a noun.

140. (D) The preposition *at* indicates a specific time. Choice (A) indicates location. Choice (B) indicates the day of the week. Choice (C) indicates a duration of time.

Part 6 (page 201)

141. (A) The word *interest* in this sentence is a noun referring to the money paid as the cost of a loan. Choices (B), (C), and (D) are all incorrect word forms.

142. (C) The phrasal verb *fill out* means *complete a form*. Choice (B) would be *fill up*, meaning *completely fill a container*. Choices (C) and (D) are not possible.

143. (C) A passive form is required here since the subject, *your application*, is not active; it is a person who will approve the application. Choices (A), (B), and (D) are all active verbs.

144. **(B)** The main verb *plan* is followed by an infinitive verb. Choice (A) is the base form. Choice (C) is the present participle. Choice (D) is a noun.

145. **(D)** Maya is giving Peter a *chance*, or *opportunity*, to look over the agenda. Choices (A), (B), and (C) look similar to the correct answer but do not make sense in this context.

146. **(B)** *Your* is a possessive adjective modifying the noun *patience*. Choice (A) is a subject pronoun. Choice (C) is a contraction of *you are*. Choice (D) is a contraction of *you have*.

147. **(A)** Available means *ready* or *offered*. Choices (B), (C), and (D) look similar to the correct answer but don't make sense in this context.

148. **(C)** *Spacious* is an adjective used to describe the offices. Choice (A) is a noun. Choice (B) is a past tense verb. Choice (D) is an adverb.

149. **(D)** This is a negative imperative verb. The ad offers an opportunity that people should not miss. Choice (A) is a base verb. Choice (B) is a gerund. Choice (C) is a negative infinitive.

150. **(D)** *Have* is used here to complete the present perfect verb *have designed*. Choice (A) does not agree with the subject. Choice (B) would cause the past participle verb *redesigned* to act as an adjective, which does not fit the context. Choice (C) does not agree with the subject.

151. **(A)** Francine's Fashions is a clothing store, and *attire* means *clothing*. Choices (B), (C), and (D) do not fit the context.

152. **(C)** The preposition *by* is correctly followed by a gerund. Choice (A) is base form. Choice (B) is an infinitive. Choice (D) is future tense.

Part 7 (page 205)

153. **(D)** The memo is about saving cab costs. Choices (A), (B), and (C) are not mentioned.

154. **(A)** The memo is to all employees. Choices (B) and (D) would not see the company's memo. Choice (C) is incorrect because the accounting department is the source of the memo.

155. **(C)** The driver should turn the meter on after you are in the cab. Choices (A), (B), and (D) are contradicted by *after, not before, you sit down in the cab.*

156. **(B)** The receipt verifies the trip. Choices (A), (C), and (D) are not the purpose of the receipt.

157. **(A)** They have a meeting known as the power breakfast. Choices (B), (C), and (D) are not mentioned.

158. **(D)** People who consider themselves too busy to meet any other time started the power breakfast. Choices (A), (B), and (C) are not mentioned.

159. **(B)** Some restaurants require reservations before 9:00 A.M. Choices (A) and (C) are possible but not mentioned. Choice (D) is not mentioned.

160. **(C)** Companies must look for a match between needs and resources. Choice (A) may not be appropriate for every company. Choices (B) and (D) are not mentioned.

161. **(B)** Tax advantages are not mentioned. Choices (A), (C), and (D) are mentioned.

162. **(D)** A pro-business attitude is essential. Choices (A), (B), and (C) are not essential for every company.

163. **(A)** It was made by credit card. Choices (B), (C), and (D) are not consistent with the information given.

164. **(D)** She requests that they credit her credit card. Choices (A), (B), and (C) are not consistent with the information given.

165. **(C)** In this context, a *slip* is a small piece of paper containing the sales information. Choices (A) and (B) are other meanings of the word *slip*, which do not fit the context. Choice (D) is associated with ordering by mail.

166. **(D)** It describes a festival. Choices (A), (B), and (C) are not consistent with the information given.

167. **(A)** The children can learn folk dances. Choices (B), (C), and (D) are not mentioned.

168. **(D)** The advertisement assumes that people will drive their cars since it is far to the fairgrounds and parking is available at no extra charge. Choice (A) is unlikely considering the distance. Choices (B) and (C) are not mentioned.

169. **(C)** The admissions fee is donated to the Preserve Our History Fund. Choices (A), (B), and (D) are not mentioned.

170. **(D)** The article encourages people to pay more attention to their pens. Choice (A) is incorrect because it tells people what to write with, not how to write. Choice (B) is incorrect because the article tells how to purchase pens, not printers. Choice (C) is incorrect because although the article

mentions that few things are written by hand, it does not encourage people to write more.

171. **(A)** The most important characteristic for determining comfort is thickness. Choice (B) is mentioned but is not as important as thickness. Choice (C) is not mentioned. Choice (D) is incorrect because size is a combination of thickness, length, and weight.

172. **(B)** An irregular flow of ink may cause skips or gaps. Choice (A) is not mentioned. Choice (C) is the result of failure of the pen to seal off the flow of ink. Choice (D) is not mentioned.

173. **(C)** The advantage of fine-line pens is that they may compensate for bad handwriting. Choice (A) is not mentioned. Choices (B) and (D) refer to pens that make a bold, dark line.

174. **(B)** *Executives* belong to ORE. Choices (A), (C), and (D) are not consistent with the information given.

175. **(A)** The purpose of ORE is to provide responsible solutions. Choices (B), (C), and (D) are not mentioned.

176. **(D)** It has been operating for five years. Choices (A), (B), and (C) are contradicted by *five years ago*.

177. **(C)** ORE *has grown fast*. Choices (A), (B), and (D) are not mentioned.

178. **(C)** It concerns *help for flood victims*. Choices (A), (B), and (D) are not consistent with the information given.

179. **(A)** *Medical supplies* are not mentioned. Choices (B), (C), and (D) are mentioned.

180. **(D)** *Volunteers* are needed. Choices (A), (B), and (C) are not consistent with the information given.

181. **(A)** In his letter, Alex Hayes states that he recently graduated from Northland College. Choice (B) is confused with his former job as an office assistant. Choice (C) is what he plans to be in the future. Choice (D) is related to his former workplace, a law firm.

182. **(D)** He is applying for a position as office manager. Choice (A) is something he plans to do but is not the purpose of the letter. Choice (B) is something he did at his former job. Choice (C) is related to his former workplace.

183. **(B)** In his letter, Alex Hayes states that he is enclosing a letter of reference. In the second passage, we see that the letter was written by Ms. Smith. Choice (A) is confused with Alex's statement that he *plans* to get a *business* degree. Choice (C) is wrong because no application form is mentioned. Choice (D) is confused with Alex's mentioning *college* and the *degree* he plans to get.

184. **(C)** Georgina Smith wrote the letter of reference because Alex used to work for her at her law firm. Choice (A) is what Alex would like to become. Choice (B) mentions the name of the college where Alex studied. Choice (D) mentions the name of the person to whom Alex is applying for a job.

185. **(A)** The main idea of Ms. Smith's letter is that Alex is a good worker and she can recommend him for a job. Choice (B) is Alex's description of himself. Choice (C) is incorrect because Ms. Smith says she can't give him a full-time job, but she doesn't say he shouldn't work full time. Choice (D) is confused with the fact that Alex worked for Ms. Smith during his school vacations.

186. **(B)** Ms. Chan is scheduled to arrive at 4:40, but she says she wants to arrive an hour and a half before that time. Choice (A) is the time she is scheduled to leave New York. Choice (C) is the time she is scheduled to arrive in San Francisco. Choice (D) is the time of her meeting.

187. **(A)** Ms. Chan says she has a meeting in San Francisco. Choices (B) and (D) are things she will do in Los Angeles. Choice (C) confuses the meaning of the word *book* as it is used in this context.

188. **(C)** The itinerary shows that she will stay at the Hightowers Hotel in Los Angeles. Choice (A) is where she will stay in San Francisco. Choice (B) is a hotel she has stayed in in the past. Choice (D) is where Mr. Kim will stay.

189. **(D)** The itinerary shows four nights in Los Angeles, but Ms. Chan says she wants to stay one more night. Choices (A), (B), and (C) are incorrect.

190. **(D)** Ms. Chan was originally scheduled to return on July 14, but she plans to stay one more day in Los Angeles, so she will return on July 15. Mr. Kim will arrive the following day. Choices (A), (B), and (C) are incorrect.

191. **(B)** Roberta is scheduled to talk about marketing goals, but she will be on a trip, so Maria wants Peter to take her place. Choice (A) is something Maria has already done. Choice (C) is what Roberta will do. Choice (D) is incorrect because Maria wants Peter to do the entire presentation himself, in place of Roberta.

192. (C) According to the meeting agenda, Tami is scheduled to talk about product development. Choices (A), (B), and (D) are topics that other people are scheduled to talk about.

193. (C) The meeting is scheduled to end at 11:45, with Ivan talking during the last half hour. Maria wants to give Ivan an extra 15 minutes to talk, which would have the meeting end at 12:00. Choice (A) is when Ivan's talk is scheduled to begin. Choice (B) is when Ivan's talk is scheduled to end. Choice (D) is not mentioned.

194. (D) Maria tells Peter that she has reserved the Board Room in place of Conference Room 3. Choice (A) is the originally scheduled location for the meeting. Choices (B) and (C) are confused with the fact that lunch will be served at the end of the meeting.

195. (A) Maria's e-mail states that a draft of the meeting agenda is attached. Choices (B), (C), and (D) are all related to things Maria mentions in her e-mail, but she did not attach any of them.

196. (A) In his letter, dated April 15, Mr. Rothman states that he read the article in yesterday's paper. Choice (B) is the date of Mr. Rothman's letter. Choice (C) is the day before the mall was opened. Choice (D) is the date the mall was opened and is mentioned in Mr. Rothman's letter.

197. (C) The article states that Ms. Johnson is a member of the City Planning Board. Choice (A) is how Mr. Rothman describes himself. Choice (B) is the person to whom Mr. Rothman addressed his letter. Choice (D) mentions the company that will do the downtown revitalization project.

198. (C) The article quotes Ms. Johnson as saying . . . *landlords will be able to earn higher profits.* Choice (A) is not mentioned. Choice (B) is incorrect because although offices are mentioned, their cost is not. Choice (D) is related to Mr. Rothman's statement that this company is only interested in profits.

199. (A) The main idea of the letter is that Mr. Rothman does not like the work of the Windsor Development Corporation. Choice (B) is the opposite of the correct answer. Choice (C) is incorrect because Mr. Rothman says he does not like the mall. Choice (D) is incorrect because Mr. Rothman states *While I agree that the business district is in desperate need of revitalization. . . .*

200. (B) Mr. Rothman does not like the Windsor Development Corporation because it destroys old buildings, and he says that the city should copy other cities that have preserved historic buildings. Choices (A) and (D) are what the Windsor Development Corporation plans to build and the reason Mr. Rothman is protesting the plans. Choice (C) is incorrect because the one mall that Mr. Rothman mentions is one he doesn't like.

Practice TOEIC Test 2

Part 1 (page 224)

1. (B) The people are walking together in the park, and a woman is holding a child's hand. The group is probably a family. Choice (A) is incorrect because the people are on level ground, not at a summit. Choice (C) is incorrect because the mother is holding the child's hand, not carrying him. Choice (D) confuses the similar-sounding *familiar* with *family* and *talk* with *walk.*

2. (C) The man wearing a tall, white hat and white uniform is holding a basket of tomatoes; he is probably a chef. Choice (A) uses the related word *lunch* and confuses the similar-sounding *chief* and *chef.* Choice (B) confuses the related *tomato sauce* with *tomatoes.* Choice (D) describes an incorrect action; the man is *showing,* not *chopping,* the vegetables.

3. (A) The people are at an airport check-in counter. There are flags above the counter. Choice (B) is incorrect because the counter is a departure area, not an arrival hall; you do not need to visit the counter when your flight arrives. It is also incorrect because the area is not empty. Choice (C) confuses the similar-sounding *tickets to the fair* with *air tickets.* Choice (D) confuses the similar-sounding *pass the port* with *passport.*

4. (D) The woman is watching the man shoot the billiard ball. Choice (A) incorrectly identifies the location; they are in a billiard hall, not on the field. Choice (B) confuses the definition of *shooting* (hunting) with *shooting* (billiards) and the definition of *game* (animal) with *game* (sport). Choice (C) confuses *swimming pool* with the game *pool* and the similar-sounding *Bill's yard* with *billiards.*

5. (D) A man and woman are talking in the hotel lobby while a bellhop takes a bag to the reception desk. Choice (A) confuses the

similar-sounding *hobby* with *lobby*. Choice (B) confuses the related word *visiting* (adj.) with *visitors* (n.) and uses the related words *rest* and to(*night*). Choice (C) confuses the similar-sounding *guess* with *guest*.

6. **(D)** The men dressed in white laboratory coats looking at the machinery are probably technicians. Choice (A) incorrectly assumes the men wearing white coats are doctors. Choice (B) incorrectly identifies the place and the action. Choice (C) confuses the similar-sounding *lazy* with *laser* and incorrectly identifies the action.

7. **(A)** The man is pointing to the book the woman is showing him. Choice (B) incorrectly identifies the location; they are in an office with a palm tree behind them, not in the forest. Choice (C) is incorrect because although the man may be a pharmacist, he is not dispensing medicine. Choice (D) identifies an incorrect action; they are not buying flowers.

8. **(A)** The men are playing drums. Choice (B) incorrectly identifies the location of the drum; the drum is not in the window. Choice (C) is incorrect because they are playing live, so they probably would not be listening to music on the radio. Choice (D) confuses the similar-sounding *freedom* with *drum*.

9. **(D)** The man is reading a newspaper. Choice (A) identifies an incorrect action; he is reading a paper, not talking on the phone. Choice (B) is incorrect because there is a lamp on the table. Choice (C) is incorrect because although the man may be a journalist, he is not reporting.

10. **(A)** People are getting out of a car and handing a bag to the bellhop. Choice (B) is incorrect because the couple just arrived and are staying, not driving away. Choice (C) is incorrect because the couple are *going up* the stairs, not *falling down* them. Choice (D) is incorrect because the car door is *open*, not *closed*.

Part 2 (page 230)

11. **(A)** *Sure. I never use it* is an appropriate response. Choice (B) confuses the word *spell* with *dictionary*. Choice (C) confuses the words *books* and *dictionary*.

12. **(C)** The agenda would include a schedule of presentations. Choice (A) confuses *plane schedule* and *lecture schedule*. Choice (B) confuses the words *speak* and *lecture*.

13. **(B)** This statement suggests training would help the problem. Choice (A) confuses the word *bad* with *problem* and *train* (n.) with *train* (v.). Choice (C) confuses *I can't* with *it wouldn't*.

14. **(B)** *I did* answers *who*. Choice (A) confuses *open* with *closed*. Choice (C) answers the question *would you like me to open the window*.

15. **(C)** *After their board meeting* answers *when*. Choice (A) answers *how is the client*. Choice (B) confuses the words *telephone* and *hear* and answers *how*.

16. **(A)** *It depends which magazines run our ads* is the best response to the question. Choice (B) confuses *fish market* with *market* (for advertising). Choice (C) confuses *right* (direction) with *right* (correct).

17. **(C)** *It was our supplier* answers *who*. Choice (A) confuses the similar-sounding *loan* with *phone*. Choice (B) confuses the words *ring* and *phone*.

18. **(A)** *No. I heard the crash and then looked up* is the best response to the question. Choice (B) confuses the words *hurt* and *accident*. Choice (C) confuses the words *police* and *accident*.

19. **(B)** This statement offers a critique of the acting in the film. Choice (A) confuses the words *movers* and *movie*. Choice (C) confuses the similar-sounding *ink* and *think*.

20. **(C)** *Actually, we went there on our honeymoon* is the best response to the question. Choice (A) confuses the similar-sounding *pair of those* with *Paris*. Choice (B) uses the incorrect pronoun.

21. **(B)** The question requires a time; it could start snowing any minute. Choice (A) uses a time marker but confuses the subject *he* with *snow*. Choice (C) uses the incorrect verb tense.

22. **(A)** This statement offers to connect the caller with a woman in the billing department. Choice (B) confuses the related word *bill* with *billing*. Choice (C) confuses the word *pay* with *bill*.

23. **(A)** *Faster computers* would increase efficiency. Choice (B) confuses the words *more* and *to increase*. Choice (C) confuses *longer way* with *a way*.

24. **(C)** *Many years ago* answers the question *have you worked with the director before?* Choice (A) is incorrect because it refers to working longer than an eight-hour day, while the statement implies the woman has worked with the director over a period of time. Choice (B) does not answer the question.

25. (B) *Yes, I'm sorry* is a polite response to the question. Choice (A) confuses the word *stand* with *sitting*. Choice (C) confuses the word *seats* with *sitting*.

26. (A) This choice is the only response that gives a time. Choice (B) answers *where*, not *when*. Choice (C) confuses the similar-sounding *cold* and *call* and answers *what*.

27. (B) *I can't. I have plans* is the best response to the question. Choice (A) confuses *early* and *late*. Choice (C) confuses the related word *later* with *late*.

28. (A) This statement uses the correct pronoun *I* and gives a possible explanation for the woman being late for the appointment. Choice (B) answers *when*. Choice (C) answers *where*.

29. (C) *Yes, thank you* is a polite response to the question. Choice (A) confuses the similar-sounding *salary* with *salad*. Choice (B) answers *when* the salad is served.

30. (B) *No, the subway* answers the question *do you take the bus*. Choice (A) answers *how much* the bus costs. Choice (C) answers the question *why*.

31. (B) *Only long enough to get a sandwich* answers the question *are you going out for lunch*. Choice (A) is an incorrect response because the question does not ask about the weather. Choice (C) confuses the similar-sounding *bunch* with *lunch*.

32. (A) *Not until one o'clock* is the best response to the question. Choice (B) confuses *close* with *open*. Choice (C) answers *when* but confuses *open the present* with *open the store*.

33. (A) Since the woman placed the order herself, she knows it was placed. Choice (B) confuses the related words *misplaced* and *placed*. Choice (C) contains the word *chicken* but does not answer the question.

34. (C) *It looks like mine* answers the question *whose*. Choice (A) confuses the word *music* with *notes*. Choice (B) confuses the word *handwriting* with *notebook*.

35. (B) *No, I won't be near a phone* is the best response to the question. Choice (A) answers *when*, not *can*. Choice (C) confuses the similar-sounding *refund* with *return*.

36. (C) *To the beach* correctly answers the question *where*. Choice (A) confuses the similar-sounding *vacancies* and *vacation*. Choice (B) answers *when* but not *where*.

37. (B) *Thanks, but I just finished it* is a polite response to the question. Choice (A) confuses the similar-sounding *report* and *reporters*. Choice (C) does not answer the question *can I help you*.

38. (A) More deck space will attract more passengers. Choice (B) confuses the similar-sounding *race* with *space*. Choice (C) confuses the similar-sounding *redecorate* with *renovate*.

39. (B) *Yes, they're posting them right now* correctly rephrases and answers the question. Choice (A) confuses the similar-sounding *cab* with *cabin*. Choice (C) confuses the word *fence* with *post*.

40. (B) *Five hundred dollars each way* is the amount of the fare. Choice (A) answers *when*. Choice (C) confuses *empty* with *full*.

Part 3 (page 231)

41. (B) The man says he'll copy his notes for the woman. Choices (A) and (C) have already been done. Choice (D) is plausible since the woman is looking for her notes, but the man never offers to do this.

42. (B) The woman refers to *Tuesday's meeting*. Choices (A) and (C) sound similar to the correct answer. Choice (D) repeats the word *afternoon*, which is when the man will give the woman a copy of his notes.

43. (A) The woman explains that she needs the notes to prepare for her presentation next Monday. Choice (B) confuses *reading* with the similar-sounding word *meeting*. Choice (C) repeats the words *notes* and *meeting*. Choice (D) is what the woman will do this afternoon.

44. (C) The man tells the woman, *The air conditioner broke down again this morning*. Choice (A) is the last time the air conditioner was fixed. Choice (B) sounds similar to *today*, which is when the man will speak with the manager. Choice (D) repeats the word *afternoon*.

45. (C) The woman says, *We should buy a new one*. Choices (A) and (D) are plausible responses to the situation but are not mentioned. Choice (B) is what was done last week.

46. (D) The man says he will speak to the manager about the problem. Choice (A) repeats the word *concentrate*. Choice (B) repeats the word *down*. Choice (C) is what the man will ask the manager to do.

47. (C) The woman is asking directions to the courthouse. Choice (A) uses the word *park* in a different context. Choice (B) is next to

the courthouse. Choice (D) confuses the similar-sounding *work* and *walk.*

48. **(A)** The woman says she will walk. Choice (B) repeats the word *car.* Choice (C) is not mentioned. Choice (D) confuses the similar-sounding *bike* and *hike.*

49. **(B)** The man says it shouldn't take her more than six minutes. Choice (A) confuses the similar-sounding *four* and *more.* Choice (C) confuses the similar-sounding *eight* and *great.* Choice (D) confuses the similar-sounding *ten* and *then.*

50. **(C)** The woman tells the man that the paper jams because it is too thin. Choice (A) confuses *rolls* with *rollers.* Choice (B) confuses the meaning of *jam* in this context. Choice (D) is the opposite of the correct answer.

51. **(B)** The man says that he needs the copies done by 3:00. Choice (A) confuses the similar-sounding *two* and *through.* Choice (C) confuses the similar-sounding *eight* and *collate.* Choice (D) confuses the similar-sounding *ten* and *then.*

52. **(D)** The woman offers to show the man how to program the machine to copy, staple, and collate. Choice (A) is what the machine does. Choice (B) mentions what the man will use, but the woman doesn't offer to buy it. Choice (C) uses the word *program* in a different context.

53. **(B)** The man is angry because the woman spilled coffee on his jacket. Choice (A) confuses *sad* with the similar-sounding word *mad.* Choice (C) repeats the word *happy.* Choice (D) repeats the word *relax.*

54. **(D)** The woman says the stain will come out if they take the jacket to the cleaners right away. Choice (A) is the man's description of the jacket. Choice (B) confuses *rain* with the similar-sounding word *stain.* Choice (C) is the opposite of what the woman says.

55. **(C)** The man says he paid more than $500 for the jacket. Choice (A) confuses *two* with *too.* Choice (B) confuses *four* with the similar-sounding word *more.* Choice (D) confuses *nine* with the similar-sounding word *fine.*

56. **(C)** The man says he is planning a camping trip. Choice (A) confuses *bike* with the similar-sounding word *hike.* Choice (B) confuses *school* with the similar-sounding word *cool.* Choice (D) uses the word *business* in a different context.

57. **(A)** The woman says the man should cancel the trip because of the rain and the cool air. Choice (B) repeats the word *long.* Choice (C) repeats the word *overnight.* Choice (D) isn't mentioned.

58. **(C)** The man says he'll decide in another day, that is, tomorrow. Choice (A) confuses *eight* with the similar-sounding word *wait.* Choice (B) confuses *tonight* with *overnight.* Choice (D) is when he wants to take the trip.

59. **(D)** This is a conversation between a waitress and a customer. Choices (A), (B), and (C) are all places where people eat, but the conversation is too formal for these settings.

60. **(A)** The man tells the woman that the fork is dirty. Choice (B) repeats the word *good.* Choice (C) repeats the word *silverware.* Choice (D) uses the word *order* in a different context.

61. **(B)** The man orders a chicken and rice casserole. Choice (A) confuses the similar-sounding words *steak* and *take.* Choice (C) confuses the similar-sounding words *fish* and *dish.* Choice (D) confuses the similar-sounding words *ice* and *rice.*

62. **(A)** The woman is making an appointment to get her teeth cleaned. Choice (B) confuses *painter* with the similar-sounding word *pain.* Choice (C) confuses *horse* with the similar-sounding word *course.* Choice (D) is not mentioned.

63. **(B)** The woman says that she gets her teeth cleaned *every six months.* Choice (A) repeats the word *month.* Choice (C) repeats the word *six.* Choice (D) repeats the word *sixteen.*

64. **(D)** The man says that he'll put her down for June 16th. Choices (A), (B), and (C) sound similar to the correct answer.

65. **(C)** The speakers agree to order balloons. Choices (A) and (B) are what they decide not to do. Choice (D) repeats the word *call.*

66. **(D)** The man says that Mrs. Green had surgery. Choice (A) sounds similar to *today,* which is when she had the surgery. Choice (B) repeats the word *home.* Choice (C) confuses the similar-sounding words *baby* and *maybe.*

67. **(C)** The woman says they can call the store to order the balloons this evening. Choice (A) confuses the similar-sounding words *four* and *before.* Choice (B) confuses the similar-sounding words *ten* and *send.* Choice (D) confuses the similar-sounding words *Tuesday* and *today.*

68. **(A)** The man says *The subway train is late again.* Choice (B) confuses the similar-sounding words *rain* and *train.* Choice (C) repeats

the word *stations*. Choice (D) repeats the word *work*.

69. **(B)** The man says that tourists *ought to wait until after rush hour to take the trains*. Choice (A) confuses the similar-sounding words *drive* and *five*. Choice (C) is related to the woman's saying *people like to visit this city*. Choice (D) confuses the similar-sounding words *bus* and *us*.

70. **(A)** The woman says that they'll be home *by seven*. Choices (B), (C), and (D) sound similar to the correct answer.

Part 4 (page 234)

71. **(B)** It is described as a *moving sidewalk*. Choices (A), (C), and (D) are not mentioned.

72. **(D)** References to *luggage* suggest an airport. Choices (A), (B), and (C) are not consistent with the information given.

73. **(A)** The speaker says, *Do not run*. Choice (B) uses the word *exercise* in a different context. Choices (C) and (D) are things users are asked to do.

74. **(C)** People should wait until *all the speakers have finished*. Choices (A), (B), and (D) are not consistent with the information given.

75. **(B)** People are asked to *step to the center of the room*. Choices (A) and (C) are contradicted by *step to the center of the room*. Choice (D) is not mentioned.

76. **(B)** The speaker says that *half an hour* will be left for questions. Choice (A) is confused with *12:15*, the time they will break for lunch. Choice (C) is confused with *1:45*, the time the afternoon session will begin. Choice (D) means the same as an hour and so is confused with *half an hour*.

77. **(A)** The ad is for *dishes*. Choices (B), (C), and (D) are not consistent with the information given.

78. **(C)** You cannot *freeze food in them*. Choices (A), (B), and (D) are explicitly mentioned.

79. **(D)** Listeners are asked to call to make their order. Choice (A) confuses *line* with *on line*. Choices (B) and (C) are mentioned as places where these products are not available.

80. **(D)** The road *leads to the business district*. Choice (A) is contradicted by *construction crews are working*. Choice (B) is not mentioned. Choice (C) is not as explicit as *business district*.

81. **(C)** Repairs will take *four weeks* (one month). Choice (A) is confused with *crews will work around the clock*. Choices (B) and (D) are contradicted by *four weeks*.

82. **(A)** They should *find alternate routes*. Choices (B), (C), and (D) are not mentioned.

83. **(B)** Madison House is *older and smaller*. Choice (A) describes the other houses on the tour. Choices (C) and (D) are not mentioned.

84. **(D)** It represents the *highest quality available at that time*. Choices (A), (B) and (C) are not mentioned.

85. **(C)** Attention is drawn to the *carved ceilings*. Choices (A), (B), and (D) are not mentioned.

86. **(B)** People can look forward to *good weather*. Choices (A), (C), and (D) are not mentioned.

87. **(A)** It will get colder *at night*. Choices (B) and (C) may be true but are not the focus here. Choice (D) is when it gets warmer.

88. **(D)** The speaker suggests that people carry a light jacket if they plan to be out after dark. Choices (A) and (B) are what the speaker says people won't need. Choice (C) is a different meaning of the word *light*.

89. **(C)** You would hear it *on a train*. Choices (A), (B), and (D) are not consistent with the information given.

90. **(D)** The information is about *seatings for dinner*. Choices (A) and (C) are not mentioned. Choice (B) is not the focus of the announcement.

91. **(C)** There are *two seatings*. Choices (A), (B), and (D) are not consistent with the information given.

92. **(B)** It discusses *survey results*. Choice (A) is the opposite of the information in the survey. Choices (C) and (D) are not consistent with the information given.

93. **(D)** Their ads are usually based on *price*. Choices (A), (B), and (C) are contradicted by *concentrate on price*.

94. **(A)** Consumers want *good repair service*. Choices (B), (C), and (D) are not mentioned.

95. **(C)** The tour participants will have lunch at the museum café. Choice (A) is what they are not allowed to do at the museum. Choice (B) is what they will do on the way to the museum. Choice (D) uses the word *spend* in a different context.

96. **(B)** The tour guide says that they will take a ride around City Gardens. Choice (A) is what they will do after they look at the gardens. Choice (C) is confused with the location of the gardens, which is right next to the park. Choice (D) is what they will do later in the afternoon.

97. (A) The tour guide says that they will return to the hotel at 7:00. Choice (B) confuses the similar-sounding words *nine* and *time*. Choice (C) confuses the similar-sounding words *ten* and *then*. Choice (D) sounds similar to the correct answer.

98. (B) The store is open Tuesday through Sunday; therefore, it is closed Monday. Choices (A), (C), and (D) are all days that the store is open.

99. (C) The recording tells us to press 2 to hear directions to the store. Choice (A) is information given in the recording. Choice (B) is heard when you press 1. Choice (D) is incorrect because although orders are mentioned, instructions for ordering are not.

100. (D) The recording tells us that book reviews are available on the website. Choice (A) is incorrect because book reviews are not mentioned in relation to the café. Choice (B) is how to hear a list of events. Choice (C) is what will happen when you press 4.

Part 5 (page 237)

101. (B) *Uniform* begins with a consonant sound and requires *a*. Choice (A) is used before a vowel sound. Choice (C) is the definite article, so it cannot be used with the indefinite *any*. Choice (D) expresses quantity.

102. (C) An action that begins in the past and continues in the present requires the present perfect. Choice (A) is a gerund or a participle form. Choice (B) is the past perfect. Choice (D) is the future perfect.

103. (A) The *document* is affected; it does not do the enclosing, so the past participle is needed. Choice (B) is the base form of the verb. Choice (C) is the present participle. Choice (D) is the infinitive.

104. (D) *Accept* means *receive*. Choice (A) means *exclude*. Choice (B) means *something that is excluded*. Choice (C) means *alter*.

105. (B) A relative clause indicating possession begins with *whose*. Choice (A) is not a relative pronoun. Choice (C) does not indicate possession. Choice (D) is not used with people except in restrictive clauses.

106. (D) The verb *requires*, in this context, should be followed by a gerund or present participle form. Choice (A) is a noun. Choice (B) is the simple form of the verb. Choice (C) is the infinitive.

107. (A) An action that occurs before a past action requires the past perfect. Choice (B) is the present perfect. Choice (C) is the future tense. Choice (D) is conditional.

108. (C) *Sensible* means *makes sense*. Choice (A) means *able to detect small differences*. Choice (B) means *perceive*. Choice (D) refers to senses of touch, sight, etc., which humans use to perceive.

109. (D) The preposition *at* indicates location when used with the verb phrase *to be held*. Choice (A) is used with days of the week. Choice (B) is used for a position within something. Choice (C) indicates possession.

110. (C) The present tense in the *if* clause of a real condition appears with a present, imperative, or future form in the main clause. Choice (A) is the past tense. Choice (B) is the present continuous but is singular. Choice (D) is the past perfect.

111. (B) *People* requires a plural verb. Choice (A) is singular. Choice (C) is the infinitive. Choice (D) is the gerund or the present participle form.

112. (D) *But* indicates a contrast between items and is used as a conjunction to introduce a clause. Choice (A) is not a conjunction. Choice (B) indicates a choice between items. Choice (C) eliminates both items.

113. (A) Adverbs of definite frequency, such as *every day*, can occur at the end of a sentence. Choices (B), (C), and (D) are adverbs of indefinite frequency.

114. (C) A relative clause indicating possession begins with *whose*. Choice (A) is a relative pronoun, but it does not indicate possession. Choices (B) and (D) are not relative pronouns.

115. (B) *Because* indicates a cause and effect and is used as a conjunction to introduce a clause. Choice (A) indicates possibility. Choice (C) indicates an unexpected result. Choice (D) indicates location.

116. (A) Non-count nouns do not use an indefinite article. Choice (B) uses the indefinite article. Choice (C) uses the definite article, which is not appropriate here. Choice (D) uses an expression of quantity.

117. (C) Comparisons of more than two things require *the* and the superlative form. Choice (A) is the simple form of the adjective. Choice (B) is an equal comparison. Choice (D) is the comparative form.

118. (B) Items joined by *and* must have the same form; both *learning* and *improving* are gerunds. Choices (A), (C), and (D) do not match *learning*.

119. (C) Relative clauses referring to people can begin with *who*. Choices (A) and (B) are not relative pronouns. Choice (D) is used when the object form of the relative pronoun is required.

120. (A) The *statement* is affecting the members, so the present participle is used. Choice (B) is the past participle. Choice (C) is a present form of the verb. Choice (D) is the past perfect.

121. (D) The comparison of two things requires the comparative form and *than*. Choice (A) uses the superlative *most*. Choices (B) and (C) are incorrect equal comparisons.

122. (B) An action that begins in the past and continues in the present requires the present perfect. Choice (A) is the present tense and is plural in number. Choice (C) is the past perfect. Choice (D) is the passive.

123. (A) Equal comparisons require *as* on both sides of the adjective. Choices (B) and (C) are incorrect comparative forms. Choice (D) is an incorrect superlative form.

124. (D) An action that interrupts a past continuous action requires the past tense. Choice (A) is the present tense. Choice (B) is the past perfect. Choice (C) is the present continuous.

125. (C) *Production* is the correct noun form. Choice (A) is the simple form of the verb. Choice (B) is the gerund or present participle form. Choice (D) is an adjective.

126. (A) The causative verb *suggest* is followed by the gerund. Choice (B) is the infinitive. Choice (C) is the future. Choice (D) is a future form with *going to*.

127. (B) A continuous action that starts in the past and continues in the present requires the present perfect continuous. Choice (A) is the present continuous. Choice (C) is the future. Choice (D) is the past perfect.

128. (D) The causative verb *forced* is followed by the infinitive. Choice (A) is the gerund or present participle form. Choice (B) is the simple form of the verb. Choice (C) is the present tense.

129. (C) The preposition *with* indicates association with something. Choice (A) means *in place of* or *on behalf of*. Choice (B) indicates direction toward a place. Choice (D) indicates representation by someone.

130. (A) The future tense in a real condition requires the present tense in the *if* clause. Choice (B) is the past tense. Choice (C) is the future tense. Choice (D) is the present perfect.

131. (D) An action that happens before a future action requires the future perfect. Choice (A) is the present tense. Choice (B) is the past tense. Choice (C) is the present perfect.

132. (B) The subject *bags* requires a plural verb. Choices (A), (C), and (D) are singular.

133. (C) *In spite of* indicates an unexpected result. Choices (A), (B), and (D) indicate cause and effect.

134. (A) A comparison between two things requires the comparative form and *than*. Choices (B) and (C) are not logical in this context. Choice (D) is an incorrect superlative comparison.

135. (B) *While* means *during the time when*. Choices (A) and (C) are prepositions and cannot be followed by a clause. Choice (D) is not logical.

136. (A) *Not only . . . but also* is a paired conjunction. Choices (B), (C), and (D) are not the proper form for the second element in the pair.

137. (C) *Damaged* refers to things. Choices (A), (B), and (D) refer to people.

138. (A) *Is* is in the present tense and, along with *whenever*, suggests habitual action. The present tense *ask* conveys habitual action. Choice (B) is the present tense but is third person and cannot be used with *I*. Choice (C) is the simple past tense. Choice (D) is the past perfect.

139. (A) *And* joins items. Choice (B) contrasts items. Choice (C) offers a choice between items. Choice (D) eliminates both items.

140. (B) Adverbs of definite frequency can appear at the beginning of the sentence. Choices (A), (C), and (D) are adverbs of indefinite frequency and appear in the middle of the sentence.

Part 6 (page 241)

141. (A) The verb *respond* is followed by the preposition *to*. Choices (B), (C),and (D) are prepositions which do not fit this context.

142. (C) Choice (C) is a noun meaning *a person who provides assistance*. Choice (A) is the base form of the verb. Choice (B) is the past tense verb. Choice (D) is another noun form, but it names the action that an assistant does.

143. (B) Ms. Ling encloses two letters of reference from people who know her and can describe her qualifications for the job. Choices (A), (C), and (D) look similar to the correct answer but have very different meanings and cannot be used in this context.

144. **(A)** This is a simple present tense verb that agrees with the plural subject. Choices (B), (C), and (D) do not agree with the subject.

145. **(C)** *Variety* means *several different kinds*. Choices (A), (B), and (D) look similar to the correct answer but have very different meanings and cannot be used in this context.

146. **(D)** *Rapidly* is an adverb of manner that describes how the rents are rising. Choice (A) is an adjective. Choice (B) is a noun. Choice (C) looks very similar to the correct answer but is a different word with a very different meaning.

147. **(B)** This is a comparative adjective comparing business class cars to economy class cars. Choices (A), (C), and (D) are adjectives but are not in the comparative form.

148. **(D)** This is passive voice; somebody provides the coffee, tea, and water, so the subject receives the action. Choices (A), (B), and (C) are active voice.

149. **(A)** This noun is the object of the verb *is advertising*, and it follows the article *the*. Choice (B) is an adjective. Choice (C) is an adverb. Choice (D) is a noun, but it has a very different meaning.

150. **(D)** Lee is talking about the location, or place, of the hotel; he says *it's close to everything*. Choices (A), (B), and (C) are things one might mention when talking about a hotel, but they don't fit the context of the sentence.

151. **(C)** This is an indirect question and requires the usual statement word order of subject-verb in the clause. Choices (A) and (B) are verbs without subjects. Choice (D) is question word order.

152. **(C)** The expression *would like* means *want*. Choices (A), (B), and (D) do not fit with *like*.

Part 7 (page 245)

153. **(B)** The bottle has a child-resistant cap. Choices (A), (C), and (D) are contradicted by *child-resistant*.

154. **(C)** The instructions say to press down. Choices (A) and (B) are not mentioned. Choice (D) is the opposite of *press downward*.

155. **(C)** The letter acknowledges conference registration. Choices (A), (B), and (D) are not mentioned.

156. **(B)** A brochure is enclosed. Choices (A) and (D) are not logical if she has already registered for the conference. Choice (C) is not mentioned.

157. **(A)** The letter says to contact the conference coordinator. Choice (B) wrote the letter. Choice (C) is where Le Ziaolie works. Choice (D) is not mentioned.

158. **(D)** It offers a range of shopper services. Choices (A), (B), and (C) are not mentioned.

159. **(B)** It is located by the Gourmet Food Shop. Choices (A), (C), and (D) may have concierge desks of their own but are not mentioned.

160. **(D)** There are direct phone lines to the Concierge Desk at the directory maps in the mall. Choices (A), (B), and (C) are not mentioned.

161. **(C)** The word *advent* means *arrival* in this context. Choices (A), (B), and (D) could fit the sentence but don't have the correct meaning in this context.

162. **(A)** It was predicted when offices began to use computers. Choices (B), (C), and (D) are not mentioned.

163. **(C)** Documents are easy to prepare on a computer, so people print more. Choice (A) is a result, not a reason. Choice (B) is not mentioned. Choice (D) may be true but is not mentioned.

164. **(D)** People prefer paper, so there will probably always be paper in offices. Choices (A), (B), and (C) are not mentioned.

165. **(C)** They are returned because they do not fit. Choice (A) is not the most common reason. Choices (B) and (D) are not mentioned.

166. **(C)** Twenty-five percent of people do not like their gifts. Choices (A), (B), and (D) are contradicted by 25%.

167. **(B)** Only 5% of items are returned because they are damaged. Choices (A), (C), and (D) are not mentioned.

168. **(A)** Commuter flights have decreased. Choices (B), (C), and (D) are not mentioned.

169. **(B)** Commuter flights have been absorbed into the regular schedule. Choices (A), (C), and (D) are not mentioned.

170. **(D)** Larger planes can now fly into these airports. Choice (A) is not mentioned. Choice (B) may be true but is not mentioned. Choice (C) is not mentioned.

171. **(A)** It is more economical to fly one plane with more passengers. Choices (B), (C), and (D) are not mentioned.

172. **(B)** The article gives reasons why commuter flights have changed. Choices (A), (C), and (D) are not mentioned.

173. **(C)** People fed their pets *leftover food from family meals*. Choices (A) and (B) are mentioned as things people eat but are not mentioned as pet food. Choice (D) is one of the special things people now give their pets.

174. **(B)** At gourmet food stores. Choices (A), (C), and (D) are not mentioned.

175. **(A)** They are supposed to be healthier. Choices (B), (C), and (D) are not mentioned.

176. **(D)** Vegetarian foods are not mentioned. Choices (A), (B), and (C) are explicitly mentioned.

177. **(B)** The word *interior* means *inside*. Choice (A) is the meaning of the similar-looking word *inferior*. Choices (C) and (D) could be used to describe the walls but are not the correct meaning.

178. **(C)** You can create space by moving the partitions. Choices (A), (B), and (D) are not mentioned.

179. **(D)** You can change the space for different office projects. Choices (A) and (C) are not mentioned. Choice (B) may be true but is not a reason.

180. **(A)** They provide privacy by absorbing sound. Choices (B), (C), and (D) describe the look of the partitions, which is not discussed in the article.

181. **(B)** Small business is mentioned several times on the conference schedule, and the workshop topics are things that would be of interest to a small business owner. Choice (A) is associated with the workshop on health insurance. Choice (C) is associated with the workshop on web pages. Choice (D) is incorrect because the conference overall is geared toward small businesses.

182. **(B)** Louise wants to attend the workshop on marketing strategies, which will be given at 10:00 in Room 5. Choices (A) and (C) are rooms that are scheduled for other workshops at 10:00. Choice (D) is where Louise will be at 11:15.

183. **(D)** Louise says that she will be giving a workshop in Room 9 right before lunch. The topic of the workshop in that room at that time is health insurance. Choices (A), (B), and (C) are topics listed for workshops in other rooms.

184. **(B)** Louise wants to meet Rick for lunch, which is scheduled for 12:30. Choice (A) is when the second workshop session ends. Choice (C) is when lunch ends. Choice (D) is when the lecture begins.

185. **(C)** Louise says she is sorry that this restaurant was chosen. Choices (A) and (B) are the opposite of the opinion she expresses. Choice (D) is incorrect because it is implied that the restaurant is in the hotel since it is near the room where Louise will give her workshop.

186. **(D)** The position is for a marketing assistant and a degree in business or marketing is required. Choices (A) and (C) are related to the fact that the company is a fashion company. Choice (B) is related to Josefa Silva's former job.

187. **(A)** Josefa Silva's letter of September 22 refers to the ad in *yesterday's paper*. Choice (B) is the date on Ms. Silva's letter. Choice (C) is the day before the job application is due. Choice (D) is the date the job application is due.

188. **(C)** Mija Kim is the human resources director to whom job applications should be sent. Choice (A) is the position advertised, and choice (B) is related to this. Choice (D) is related to the work of the company.

189. **(D)** Ms. Silva states in her letter that she worked for River Run Publishers. Choice (A) is where she studied. Choice (B) is related to the advertised position. Choice (C) is where she wants to work.

190. **(D)** The ad asks for five years of experience, and Ms. Silva only mentions three years. Choice (A) is incorrect because she has a degree from Clifton College. Choice (B) is confused with *competitive salary*. Choice (C) is incorrect because she has taken several fashion courses.

191. **(A)** The letter does not mention a restaurant or any other sort of eating facility. Choice (B) is incorrect because there is an indoor running track. Choice (C) is incorrect because there are swimming classes. Choice (D) is incorrect because there is a store that sells sports equipment.

192. **(D)** Mr. Siebold will pay the full price for his one-year membership because his application was filled out after the special offer expired. Choice (A) would be the price of a six-month membership with discount. Choice (B) is the full price of a six-month membership. Choice (C) is the price of a one-year membership with discount.

193. **(B)** On his application, Mr. Siebold indicates that he wants to take tennis lessons. Choices (A),

(C), and (D) are other activities that are available at the health club.

194. (B) On his application, Mr. Siebold indicates that he is an accountant. Choices (A) and (C) are people who would work at the health club. Choice (D) is related to sports activities.

195. (C) On his application, Mr. Siebold indicates that he wants a locker, and the letter says that people have to call to find out about locker availability. Choice (A) is incorrect because there is a space on the application to sign up for classes. Choice (B) is incorrect because Mr. Siebold already has an application, which was enclosed with the letter. Choice (D) is incorrect because it is too late to get a discount.

196. (B) Mr. Watson states *your website did not have any information on volume discounts*. Choice (A) is incorrect because Mr. Watson mentions a *detailed price list*. Choice (C) is not mentioned as a problem. Choice (D) is incorrect because Mr. Watson's e-mail is not addressed to the sales department.

197. (A) The price of three large boxes is $225, and there is no charge for shipping on orders over $200. Choice (B) is 10% (the usual shipping charge) of the price of one large box. Choice (C) is 10% of the price of three small boxes. Choice (D) is 10% of the price of three large boxes.

198. (D) Five lamps cost $50, five organizers cost $40, and shipping is $9, or 10% of the total order. Choice (A) is the price plus shipping of the organizers. Choice (B) is the price plus shipping of the lamps. Choice (C) is the price of Mr. Watson's order without shipping.

199. (A) Ms. Burke's e-mail says that office furniture, such as lamps and organizers, does not have a discount. Choice (B) is incorrect because the lamps are described as *energy-saving*. Choice (C) is confused with the desks and chairs that are made of recycled materials. Choice (D) is incorrect because a lamp costs $2 more than an organizer.

200. (D) Mr. Watson says he likes this company's products because they are environmentally friendly. Since the desks and chairs are made of 100% recycled materials, they are environmentally friendly. Choice (A) is not mentioned. Choice (B) is incorrect because free shipping is available according to the price of the order and can be applied to any product. Choice (C) is incorrect because there is no discount for furniture.

Practice TOEIC Speaking Test 1 (page 263)

Sample answers

3. A man and a woman are talking about something. They may be architects or engineers. Both of them are wearing hard hats. The man is holding some rolled-up plans. They are outdoors at a building site, and there is a large crane in the background. The man is pointing to something.

4. I prefer to eat at home. It is cheaper than eating at a restaurant. It is also a lot more convenient because I am already at home. I like to eat at restaurants sometimes, like when I go out with friends on weekends, but most of the time I prefer to eat at home.

5. I like restaurants that serve food from different countries. I like to try food from all around the world. It is interesting to eat things that you have never heard of before.

6. My favorite restaurant is called Tony's. It is very close to my house. I like it because it is small and comfortable and it isn't very expensive. The food is not the best, but it is good. The people there are very friendly. Most important, they have great desserts.

7. We have two word processing classes for beginners. They are both on Monday and Wednesday evenings. The first starts at 5:00 and ends at 6:30. The second goes from 7:00 to 8:30.

8. All of our classes cost $250 for an eight-week session. You will also have to pay $50 for books.

9. We have three classes on Saturdays. For adults we have Using the Internet, which goes from 9:00 to 12:00. We also have an advanced word processing class. It goes from 1:00 to 4:00. For children, we have Using the Internet, from 10:30 until 12:00.

10. Good evening. This is a message for Mr. Jones from the front desk. We are very sorry to hear about your accident. We do have a cleaning service in the hotel. If you leave your suit outside the door tonight, someone will pick it up early in the morning and take it to the cleaners. However, we can't have it back to you until tomorrow evening. Since you need it sooner, I suggest you take it to the cleaners yourself early tomorrow morning. They are located in the hotel basement, and they open at 5:00 A.M. If you give them your suit then, I am sure they can have it ready for you before your meeting. Let me know if you need any further assistance.

11. I think it is much better to live in a city than in the countryside. First of all, a city has many more opportunities. There are a lot of jobs in a city. There are very few jobs in the countryside, unless you want to be a farmer. Also, in a city there are more opportunities for education. Most cities have a lot of schools and universities. You can also find places that give classes in art, music, or whatever your special interest is. In the countryside, however, there are very few schools. You might have to travel far from your home to study something. Another reason a city is better is that you can meet a lot of interesting people there. In the countryside there are very few people, and they are probably all the same. I think life in a city is very interesting. I would never live in the countryside.

Practice TOEIC Speaking Test 2 (page 273)

Sample answers

3. A man is washing a large window outside a restaurant. The man is wearing a uniform over his clothes to keep them clean. He's also wearing a baseball cap. The restaurant looks like it would be a nice place to eat. Inside, there is a table with a checked tablecloth. Outside the building there are several plants, including a bush and some flowers. The flowers are in a nice pot hanging on the wall of the restaurant.
4. In my country, birthday celebrations are important for children. People pay a lot of attention to children on their birthdays. For adults, birthdays are usually not as important. Sometimes adults celebrate significant birthdays such as when they turn 30, 40, or 50 years old.
5. When a child has a birthday, the parents give a party and invite other children. They serve cake and ice cream and play games and everyone gives the child presents. Adults might invite some friends over for dinner. Sometimes adults have big birthday parties, but not always.
6. In my country, people think it is bad to get old. They dye their hair so it doesn't look gray. Sometimes they have surgery to remove wrinkles. They lie about their age. They do everything they can to look young. People don't respect old people in my country. People don't pay attention to older people.
7. Let me see. The first speaker is Martin Brown. He'll speak from 9:15 to 9:45, so, half an hour.
8. Two people will give the sales report. Martha Warren will speak first. Then Robert Jones will give Part 2 of the report.
9. After lunch, from 1:00 to 3:00, there will be a planning discussion for everybody. Then from 3:00 until 3:30 a video called "The Creation of a Company" will be shown. There will be coffee and snacks in the Board Room from 3:30 until 4:00.
10. Hello, I'm calling for Sam Lee from the karate school. I got your message about classes for your son. We give classes for children every Saturday morning from 9:00 to 12:00. Most of the children in this class are nine or ten years old, so your son is the right age. However, the class is very large. There are 16 students in it. We still have room for more students if your son wants to take it. If he doesn't want to be with a large group, I have another suggestion for you. Some of our instructors give private lessons. This might be best for your son if he is very shy. If you are interested in this, please call me back and I will give you the names of some of our instructors who give private lessons.
11. I wouldn't take a job that pays a high salary if I don't like the job. I think this is a very bad idea. First, it will make you unhappy. You spend all day at your job. If you don't like your job, you will be unhappy all day. It is a terrible way to spend your time. Second, you have to think about the importance of money. We all need money for food, clothes, and a house. We like to have a little extra for entertainment and travel. You can earn enough money to pay for these things at most jobs. If you have a high salary, you can have a bigger house and better clothes and you can take more trips. However, these things won't make you happy if you don't like going to your job every day. Another reason is, if you don't like your job, you probably won't do it well. This will make you even more unhappy. It is better to spend your days at a job that you can do well and enjoy. This is much more important than money.

Practice TOEIC Writing Test 1 (page 283)

Sample answers

1. The man is riding his bicycle down the street.
2. The food in the pots is very hot.
3. They want to buy tickets so they can see the show.
4. They discussed the project while they ate lunch.
5. When the bus arrives, everyone will get on it.
6. Dear Ms. Rich:
   I am happy to be a member of the City Sports and Fitness Club. There are some things I would like to know about the club. I like to go swimming early every morning before work. How early does the pool open on weekdays? Also, although I am a very good swimmer, I am a very bad tennis player. I would like to improve my game. Do you have tennis lessons at the club? I would have time for lessons on Saturdays or Sundays. I don't have a tennis racket, so I am planning to buy one at the club store. I don't know how to choose one. Is there someone in the store who knows a lot about tennis rackets and can help me choose the best one for me? I really appreciate your help.

7. Dear Ms. Andrews:
I have received your e-mail asking me to explain why I don't wish to renew your lease. In your lease, it clearly states that rent is due by the 5th day of the month. For the past three months, you have made your rent payment as late as the 15th. I have already written you a letter stating that this is unacceptable. In addition, it has come to my attention that you have been allowing clients to bring pets into the office. This is a violation of the lease, which states that no animals are allowed on the premises. I will consider renewing your lease if you wish. However, in order to do so, I would like you to pay three months' rent in advance. If you bring me a check for three months' rent before the end of this month, I will renew your lease for one year.

Sincerely,
John Munro

8. Many people like to work in a group. My preference, however, is to work alone. When I work alone, I can get my work done more efficiently, I can follow my own schedule, and I think much better.

I work much more efficiently when I work alone. When people work together, they use up time talking about things that aren't related to work. They also use up time trying to find a way to agree about things. When I work alone, I don't have to do any of this. I just sit down at my desk and start working. All my work time is for work, and when I am finished, I have time to do something else.

I can follow my own plan when I work alone. I can choose to work on one part of a project today and on a different part tomorrow. I don't have to follow another person's plan or wait for someone to finish his or her part so that I can then do my part. Working this way is much more enjoyable for me.

I think much better when I work alone. I am not distracted by other people's ideas or ways of doing things. I look an assignment over and start thinking of ways to approach it. I don't have to worry about what other people think or how they might want to do the job. That takes my concentration away from my work, but when I work alone, I only have to think about the assignment in front of me.

A lot of people prefer to work in groups. They like to feel the energy and the support of the group. They like to share responsibilities and ideas. For me, however, it is preferable to work alone. I do much better work this way.

Practice TOEIC Writing Test 2 (page 291)

Sample answers

1. The woman is opening the door.
2. There are a lot of people waiting for the train in the station.
3. They are carrying umbrellas because it is raining.
4. The man's luggage is so heavy that he needs to use a cart.
5. She is pouring some juice so that she can have a drink.
6. Dear Ms. Mills:
I am very happy to hear that the library is finally open. I look forward to using it. I have a few questions about library services. Does the library provide Internet access? I have Internet access at work but not at home, and sometimes I like to do online research on weekends. I would also like to know about your magazine collection. I am interested in reading magazines about world cultures. Does the library subscribe to magazines that deal with this topic? Finally, would you mind sending me a schedule of the library's hours? My whole family is eager to use the library, and we need to know what hours it is open. Thank you very much for your help.
7. Dear Mr. Hamm:
I received your message asking about my canceled subscription to *World Economic News* magazine. Please don't think that I have found any problem with your magazine. I enjoy it very much, but it is very long and I just don't have enough time to read it. In addition, although the content of the magazine is very good and worth every penny of the subscription price, I just cannot afford to pay so much money for a magazine. I will miss your magazine. May I suggest that you consider developing another magazine in addition to this one? If you published a shorter magazine, busy people like me might have time to read it. Let me know what you think of my idea.

Sincerely,
Marilyn Hughes

8. Many people enjoy sports. Some people like to watch sports, other people like to play them, and some people like to do both. Sports are an important part of society for a number of reasons.

First, sports are good for our health. Everybody needs to get physical exercise, and playing sports is a good and enjoyable way to do this. Sports motivate us to be active. Playing sports gives us a focus for our physical exercise and allows us to exercise together with other people. People who watch sports may be encouraged to start a plan of physical exercise for themselves.

In addition, sports bring people together. They give people a sense of community. People who play sports are part of a team, and they identify with other people who play the same sport. People who watch sports are connected to other people who enjoy the same sport and support the same teams. Students come together when they support their school teams, and residents of a city are brought together when they support their local teams.

Furthermore, sports are an important part of education. When children play sports in school, they learn to work with a team. They learn to set goals and work for these goals. They learn to deal with winning and losing. These are skills that will help them not only in sports, but in other areas of their lives as well.

Sports are good for our health, for our sense of community, and for our education. Sports have an important place in society for everybody.

ANSWER SHEET—Practice TOEIC Test 1

Mark all answers by completely filling in the circle. Mark only <u>one</u> answer for each question. If you change your mind about an answer after you have marked it on your answer sheet, completely erase your old answer and then mark your new answer. You must mark the answer sheet carefully so that the test-scoring machine can accurately record your test score.

Listening Comprehension

Part 1		Part 2						Part 3						Part 4					
	Answer		Answer		Answer		Answer		Answer		Answer		Answer		Answer		Answer		Answer
	A B C D		A B C		A B C		A B C		A B C D		A B C D		A B C D		A B C D		A B C D		A B C D
1	Ⓐ Ⓑ Ⓒ Ⓓ	11	Ⓐ Ⓑ Ⓒ	21	Ⓐ Ⓑ Ⓒ	31	Ⓐ Ⓑ Ⓒ	41	Ⓐ Ⓑ Ⓒ Ⓓ	51	Ⓐ Ⓑ Ⓒ Ⓓ	61	Ⓐ Ⓑ Ⓒ Ⓓ	71	Ⓐ Ⓑ Ⓒ Ⓓ	81	Ⓐ Ⓑ Ⓒ Ⓓ	91	Ⓐ Ⓑ Ⓒ Ⓓ
2	Ⓐ Ⓑ Ⓒ Ⓓ	12	Ⓐ Ⓑ Ⓒ	22	Ⓐ Ⓑ Ⓒ	32	Ⓐ Ⓑ Ⓒ	42	Ⓐ Ⓑ Ⓒ Ⓓ	52	Ⓐ Ⓑ Ⓒ Ⓓ	62	Ⓐ Ⓑ Ⓒ Ⓓ	72	Ⓐ Ⓑ Ⓒ Ⓓ	82	Ⓐ Ⓑ Ⓒ Ⓓ	92	Ⓐ Ⓑ Ⓒ Ⓓ
3	Ⓐ Ⓑ Ⓒ Ⓓ	13	Ⓐ Ⓑ Ⓒ	23	Ⓐ Ⓑ Ⓒ	33	Ⓐ Ⓑ Ⓒ	43	Ⓐ Ⓑ Ⓒ Ⓓ	53	Ⓐ Ⓑ Ⓒ Ⓓ	63	Ⓐ Ⓑ Ⓒ Ⓓ	73	Ⓐ Ⓑ Ⓒ Ⓓ	83	Ⓐ Ⓑ Ⓒ Ⓓ	93	Ⓐ Ⓑ Ⓒ Ⓓ
4	Ⓐ Ⓑ Ⓒ Ⓓ	14	Ⓐ Ⓑ Ⓒ	24	Ⓐ Ⓑ Ⓒ	34	Ⓐ Ⓑ Ⓒ	44	Ⓐ Ⓑ Ⓒ Ⓓ	54	Ⓐ Ⓑ Ⓒ Ⓓ	64	Ⓐ Ⓑ Ⓒ Ⓓ	74	Ⓐ Ⓑ Ⓒ Ⓓ	84	Ⓐ Ⓑ Ⓒ Ⓓ	94	Ⓐ Ⓑ Ⓒ Ⓓ
5	Ⓐ Ⓑ Ⓒ Ⓓ	15	Ⓐ Ⓑ Ⓒ	25	Ⓐ Ⓑ Ⓒ	35	Ⓐ Ⓑ Ⓒ	45	Ⓐ Ⓑ Ⓒ Ⓓ	55	Ⓐ Ⓑ Ⓒ Ⓓ	65	Ⓐ Ⓑ Ⓒ Ⓓ	75	Ⓐ Ⓑ Ⓒ Ⓓ	85	Ⓐ Ⓑ Ⓒ Ⓓ	95	Ⓐ Ⓑ Ⓒ Ⓓ
6	Ⓐ Ⓑ Ⓒ Ⓓ	16	Ⓐ Ⓑ Ⓒ	26	Ⓐ Ⓑ Ⓒ	36	Ⓐ Ⓑ Ⓒ	46	Ⓐ Ⓑ Ⓒ Ⓓ	56	Ⓐ Ⓑ Ⓒ Ⓓ	66	Ⓐ Ⓑ Ⓒ Ⓓ	76	Ⓐ Ⓑ Ⓒ Ⓓ	86	Ⓐ Ⓑ Ⓒ Ⓓ	96	Ⓐ Ⓑ Ⓒ Ⓓ
7	Ⓐ Ⓑ Ⓒ Ⓓ	17	Ⓐ Ⓑ Ⓒ	27	Ⓐ Ⓑ Ⓒ	37	Ⓐ Ⓑ Ⓒ	47	Ⓐ Ⓑ Ⓒ Ⓓ	57	Ⓐ Ⓑ Ⓒ Ⓓ	67	Ⓐ Ⓑ Ⓒ Ⓓ	77	Ⓐ Ⓑ Ⓒ Ⓓ	87	Ⓐ Ⓑ Ⓒ Ⓓ	97	Ⓐ Ⓑ Ⓒ Ⓓ
8	Ⓐ Ⓑ Ⓒ Ⓓ	18	Ⓐ Ⓑ Ⓒ	28	Ⓐ Ⓑ Ⓒ	38	Ⓐ Ⓑ Ⓒ	48	Ⓐ Ⓑ Ⓒ Ⓓ	58	Ⓐ Ⓑ Ⓒ Ⓓ	68	Ⓐ Ⓑ Ⓒ Ⓓ	78	Ⓐ Ⓑ Ⓒ Ⓓ	88	Ⓐ Ⓑ Ⓒ Ⓓ	98	Ⓐ Ⓑ Ⓒ Ⓓ
9	Ⓐ Ⓑ Ⓒ Ⓓ	19	Ⓐ Ⓑ Ⓒ	29	Ⓐ Ⓑ Ⓒ	39	Ⓐ Ⓑ Ⓒ	49	Ⓐ Ⓑ Ⓒ Ⓓ	59	Ⓐ Ⓑ Ⓒ Ⓓ	69	Ⓐ Ⓑ Ⓒ Ⓓ	79	Ⓐ Ⓑ Ⓒ Ⓓ	89	Ⓐ Ⓑ Ⓒ Ⓓ	99	Ⓐ Ⓑ Ⓒ Ⓓ
10	Ⓐ Ⓑ Ⓒ Ⓓ	20	Ⓐ Ⓑ Ⓒ	30	Ⓐ Ⓑ Ⓒ	40	Ⓐ Ⓑ Ⓒ	50	Ⓐ Ⓑ Ⓒ Ⓓ	60	Ⓐ Ⓑ Ⓒ Ⓓ	70	Ⓐ Ⓑ Ⓒ Ⓓ	80	Ⓐ Ⓑ Ⓒ Ⓓ	90	Ⓐ Ⓑ Ⓒ Ⓓ	100	Ⓐ Ⓑ Ⓒ Ⓓ

Reading

Part 5								Part 6				Part 7							
	Answer		Answer		Answer		Answer		Answer		Answer		Answer		Answer		Answer		Answer
	A B C D		A B C D		A B C D		A B C D		A B C D		A B C D		A B C D		A B C D		A B C D		A B C D
101	Ⓐ Ⓑ Ⓒ Ⓓ	111	Ⓐ Ⓑ Ⓒ Ⓓ	121	Ⓐ Ⓑ Ⓒ Ⓓ	131	Ⓐ Ⓑ Ⓒ Ⓓ	141	Ⓐ Ⓑ Ⓒ Ⓓ	151	Ⓐ Ⓑ Ⓒ Ⓓ	161	Ⓐ Ⓑ Ⓒ Ⓓ	171	Ⓐ Ⓑ Ⓒ Ⓓ	181	Ⓐ Ⓑ Ⓒ Ⓓ	191	Ⓐ Ⓑ Ⓒ Ⓓ
102	Ⓐ Ⓑ Ⓒ Ⓓ	112	Ⓐ Ⓑ Ⓒ Ⓓ	122	Ⓐ Ⓑ Ⓒ Ⓓ	132	Ⓐ Ⓑ Ⓒ Ⓓ	142	Ⓐ Ⓑ Ⓒ Ⓓ	152	Ⓐ Ⓑ Ⓒ Ⓓ	162	Ⓐ Ⓑ Ⓒ Ⓓ	172	Ⓐ Ⓑ Ⓒ Ⓓ	182	Ⓐ Ⓑ Ⓒ Ⓓ	192	Ⓐ Ⓑ Ⓒ Ⓓ
103	Ⓐ Ⓑ Ⓒ Ⓓ	113	Ⓐ Ⓑ Ⓒ Ⓓ	123	Ⓐ Ⓑ Ⓒ Ⓓ	133	Ⓐ Ⓑ Ⓒ Ⓓ	143	Ⓐ Ⓑ Ⓒ Ⓓ	153	Ⓐ Ⓑ Ⓒ Ⓓ	163	Ⓐ Ⓑ Ⓒ Ⓓ	173	Ⓐ Ⓑ Ⓒ Ⓓ	183	Ⓐ Ⓑ Ⓒ Ⓓ	193	Ⓐ Ⓑ Ⓒ Ⓓ
104	Ⓐ Ⓑ Ⓒ Ⓓ	114	Ⓐ Ⓑ Ⓒ Ⓓ	124	Ⓐ Ⓑ Ⓒ Ⓓ	134	Ⓐ Ⓑ Ⓒ Ⓓ	144	Ⓐ Ⓑ Ⓒ Ⓓ	154	Ⓐ Ⓑ Ⓒ Ⓓ	164	Ⓐ Ⓑ Ⓒ Ⓓ	174	Ⓐ Ⓑ Ⓒ Ⓓ	184	Ⓐ Ⓑ Ⓒ Ⓓ	194	Ⓐ Ⓑ Ⓒ Ⓓ
105	Ⓐ Ⓑ Ⓒ Ⓓ	115	Ⓐ Ⓑ Ⓒ Ⓓ	125	Ⓐ Ⓑ Ⓒ Ⓓ	135	Ⓐ Ⓑ Ⓒ Ⓓ	145	Ⓐ Ⓑ Ⓒ Ⓓ	155	Ⓐ Ⓑ Ⓒ Ⓓ	165	Ⓐ Ⓑ Ⓒ Ⓓ	175	Ⓐ Ⓑ Ⓒ Ⓓ	185	Ⓐ Ⓑ Ⓒ Ⓓ	195	Ⓐ Ⓑ Ⓒ Ⓓ
106	Ⓐ Ⓑ Ⓒ Ⓓ	116	Ⓐ Ⓑ Ⓒ Ⓓ	126	Ⓐ Ⓑ Ⓒ Ⓓ	136	Ⓐ Ⓑ Ⓒ Ⓓ	146	Ⓐ Ⓑ Ⓒ Ⓓ	156	Ⓐ Ⓑ Ⓒ Ⓓ	166	Ⓐ Ⓑ Ⓒ Ⓓ	176	Ⓐ Ⓑ Ⓒ Ⓓ	186	Ⓐ Ⓑ Ⓒ Ⓓ	196	Ⓐ Ⓑ Ⓒ Ⓓ
107	Ⓐ Ⓑ Ⓒ Ⓓ	117	Ⓐ Ⓑ Ⓒ Ⓓ	127	Ⓐ Ⓑ Ⓒ Ⓓ	137	Ⓐ Ⓑ Ⓒ Ⓓ	147	Ⓐ Ⓑ Ⓒ Ⓓ	157	Ⓐ Ⓑ Ⓒ Ⓓ	167	Ⓐ Ⓑ Ⓒ Ⓓ	177	Ⓐ Ⓑ Ⓒ Ⓓ	187	Ⓐ Ⓑ Ⓒ Ⓓ	197	Ⓐ Ⓑ Ⓒ Ⓓ
108	Ⓐ Ⓑ Ⓒ Ⓓ	118	Ⓐ Ⓑ Ⓒ Ⓓ	128	Ⓐ Ⓑ Ⓒ Ⓓ	138	Ⓐ Ⓑ Ⓒ Ⓓ	148	Ⓐ Ⓑ Ⓒ Ⓓ	158	Ⓐ Ⓑ Ⓒ Ⓓ	168	Ⓐ Ⓑ Ⓒ Ⓓ	178	Ⓐ Ⓑ Ⓒ Ⓓ	188	Ⓐ Ⓑ Ⓒ Ⓓ	198	Ⓐ Ⓑ Ⓒ Ⓓ
109	Ⓐ Ⓑ Ⓒ Ⓓ	119	Ⓐ Ⓑ Ⓒ Ⓓ	129	Ⓐ Ⓑ Ⓒ Ⓓ	139	Ⓐ Ⓑ Ⓒ Ⓓ	149	Ⓐ Ⓑ Ⓒ Ⓓ	159	Ⓐ Ⓑ Ⓒ Ⓓ	169	Ⓐ Ⓑ Ⓒ Ⓓ	179	Ⓐ Ⓑ Ⓒ Ⓓ	189	Ⓐ Ⓑ Ⓒ Ⓓ	199	Ⓐ Ⓑ Ⓒ Ⓓ
110	Ⓐ Ⓑ Ⓒ Ⓓ	120	Ⓐ Ⓑ Ⓒ Ⓓ	130	Ⓐ Ⓑ Ⓒ Ⓓ	140	Ⓐ Ⓑ Ⓒ Ⓓ	150	Ⓐ Ⓑ Ⓒ Ⓓ	160	Ⓐ Ⓑ Ⓒ Ⓓ	170	Ⓐ Ⓑ Ⓒ Ⓓ	180	Ⓐ Ⓑ Ⓒ Ⓓ	190	Ⓐ Ⓑ Ⓒ Ⓓ	200	Ⓐ Ⓑ Ⓒ Ⓓ

ANSWER SHEET—Practice TOEIC Test 2

Mark all answers by completely filling in the circle. Mark only <u>one</u> answer for each question. If you change your mind about an answer after you have marked it on your answer sheet, completely erase your old answer and then mark your new answer. You must mark the answer sheet carefully so that the test-scoring machine can accurately record your test score.

Listening Comprehension

Part 1		Part 2						Part 3						Part 4					
	Answer A B C D		Answer A B C		Answer A B C		Answer A B C		Answer A B C D		Answer A B C D		Answer A B C D		Answer A B C D		Answer A B C D		Answer A B C D
1	Ⓐ Ⓑ Ⓒ Ⓓ	11	Ⓐ Ⓑ Ⓒ	21	Ⓐ Ⓑ Ⓒ	31	Ⓐ Ⓑ Ⓒ	41	Ⓐ Ⓑ Ⓒ Ⓓ	51	Ⓐ Ⓑ Ⓒ Ⓓ	61	Ⓐ Ⓑ Ⓒ Ⓓ	71	Ⓐ Ⓑ Ⓒ Ⓓ	81	Ⓐ Ⓑ Ⓒ Ⓓ	91	Ⓐ Ⓑ Ⓒ Ⓓ
2	Ⓐ Ⓑ Ⓒ Ⓓ	12	Ⓐ Ⓑ Ⓒ	22	Ⓐ Ⓑ Ⓒ	32	Ⓐ Ⓑ Ⓒ	42	Ⓐ Ⓑ Ⓒ Ⓓ	52	Ⓐ Ⓑ Ⓒ Ⓓ	62	Ⓐ Ⓑ Ⓒ Ⓓ	72	Ⓐ Ⓑ Ⓒ Ⓓ	82	Ⓐ Ⓑ Ⓒ Ⓓ	92	Ⓐ Ⓑ Ⓒ Ⓓ
3	Ⓐ Ⓑ Ⓒ Ⓓ	13	Ⓐ Ⓑ Ⓒ	23	Ⓐ Ⓑ Ⓒ	33	Ⓐ Ⓑ Ⓒ	43	Ⓐ Ⓑ Ⓒ Ⓓ	53	Ⓐ Ⓑ Ⓒ Ⓓ	63	Ⓐ Ⓑ Ⓒ Ⓓ	73	Ⓐ Ⓑ Ⓒ Ⓓ	83	Ⓐ Ⓑ Ⓒ Ⓓ	93	Ⓐ Ⓑ Ⓒ Ⓓ
4	Ⓐ Ⓑ Ⓒ Ⓓ	14	Ⓐ Ⓑ Ⓒ	24	Ⓐ Ⓑ Ⓒ	34	Ⓐ Ⓑ Ⓒ	44	Ⓐ Ⓑ Ⓒ Ⓓ	54	Ⓐ Ⓑ Ⓒ Ⓓ	64	Ⓐ Ⓑ Ⓒ Ⓓ	74	Ⓐ Ⓑ Ⓒ Ⓓ	84	Ⓐ Ⓑ Ⓒ Ⓓ	94	Ⓐ Ⓑ Ⓒ Ⓓ
5	Ⓐ Ⓑ Ⓒ Ⓓ	15	Ⓐ Ⓑ Ⓒ	25	Ⓐ Ⓑ Ⓒ	35	Ⓐ Ⓑ Ⓒ	45	Ⓐ Ⓑ Ⓒ Ⓓ	55	Ⓐ Ⓑ Ⓒ Ⓓ	65	Ⓐ Ⓑ Ⓒ Ⓓ	75	Ⓐ Ⓑ Ⓒ Ⓓ	85	Ⓐ Ⓑ Ⓒ Ⓓ	95	Ⓐ Ⓑ Ⓒ Ⓓ
6	Ⓐ Ⓑ Ⓒ Ⓓ	16	Ⓐ Ⓑ Ⓒ	26	Ⓐ Ⓑ Ⓒ	36	Ⓐ Ⓑ Ⓒ	46	Ⓐ Ⓑ Ⓒ Ⓓ	56	Ⓐ Ⓑ Ⓒ Ⓓ	66	Ⓐ Ⓑ Ⓒ Ⓓ	76	Ⓐ Ⓑ Ⓒ Ⓓ	86	Ⓐ Ⓑ Ⓒ Ⓓ	96	Ⓐ Ⓑ Ⓒ Ⓓ
7	Ⓐ Ⓑ Ⓒ Ⓓ	17	Ⓐ Ⓑ Ⓒ	27	Ⓐ Ⓑ Ⓒ	37	Ⓐ Ⓑ Ⓒ	47	Ⓐ Ⓑ Ⓒ Ⓓ	57	Ⓐ Ⓑ Ⓒ Ⓓ	67	Ⓐ Ⓑ Ⓒ Ⓓ	77	Ⓐ Ⓑ Ⓒ Ⓓ	87	Ⓐ Ⓑ Ⓒ Ⓓ	97	Ⓐ Ⓑ Ⓒ Ⓓ
8	Ⓐ Ⓑ Ⓒ Ⓓ	18	Ⓐ Ⓑ Ⓒ	28	Ⓐ Ⓑ Ⓒ	38	Ⓐ Ⓑ Ⓒ	48	Ⓐ Ⓑ Ⓒ Ⓓ	58	Ⓐ Ⓑ Ⓒ Ⓓ	68	Ⓐ Ⓑ Ⓒ Ⓓ	78	Ⓐ Ⓑ Ⓒ Ⓓ	88	Ⓐ Ⓑ Ⓒ Ⓓ	98	Ⓐ Ⓑ Ⓒ Ⓓ
9	Ⓐ Ⓑ Ⓒ Ⓓ	19	Ⓐ Ⓑ Ⓒ	29	Ⓐ Ⓑ Ⓒ	39	Ⓐ Ⓑ Ⓒ	49	Ⓐ Ⓑ Ⓒ Ⓓ	59	Ⓐ Ⓑ Ⓒ Ⓓ	69	Ⓐ Ⓑ Ⓒ Ⓓ	79	Ⓐ Ⓑ Ⓒ Ⓓ	89	Ⓐ Ⓑ Ⓒ Ⓓ	99	Ⓐ Ⓑ Ⓒ Ⓓ
10	Ⓐ Ⓑ Ⓒ Ⓓ	20	Ⓐ Ⓑ Ⓒ	30	Ⓐ Ⓑ Ⓒ	40	Ⓐ Ⓑ Ⓒ	50	Ⓐ Ⓑ Ⓒ Ⓓ	60	Ⓐ Ⓑ Ⓒ Ⓓ	70	Ⓐ Ⓑ Ⓒ Ⓓ	80	Ⓐ Ⓑ Ⓒ Ⓓ	90	Ⓐ Ⓑ Ⓒ Ⓓ	100	Ⓐ Ⓑ Ⓒ Ⓓ

Reading

Part 5								Part 6				Part 7							
	Answer A B C D		Answer A B C D		Answer A B C D		Answer A B C D		Answer A B C D		Answer A B C D		Answer A B C D		Answer A B C D		Answer A B C D		Answer A B C D
101	Ⓐ Ⓑ Ⓒ Ⓓ	111	Ⓐ Ⓑ Ⓒ Ⓓ	121	Ⓐ Ⓑ Ⓒ Ⓓ	131	Ⓐ Ⓑ Ⓒ Ⓓ	141	Ⓐ Ⓑ Ⓒ Ⓓ	151	Ⓐ Ⓑ Ⓒ Ⓓ	161	Ⓐ Ⓑ Ⓒ Ⓓ	171	Ⓐ Ⓑ Ⓒ Ⓓ	181	Ⓐ Ⓑ Ⓒ Ⓓ	191	Ⓐ Ⓑ Ⓒ Ⓓ
102	Ⓐ Ⓑ Ⓒ Ⓓ	112	Ⓐ Ⓑ Ⓒ Ⓓ	122	Ⓐ Ⓑ Ⓒ Ⓓ	132	Ⓐ Ⓑ Ⓒ Ⓓ	142	Ⓐ Ⓑ Ⓒ Ⓓ	152	Ⓐ Ⓑ Ⓒ Ⓓ	162	Ⓐ Ⓑ Ⓒ Ⓓ	172	Ⓐ Ⓑ Ⓒ Ⓓ	182	Ⓐ Ⓑ Ⓒ Ⓓ	192	Ⓐ Ⓑ Ⓒ Ⓓ
103	Ⓐ Ⓑ Ⓒ Ⓓ	113	Ⓐ Ⓑ Ⓒ Ⓓ	123	Ⓐ Ⓑ Ⓒ Ⓓ	133	Ⓐ Ⓑ Ⓒ Ⓓ	143	Ⓐ Ⓑ Ⓒ Ⓓ	153	Ⓐ Ⓑ Ⓒ Ⓓ	163	Ⓐ Ⓑ Ⓒ Ⓓ	173	Ⓐ Ⓑ Ⓒ Ⓓ	183	Ⓐ Ⓑ Ⓒ Ⓓ	193	Ⓐ Ⓑ Ⓒ Ⓓ
104	Ⓐ Ⓑ Ⓒ Ⓓ	114	Ⓐ Ⓑ Ⓒ Ⓓ	124	Ⓐ Ⓑ Ⓒ Ⓓ	134	Ⓐ Ⓑ Ⓒ Ⓓ	144	Ⓐ Ⓑ Ⓒ Ⓓ	154	Ⓐ Ⓑ Ⓒ Ⓓ	164	Ⓐ Ⓑ Ⓒ Ⓓ	174	Ⓐ Ⓑ Ⓒ Ⓓ	184	Ⓐ Ⓑ Ⓒ Ⓓ	194	Ⓐ Ⓑ Ⓒ Ⓓ
105	Ⓐ Ⓑ Ⓒ Ⓓ	115	Ⓐ Ⓑ Ⓒ Ⓓ	125	Ⓐ Ⓑ Ⓒ Ⓓ	135	Ⓐ Ⓑ Ⓒ Ⓓ	145	Ⓐ Ⓑ Ⓒ Ⓓ	155	Ⓐ Ⓑ Ⓒ Ⓓ	165	Ⓐ Ⓑ Ⓒ Ⓓ	175	Ⓐ Ⓑ Ⓒ Ⓓ	185	Ⓐ Ⓑ Ⓒ Ⓓ	195	Ⓐ Ⓑ Ⓒ Ⓓ
106	Ⓐ Ⓑ Ⓒ Ⓓ	116	Ⓐ Ⓑ Ⓒ Ⓓ	126	Ⓐ Ⓑ Ⓒ Ⓓ	136	Ⓐ Ⓑ Ⓒ Ⓓ	146	Ⓐ Ⓑ Ⓒ Ⓓ	156	Ⓐ Ⓑ Ⓒ Ⓓ	166	Ⓐ Ⓑ Ⓒ Ⓓ	176	Ⓐ Ⓑ Ⓒ Ⓓ	186	Ⓐ Ⓑ Ⓒ Ⓓ	196	Ⓐ Ⓑ Ⓒ Ⓓ
107	Ⓐ Ⓑ Ⓒ Ⓓ	117	Ⓐ Ⓑ Ⓒ Ⓓ	127	Ⓐ Ⓑ Ⓒ Ⓓ	137	Ⓐ Ⓑ Ⓒ Ⓓ	147	Ⓐ Ⓑ Ⓒ Ⓓ	157	Ⓐ Ⓑ Ⓒ Ⓓ	167	Ⓐ Ⓑ Ⓒ Ⓓ	177	Ⓐ Ⓑ Ⓒ Ⓓ	187	Ⓐ Ⓑ Ⓒ Ⓓ	197	Ⓐ Ⓑ Ⓒ Ⓓ
108	Ⓐ Ⓑ Ⓒ Ⓓ	118	Ⓐ Ⓑ Ⓒ Ⓓ	128	Ⓐ Ⓑ Ⓒ Ⓓ	138	Ⓐ Ⓑ Ⓒ Ⓓ	148	Ⓐ Ⓑ Ⓒ Ⓓ	158	Ⓐ Ⓑ Ⓒ Ⓓ	168	Ⓐ Ⓑ Ⓒ Ⓓ	178	Ⓐ Ⓑ Ⓒ Ⓓ	188	Ⓐ Ⓑ Ⓒ Ⓓ	198	Ⓐ Ⓑ Ⓒ Ⓓ
109	Ⓐ Ⓑ Ⓒ Ⓓ	119	Ⓐ Ⓑ Ⓒ Ⓓ	129	Ⓐ Ⓑ Ⓒ Ⓓ	139	Ⓐ Ⓑ Ⓒ Ⓓ	149	Ⓐ Ⓑ Ⓒ Ⓓ	159	Ⓐ Ⓑ Ⓒ Ⓓ	169	Ⓐ Ⓑ Ⓒ Ⓓ	179	Ⓐ Ⓑ Ⓒ Ⓓ	189	Ⓐ Ⓑ Ⓒ Ⓓ	199	Ⓐ Ⓑ Ⓒ Ⓓ
110	Ⓐ Ⓑ Ⓒ Ⓓ	120	Ⓐ Ⓑ Ⓒ Ⓓ	130	Ⓐ Ⓑ Ⓒ Ⓓ	140	Ⓐ Ⓑ Ⓒ Ⓓ	150	Ⓐ Ⓑ Ⓒ Ⓓ	160	Ⓐ Ⓑ Ⓒ Ⓓ	170	Ⓐ Ⓑ Ⓒ Ⓓ	180	Ⓐ Ⓑ Ⓒ Ⓓ	190	Ⓐ Ⓑ Ⓒ Ⓓ	200	Ⓐ Ⓑ Ⓒ Ⓓ

Audio CD Tracking List

CD 1

Track	Activity
1	Program Introduction

Listening Comprehension Practice

Track	Activity
2	Part 1: Directions
3	Part 1: Questions 1–6
4	Part 2: Directions
5	Part 2: Questions 1–10
6	Part 3: Directions
7	Part 3: Questions 1–3
8	Part 3: Questions 4–6
9	Part 3: Questions 7–9
10	Part 3: Questions 10–12
11	Part 4: Directions
12	Part 4: Questions 1–3
13	Part 4: Questions 4–6

Speaking Practice

Track	Activity
14	Speaking Questions 7–9: Directions
15	Speaking: Questions 7–9
16	Speaking Question 10: Directions
17	Speaking: Question 10

Practice TOEIC Test 1 – Listening Test

Track	Activity
18	Part 1: Directions
19	Part 1: Questions 1–10
20	Part 2: Directions
21	Part 2: Questions 11–20
22	Part 2: Questions 21–30
23	Part 2: Questions 31–40
24	Part 3: Directions
25	Part 3: Questions 41–43
26	Part 3: Questions 44–46
27	Part 3: Questions 47–49
28	Part 3: Questions 50–52
29	Part 3: Questions 53–55
30	Part 3: Questions 56–58
31	Part 3: Questions 59–61
32	Part 3: Questions 62–64
33	Part 3: Questions 65–67
34	Part 3: Questions 68–70
35	Part 4: Directions
36	Part 4: Questions 71–73
37	Part 4: Questions 74–76

Track	Activity
38	Part 4: Questions 77–79
39	Part 4: Questions 80–82
40	Part 4: Questions 83–85
41	Part 4: Questions 86–88
42	Part 4: Questions 89–91
43	Part 4: Questions 92–94
44	Part 4: Questions 95–97
45	Part 4: Questions 98–100

CD 2

Track	Activity
	Practice TOEIC Test 2 – Listening Test
1	Part 1: Directions
2	Part 1: Questions 1–10
3	Part 2: Directions
4	Part 2: Questions 11–20
5	Part 2: Questions 21–30
6	Part 2: Questions 31–40
7	Part 3: Directions
8	Part 3: Questions 41–43
9	Part 3: Questions 44–46
10	Part 3: Questions 47–49
11	Part 3: Questions 50–52
12	Part 3: Questions 53–55
13	Part 3: Questions 56–58
14	Part 3: Questions 59–61
15	Part 3: Questions 62–64
16	Part 3: Questions 65–67
17	Part 3: Questions 68–70
18	Part 4: Directions
19	Part 4: Questions 71–73
20	Part 4: Questions 74–76
21	Part 4: Questions 77–79
22	Part 4: Questions 80–82
23	Part 4: Questions 83–85
24	Part 4: Questions 86–88
25	Part 4: Questions 89–91
26	Part 4: Questions 92–94
27	Part 4: Questions 95–97
28	Part 4: Questions 98–100
	Practice TOEIC Speaking Test 1
29	Speaking Questions 7–9: Directions
30	Speaking: Questions 7–9

31 Speaking Question 10: Directions
32 Speaking: Question 10

Practice TOEIC Speaking Test 2

33 Speaking Questions 7–9: Directions
34 Speaking: Questions 7–9
35 Speaking Question 10: Directions
36 Speaking: Question 10